T0295949

Entrepreneurship and Green Finance Practices

Entrepreneurship and Green Finance Practices: Avenues for Sustainable Business Start-ups in Asia

EDITED BY

SYED ALI RAZA
Iqra University, Pakistan

MUHAMMAD NAWAZ TUNIO
University of Sufism and Modern Sciences, Pakistan

MUHAMMAD ALI
UCSI University, Malaysia

AND

CHIN-HONG PUAH
University Malaysia Sarawak, Malaysia

United Kingdom – North America – Japan – India – Malaysia – China

Emerald Publishing Limited
Emerald Publishing, Floor 5, Northspring, 21-23 Wellington Street, Leeds LS1 4DL

First edition 2024

British Library Cataloguing in Publication Data
A catalogue record for this book is available from the British Library

ISBN: 978-1-80455-679-5 (Print)
ISBN: 978-1-80455-678-8 (Online)
ISBN: 978-1-80455-680-1 (Epub)

INVESTOR IN PEOPLE

We dedicate this book with sincere gratitude and deep admiration to our families, whose unfailing love and support served as the cornerstone of our journey.

Contents

List of Contributors

Wasim Ahmad	UCSI University, Malaysia
Syed Haider Ali Shah	Bahria University, Pakistan
Tehzeeb Sakina Amir	Bahria University, Pakistan
Muhammad Asim	Karachi University Business School, Pakistan
Nazish Baladi	National University of Modern Languages, Pakistan
Shuvasree Banerjee	Chandigarh University, India
Salman Bashir	Shaheed Benazir Bhutto University, Pakistan
Prashanth Beleya	INTI International University, Malaysia
Mehwish Bhatti	National University of Modern Languages, Pakistan
Lee-Yen Chaw	UCSI University, Malaysia
Noshin Fatima	UCSI University, Malaysia
Irfan Hameed	UCSI University, Malaysia
Zahid Hussain	Shaheed Benazir Bhutto University, Pakistan
Naveed R. Khan	UCSI University, Malaysia
Muhammad Rahies Khan	Bahria University, Pakistan
Sadia Mehfooz Khan	Iqra University, Pakistan
Jia Le Germaine Chee	Peninsula College Georgetown, Malaysia
Choi-Meng Leong	UCSI University, Malaysia
Eva Lim	UCSI University, Malaysia
Tze-Yin Lim	Swinburne University of Technology, Malaysia
Farhan Mirza	University of Management and Technology, Pakistan

Sasidharan Raman Nair	Open Universiti Malaysia, Malaysia
Shishi Kumar Piaralal	Open Universiti Malaysia, Malaysia
Eman Zameer Rahman	Bahria University, Pakistan
Jagathiswary Ravichandran	UCSI University, Malaysia
Hamad Raza	Government College University, Pakistan
Ahsan Riaz	Government College University, Pakistan
Nimra Riaz	Government College University, Pakistan
Mohd Rushidi bin Mohd Amin	INTI International College, Malaysia
Rabia Sabri	IOBM, Pakistan
Muhammad Furqan Saleem	Iqra University, Pakistan
Abdul Samad	Shaheed Benazir Bhutto University, Pakistan
Erum Shaikh	Shaheed Benazir Bhutto University, Pakistan
Saba Shaikh	National University of Modern Languages, Pakistan
Sadia Shaikh	Benazir Bhutto Shaheed University, Pakistan
Ghazala Shaukat	University of Sindh, Pakistan
Vinesh Maran Sivakumaran	INTI International College, Malaysia
Rana Muhammad Sohail Jafar	Guangzhou University, China
Yu Qing Soong	Universiti Sains Malaysia, Malaysia
Muhammad Faisal Sultan	Khadim Ali Shah Bukhari Institute of Technology (KASBIT), Pakistan
Sumaiya Syed	Shah Abdul Latif University, Pakistan
Mcxin Tee	INTI International University, Malaysia
Bak Aun Teoh	Universiti Teknikal Malaysia Melaka (UTeM), Fakulti Pengurusan Teknologi Dan Teknousahawanan (FPTT), Centre of Technopreneurship Development (CTeD), Malaysia
Muhammad Nawaz Tunio	University of Sufism and Modern Sciences, Pakistan
Geetha Veerappan	Universiti Tunku Abdul Rahman, Malaysia

Preface

Hello and welcome to the fascinating world of Asia's sustainable business. To promote sustainable economic growth and environmental stewardship, this book attempts to explore the critical junction between green finance and entrepreneurship.

The need for companies to implement environmentally friendly practices has become increasingly pressing in today's quickly changing global environment. With the introduction of creative and sustainable business models, entrepreneurs have emerged as major change-makers, driven by their passion and vision. This book aims to shine attention on green entrepreneurship's enormous potential as a driver of favourable environmental and social change.

This book shed light on how financial systems and institutions can effectively support the expansion of sustainable start-ups as we delve into the world of green finance practices in the book chapters. This book offers entrepreneurs the knowledge and resources they need to successfully negotiate the complex financial landscape and secure funding for their sustainable ventures by highlighting the importance of specialized financing options, funding mechanisms and investment strategies for green businesses.

This book is equipped with a thorough examination of the Asian business environment, with a focus on start-ups with a sustainable business model. This book also stresses the value of cooperation and information exchange among participants in the ecosystem of green entrepreneurship. The book chapters emphasize the need of building partnerships and gaining access to mentorship to promote growth, innovation and sustainability. This applies to incubators, accelerators, industry networks and organizations that focus on sustainability. This book also discusses the difficulties and barriers experienced by green business owners, offering solutions and doable plans of action. We examine the difficulties involved in starting a sustainable company and provide recommendations for long-term success, covering everything from risk management and securing funding to interacting with moral clients and developing a sustainable brand.

In the end, the mission is to motivate and enable business leaders, financiers, policymakers and academics to adopt green business and green finance practices as the cornerstones of Asia's sustainable growth. The editors do not doubt that the knowledge from this book can create a greener, more inclusive and affluent future for future generations if the world harnesses the force of entrepreneurship and matches financial systems with environmental objectives.

Let's work together to create a future for our planet and our communities that is more robust and sustainable.

Acknowledgement

We want to express our sincere gratitude to the distinguished chapter authors for their essential contributions to this book. Your knowledge, commitment and enthusiasm have changed the information and contributed a variety of viewpoints that contribute to a deeper understanding of green entrepreneurship and sustainable business methods.

Your knowledge and perceptions have shed light on a variety of topics in the industry, including sustainable business practices, supply chain management, green marketing, innovation, etc. A thorough and stimulating resource for readers interested in sustainable business start-ups has been made possible thanks to the amount of information and research given in each chapter.

We would also like to thank the reviewers for their thorough analysis of the chapters, thoughtful criticism and insightful recommendations. Your thorough review procedure was crucial in making sure the content was accurate, coherent and pertinent. Your knowledge and critical thinking skills have made a significant impact on this book's overall quality.

We sincerely appreciate all the time, work and knowledge that each author and reviewer provided. It is admirable and strongly valued that you are committed to advancing knowledge in the areas of green entrepreneurship and sustainable company practices.

We also want to express our gratitude to the Emerald editorial and publishing staff for their professionalism, direction and assistance throughout the publication process. Your commitment to quality and keen eye for detail have greatly influenced the final shape of this book.

Finally, we want to thank our families, friends and other loved ones for their unfailing help and compassion. Your support and confidence in our work have inspired us to start this project and see it through to completion.

We recognize the collaborative efforts of the chapter authors and reviewers with the utmost gratitude and admiration. Without your knowledge, dedication and collaborative attitude, this book would not have been feasible. We are privileged to have collaborated with such gifted people who are bringing about positive change in the area of sustainable business.

We appreciate your efforts and participation in this critical journey towards a greener and more sustainable future.

Part 1
From Business Perspective

Chapter 1

The Grass Is Greener Where You Water It!

Tehzeeb Sakina Amir and Rabia Sabri

Abstract

This chapter *The Grass Is Greener Where You Water It!* delves deeper into explicating Employee Green Behaviour (EGB), which outlines the eco-friendly behaviours practiced by employees. The section provides a more thorough explanation of EGB, including its origins, theoretical foundations, and practical applications in a social and physical environment to create environmentally conscious workplaces. The in-role and extra-role of EGB are discussed to strengthen its execution, and its significance considering the present ecological exigency. This chapter outlines the five-features-hierarchical framework for EGB: Sustainability Initiatives, Non-Harmful Action, Resource Conservation, Peer Influence, and Individual Commitment. The environmental history, ecosystems, and biodiversity and their interaction with humans from the ancient period to the present day are provided. The later unit explores organizational plans to encourage EGB, focussing on the role of HR policies, practices, and systems in nurturing the culture of sustainability within organizations. This chapter reviews current studies on EGB, emphasizing the role of employee engagement, transformational environmental leadership, and corporate culture in promoting green practices. It contributes to the academic literature by analyzing EGB, its relevance, and the effects it can have on organizations and society. It is a great tool for academics, government officials, and business heads to make workplaces environmentally friendly.

Keywords: Green behaviour; Employee Green Behaviour; sustainability initiatives; eco-friendly workplace; HR green practices; conservation efforts

1. Green Behaviour

Green behaviour is the behaviour where an individual attempts to conserve natural resources and at the same time tries to protect the environment from different

Entrepreneurship and Green Finance Practices, 3–19
Copyright © 2024 Tehzeeb Sakina Amir and Rabia Sabri
Published under exclusive licence by Emerald Publishing Limited
doi:10.1108/978-1-80455-678-820231001

types of pollution. It could be a simple act of saving energy by switching off extra lights and fans, carrying a cloth bag when going out for groceries, avoiding use of plastics in whichever way possible, cutting down on use of paper, turning off tap while brushing teeth, etc.

When similar behaviours are practiced by an employee at the workplace, it is called *Employee Green Behaviour (EGB)*. It is the environmentally friendly behaviour an individual carries at workplace (Dumont et al., 2017; Norton et al., 2015). Stemming out of the term 'green behaviour' are concepts like The Green Consumer Behaviour, Employee Green Behaviour, Organizational Green Behaviour, etc. Further, there is also the Green Innovative Work Behaviour which is generating and implementing new environmentally friendly ideas which impact products, processes, and norms of the organizations (Aboramadan, 2020). EGB includes activities like turning off lights/fans when leaving office, using soft copies, informing any water/gas leaks, video conferencing, using backside of printed papers to take notes, avoid single-use plastic items, procuring sustainable products like glass or steel straws (Norton et al., 2017).

EGB is a comparatively newer concept and so far, has produced some ground-breaking and enlightening research. However, a lot still needs to be done to reinforce the concept and its implementation. EGB offers fertile ground for researchers to come up with different approaches from both organizations and individual perspectives. Especially if one looks at the regular updates on depleting environmental conditions, the need to carry out studies to encourage 'green behaviours' and correct the opposite behaviours is immense. The focus of studies should not only be towards organizational green strategies but also to explain, understand, predict, and control human behavioural factors.

1.1. Understanding Employee Green Behaviour

One of the popular definitions of EGB is *'scalable actions and behaviours that employees engage in that are linked with and contribute to or detract from environmental sustainability'* (Ones & Dilchert, 2013, pp. 115–148). The definition focusses on employees as the major players taking off the responsibility of the organization shoulders – and frame EGB as behaviours to be adopted, adapted, and acted intrinsically by the employees. Secondly, it doesn't mention anything about the consequences of those behaviours which are not under the control of the employees and are influenced by the actions of the teams/groups or departments internally and communities or governments externally. Third, the definition states 'scalable actions and behaviours' – employees sustainable behaviours need to be assessed in terms of their contribution which can vary from employee to employee. Lastly, the definition recognizes that not all behaviours can be beneficial to the environment, in simpler words, employee behaviours could harm the environment which is the darker side of the EGB construct. Sustainable acts are those which reinforce the behaviours resulting in environmental conservation and refraining from the acts which result in environmental pollution and damage. The definition raises an important query which is whether green behaviours are part of the job behaviours and organizational goals or not.

Fig. 1.1.   Three Dimensions of EGB.

Green behaviours encompass three 'R's' i.e. *Reduce, Reuse,* and *Recycle* (Fig. 1.1). But not all green behaviours at workplace can be put into these dimensions (Paillé & Boiral, 2013).

1.1.1. In-Role and Extra-Role Green Behaviours

It is advised that EGBs should not be left as optional behaviour at workplace; with corporate world getting into the concept, EGB becomes significant. When the green behaviour is driven by the workplace policies and linked to the performance assessment criteria, it becomes a mandatory performance indicator for the employee. A voluntarily displayed EGB is where the employee intrinsically feels responsible and avoids getting involved in any act of polluting the environment. They are called *in-role and extra-role green behaviours*; HR practices have found to influence in-role green behaviours both directly and indirectly which can be further strengthened by the psychological green climate of the individual (Dumont et al., 2017). Organizational performance enhanced because of voluntary (Chen et al., 2014a, 2014b) and controlled green behaviours of the employees (Paillé et al., 2014). When an organization shares environmental knowledge, it creates a positive impact on EGB (Zhang, Xu et al., 2021).

To broaden the horizon of EGB, the concept of Green Human Resource Management (GHRM) originated. These are the strategies to promote environmental awareness at workplace, these include green recruitment, green training, green rewarding, and the green performance appraisal (Pham et al., 2019; Ren et al., 2018). Green recruitment signifies hiring employees with awareness and knowledge of green practices in the workplace. Green training means developing green skills in employees. And green performance appraisal means setting up green criteria for performance assessment linked with green rewards to incentivize employees.

1.2. Multilevel Model for EGB

The model has five dimensions, (1) Working Sustainably, (2) Avoiding Harm, (3) Conserving, (4) Influencing Others, and (5) Taking Initiative (Fig. 1.2).

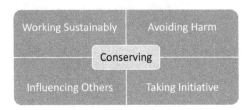

Fig. 1.2.   Multilevel Model for EGB by Ones and Dilchert.

The model establishes EGB as voluntary as well as interdependent to encompass the whole organization. Employees are encouraged to go beyond the set green policies and take personal initiatives (Fig. 1.3). A maximum of 29% of EGBs must be designed as part of employees' duties and performance management (Norton et al., 2015).

2. Historical Background

The movement of environment preservation was initiated by Europe in the mediaeval era led by United States of America. The environmentalist movement was initially focussed on forestry leading to fisheries, protected hunting grounds, and preserving wilderness. Henry D. Thoreau said, 'in wilderness is the preservation of the world'. In the early 1800s, industrial revolution gave rise to the use of coal; movement took speed and awareness started worldwide of pollution and depletion of natural resources. In the United States, national parks started to appear to counter pollution and its effect on the environment. During the 20th century, the world generally ignored green behaviour due to the two world wars and Great Depression. The first Earth Day was celebrated on 22 April 1970, and since then the green movement is much talked about resulted in actions for preservation of nature by socialist, politicians, religious leaders, and business organizations (Lallanilla, 2020).

Attitudinal - individuals are likely to manifest EGB when it corresponds well with their personal internal attitudes. Employees with internal commitment towards environment will probably adhere to the organizational green policies.

Normative – employees will display it more often to earn social gains. At workplace these behavioral norms are formed through organizational rewards & recognition policies.

Exchange – employees are most likely to involve in EGBs when their leader show commitment towards green behavior and policies (Cropanzano & Mitchell, 2005).

Motivational – employees do not only generate the drive to engage in EGB but to intensify the efforts and continuation of the efforts no matter if the impact is low and taking time to reap the benefits.

Fig. 1.3.   Norton et al. (2015) – Four Theoretical Explanations of the Whys and Hows of EGBs.

2.1. Organizational EGB Strategies

Organizations these days are focussing on integration of green-oriented pro-grammes. The management vows to practice green policies and make it part of their mission and vision statements (Unsworth et al., 2021). For example, Toyota Global Vision states 'Toyota will lead the future mobility society, enriching lives around the world with the safest and most responsible ways of moving people. Through our commitment to quality, ceaseless innovation, and *respect for the planet*, we strive to exceed expectations and be rewarded with a smile'. Educational institutes seem to take a leading role in identifying needs and tackling challenges of environmental concerns (Finlay & Massey, 2012). They must set a precedent for the future workforce to get into the habit of taking care of and conserving the environment (Fig. 1.4).

3. Literature Review

Deci and Ryan (2008) in their self-determination theory gave the concept of autonomous and controlled motivations. In this context, employees will be motivated to display more and more EGB if they feel personally satisfied and they expect that they will be rewarded by the organization. The employees' personal

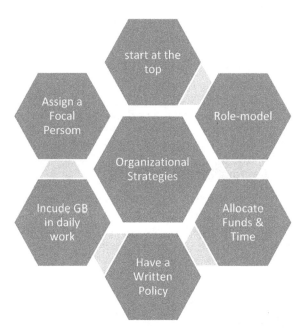

Fig. 1.4.   Organizational Strategies to Keep Employees Engaged in Green Behaviour.

attitudes and values (autonomous motivation) and organizational reward system (controlled motivators) together will generate a strong commitment towards green behaviours (Gagné & Deci, 2005). Controlled and autonomous motivation mediates the relationships between pro-environmental and voluntary and required green behaviours (Tian et al., 2020).

A joint effort of management, policy makers, leaders, workers, peers can influence and promote EGB (Norton et al., 2015). Employee involvement is very crucial for implementation of green behaviour (Mousavi et al., 2019). The group norms and behaviours in an organization strongly impact the EGB. Perceived coworker's support and appreciation create a positive indirect effect on eco-helping behaviours (Paillé & Boiral, 2013) on both mandatory and voluntary behaviours.

The empirical evidence establishes that GHRM is positively related to green task behaviour, green employee empowerment, green job crafting, and organizational citizenship behaviour towards the environment (Chaudhary, 2019; Fawehinmi et al., 2020; Hameed et al., 2020). GHRM further promotes innovative behaviour from employees as they think and act in various innovative ways to promote it (Luu, 2019). GHRM predicts both voluntary and task-based EGBs with organizational identification as an important mediating factor (Chaudhary, 2020), environmental beliefs further mediate the positive relationship between GHRM and voluntary behaviours (Zhu et al., 2021).

Wilson et al. (2016) found that feedback interventions and educating employees about sustainable environment solutions resulted in significant decreased energy consumption. Training enhances employees' level of awareness and their commitment towards green behaviours. It enables employees to take pro-environmental actions at workplace voluntary (Saeed et al., 2019; Sammalisto & Brorson, 2008; Zibarras & Coan, 2015). Green culture, green practices, and digitalisation are the key outcomes of EGBs (Khattak & Khalid, 2022). Training employees and initiating development programmes result in employees' awareness (Iqbal et al., 2018).

4. Personality Factors Influencing EGB

Personality factors, early habits, and personal norms regarding environmental concerns result in voluntary green behaviours at workplace (AlSuwaidi et al., 2021). Though Zhang et al. (2014) reported no effect of personal norms on EGB. Job characteristics like autonomy, affective commitment to the organization, and perceived support on citizenship behaviours have positive effect on eco-helping behaviours (Paillé et al., 2014).

5. Leadership and Employee Green Behaviour

Managers/leaders play a crucial role between the 'organization' and the 'employees'; they provide meaning to this relationship. The pro-environmental decisions are therefore largely affected by how the manager interpret and perceive the same (Hanh et al., 2014; Larsson et al., 2016). If the managers view EGB as an integral part of the business, the employees will also take it as a serious job performance criterion, but if the managers feel that EGB is something out of company's processes and a more societal external pressure, the employees will not give a heed to *required* green behaviours (Del Giudice et al., 2017). Sceptical managers will make the green behaviours appear impossible to attain for the employees (Demers & Gond, 2020). Employee voluntary green behaviour is nurtured through responsible and transformational leadership and supervisory support (Ramus & Steger, 2000; Zhang, Ul-Durar et al., 2021).

The term 'environmental transformational leadership (ETFL)' encompasses pro-environmental behaviours through transformational leadership concept (Roberson & Barling, 2013). ETFL influences employees' view about green behaviours and its significance (Kim et al., 2019). Persuasive leadership and supportive peer groups are likely to change an employee's take on green behaviours and how he can contribute to environment sustainable actions (Robertson & Carleton, 2018; Wesselink et al., 2017). Though no significant relationship is reported between ethical leadership and EGB (Adnan, 2021); environment-specific ethical leadership results in greater committed EGB and foster psychological green climate (Khan et al., 2022; Saleem et al., 2021). Servant leadership influences psychological empowerment and autonomous motivation for the environment results in voluntary EGB (Ying et al., 2020).

A leader, Paul Polman and Bhattacharya (2016) ex-CEO of Unilever – a company committed to sustainability summed up 8-ways to keep employees engaged in the organization's efforts on sustainability and pro-environment behaviours:

(1) Define the company's long-term purpose – include 'doing-good' to society and community where they operate. This way employees feel part of the bigger picture and at the same time accept that the impact of sustainable efforts will take time to show and hence feel persistent in their efforts.

(2) Spell out economic case for sustainability – highlight the economical aspect of sustainability – making your employees aware of the economic impact like energy saving, decrease in wastage, reduced medical expenses, etc., all resulting in a green line to the profits means more bonuses, benefits, and better lifestyle for the employees.

(3) Create sustainability knowledge and competence – keep employees informed why sustainability is important for the company and how they can contribute. This can be achieved through training the employees as to how they play their part in this important business aspect.

(4) Make every employee a sustainable champion – get every employee onboard with sustainability by making them understand and provide them with training for a successful implementation.

(5) Co-create sustainable practices with employees – give the employees voice to participate in the sustainability decisions. Participatory approach inculcates commitment and sustained efforts from the employees. You already get a buy-in!

(6) Encourage healthy competition among employees – announce awards and rewards for healthy competition amongst departments and employees. Healthy competitions are at times fun also, so the organization gets an added benefit of employee engagement with happy work force. Announcing recognition as well as monetary rewards will work for e.g. extra bonus for the department with the highest reduction in energy bills, picnic or trips, appreciation letters, e-mails, and/or a medal/cap/jacket for an 'EGB champion'.

(7) Make sustainability visible inside and outside the company – communicate sustainable behaviours and keep reviews and feedback available for the employees. Celebrate success! Also create voice in the industry and outside company through your website, advertisement – your customer will be happy to learn about pro-environmental behaviours of the organization, this leaves a soft feeling in their attitudes and hearts… means more business!

(8) Showcase higher purpose by creating transformational change – bring in sustainability as a transform change by changing the way business is conducted. Making sustainability an embedded part of the business.

6. Theoretical Framework

Theory of Planned Behaviour is the positive or negative attitude towards the behaviour, social pressure to execute or not to execute the behaviour, and the perception of ease or difficulty to perform the behaviour. When employees have time to plan their green behaviours, the underlying force is the intention, and the intention is determined by attitude, perceived control, and subjective norms. Intentions to consume green products is positively affected by perceived behavioural control and attitudes (Al Mamun et al., 2018).

Theory of Social Exchange suggests that humans calculate a cost–benefit ratio in a relationship to determine its worth (Cook et al., 2013). Once employees realize that their acts of sustainability and green behaviours would be beneficial for the larger community as well as for themselves in short- and long-term manners, they tend to be more committed with it. Cost would be the time and effort to get involved in the EGB and benefits would be social approvals, cleaner environment, etc.

Linear Theory of Social Change states that society moves to a more civilized way gradually. The movement is in the direction of improvement (Qing, 2010). Out of the three stages presented by Comte: The Theological, The Metaphysical, and The Positive; it is believed that man is currently at the Positive stage. At this stage now man is carrying a positive attitude to understand environmental and social dynamics. Man is seeking empirical causes and facts and figures to explain life phenomena. Human society is progressing towards a better improved state (Turner et al., 2002).

These theories cultivate and direct human behaviour as an outcome of their negative or positive attitude towards green behaviour. A positive attitude could be determined by the cost–benefit analysis by individual regarding the behaviour. So, if an employee gets to know the cost and benefits attached to the green behaviours (through organizational policies), this will greatly impact his attitude towards EGB. The cost and benefit analysis will further help in long-term sustainability of the green behaviours – outside the workplace and more as an outcome of voluntary behaviour engagement. All of it will pursue society's efforts towards improvement and betterment of humans.

Most recently, at The World Economic Forum 2022, Anna Brog (President and CEO of Vattenfall) in the Accelerating and Scaling Up Climate Innovation session quipped '*Businesses can't afford to not change when the world around you are changing*'. The significance of transition to clean energy was emphasized by German Chancellor Scholz and Fatih Birol (Executive Director IEA) that the effects of climate change are felt across the globe and achieving net-zero through energy waste reduction by 2050 is a humongous task.

7. Organizational Benefits of EGB

EGB contributes to building an environmentally friendly and socially responsible organization image in addition to culture and ethical practices of the organization (Zientara & Zamojska, 2018). Organizational CSR activities though promote emotional and environmental well-being but not necessarily the specific employees' behaviours which CSR outlines (Süßbauer & Schäfer, 2019). Organization CSR activities significantly increase the likelihood of employees behaving in a socially responsible manner outside the organization as well. EGB has positive relationships with CSR, green psychological climate, and pro-environmental behaviours (Katz et al., 2022). With COVID-19 workplace dynamics change. The effects are far reaching and long-lasting (Davis et al., 2021) (Table 1.1). Employees are becoming health focussed and showed dissatisfaction with existing health policies prevalent in the organizations. At the same time, they realize that they can contribute to the overall health-eco-system which gives rise to EGB and organization environment sustainable policies (Azizi et al., 2021).

Table 1.1. Some Benefits of Green Culture for the Organization (Harris & Crane, 2002).

1.	Helps with recruitment – a company with green culture becomes a likeable place for work hence inviting good potential candidates.
2.	Improves morale and productivity – green initiatives promote loyalty and commitment of employees and hence improving their performance and overall morale.
3.	Giving a sense of community care – green culture inculcates a sense of community care amongst the employees of that organization, and they take pride in working for such a company.
4.	Builds pride – employees are satisfied and feel proud to be part of an organization having a green culture. Simply it is called a 'good' business!
5.	Reducing cost and enhance profit lines.

8. Measuring EGB

Organizations measure EGBs through their own records, energy consumption patterns, audit reports, and procurement details (Davis et al., 2020). Organizations conduct energy audits to analyze energy consumption, flow, and conservation. Such audits are aimed at reducing or managing energy used without effecting productivity.

8.1. List of EGB Instruments

Several psychometric tools have been developed to measure EGB and its related constructs. These tools help to determine the EGB objectively and scientifically. Some of them are listed below in Table 1.2:

Table 1.2. Instruments of EGB.

Instrument Name	Author(s)/Year
Employee Green Behaviour Descriptive Norms Scale	McConnaughy (2014)
Green Human Resource Management Scale	Guiyao et al. (2017)
Green Work Engagement Scale	Schaufeli et al. (2006)
Green In-role and Extra-role Behaviour Scale	Francoeur et al. (2021)
Pro-Environmental Behaviour Scale	Markle (2013)

9. EGB Real-Time Examples

(1) *Unilever* – arrange 'lunch/tea and talk' sessions on sustainability, announced awards and rewards at department and employees' for green behaviours. Play green behaviour videos in the reception, lunch/cafeteria areas, employees' portals. Keep a separate budget for EGB trainings, make sustainability a part of decision-making process, form cross-functional green teams for exchange of ideas and taking decisions, take regular feedbacks, seeking ideas for improvements.

(2) *Patagonia* (a sportswear designer company) – *the greener they go, the larger they grow*, with only 4% turnover rate which they attribute to their 'Employee Internship Programme', where they promote employees to work for the planet earth through activism. From 5 km runs to bike-to-work and other various community volunteer opportunities they encourage employees to raise money and actively work for sustainability of the planet. Their manufacturing, distribution, and recycling functions are based on eco-friendly practices. Conducting waste audits is also their way to know the potential recycled material.

(3) *Nike*: The Lunch Programme – Their 'reusable dishware programme' discourages employees to buy and bring disposable lunch boxes to work. The results are 11.5% reduction in waste per employee at the year end and reduction in single-use food containers by 16,000 pounds per quarter.

(4) *Disney* – Food Waste Energy – the most successful food waste recycling programme and created biogas. Disney biogas facility produces power enough to light 2000 homes and lowers down Disney own power consumption.

(5) *Coca-Cola*: 'Do One Thing' campaign focussed on educating and creating awareness among their employees about the sustainability programmes at the company. Employees were asked to come up with 'one thing' they would do for the planet Earth on its day. They gave employees access to the 'Ask Milo' tool which tells them immediately if the item can or cannot be recycled. They created a circular economy by collecting and recycling their bottle or can. This reduces their cost of buying new material. Their 'World Without Waste Programme' resulted in 80% of their packaging is recyclable which is a great achievement. Their future goal is to make their packaging 100% recyclable by 2025.

(6) *Intel*: E-Waste Recycling Bins – Intel recycles 75% of their total waste. They introduced a reward programme for employees showing sustainable behaviour, they placed recycled bins for employees to dispose-off their digital waste. The result is a highly motivated work force making Intel a zero-waste company.

(7) *GE* with the launch of its *ecomagination* initiative in 2005, they had successfully sold 70 billion dollars of green products and services by 2011. The company is now committed to double its investment in its green projects.

(8) *Walmart* built its facility with a skylight/dimming system. As the day progresses, it allows Walmart to dim or turn off the lights, saving electricity during peak business hours.

(9) *Burger King* (Spain) combined energy management with employee engagement, they provided awareness sessions to the employees which resulted in consumption usage.

(10) *Prius* car by Toyota was the first hybrid car to reduce carbon emissions.

(11) *McDonald* plans to switch to recycled material for all its packaging by 2025.

(12) *Dunkin'* has switched from foam cup to paper cup for its coffee.

(13) *Hewlett Packard* is working on making every item of the products completely recyclable.

The efforts by various organizations highlight the importance of green behaviours in the workplace. Research must aim to provide the outcomes of such activities to strengthen the management commitment and perseverance towards green policies. What needs to be done is to form an integrated approach among organization, employees, and society for more sustainable actions which can be achieved through research-oriented approaches.

In a nutshell

- EGB (see Fig. 1.5) is everyone's responsibility inside and outside the organization. At individual level, one must display green behaviours and take responsibility of the actions which are harmful for the environment.
- Awareness of green behaviours should start from early education years and would be then easier to adopt the same in workplace.
- Organizations must undertake actions to integrate EGBs with performance management, role and tasks descriptions, organizational change towards green practices, and hiring people having pro-green attitudes or beliefs. Rather than perceiving green culture as an expense, organizations need to change their perspective to an investment for the betterment of business and society.
- Researchers/behavioural scientists have enough room to carry out empirical studies to further strengthen the significance of EGBs. These studies on the one hand enlighten the organizations to understand and implement green policies in their businesses. On the other hand, the findings could be used to influence the policy makers to come up with sustainable development plans. More so, at the individual level, awareness can generate more green behaviours in their personal and social lives other than workplace.
- A qualitative approach should be adopted towards understanding human behavioural dynamics as it will provide us with in-depth understanding of what and how to drive (green) human behaviours.

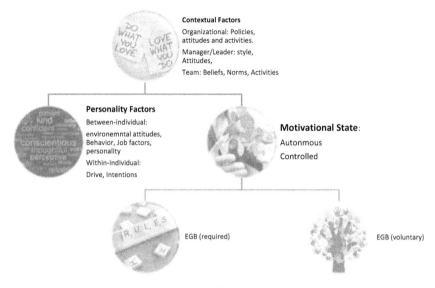

Fig. 1.5.   Visual Summary of EGB. *Source*: Images are taken from
Google Images.

References

Aboramadan, M. (2020). The effect of green HRM on employee green behaviors in higher education: The mediating mechanism of green work engagement. *International Journal of Organizational Analysis*, *30*, 7–23.

Adnan, M. (2021). Employee's performance as a consequence of employee green behavior as a consequence of green HRM practices and ethical leadership: The mediating role of green self efficacy. *Journal of Business and Social Review in Emerging Economies*, *7*(3), 599–612.

Al Mamun, A., Mohamad, M. R., Yaacob, M. R. B., & Mohiuddin, M. (2018). Intention and behavior towards green consumption among low-income households. *Journal of Environmental Management*, *227*, 73–86.

AlSuwaidi, M., Eid, R., & Agag, G. (2021). Understanding the link between CSR and employee green behavior. *Journal of Hospitality and Tourism Management*, *46*, 50–61.

Azizi, M. R., Atlasi, R., Ziapour, A., Abbas, J., & Naemi, R. (2021). Innovative human resource management strategies during the COVID-19 pandemic: A systematic narrative review approach. *Heliyon*, *7*(6), e07233.

Chaudhary, R. (2019). Green human resource management and job pursuit intention: Examining the underlying processes. *Corporate Social Responsibility and Environmental Management*, *26*(4), 929–937.

Chaudhary, R. (2020). Green human resource management and employee green behavior: An empirical analysis. *Corporate Social Responsibility and Environmental Management*, *27*(2), 630–641.

Chen, Y., Tang, G., Jin, J., Li, J., & Paillé, P. (2014a). Linking market orientation and environmental performance: The influence of environmental strategy, employee's environmental involvement, and environmental product quality. *Journal of Business Ethics, 127*, 479–500. https://doi.org/10.1007/s10551-014-2059-1

Chen, Y., Wang, Y., Nevo, S., Jin, J., Wang, L., & Chow, W. S. (2014b). IT capability and organizational performance: The roles of business process agility and environmental factors. *European Journal of Information Systems, 23*(3), 326–342.

Cook, K. S., Cheshire, C., Rice, E. R., & Nakagawa, S. (2013). Social exchange theory. In J. DeLamater & A. Ward (Eds.), *Handbook of social psychology* (pp. 61–88). Springer.

Davis, E. B., McElroy-Heltzel, S. E., Lemke, A. W., Cowden, R. G., VanderWeele, T. J., Worthington, E. L., Jr, … Aten, J. D. (2021). Psychological and spiritual outcomes during the COVID-19 pandemic: A prospective longitudinal study of adults with chronic disease. *Health Psychology, 40*(6), 347.

Davis, M. C., Unsworth, K. L., Russell, S. V., & Galvan, J. J. (2020). Can green behaviors really be increased for all employees? Trade-offs for "deep greens" in a goal-oriented green human resource management intervention. *Business Strategy and the Environment, 29*(2), 335–346.

Deci, E. L., & Ryan, R. M. (2008). Self-determination theory: A macrotheory of human motivation, development, and health. *Canadian psychology/Psychologie canadienne, 49*(3), 182.

Del Giudice, M., Khan, Z., De Silva, M., Scuotto, V., Caputo, F., & Carayannis, E. (2017). The microlevel actions undertaken by owner-managers in improving the sustainability practices of cultural and creative small and medium enterprises: A United Kingdom–Italy comparison. *Journal of Organizational Behavior, 38*(9), 1396–1414.

Demers, C., & Gond, J. P. (2020). The moral micro foundations of institutional complexity: Sustainability implementation as compromise-making at an oil sands company. *Organization Studies, 41*(4), 563–586.

Dumont, J., Shen, J., & Deng, X. (2017). Effects of green HRM practices on employee workplace green behavior: The role of psychological green climate and employee green values. *Human Resource Management, 56*(4), 613–627.

Fawehinmi, O., Yusliza, M. Y., Mohamad, Z., Faezah, J. N., & Muhammad, Z. (2020). Assessing the green behavior of academics: The role of green human resource management and environmental knowledge. *International Journal of Manpower, 41*(7), 879–900.

Finlay, J., & Massey, J. (2012). Eco-campus: Applying the ecocity model to develop green university and college campuses. *International Journal of Sustainability in Higher Education, 13*(2), 150–165.

Francoeur, V., Paillé, P., Yuriev, A., & Boiral, O. (2021). The measurement of green workplace behaviors: A systematic review. *Organization & Environment, 34*(1), 18–42.

Gagné, M., & Deci, E. L. (2005). Self-determination theory and work motivation. *Journal of Organizational Behavior, 26*(4), 331–362.

Guiyao, T., Chen, Y., Jiang, Y., Paillé, P., & Jia, J. (2017). Green human resource management practices: Scale development and validity. *Asia Pacific Journal of Human Resources, 56*(1), 31–55. https://doi.org/10.1111/1744-7941.12147

Hameed, Z., Khan, I. U., Islam, T., Sheikh, Z., & Naeem, R. M. (2020). Do green HRM practices influence employees' environmental performance? *International Journal of Manpower, 41*(7), 1061–1079.

Hanh, T., Preuss, L., Pinkse, J., & Figge, F. (2014). Cognitive frames in corporate sustainability: Managerial sensemaking with paradoxical and business case frame. *Academy of Management Review, 39*(4), 463–487.

Harris, L. C., & Crane, A. (2002). The greening of organizational culture: Management views on the depth, degree, and diffusion of change. *Journal of Organizational Change Management, 15*(3), 214–234. https://doi.org/10.1108/09534810210429273

Iqbal, Q., Hassan, S., Akhtar, S., & Khan, S. (2018). Employee's green behavior for environmental sustainability: A case of banking sector in Pakistan. *World Journal of Science, Technology and Sustainable Development, 15*, 118–130. https://doi.org/10.1108/WJSTSD-08-2017-0025

Katz, I. M., Rauvola, R. S., Rudolph, C. W., & Zacher, H. (2022). Employee green behavior: A meta-analysis. *Corporate Social Responsibility and Environmental Management, 29*, 1146–1157. https://doi.org/10.1002/csr.2260

Khan, N. U., Cheng, J., Yasir, M., Saufi, R. A., Nawi, N. C., & Bazkiaei, H. A. (2022). Antecedents of employee green behavior in the hospitality industry. *Frontiers in Psychology, 13*, 836109. https://doi.org/10.3389/fpsyg.2022.836109

Khattak, A. N., & Khalid, M. M. (2022). Employee green behavior and the role of a green sustainable recruitment and selection plan. A call for action. *Webology, 19*(2), 5093–5105.

Kim, Y. J., Kim, W. G., Choi, H. M., & Phetvaroon, K. (2019). The effect of green human resource management on hotel employees' eco-friendly behavior and environmental performance. *International Journal of Hospitality Management, 76*, 83–93.

Lallanilla, M. (2020, December 30). *The effects of war on the environment.* Treehugger. https://www.treehugger.com/the-effects-of-war-on-environment-1708787

Larsson, M., Milestad, R., Hahn, T., & Von Oelreich, J. (2016). The resilience of a sustainability entrepreneur in the Swedish food system. *Sustainability, 8*(6), 550. https://doi.org/10.3390/su8060550

Luu, T. T. (2019). Green human resource practices and organizational citizenship behavior for the environment: The roles of collective green crafting and environmentally specific servant leadership. *Journal of Sustainable Tourism, 27*(8), 1167–1196.

Markle, G. L. (2013). Pro-environmental behavior: Does it matter how it's measured? Development and validation of the pro-environmental behavior scale (PEBS). *Human Ecology, 41*(6), 905–914.

McConnaughy, J. C. (2014). Development of an employee green behavior descriptive norms scale. *Electronic Theses, Projects, and Dissertations, 83*. https://scholarworks.lib.csusb.edu/etd/83

Mousavi, S., Bossink, B., & van Vliet, M. (2019). Microfoundations of companies' dynamic capabilities for environmentally sustainable innovation: Case study insights from high-tech innovation in science-based companies. *Business Strategy and the Environment, 28*(2), 366–387. https://doi.org/10.1002/bse.2255

Norton, T. A., Parker, S. L., Zacher, H., & Ashkanasy, N. M. (2015). Employee green behavior: A theoretical framework, multilevel review, and future research agenda. *Organization & Environment, 28*(1), 103–125.

Norton, T. A., Zacher, H., Parker, S. L., & Ashkanasy, N. M. (2017). Bridging the gap between green behavioral intentions and employee green behavior: The role of green psychological climate. *Journal of Organizational Behavior*, *38*(7), 996–1015.

Ones, D. S., & Dilchert, S. (2013). *Measuring, understanding, and influencing employee green behaviors. Green organizations: Driving change with IO psychology.* Taylor & Francis. https://doi.org/10.4324/9780203142936

Paillé, P., & Boiral, O. (2013). Pro-environmental behavior at work: Construct validity and determinants. *Journal of Environmental Psychology*, *36*, 118–128.

Paillé, P., Chen, Y., Boiral, O., & Jin, J. (2014). The impact of human resource management on environmental performance: An employee-level study. *Journal of Business Ethics*, *121*(3), 451–466.

Pham, N. T., Tučková, Z., & Jabbour, C. J. C. (2019). Greening the hospitality industry: How do green human resource management practices influence organizational citizenship behavior in hotels? A mixed-methods study. *Tourism Management*, *72*, 386–399.

Polman, P., & Bhattacharya, C. B. (2016). Engaging employees to create a sustainable business. *Stanford Social Innovation Review*, *14*(4), 34–39.

Qing, H. (2010). Progress theory: The constraint on China's cultural renaissance. In *Culture and social transformations in reform era China* (pp. 285–295). Brill.

Ramus, C. A., & Steger, U. (2000). The roles of supervisory support behaviors and environmental policy in employee "Ecoinitiatives" at leading-edge European companies. *Academy of Management Journal*, *43*(4), 605–626.

Ren, S., Tang, G., & Jackson, S. E. (2018). Green human resource management research in emergence: A review and future directions. *Asia Pacific Journal of Management*, *35*(3), 769–803.

Roberson, J., & Barling, J. (2013). Greening organizations through leaders' influence on employees' pro-environmental behaviors. *Journal of Organizational Behavior*, *34*, 176–194. https://doi.org/10.1002/job.1820

Robertson, J. L., & Carleton, E. (2018). Uncovering how and when environmental leadership affects employees' voluntary pro-environmental behavior. *Journal of Leadership & Organizational Studies*, *25*(2), 197–210. https://doi.org/10.1177/1548051817738940

Saeed, B. B., Afsar, B., Hafeez, S., Khan, I., Tahir, M., & Afridi, M. A. (2019). Promoting employee's pro-environmental behavior through green human resource management practices. *Corporate Social Responsibility and Environmental Management*, *26*(2), 424–438.

Saleem, M., Qadeer, F., Mahmood, F., Han, H., Giorgi, G., & Ariza-Montes, A. (2021). Inculcation of green behavior in employees: A multilevel moderated mediation approach. *International Journal of Environmental Research and Public Health*, *18*(1), 331. https://doi.org/10.3390/ijerph18010331

Sammalisto, K., & Brorson, T. (2008). Training and communication in the implementation of environmental management systems (ISO 14001): A case study at the University of Gävle. Sweden. *Journal of Cleaner Production*, *16*(3), 299–309. https://doi.org/10.1016/j.jclepro.2006.07.029

Schaufeli, W. B., Bakker, A. B., & Salanova, M. (2006). The measurement of work engagement with a short questionnaire: A cross-national study. *Educational and Psychological Measurement*, *66*(4), 701–716.

Süßbauer, E., & Schäfer, M. (2019). Corporate strategies for greening the workplace: Findings from sustainability-oriented companies in Germany. *Journal of Cleaner Production, 12*, 564–577. https://doi.org/10.1016/j.jclepro.2019.04.009

Tian, H., Zhang, J., & Li, J. (2020). The relationship between pro-environmental attitude and employee green behavior: The role of motivational states and green work climate perceptions. *Environmental Science and Pollution Research, 27*(7), 7341–7352.

Turner, J. H., Beeghley, L., & Powers, C. H. (2002). The sociology of Herbert Spencer. In J. H. Turner, L. Beeghley, & C. H. Powers (Eds.), *The emergence of sociological theory* (5th ed., pp. 54–89). Wadsworth Thomson Learning.

Unsworth, K. L., Davis, M. C., Russell, S. V., & Bretter, C. (2021). Employee green behaviour: How organizations can help the environment. *Current Opinion in Psychology, 42*, 1–6.

Wesselink, R., Blok, V., & Ringersma, J. (2017). Pro-environmental behaviour in the workplace and the role of managers and organisation. *Journal of Cleaner Production, 168*, 1679–1687.

Wilson, G. T., Bhamra, T., & Lilley, D. (2016). Evaluating feedback interventions: A design for sustainable behaviour case study. *International Journal of Design, 10*(2).

Ying, M., Faraz, N. A., Ahmed, F., & Raza, A. (2020). How does servant leadership foster employees' voluntary green behavior? A sequential mediation model. *International Journal of Environmental Research and Public Health, 17*(5), 1792. https://doi.org/10.3390/ijerph17051792

Zhang, J., Ul-Durar, S., Akhtar, M. N., Zhang, Y., & Lu, L. (2021). How does responsible leadership affect employees' voluntary workplace green behaviors? A multilevel dual process model of voluntary workplace green behaviors. *Journal of Environmental Management, 296*, 113205. https://doi.org/10.1016/j.jenvman.2021.113205

Zhang, W., Xu, R., Jiang, Y., & Zhang, W. (2021). How environmental knowledge management promotes employee green behavior: An empirical study. *International Journal of Environmental Research and Public Health, 18*(9), 4738.

Zhang, Y., Wang, Z., & Zhou, G. (2014). Determinants of employee electricity saving: The role of social benefits, personal benefits and organizational electricity saving climate. *Journal of Cleaner Production, 66*, 280–287.

Zhu, J., Tang, W., Wang, H., & Chen, Y. (2021). The influence of green human resource management on employee green behavior—A study on the mediating effect of environmental belief and green organizational identity. *Sustainability, 13*(8), 4544.

Zibarras, L. D., & Coan, P. (2015). HRM practices used to promote pro-environmental behavior: A UK survey. *International Journal of Human Resource Management, 26*(16), 2121–2142. https://doi.org/10.1080/09585192.2014.972429

Zientara, P., & Zamojska, A. (2018). Green organizational climates and employee pro-environmental behavior in the hotel industry. *Journal of Sustainable Tourism, 26*(7), 1142–1159. https://doi.org/10.1080/09669582.2016.1206554

Chapter 2

Challenges of Sustainable Finance in Transitions Economy

Mehwish Bhatti, Saba Shaikh and Nazish Baladi

Abstract

The main objective of this chapter is to figure out various challenges emerging, or transition economies face in fostering sustainable finance. In this regard, extensive review of the extant and relevant literature is conducted with specification of time range, online database, and keywords. The findings suggest the various financing barriers experienced by emerging and transition economies in implementing the sustainable development goals (SDGs). Furthermore, this chapter triggers further debate on green financing initiatives that can help in dealing with the challenges of sustainable finance. It is found that green financing initiatives offer significant solutions in emerging and transition economies. In addition, this chapter provides policy implications to academia, practitioners, financial institutions, and government agencies to promote sustainable finance.

Keywords: Sustainable finance; green initiatives; transition economies; challenges; sustainable development goals (SDGs); small- and medium-sized enterprises (SMEs)

1. Introduction

Currently, the world faces numerous social, environmental, and economic issues that must be resolved. The reduction of economic inequality, the fight against climate change, eradicating poverty, and more recently, mitigating pandemic risks all call for significant financial resources and investments (Pisani & Russo, 2021). As a result, financial institutions provide green solutions to businesses to help offset the problems and to attain sustainable development goals.

Zhang et al. (2019) mentioned that financial development is a key factor in determining how far China's renewable energy sector will advance. The Green Climate Fund (GCF), which 194 nations formed in 2010, aims to give developing

Entrepreneurship and Green Finance Practices, 21–45
Copyright © 2024 Mehwish Bhatti, Saba Shaikh and Nazish Baladi
Published under exclusive licence by Emerald Publishing Limited
doi:10.1108/978-1-80455-678-820231002

nations financial assistance so they may reduce their greenhouse gas emissions and prepare for climate change. Since then, both international organizations (such as the IFC, 2017) and national governments have frequently used the term 'green financing' in their reports. Academics have also given pertinent discussions a great deal of attention. However, green finance as a whole is still ill-defined and frequently combined with climate finance.

Sustainable financing is gaining the increased attention of businesses as well as environmentalists. Companies, non-governmental organizations, and developed or underdeveloped countries widely advocate sustainable finance initiatives to address sustainability challenges (Cunha et al., 2021). The question arises here about how finance can contribute to sustainable development. The primary function of the financial system is to allocate funds to the most productive uses. Finance can take the lead in investing in sustainable businesses, accelerating the transition to a low-carbon, circular economy (Schoenmaker & Schramade, 2019). Sustainable finance explores the interactions of finance (investment and lending) with economic, social, and environmental challenges.

Sustainable finance can play a significant role in the growth and progress of developing economies. Developed countries are better at regulating the environmental impacts of economic expansion because the laws that firms must follow are defined and enforced. While it is true that excessive use of resources and energy in developed countries causes the global environmental catastrophe, the global ecological crisis is also perpetuated by sluggish laws in developing countries. When ties with underdeveloped nations are created through international trade, they contribute to global environmental concerns. Environmental problems are much worse in developing countries because they don't follow business rules. It includes not getting rid of industrial waste, using old equipment, not keeping plants and equipment in good shape, and a lack of accountability of government bodies (Mumtaz & Smith, 2019).

Sustainable finance discusses the consideration of environmental, social, and governance factors while taking crucial investment decisions. Therefore, it grabbed the attention of many researchers who studied it from different perspectives. However, no attempt has been made to present a bibliographic study demonstrating how the topic has changed through time and the associated difficulties that developing and transitioning countries face. This study aims to highlight the knowledge regarding challenges faced by emerging and transition economies in promoting sustainable finance by evaluating existing literature. Further, it will discuss the possible solutions to the identified problems.

2. Background

2.1 History of Sustainability

Sustainability was not a key priority for many in the finance industry 20 years ago. There were, in fact, socially conscious investors. Some of them had developed from charitable trusts or religious organizations, while others had been founded as the US mutual fund sector began to boom in the 1960s. For corporations, the situation was comparable. In the 1980s and 1990s, capital market growth helped many businesses strengthen their governance, but societal and ecological concerns were not a priority. The year is 2019, and a lot has changed. The economic and political landscape has changed as a result of the financial crisis. The environmental, social, and governance (ESG) issues facing the world have changed. As a recent illustration, governments all around the world have responded to public calls for action on plastic pollution in our oceans by outlawing or taxing single-use plastics (Cooper, 2019).

2.2 Sustainable Finance

The financial sector has made adjustments in response to shifting public and legislative sentiment. Investors, banks, and companies all across the world are particularly interested in the idea of sustainable financing. Without taking environmental concerns into account, economic expansion would not be sustainable. Without adequate reversal of plans to finance such initiatives, international trade in ecological goods and services would not prove sufficient for environmental protection. The sustainable evaluation in finance will benefit numerous stakeholders and policymakers (Sarma & Roy, 2021).

When making investment decisions in the financial sector, environmental, social, and governance (ESG) factors are taken into consideration. This process encourages longer-term investments in sustainable economic activities and projects (Nicholls & Edmiston, 2019).

In order to move to a green economy with low emissions and resource efficiency, based on clean technology and other generally recognized solutions known as eco-innovation, the sustainability transition idea is typically proposed. Financial sector is significantly impacted by sustainability transition (Ryszawska, 2016). Economic progress is severely hampered by the current issues, both social and environmental (mainly related to extreme wealth inequality) and environmental (such as climate change, biodiversity loss, and resource depletion).

2.3 Rationale of the Study

Sustainable finance performs a vital part in the growth and progress of developing economies. Developed countries are better at regulating the environmental impacts of economic expansion because the laws that firms must follow are defined and enforced. While it is true that excessive use of resources and energy in developed countries causes the global environmental catastrophe, the global ecological crisis is also perpetuated by sluggish laws in developing countries. When ties with underdeveloped nations are created through international trade, they contribute to global environmental concerns.

The aim of this research chapter is to diagnose various challenges emerging, or transition economies face in fostering sustainable finance. In this regard, extensive review of the extant and relevant literature is conducted with specification of time range, online database, and keywords. The findings suggest the various financing barriers experienced by emerging and transition economies in implementing the sustainable development goals (SDGs).

3. Methodology

Research methodology is a strategy for scientifically overcoming the research problem. The study of scientific research methods might be how one would describe it. In scientific research methods, we look at the methods generally employed by researchers to analyze their research problems, as well as the justifications for these methods. In addition to research methodologies and procedures, the researcher needs to be knowledgeable with methodology (Donthu et al., 2021).

Step 1 – research preparation and data collection

At the outset, we do a comprehensive literature search on the subject at hand. Keywords like 'financing', 'Sustainable finance', 'challenges', 'emerging', and 'transition' countries are used to identify the most relevant literature in the time span of 2017–2022. These terms are used independently and in conjunction to identify the appropriate literature. Numerous people have worked on this subject, and many articles have been written about it; however, you can only read the complete versions of the articles that you find by searching for the keywords online database google scholar and time frame.

Step 2 – data analysis and presentation

The second phase begins with a bibliographic analysis, which provides the current state of the pertinent work based on the sustainable finance. Second, previous research is shown in Table 2.1, which includes pertinent studies from transition economies. Discussion is had regarding the results and conclusions of previous researches.

This research is based on bibliometric analysis. Large-scale scientific data can be explored and analyzed using the popular and accurate bibliometric analysis technique. It gives us the chance to explore the subtleties of an evolutionary process in a particular subject while emphasizing its horizons. Yet, it has only recently and frequently been used to business research. Therefore, we intended to provide a summary of the bibliometric methodology, with a special emphasis on its many methodologies, while providing step-by-step instructions that can be used to meticulously conduct bibliometric analysis with conviction (Persson et al., 2009).

4. Results and Findings

4.1 Bibliography Analysis

The literature on the greening of the industry is significantly lacking despite the major contribution that green efforts have made to environmental sustainability. Few published studies have looked at this important contemporary topic in the financial sector. Furthermore, very few studies have described the difficulties that emerging economies confront in implementing sustainable finance. As a result, it is critical to identify, assess, and compare the challenges emerging and

Table 2.1. Existing Research.

SR. No.	Title	Author/Year	Journal	Year	Country	Objective	Methodology	Key Findings
1	Past, present, and future of sustainable finance: insights from big data analytics through machine learning of scholarly research	Kumar et al. (2022)	Annals of Operations Research		India	This study intends to perform a thorough analysis of scholarly research employing big data analytics and machine learning in the field of sustainable finance.	Bibliometric data on sustainable finance research.	This research sheds light on seven key topics in sustainable finance research: socially responsible investing, climate finance, green finance, impact investing, carbon finance, energy finance, and governance of sustainable investing and financing.
2	A taxonomy of sustainable finance taxonomies	Torsten Ehlers, Diwen (Nicole) Gao, Frank Packer (2021)	BIS Papers No 118 Monetary and Economic Department	2021	Paris	(1) Alignment with high-level policy goals. (2) Independence versus co-dependence.	The methodology transforms the temperatures provided by businesses as emission objectives. With respect to a metric (such as absolute carbon	The analysis's main policy recommendations are to i. Work to align transition taxonomies with the Paris Agreement's goals; ii. Encourage the development of

(Continued)

Table 2.1. (*Continued*)

SR. No.	Title	Author/Year	Journal	Year	Country	Objective	Methodology	Key Findings
							emissions of carbon intensity), each target corresponds to a linear annual reduction rate from the base year to the target year. Data for regressions that yield a point temperature estimate for any trend specified by the objective are acquired from a vast number of climate scenarios that map short, medium, and	such taxonomies; iii. Monitor and oversee the development of certification and verification procedures; and iv. Make impact reporting for green bonds mandatory.

| 3 | The green economy transition: the challenges of technological change for sustainability | Patrik Söderholm (2020) | 2020 | Söderholm Sustainable Earth | Discuss a number of challenges like a. Dealing with diffuse – and ever more global – environmental risks; b. Achieving radical and not just incremental sustainable technological change; c. Green capitalism and the uncertain long-term trends of absolute carbon emissions or emissions intensities into anticipated global warming in 2100. | The methodology of this paper is depends on comparative analysis and policy analysis of challenges literature. | The extent and type of the societal issues that result from environmental and climate risks are intricate and multifaceted. Even though the precise remedies may vary based on context, these problems are universal and should concern most nations and areas. Future research should focus more |

(Continued)

Table 2.1. (*Continued*)

SR. No.	Title	Author/Year	Journal	Year	Country	Objective	Methodology	Key Findings
						business-as-usual scenario; d. The role of the state and designing appropriate policy mixes; and e. Dealing with distributional concerns and impacts encountered when pursuing sustainable technological change.		on green innovation in the public sector.
4	Environmental Finance and Impact Investing: Status Quo And Future research	Christoph Bertle (2016)	ACRN Oxford Journal of Finance and Risk Perspectives	2016	Austria	With the aid of a thorough literature analysis, identify and list the current environmental finance streams,	In order to provide comprehensive and accurate insights into EF, markets,	Comparative research could be useful to validate the findings of this article. Additionally,

challenges, and potential future research areas.	and the impact investing areas with current streams, barriers, and future research proposals, a systematic literature review is conducted initially. Second, to ensure that only peer-reviewed and high-quality publications are used, the **ABS** 4th list (Harvey et al., 2010) is used to portray the overall picture.	extensive quantitative research and eventually sector specific research would provide the area with useful knowledge about things like the prerequisites for company formation and available funding options for businesses operating globally in the environmental sector. The distinction between the financial and environmental impact markets, as well as the distinction between the markets' right monetary and transparent measurement, have practical ramifications. Supply and demand

(Continued)

Table 2.1. (*Continued*)

SR. No.	Title	Author/Year	Journal	Year	Country	Objective	Methodology	Key Findings
								might gradually balance as jargon clears up and usage increases, in particular.
5	Sustainable Financing for New Vaccines in Indonesia: Challenges and Strategies	Fonjungo et al. (2020)	Sustainability	2020	Switzerland	Overcome the issue of sustainable financing for new vaccines in Indonesia. Practical solutions must be developed and implemented to increase budget flexibility for paying vaccines without compromising the requirements of the current healthcare system as the current immunization system transforms.	Secondary data is collected in this paper on the basis of strategies and methodologies of a COVID-19 vaccine and immunization system of various countries.	Vaccinations have the ability to improve the means of implementation for the SDGs because they are the most economical medical intervention. Sustainable financing for new vaccines is essential to ensuring that immunization systems can provide every targeted population with the vaccinations they need, and the issue

of financing is especially important as Indonesia moves away from intensive Gavi support and towards a self-financing immunization system. Hence, at this crucial moment, strong financial solutions and system structuring techniques are essential. To generate money for its immunization system, Indonesia may need to look into alternative options. Three strategies – general revenue from the central government, a sector-wide approach to finance, and a national trust fund – have been identified in a

(Continued)

Table 2.1. (*Continued*)

SR. No.	Title	Author/Year	Journal	Year	Country	Objective	Methodology	Key Findings
								number of published studies as potentially useful and doable to implement.
6	Too risky – The role of finance as a driver of sustainability transitions	Bjorn Nykvist, Aaron Maltais	Environmental Innovation and Societal Transitions	2022		So, the study's main objective is not to transition the financial industry per se, but rather to learn more about how finance functions as a key element of sustainability changes in larger economic activity. It is unclear if sustainable finance would alter financial players' traditional roles as efficient brokers of	Actors in the Swedish financial system regime are interviewed.	Sustainability is valued and obviously on the agenda in the Swedish finance sector, which has passed the point of no return. A considerable portion of capital is currently being screened or using ESG variables as a result of the sharp decline in the value of coal assets, increased awareness of climate hazards,

capital allocation and, consequently, how transitioning societies are financed.

and the rapid expansion of the renewable energy industry. Nearly all of our informants concurred that sustainable investment is both beneficial and essential, and that the financial industry is perhaps beginning to up to the task of facilitating the enormous amount of capital required. In the future decades, the finance sector will play a critical role in aiding sustainable transformations, but playing the usual mediator is indeed not the same as acting as a catalyst.

(Continued)

Table 2.1. (*Continued*)

SR. No.	Title	Author/Year	Journal	Year	Country	Objective	Methodology	Key Findings
7	Classification Scheme for Sustainable Investments	Timo Busch Victor van Hoorn Matthias Stapelfeldt Eric Pruessner	Classification Scheme for Sustainable Investments	2022	Hamburg/ Brussels,	Proposed a transition-focussed classification for investments.	The European Sustainable Investment Forum (Eurosif), the Global Sustainable Investment Alliance (GSIA), and the United Nations Principles for Responsible Investment (PRI) are widely used approaches for sustainable investment strategies. The applied strategy was built on these approaches and incorporate classification suggested by the impact task	Based on their desire to support a more sustainable economy, the categories of sustainable investments are categorized in this paper. It combines additional aspects from the classification proposed by the impact task force established by the G7 (ITF, 2021) and uses existing sustainable investment methods like exclusions or involvement as defining criteria. This classification is based on Busch et al. (2022). It is possible to seamlessly incorporate

#	Title	Author	Journal	Year	Country	Methodology	Description	Findings
							force established by the G7 (ITF, 2021), which is based on Busch et al. (2022).	regulatory strategies like PAIs and the EU Taxonomy alignment.
8	Defining transition finance and embedding it in the post-Covid-19 recovery	Ben Caldecott	Journal of Sustainable Finance and Investment	2020	UK	Literature review analysis.	In this article, the author makes the case that all future commercial and governmental financial institutions must put 'transition finance' at the forefront of any financing supplied as part of post-COVID-19 stimulus and bailouts. Furthermore, author defends his argue with literature support.	An exceptional challenge and opportunity are presented by the COVID-19-related stimulus and bailouts, as well as the significant rise in government-backed funding facilities for counterparties. As quickly as feasible, we must make sure Transition Finance is integrated into the structure of these funding facilities. This will hasten the mainstreaming and widespread acceptance of Transition Finance. Any COVID-19

(Continued)

Table 2.1. (*Continued*)

SR. No.	Title	Author/Year	Journal	Year	Country	Objective	Methodology	Key Findings
								loans supported by governments should be required to be SLLs, with a set of straightforward off-the-shelf sustainability performance measures adapted to sectoral and national benchmarks. This would be a straightforward action that could be performed right away.
9	Dirty Banking: Probing the Gap in Sustainable Finance	Dirty Banking: Probing the Gap in Sustainable Finance Michael A. Urban * and Dariusz Wójcik	Sustainability	2019	Switzerland	This paradox is underpinned by a major gap in the way sustainability has permeated primary and secondary markets which, we argue,	To evaluate the viability of investment banks' underwriting services, the analysis combines data	Investment banks do not hesitate to underwrite businesses that have been accused of serious environmental, social, and

No.	Title	Authors		Journal	Year	Country			
							calls for a serious rethinking of the sustainability transition in finance.	from Dealogic and the Norwegian Government Pension Fund Global (GPF-G).	governance violations, nor do they hesitate to underwrite businesses that produce divisive goods like tobacco, coal, and nuclear weapons. Moving forward, we make recommendations on how to solve this issue and urge more investigation into the role and agency of finance and advanced business services companies in sustainability transitions.
10	Green New Deal Policy of South Korea: Policy Innovation for a Sustainability Transition	Jae-Hyup Lee and Jisuk Woo	1	Sustainability	2020	Switzerland	The Green New Deal is a sustainability-focussed plan for building an pemission-free and climate-neutral economy that was put forth as a	Eight goals are outlined in a literature review analysis based on the Green New Deal in three crucial areas: low-carbon	The COVID-19–related stimulus and bailouts, with the attendant massive increase in government-backed financing facilities for counterparties, creates an

(Continued)

Table 2.1. *(Continued)*

SR. No.	Title	Author/Year	Journal	Year	Country	Objective	Methodology	Key Findings
						post-COVID-19 stimulus package.	decentralized energy, creative green industry, and green urban development. The Deal also includes safeguards for groups and industries that are more susceptible to being left behind during the process of the economy's transition.	unprecedented challenge and opportunity. One simple step that could be taken now, without much difficulty, is requiring ns backed by governments to be SLLs, with a series of simple off the shelf sustainability performance indicators tailored to sectoral and country benchmarks.

transitioning countries face in adopting sustainable financing and to come up with workable solutions. These investigations are especially important in developing countries where environmental concerns are rising and laws are not being adhered to exactly.

Wang and Zhi (2016) identified various insufficiencies in the elasticity of green money for renewable energy. They are concerned with how the market is doing and how policies are being created. They are impulsively suggested for more effectively establishing environmental balance while expressing internal disputes between green finance and environmental protection.

According to Koscielniak and Gorka (2016), public and private partnership processes (PPPs) scale and nature in the development of the Silesia state. PPP solutions as a framework determinant of sustainable development based on the choice on the aforementioned themes. The report described the PPP project for sustainable urban transportation that was put into place in the studied areas.

The most benefits for the strategic components of green banking were the major difficulty that Choudhury (2015) underlined. The green banking system is being built for the first time in Bangladesh, and another effort is being made to determine the regulatory, managerial, and environmental stakeholder pressures that can affect the bank that is being controlled by Bangladesh's government's deliberate environmental behaviour. Choudhary and their colleagues suggested that banks take an active part in preserving the environment, aggressively adopt environmental banking practices, and modify client banking practices. In addition to being beneficial for the environment, the application of proper environmental technology and management techniques will also result in better functioning. The study recommends that needs of stakeholders in the Green Banking system and offers some advice for the government, the entire banking industry, and the business community after applying both descriptive and accredited statistical analysis.

Keerthi (2013) emphasized the benefits and problems of green finance in India's developing economy. According to the report, the national government may assist the cities by boosting financing that is suitable for energy conservation and is also locally administered. The coordination between adjacent municipalities, regions, and the federal government is of utmost importance due to the various mandates, specializations, and multijurisdictional fluidity of the majority of environmental problems. The study also recommended new regulations for the local governments on the issue of emission permits as well as/or for the monitoring, reporting, and verification of emissions. The findings of this study open up possibilities for the green financing system, including the issuing of green bonds, improvements in banking, various green financing banking units, environmental risk adjustment with the primary risk, and other opinion formation procedures.

Mumtaz and Smith (2019) demonstrated Pakistan's tendency towards green financing. They emphasized that wealthier countries have more straightforward procedures for implementing the new forms of financing than poor nations do. This article analyzes the green finance mechanism for sustainable development in Pakistan by looking at the supply side of the green banking approach, which encompasses numerous issues faced by banks and DFIs, and the demand side, which refers to borrowers' compliance with green banking norms. Additionally, it examined the green finance policies that emerging nations had put in place and found that China and India were significantly superior at designing and putting green banking methods into effect. They advise that it is crucial to evaluate the comprehensive strategy on green funding if Pakistan is to make quick progress towards a greener environment and sustainable economic growth.

Setyowati (2020) published the practice of sustainable finance in Indonesia. The study looked at how Indonesia's sustainable finance roadmap had developed locally and looked into the major obstacles to its successful implementation. According to the study, financial institutions have developed sustainable finance action plans and submitted yearly sustainability reports to the financial regulator with a high level of procedural compliance. Yet, there is a lot of variance and inconsistency in how financial institutions define what counts as a 'green' initiative, allowing few financial institutions to participate more than involving only in token gestures. With the current level of regulatory scrutiny, it is difficult to understand how financial institutions could be encouraged to do more or how specific sustainability objectives could be achieved. This article suggests potential solutions to some of the roadblocks to the roadmap's implementation, including further action by Indonesia's central bank to encourage climate funding.

Kumar (2022) looked at the body of literature regarding financial incentives for going green in developing nations. The leading public sector banks and public sector enterprises that promote products, processes, and technology that helps lower carbon footprint in the environment were critically reviewed. He particularly concentrated on green bonds, including their primary forms and the contribution they make to uphold the Sustainable Development Goals. Additionally, the main obstacles to adopting green finance efforts in developing nations like India were explored.

The paper by Wakeford et al. (2017) explores Ethiopia's cement, skin, and textile industries, innovative system, and green industrialization based on nine semi-structured interviews with researchers looking into the country's green innovation and industrialization and a survey of 117 businesses in order to determine how effective they are in promoting industrialization. The findings revealed lower levels of product and process innovation among Ethiopian businesses. The high cost of technology, a lack of funding, and a lack of information are the key barriers to innovation. Reduced environmental impact and fewer environmental laws are among the least important motives for new invention among the powerful, and thus supports the rise of interaction between the powerful government and other players. Studies have demonstrated the importance of environmental regulation, financial support for organizations, and cooperation amongst key players.

4.2 Major Challenges

Following are the main challenges that sustainable finance is facing in meeting sustainable development goals that is being identified by the extensive literature review.

4.3 Disparities in Financial Access

According to Wakeford and their colleagues (2017), advanced economies now account for 97% of newly emerged sustainable investing funds are holding 80% of the world's assets under management. Sub-Saharan Africa accounts for only 0.3% in terms of value but 1.5% of all green bonds. The increased demand for sustainable recovery financing and the rising pressure on interest rates brought on by stimulus packages in advanced economies may have an influence on other countries' ability to recruit capital. Due to their tight fiscal space and severe debt sustainability restrictions, low-income countries (LICs) were only capable of investing 2.5% of their GDP on stimulus programs during the COVID-19 crisis, compared to 16% in HICs.

4.4 Regulatory Obstacles

The effectiveness of the current legal frameworks in providing financial institutions with clear guidance to construct their sustainable finance action plans and in finding activities capable of mainstreaming it into their business practices has been relatively limited. Even though a technical guideline to help financial institutions comply with the sustainable finance legislation has been released, 80% of financial institution representatives who were interviewed say they find it extremely difficult to understand what the guideline is trying to accomplish. Additionally, the guideline lacks any distinct metrics to assess compliance performance (Setyowati & Quist, 2022).

4.5 Inadequate Risk Management

One of the most effective methods for reducing the threats that climate change poses to the financial markets is proper risk management (Carney, 2015). Risk management in investment and lending decision-making is critical to maintain not only sustainability but also broader macroeconomic and financial sustainability, according to central banks and financial authorities around the world. Additionally, research indicates that financial organizations that use ESG criteria in business choices perform financially better than those that do not (Nizam et al., 2019).

4.6 Political Obstacles

This study reveals that various interests within financial institutions and regulatory authorities pose unique difficulties for implementing a sustainable plan. The conduct of banks and other financial institutions generally has not mainstreamed sustainable financing. Despite an increase in the proportion of financial portfolios going towards sustainable investments, these investments still make up a modest portion of financial institutions' overall financial portfolios. An official from the financial regulatory body particularized on the challenges of setting and enforcing more aggressive performance goals in the sustainable finance roadmap due to worries that doing so might reduce financial institutions' competitiveness and result in unplanned negative effects on the nation's economy.

4.7 Lack of Information on Environmental, Social, and Governance

In most developing nations, environmental, social, and governance (ESG) information is lacking, which may hide prospects and intensify the income bias in investment decisions. The level of development of a nation account for about 90% of its sovereign ESG score; if this bias is not taken into consideration while making investment decisions, money may be diverted to HICs at the expense of less developed nations. The push for sustainability might offer the long overdue reform of credit and risk ratings, as well as the battle against SDG-washing in HICs, a practice that unnecessarily diverts investors away from emerging countries, a fresh lease on life.

4.8 Green Financing Initiatives

The most innovative green finance projects over the past 10 years that have provided strategies to stabilize the current environmental situation have been green bonds. The only distinction between green bonds and conventional bonds is how the proceeds are used. The green projects would be financed with the funds raised by the green bonds.

4.9 Policy Implications

This study aims to highlight the knowledge regarding challenges faced by emerging and transition economies in promoting sustainable finance by evaluating existing literature. The breadth and character of the societal issues that result from environmental and climate concerns are intricate and multifaceted. Achieving sustainable development goals, converting the economy to one that is green, low carbon, and resource efficient, and addressing climate change are all part of the multilayered sustainability transition process. Sustainable, environmental, and climate finance are used to promote this process (Söderholm, 2020). This research developed a thorough grasp of sustainable finance and its contribution to the development of transition economies. This study provides valuable insights for policymakers in terms of the importance of sustainable finance in transitioning economies and the need for specific policies and regulations to promote its adoption. This can help in shaping the policy framework for sustainable finance in these economies and ensuring that the right incentives are in place to encourage the growth of sustainable finance practices. The policy environment typically relies on the scale of the project, be it large or micro. Improve the organs and develop the skills at the micro level, especially while forming agencies positive innovation to create green financial businesses comes next. Risk management, particularly financial risk management for carbon i.e. the adaptable operation to handle the switch to green finance. Financial institutions must thus pay particular attention to any changes in policy. Green financial institutions must cooperate with one another, improve new services and products, promote education, and improve their ability to adapt to and respond to fluctuations in the green financing model. China sustains a notable position for green financing at the continental level in Asia. As a result, the relevant ministries and commissions must strengthen the harmony as well as continue to build and update operation guidelines and pertinent laws and regulations. Typically, green finance and credit are at odds with one another. The government must create a logical preferential policy and provide incentives for the growth of green finance in order to overcome barriers; at the moment, policies and principles alone are insufficient. The platform must be developed to sustain the interchange of environmental energy while simultaneously lowering transaction costs. The majority of green financial services require the expert assistance of intermediate firms in order to carry out projects. This study will support incorporating environmentally friendly practices and addressing current policy-related difficulties. The research community, regulators, and officials may benefit greatly from these discoveries. This can help in creating awareness among the general public and promoting the use of sustainable finance practices.

5. Conclusion

This chapter's major goal is to identify the numerous obstacles that developing and transitioning economies must overcome in order to implement sustainable finance. This chapter also offers a thorough discussion of that might be used to address the current problems.

Developing or transitioning economies are at a disadvantage because they must overcome numerous challenges and obstacles in order to put sustainable finance policies into practice and achieve sustainable development objectives. According to research, in order to use green finance effectively, both banks and borrowers should gain a thorough awareness of green policies and comprehend how this mechanism may be made stronger over time.

This chapter has brought up a lot of intriguing new directions for future research on green finance efforts that earlier studies have missed. These new avenues will also offer a lot of opportunities for green finance of developing and transitional economies. This chapter has a limitation because of its use of specified keywords, a limited search time span, and the use of only one leading database.

References

Busch, T., van Hoorn, V., Stapelfeldt, M., & Pruessner, E. (2022, September). Classification scheme for sustainable investments – Accelerating the just and sustainable transition of the real economy. SSRN. https://ssrn.com/abstract=4217864 or https://doi.org/10.2139/ssrn.4217864

Carney, M. (2015, September 29). Breaking the tragedy of the Horizon – Climate change and financial stability. [Speech]. Lloyd's of London.

Choudhury, M. A. (2015). Monetary and fiscal (spending) complementarities to attain socioeconomic sustainability. *ACRN Journal of Finance and Risk Perspectives, Special Issue of Social and Sustainable Finance, 4*(3), 63–80.

Cooper, S. (2019). The evolution of sustainable finance. *Standard Chartered.* Https://Www.Sc.Com/En/Feature/the-Evolution-of-Sustainable-Finance

de Cunha, F. A. F. S., Meira, E., & Orsato, R. J. (2021). Sustainable finance and investment: Review and research agenda. *Business Strategy and the Environment, 30*(8), 3821–3838.

Donthu, N., Kumar, S., Mukherjee, D., Pandey, N., & Lim, W. M. (2021). How to conduct a bibliometric analysis: An overview and guidelines. *Journal of Business Research, 133*, 285–296. https://doi.org/10.1016/j.jbusres.2021.04.070

Fonjungo, F., Banerjee, D., Abdulah, R., Diantini, A., Kusuma, A. S. W., Permana, M. Y., & Suwantika, A. A. (2020). Sustainable financing for new vaccines in Indonesia: Challenges and strategies. *Sustainability, 12*(21), 9265. https://doi.org/10.3390/su12219265

Harvey, C., Morris, H., & Rowlinson, M. (2010). *Academic journal quality guide version 4.* The Association of Business Schools.

IFC. (2017). *Green bond impact report: Financial year 2017.* https://www.ifc.org/content/dam/ifc/doc/mgrt/201710-ifc-green-bond-impact-report-fy17-v2.pdf

ITF. (2021). *Financing a better world requires impact transparency, integrity and harmonisation.* https://www.impact-taskforce.com/workstreams/impact-transparency/

Keerthi, B. S. (2013). A study on emerging green finance in India: Its challenges and opportunities. *International Journal of Management and Social Sciences Research (IJMSSR), 2*(2), 49–53.

Koscielniak, H., & Gorka, A. (2016). Green cities PPP as a method of financing sustainable urban development. *Transportation Research Procedia, 16*, 227–235.

Kumar, S. (2022). Critical assessment of green financing initiatives in emerging market: A review of India's green bond issuances. *Academy of Marketing Studies Journal, 26*(5).

Kumar, S., Sharma, D., Rao, S. et al. (2022). Past, present, and future of sustainable finance: Insights from big data analytics through machine learning of scholarly research. *Annals of Operations Research.* https://doi.org/10.1007/s10479-021-04410-8

Mumtaz, M. Z., & Smith, Z. A. (2019). Green finance for sustainable development in Pakistan. *IPRI Journal, 19*(2), 1–34.

Nicholls, A., & Edmiston, D. (2019). Social innovation policy in the European Union. In A. Nicholls & R. Ziegler (Eds.), *Creating economic space for social innovation.* Oxford Academic. https://doi.org/10.1093/oso/9780198830511.003.0011

Nizam, E., Ng, A., Dewandaru, G., Nagayev, R., & Nkoba, M. A. (2019). The impact of social and environmental sustainability on financial performance: A global analysis of the banking sector. *Journal of Multinational Financial Management, 49*(C), 35–53.

Persson, O., Danell, R., & Wiborg Schneider, J. (2009). How to use Bibexcel for various types of bibliometric analysis. In *Celebrating scholarly communication studies: A Festschrift for Olle Persson at his 60th birthday* (vol. 5, pp. 9–24).

Pisani, F., & Russo, G. (2021). Sustainable finance and COVID-19: The reaction of ESG funds to the 2020 crisis. *Sustainability, 13*(23), 13253.

Ryszawska, B. (2016). Sustainability transition needs sustainable finance. *Copernican Journal of Finance & Accounting, 5*(1), 185–194.

Sarma, P., & Roy, A. (2021). A Scientometric analysis of literature on green banking (1995–March 2019). *Journal of Sustainable Finance & Investment, 11*(2), 143–162.

Schoenmaker, D., & Schramade, W. (2019). Investing for long-term value creation. *Journal of Sustainable Finance & Investment, 9*(4), 356–377.

Setyowati, A. B. (2020). Governing sustainable finance: Insights from Indonesia. *Climate Policy*, 1–14.

Setyowati, A. B., & Quist, J. (2022). Contested transition? Exploring the politics and process of regional energy planning in Indonesia. *Energy Policy, 165*, 112980. https://doi.org/10.1016/j.enpol.2022.112980

Söderholm, P. (2020). The green economy transition: The challenges of technological change for sustainability. *Sustainable Earth, 3*(1). https://doi.org/10.1186/s42055-020-00029-y

Wakeford, J. J., Gebreeyesus, M., Ginbo, T., Yimer, K., Manzambi, O., Okereke, C., Black, M., & Mulugetta, Y. (2017). Innovation for green industrialisation: An empirical assessment of innovation in Ethiopia's cement, leather and textile sectors. *Journal of Cleaner Production, 166*, 503–511.

Wang, Y., & Zhi, Q. (2016). The role of green finance in environmental protection: Two aspects of market mechanism and policies. *Energy Procedia, 104*, 311–316.

Zhang, D., Zhang, Z., & Managi, S. (2019). A bibliometric analysis on green finance: Current status, development, and future directions. *Finance Research Letters, 29*, 425–430.

Chapter 3

Green Entrepreneurial Practices Among Small and Medium Enterprises in Karachi, Pakistan

Zahid Hussain

Abstract

Globally, environmental concerns affect all aspects of human activity, and the economy for environmentally and socially aware goods and services is expanding. Entrepreneurs today are adapting their business practices to address new environmental problems or other environmental risks impacting their business. To bring about the transformation towards green economic systems, all green entrepreneurs are encouraged. Evidence from around the world shows that people's concerns for the environment are growing, and they are constantly adapting their behaviour to reflect these concerns. The objectives of the study were to assess the prevalence of green business practices among SMEs and also identify the elements that support these practices in Karachi, Pakistan. The study used a descriptive questionnaire as its research methodology. Self-completed questionnaires were used to collect primary data. The conclusions of the article stated that SMEs were using green business practices in their business areas. This can be explained by the great appreciation for green entrepreneurship in Pakistan. The variables that influence green entrepreneurship have been found to have different effects in practice. Stakeholders were advised to develop initiatives to promote adoption and use by most entities, including SMEs, as green business practices by SMEs in Karachi were still in their infancy. Through relevant authorities and green entrepreneurship, shareholders should lobby to provide them with a stronger negotiating strategy with other stakeholders. This study has some limitations. They study law in Karachi. Results are based on scenario-based surveys and methods and their applicability in a more complex relationship between green entrepreneurship practices and the performance of small- and medium-sized businesses.

Entrepreneurship and Green Finance Practices, 47–76
Copyright © 2024 Zahid Hussain
Published under exclusive licence by Emerald Publishing Limited
doi:10.1108/978-1-80455-678-820231003

Keywords: Green entrepreneurship; technology; sustainability; small–medium enterprises; Karachi; Pakistan

1. Introduction

Environmental concerns affect all aspects of human activities around the world, and the market for environmentally friendly and socially responsible goods and services is growing. Entrepreneurs are already adapting their business strategies to deal with new environmental or other issues affecting their businesses (Walley et al., 2010). In order to achieve the transformation towards green economic systems, green entrepreneurs are encouraged. Evidence from around the world shows that people are increasingly concerned about the environment and are therefore constantly changing their behaviour (Walley et al., 2010).

The main characteristic that distinguishes the green entrepreneur from the traditional entrepreneur is that the latter strives to establish a business strategy that is both economically successful and brings environmental and social benefits. The green entrepreneur achieves this by participating in projects such as ecotourism, recycling, energy conservation, sustainable transportation, organic agriculture, and renewable energy, among others. These new projects also create many job opportunities (Lacroix et al., 2007).

The current approach to developing non-ecological fuel in Pakistan is giving way to a limited and more environmentally friendly approach. The integration and application of different implementations of green practices on natural assets is a distinctive feature of green modelling techniques. For example, to encourage the establishment of a sustainable national economic programme for the country, the Ministry of the Environment and Mineral Reserves set up an interministerial committee in 2020. The ministry has also introduced several green initiatives to help organizations in river basins, seedlings of trees and cultivate them to refinement by setting up nurseries and collecting rainwater from the roofs (UNEP, 2019). In Pakistan, the economic environment usually tends to 'green' business development. Entrepreneurs are not yet excluded because they are encouraged to create 'green' businesses. In this article, we look at the different aspects of green entrepreneurship that impact SMEs in Karachi.

2. Literature Review

2.1 Green Entrepreneurship

In order to address the ongoing environmental issues, some action must be taken. In order to utilize our natural environment and develop long-lasting solutions for the environmental problems we face, both the government and the people must work together. The goal of sustainable development, also known as sustainability or sustainable solutions, is to use the resources that are at our disposal without compromising the ability of future generations to fulfil their own requirements. The term 'green' refers to sustainable actions that have a positive impact on the environment. Based on the participant's actual intention, the term 'green' can be used both relatively and universally. The word 'green' is often used in both objective truth and relative perception. Green can describe a method or an object. The concept of 'green' is used to denote a movement towards eco-friendly or eco-friendly development (Pearce et al., 2013).

The actions taken to improve our environment, or 'green initiatives', can range from simple tree planting, wastewater treatment, and the conservation of natural resources such as water and energy to the adoption of innovative and cost-effective production techniques, mass recycling and reuse, energy-efficient buildings, environmentally friendly goods and services, etc. Due to their tremendous power to produce and pollute, corporations can make a significant contribution in this regard (Keter, 2012). They have the resources and the ability to make investments that will benefit our environment. If they have the proper vision and the motivation to protect our environment, entrepreneurs, as a standalone business unit, could make a significant contribution (Omano, 2012). Just as each country's p'ogress depends on its entrepreneurs' ca'abilities, so does sustainable and green development. They may trigger a series of green initiatives and behaviours that have a good and considerable impact on the environment.

Regarding the technological level and scope of a specific business that qualifies as entrepreneurial, there doesn't s'em to be a specific definition of what it means to be an entrepreneur. Entrepreneurs, on the other hand, are business owners who take risks to turn their ideas into profitable investments and new business opportunities. An entrepreneur would then infuse economic growth with technology, implementations, and new concepts. In business, we talk about 'structural change'. This is due to the ability of entrepreneurs to transform the economic and business environment and replace outdated business practices (Ulijn & Weggeman, 2011). According to Thornton et al. (2011), entrepreneurship is the creation of new businesses, which requires a certain level of creativity and scale. This production results from a contextual, socioeconomic, and institutional system.

Due to the lack of literature on the subject, it is difficult to define 'green entrepreneurship' and to understand how to distinguish green entrepreneurship from non-green entrepreneurship. The terms 'environmental entrepreneur' and 'environmentally friendly entrepreneur' had previously been used by Bennet (1991). From their point of view, green entrepreneurs are the ones who take on new market opportunities and risky ventures (Tripathi et al., 2020). Furthermore, driven by intrinsic motivations, environmentally friendly entrepreneurs actively fight for a different and more sustainable future, also having a positive impact on the environment and the economy (Waweru, 2017).

2.2 Typology of Green Entrepreneurs

To anticipate the motivating factors behind green entrepreneurship, Taylor and Walley (2013) divided green entrepreneurs into four categories: local ad hoc enviro-preneur, creative opportunist, moral enabler, and trailblazing champion. A kind of involuntary green entrepreneur seems to be the ad hoc local enviro-preneur. The ad hoc environmental entrepreneur is driven by money rather than principle. In addition, their networking activities, families, and friends are instrumental in setting them up to start green businesses (Ikram et al., 2019). Motivating factors such as regulatory oversight that can help the creative opportunistic entrepreneur spot a green market opportunity can have a major impact. The creative opportunist is similar to a businessman with a financial focus who recognizes a potential market or ecological niche. The impactful and sustainable entrepreneurship-oriented approach is what the pioneer champion includes. This entrepreneur's goal was to change the status quo (Mahmood et al., 2022). He lives at the forefront and has the ambition of a sustainable society with far-reaching system reforms. Moral misfits also outsource their activities with environmental goals, but prefer to avoid conventional initiatives; friends, connections, and past experiences have a significant impact on how a company is formed (Jun et al., 2019). These eco-entrepreneurs often seem to start their business here on the fringes of the industry because they are not motivated by the transformation of the world (Taylor & Walley, 2013).

2.3 Green Entrepreneurial Practices

The main characteristic that distinguishes the green entrepreneur from the conventional entrepreneur is that the former works to develop a business strategy that is both commercially successful and contributes to the environment and society. The green entrepreneur achieves this by promoting initiatives such as ecotourism, recycling, energy saving, sustainable transport, organic farming and renewable energy, among others, and by increasing the number of green jobs related to these new initiatives (Lacroix et al., 2017).

Implementing green practices can lower prices, minimize risk, or help a company differentiate itself from the competition, say Ambec and Lanoie (2018). Selling advanced pollution prevention technologies, assessing risks, and reducing costs are just a few of the ways companies can combat environmental degradation. Activities related to products or mechanisms, resources for industrial, environmental, and managerial approach are designated in this study as green business practices (Stevenson & St-Onge, 2015). These practices include energy conservation, environmental protection, recycling and reuse, environmentally friendly product design, and corporate environmental protection.

2.4 Small and Medium Enterprises in Pakistan

Small- and medium-sized enterprises (SMEs) can range from fast-growing companies to private family-owned businesses that have remained broadly unchanged for years. SMEs can also be autonomous companies, companies engaged in advanced technologies, and companies with international investment partners (Holt, 2011). They can also be companies that work part-time without employees and manufacturers that hire hundreds of employees. Many academics measure the size of SMEs by the number of people who work there. For example, Storey (1994) defines micro-enterprises as companies with 0–9 employees, small companies as companies with 10–99 employees, and medium-sized companies as companies with 100–499 employees. SMEs should be defined in terms of the economic systems in which they operate, according to Gunasekaran et al., 2010. Pakistani SMEs are active in the manufacturing, trade, and service sectors of the economy. Small businesses (SMEs) include both legally licenced and unregistered businesses, including grocery stores, wholesalers, and transportation companies. The amount of money invested in SMEs ranges from a measly 10,000 Pakistani rupees to around 5,000,000 Pakistani rupees. Only about a third of Pakistani SMEs are located in cities, while almost two-thirds of them live in remote areas. 16% of SMEs were located in Lahore and Karachi (Central Bureau of Statistics et al., 2020). SMEs make up nearly 70% of all businesses.

2.5 A Subjective Vision of Entrepreneurship

According to the subjectivist perspective of Penrose and Penrose (1959), it takes time for useful arrangements of resources to be realized. Like those who manage resources, management makes arbitrary decisions in terms of efficiency, innovation, and ongoing maintenance. Entrepreneurs think about new forms of resource use that will lead to the creation of future energy properties (Sassetti et al., 2018). Penrose argued that the services a resource might provide, rather than the resources consumed by individuals, make them inputs into the production process. The ability to separate different services from comparable resources also makes companies diverse and also describes their distinctiveness. This theory is central to this research because it suggests that business owners would become sustainable if they could understand how using green products and processes can transform their businesses relative to the competition. The ability of assets and processes to meet multiple needs (Hameed et al., 2021).

2.6 Resource Dependence Theory

According to the resource dependency theory, successful organizations maximize their authority (Pfeffer & Pfeffer, 1981). According to the resource dependency theory, characters who do not have the necessary resources would then try to connect with other individuals to acquire those resources.

In addition, companies reduce their dependence on other people or increase other companies' dependence on them. According to this view, organizations are seen as alliances that sense their organizational structures and role models to protect and preserve the necessary external resources. According to the resource dependency theory, organizations strive to gain authority over resources that reduce other organizations' dependence on them, pollution, professional services based on call centres and renewable energy reusable green initiatives, such as pathogenic micro-advanced technologies, bioethanol techniques, algae for the production of biofuels, biomass fuels, improved induction hobs, thermal protection of energy production, lighting Christmas solar, and thermoelectric techniques (Sakundarini & Udin, 2021). Based on their perception that involvement in green businesses gives them more autonomy and independence, the above could then be used to describe the behaviour of businesses in this regard.

2.7 Structure–Action Model

Giddens (1984) defined structure as a base of resources and rules that become evident only when applied according to the Structure–Action framework. When individuals communicate, elements of their own perspective and behaviour are understood in ways that affect the social structures of other people. People who are considered expert actors always keep an eye on how they interact with their environment (Barle, 1993). Consequently, and through people's daily behaviour, existing structures are strengthened or transformed. Therefore, people can choose whether to keep the current situation or act differently. This model is relevant for this research because it clarifies why entrepreneurs choose sustainability or not. It provides the fundamental reason why a person's actions can also recreate existing structures or try something completely new.

To fully understand sustainable green practices, one must consider making conceptual advances to understand how such an interdependent structure–action model might satisfactorily improve over time and distance.

2.8 Research Problem

Globally, green entrepreneurship is increasingly seen as the direction of business. Describing 'green entrepreneurship' and understanding how to distinguish between green and non-green entrepreneurship is difficult due to a lack of literature on the subject. Different perspectives on green entrepreneurs are characterized by taking on new market opportunities and risky ventures. Furthermore, green entrepreneurs are internally motivated, and their activities are good for the environment, promote the sustainability of the company, and deliberately focus attention on a more sustainable society. Karachi is strategically crucial as Pakistan's gateway. It is a rapidly growing city that is increasingly burdened by the challenges of urbanization. Consequently, the province must ensure that green practices are incorporated into its development strategy to preserve the environment and support people's lives. This requires considering green entrepreneurship in business operations. This could be achieved if research is conducted to determine the elements that favourably or unfavourably influence green entrepreneurship in Karachi. Despite this, green entrepreneurship has not been studied much in Pakistan or the world at large. The concepts 'environmental entrepreneur' and 'eco-responsible entrepreneur' were previously used by Bennet (1991). The relatively limited literature currently in print that focusses specifically on what drives green entrepreneurship yields conflicting results. According to research by Baum et al. (2014), the characteristics, skills, and inspirations of entrepreneurs were both important direct and indirect factors contributing to green entrepreneurship (Mat et al., 2010). In the United States have shown that perspectives are readily available and have a significant impact on entrepreneurship programmes. Another study conducted in Indiana, USA (Marshall et al., 2016), found that entrepreneurs' access to capital is crucial. Another study conducted in Finland by Harju and Kosonen (2012) found that lower taxes stimulate more business activity. According to a study by Kim et al. (2016), financial resources were not strongly related to the emergence of entrepreneurship. In Malaysia, Ahmed et al. (2016) showed that only certain rewards encourage entrepreneurship, while others seem not to have.

2.9 Objectives of the Study

The overall objective of the study was to establish the Green Entrepreneurial Practices among Small and Medium Enterprises in Karachi, Pakistan.

The specific objectives of the study are:

i. Determining the extent of Green Entrepreneurial Practices among SMEs in Karachi, Pakistan.
ii. Determining the factors that influence Green Entrepreneurial Practices among SMEs in Karachi, Pakistan.
iii. The main focus of the study was to identify green implementation practices among SMEs in Karachi, Pakistan.
iv. Evaluating the prevalence of green business practices among SMEs in Karachi, Pakistan, was one of the specific objectives of the article.
v. Analyze the variables influencing green business practices among SMEs in Karachi, Pakistan.

2.10 Scope of Study

Researchers, many scientists, policy makers, and also investment firms should take note of this research. Few academic studies have been conducted to establish the reasons why green entrepreneurship in Pakistan has not yet blossomed. The results of this research would therefore provide information on the variables that influence green entrepreneurship in Karachi. Therefore, it will contribute to future studies or conversations that consider research relevant in the scientific community.

This research will be useful for the development of a government economic strategy regarding green entrepreneurship. The Pakistani government wants to promote economic expansion through companies that consider the sustainability of Pakistan's natural environment. To create policies that can drive productivity growth through green entrepreneurship, policymakers in this area need access to accurate data. Understanding the variables and issues that need to be addressed to promote green entrepreneurship will enable initiatives to deliver the best results. This research is critical because it identifies both the obstacles companies face in implementing green entrepreneurship, and the factors that can contribute to it.

This research is crucial for both domestic and international eco-friendly investment firms. Investors want to be sure they are receiving dividends from their investments, but also, at the very least, to be protected. Furthermore, they also need to understand what to do to integrate green entrepreneurship in and out of their work. As a result, they would be prepared for difficulties and would understand how to deal with them so that they could benefit from their own business activities while trying to take care of both the environment in which they work.

2.11 Green Entrepreneurship-Related Factors

There are numerous factors that lead to green entrepreneurship, so this section discusses how some factors, as shown by research findings, could include business skills, possibilities for green entrepreneurship, access to finance for green entrepreneurship, rewards for green entrepreneurship, and entrepreneur inspiration.

2.11.1 Entrepreneurial Skills

Baum et al. (2014) carried out a study to determine the link between entrepreneurial characteristics and skills and resulting business growth. The study focussed on three skills: Diligence, Bravery, and New Exploration Skills. Information from 229 senior merchant executives, as well as 106 affiliates of a given company, was collected over a six-year period and used for the longitudinal survey. According to the study, certain characteristics, skills, and motivators of business owners were significant predictors, directly or indirectly, of starting a business for a period of six years after the initial assessment. Another study by Lee et al. (2015) examined the impact of entrepreneurship education in Korea and America. It was believed that through entrepreneurship education, educators would acquire the drive, information, and skills needed to start a profitable joint venture. A survey of students at the University of Nebraska-Lincoln in the United States was divided into two teams, Team A (60 students) and Team A (102 students). Team C (102 students) and Team D (115 students), both from Kyonggi University in South Korea. Self-completed questionnaires were answered by the students. Structural equation models and Anova tests were used for the evaluation. Between students enroled in an undergraduate programme and those who have not, research reveals a significant difference. This showed how entrepreneurship was influenced by skills.

To determine the strategic business skills needed for better performance of small businesses operating in both Oyo and Osun in the western regions of Nigeria, Akande (2012) conducted an exploratory case study. The survey provided insight into the impact of strategic business skills on those services provided by smaller Nigerian companies. The study used a multi-stage probability method on select square holdings in the state of Osun in western Nigeria. Key information for the study was gathered using self-completed survey questions on 240 block manufacturing companies. The information collected was submitted to both the chi-squared and ANOVA. The results showed a strong correlation between business performance and tactical capabilities.

According to the aforementioned research, there is a correlation between an entrepreneur's skills and his or her business success. Since a businessman's skills vary slightly from place to place, the results can be applied to all contexts.

Neither study shows whether conclusions are influenced by specific competencies. The results may not apply to Karachi where this research was conducted.

2.11.2 Chances for Green Entrepreneurship

Mat et al. (2010) carried out a research study with the aim of examining the mediating effect of entrepreneurial opportunities on the borrowing and success of female entrepreneurs. The research study used in-depth interview questions and a self-administered questionnaire method to elicit responses from women business owners. Secondary research on microfinance services was also used. Data analysis used descriptive statistical analysis. The research found that women had slightly more opportunities for their businesses than other female entrepreneurs. Giacomin et al. (2011) carried out a research to show the influence of an entrepreneur's socio-cultural characteristics in aligning their entrepreneurial complexity with a need or benefit. The study was derived from a survey of 538 business owners. Based on the results of this study, business owners can obviously be ranked according to the opportunities they encounter. Possibilities therefore determined what kind of businessman one could be.

Such research shows a beneficial association between identifying opportunities. Because the research was conducted outside of Pakistan, the results may not be generalizable. This provides sufficient justification for the possibility that the results might differ if the study had been conducted in Pakistan.

2.11.3 Accessibility to Capital for Green Entrepreneurship

The accessibility of different funding sources, as well as their implications for the entrepreneurial trend, were mainly compared in one study (Ho & Wong, 2017). In the study, they used a composite measure with World Bank data to examine the impact of business spending. Unofficial securities and three different forms of financing. The study found that the impact of unofficially invested money on the entrepreneurial trend made statistical sense. The operational costs of regulation have been found to discourage random forms of enterprise but have no effect on need-driven entrepreneurship. In a study by Marshall et al. (2016), researchers sought to understand the human and financial capital variables that influenced entrepreneurs in urban areas and rural environments. The information for the survey was gathered from a self-administered questionnaire that was provided to the participants in the session where their results would be presented. 84 entrepreneurs volunteered to fill out the survey. Research shows that entrepreneurs' access to capital played a pivotal role in their decision to start a business. A company to be formed previously included entrepreneurs up to moderate and higher levels of total wealth. Kim et al. (2016) conducted research to explore the hypothesis that having individual financial resources was crucial to becoming an entrepreneur.

Information from the representative sample of entrepreneurship development dynamics was used in the study. Those who therefore looked at the impact of available capital, including home equity and income, on individuals' decisions to start their own business. Research shows that financial capability has little impact on the likelihood of starting a business.

The results of these studies on the impact of fixed assets on entrepreneurship are contradictory. Although some research provides encouraging results, others show no correlation. Therefore, it is also acceptable to say that it is impossible to predict the impact of cash on green entrepreneurship among Karachi SMEs using the systematic review of this nexus between finance and entrepreneurship which is currently available. Unfortunately, only research could prove this.

2.11.4 Incentives Schemes for Green Entrepreneurship
To determine the extent to which the incentive programme affected entrepreneurship during economic growth, Harju and Kosonen (2012) conducted a research. The Finnish tax credit was the focus of the investigation. They took a close look at how the Finnish tax changes of 1997 and 1998 affected the hiring decisions of small- and medium-sized enterprises. The tax changes have attracted attention, even though they have reduced income tax for small business owners and only done so for sole proprietors.

The results showed that lower taxes increased profit margins, as landlords were perceived to be tougher as a direct result of lower taxes. This meant that the tax cut could be a motivator for more entrepreneurship. In Mumbai, in the Indian industrial zone of Taloja, a small drug manufacturer conducted a study of Nandanwar et al. (2016). The purpose of the study would be to determine how incentives affect a company's motivation to expand effectively. The subject of the study was a study population of the company's 112 employees. All relevant studies were used in the study. The analysis was performed using statistical results. It must have been found that reward systems, both financial and non-monetary, seem to have a significant impact on organizational performance. The company's entrepreneurial environment was influenced by the type and combination of rewards. Another study by Ahmed et al. (2016) examined the export subsidies faced by Malaysian business owners when doing business internationally. The research included a survey of 214 industrial manufacturing companies in Malaysia. A one-sided analysis of variance was used during the evaluation. According to the study, only 13 of the export subsidies assessed in the study were found to be significant for Malaysian entrepreneurs. Lower tariff barriers in international markets, attractive export subsidies from home country authorities, the appearance of an administration being published, the assumption of economies of scale resulting of higher overall trade, favourable profits and opportunities in international markets, the possibility of expanding into emerging markets, proof of purchase, mutual instructions from foreign buyers, the availability of effective means and economical to ship to international markets, and the relaxation of commodity regulations were examples of such rewards. In some situations, certain rewards may inspire business owners, while in other situations, they may not. Without study, it is impossible to determine how Pakistani mechanisms affect green entrepreneurship in Karachi.

2.11.5 Entrepreneur Motivation
In a study by Kiss et al. (2018), they examined the direct and indirect consequences of motivation on the internationalization of companies from a cognitive point of

view. Small- and medium-sized businesses in a large southern United States metropolitan area are where surveys were conducted to collect data. A mediated correlation method was used to examine the data, which allows simultaneous assessment of direct and indirect influences of motivational variables on this internationalization context. Although the research found that motivation had an impact on globalizing the business context, it also shows that proactive and reactionary motivators had different impacts on the global context, but risk perception had an impact significant. Blue (1990), conducted research that made a significant contribution to the success of entrepreneurship in Nigeria. Development and income have been used as performance indicators in research. According to whether entrepreneurs are either inspired from within or from outside, this study categorized entrepreneurial motivations. The study shows that externally motivated businesses are much more likely to achieve high levels of revenue because both internally and externally inspired entrepreneurs are tested before growth and profit. In contrast, intrinsically motivated entrepreneurs were much more likely than extrinsically motivated entrepreneurs to experience high levels of expansion. Collins et al. (2014) aimed to establish a link between factors related to entrepreneurial behaviour and motivation to succeed. This research was a meta-analysis of numerous studies examining the relationship between entrepreneurial behaviour and outcome expectations. Research has found a strong association between self-efficacy and the decision to pursue a career and entrepreneurial success. These studies have shown a link between entrepreneurial motivation and behaviour. However, they have not yet shown whether entrepreneurship is strongly linked to motivation or not. Although motivation is a behavioural issue that varies by meaning and stimulation, the results cannot be interpreted as universal. The results of the literature review clearly show a correlation between the dependent variable entrepreneurship and the independent variables entrepreneurial skills, opportunities, access to finance, rewards, and inspiration. However, the findings are case specific and cannot be taken as a clear and explicit prognosis of the situation of SMEs in Karachi. This is despite the fact that, unlike several of the studies mentioned in the previous section, the article still focusses on green entrepreneurship. The purpose of this research is to describe whether recognized factors have a positive or negative impact on the conduct of business in Karachi.

3. Research Methodology

3.1 Research Design

This study is a descriptive study. According to Mugenda and Mugenda (1999), a survey by questionnaire consists of asking people about their perceptions, ways of thinking, behaviours, or beliefs in order to explain an existing situation and to obtain information from the available population. By completing a survey, the researchers looked at the actual situation of a few variables at a given time. This method was chosen because the primary data collected from this type of resident is much more reliable and up to date.

This descriptive survey aims to improve a comprehensive explanation of the issues and barriers faced by green entrepreneurship among Karachi SMEs that is as credible, acceptable, and effective as possible. Growth and sustainability, entrepreneurial skills, investment opportunities, access to finance, rewards, and entrepreneurial inspiration are some of the factors examined.

3.2 Study Population

According to the schedule of registered enterprises in Karachi since about 30 June 2022, the targeted audience is 36,694 SMEs. The classifications of SMEs in Karachi since about 30 August 2022 are shown in Table 3.1.

Table 3.1. Small and Medium Enterprises in Karachi.

Category	Number
General Commerce, Distribution, Retail Markets	21,955
Informal Industry	352
Transport Services, Warehouses, and Information Exchange	1,441
Agricultural Services, Natural Resources	1,470
Both Accommodation and Hospitality	2,708
Technical or Professional Services	4,584
Academies, Healthcare, and Amusements	1,483
Industrial Facilities, Plants, and Garages	2,619
Total	36,612

Source: Municipal Corporation of Karachi (2023).

3.3 Sampling Design

120 SMEs in the range specified by Saddar, Empress Bazar, Boltan Market, University Road, and Korangi Road were the sample of the article. Within the Karachi district, there appear to be 31 streets and 6 SMEs would be randomly chosen for interviews in each street. As long as there are a total of 120 SMEs, the relatively long roads will receive an extra PMI. According to Mugenda and Mugenda (1999), a sample of at least 30 people from both populations can be used to fairly indicate the characteristics of the population. Furthermore, Mungaya et al. (2012) also used a survey of 120 SMEs in an earlier study. The research was a descriptive study of the impact of Karachi Municipality Tax System on the expansion of Small and Medium Enterprises (SMEs).

The 120 SMEs are divided into the 8 strata shown in Table 3.2 below. The proportion column shows the breakdown of the contribution of each stratum to the 36,694 SMEs.

Table 3.2. A Sample of the Research.

Category	Number	Proportion	Sample
General Commerce, Distributions, Retail Markets	21,955	0.59	71
Informal Industry	361	0.02	2
Transport Services, Warehouses, and Information Exchange	1,482	0.04	5
Agricultural Services, Natural Resources	1,493	0.04	5
Both Accommodation and Hospitality	2,708	0.07	8
Technical or Professional Services	4,584	0.13	15
Academies, Healthcare, Amusements	1,492	0.04	5
Industrial Facilities, Plants, Garages	2,619	0.07	9
Total	36,694	1	120

Source: Planned by a researcher using information from the Karachi Municipal Corporation (2023).

The survey within each classification was spread across 35 streets, with the specific PMI randomly selected to determine the number of SMEs that would respond to the survey. The positions of the participants also served as a guideline for SMEs. The distribution for one street was moved to another street, subject to the total contribution, if a particular participant did not live on that street. A single participant, ideally the supervisor or other person responsible for the day-to-day operations of an SME, completed the survey.

3.4 Data Collection

Primary data are used in this research. The SME supervisor and perhaps an employee willing to take over the day-to-day administration of the company received self-reported survey questions to complete. The survey is there at the PMI to be collected later.

Sections A and B are the survey used to collect primary data. Valuations of the SME's assets, estimates of the researchers' annual revenues, the companies it serves, and even ownership were collected in Section A. Other data included the number of employees, the number of years the SME has been in business, and also the number of employees. The second part of the survey focusses on the variables that influence environmentally friendly entrepreneurship. The variables were divided into four categories: eco-entrepreneurial skills, eco-entrepreneurial opportunities, eco-friendly, and eco-inspired rewards. The survey is presented as in Appendix 1.

3.5 Data Analysis

The responses to the questionnaire were adequate for accuracy and completeness. Subsequently, the data were classified and revised for errors and omissions. The data were examined using descriptive statistics.

The mean and mean variances were two of the descriptive statistics used. To determine the relative significance and weight of various factors, the reports were used to analyze participant information. The most common development of sustainable practices among many SMEs in Karachi has been identified using factor analysis. A descriptive study was conducted with the owners and/or top management of various SMEs in Karachi as a target group. 120 SMEs were chosen through a random selection from a wide range of categories according to the Karachi scheme of licenced companies as of 30 June 2022, shown in Appendix 2. 90% of the selected population is now packed and answered the questionnaires, which means 108 of the 120 focussed participants. The result of the SPSS version 17 analysis of the collected information was presented as frequency distribution tables. The data were interpreted using the mean and standard deviation of the statements here on a Likert-type scale. The most common implementation of green practices among SMEs in Karachi was identified by factor analysis. The section is divided into three sections for ease of analysis: demographic profile, level of green business practices, and factors that have influenced those practices.

4. Participant Companies Profiled

The demographic data obtained from the questionnaire and their entities are defined in this section. The researcher was interested in finding out the number of employees, how long the SME had been in business, how much the organization's resources were worth, and what their annual revenues were. The involvement also focussed on the ownership of the company and the sector in which it was active.

4.1 Dimensions as Determined by the Quantity of Workers

The number of workers in each participant's company was requested. Most SMEs, according to the survey, employed between 1 and 10 people. About 89% of them employ one to five people.

11% of SMEs also have jobs and more than 10 people. Table 3.3 provides an overview of these data.

Table 3.3. Number of Workers.

No. of Workers	1–5	5–10	Over 10
Results	78	18	12
Percentage	70	19	1
Cumulative	70	89	100

Source: Research data 2023.

4.2 *Duration in Business*

The period of time in which the companies of the participants carried out in activity was recommended. On the basis of the study, most of the participants, or 62%, said that their companies had been in use between one and five years, 16% said that their companies had been operated between 6 and 10 years. In addition to 22% there have been more than 10 years of the SME companies. Since most of the companies were much less in the operating state, the above suggests that relatively few SMEs will continue to exist after their fifth year.

4.3 *Value of Assets*

According to the survey respondents, 46% of SMEs have large assets of around Rs. 500,000.00 only and 22% have large assets between Rs. 500,000.00 and Rs. 000,000.00 under rupees 3,000,000.00 but also rupees 3,000,000.00 seems to be 19%. 5,000,000.00 rupees at 5% and above. 5,000,000.00 due at 8%. This shows that 68% of SMEs are SMEs with an investment portfolio of less than Rs 1 million.

4.4 *Annual Turnover*

The study examines the annual turnover of companies. 57% of the survey participants had a profitability of nearly rupees per year, 1,000,000.00. However, it was established that companies with a turnover exceeding the rupees. Higher than those who have rupees, 5,000,000.00. One million dollars and rupees 5,000,000.00.

4.5 *Ownership*

Ownership of a business was questioned by survey participants. 70% of participants' businesses were also sole proprietorships, while 27% are partnerships. Limited liability companies represent only 3% of SMEs. This suggests that almost all small businesses are controlled by one person and may be subsidiaries or start-up individuals.

5. The Percentage of SMEs in Karachi, Pakistan, That Are Developing Sustainable Practices

The initial aim of the article was to find out how widespread the development of sustainable practices is among SMEs in Karachi. A study of green business practices was conducted using 15 statements with different Likert scales. Factor analysis was used to identify the main SMEs developing sustainable practices. The results are presented in Tables 3.3 and 3.4.

The correlation (0.689) for these components was just sufficient for the principal component analysis according to Table 3.5, which contains the KMO results as well as Bartlett's test for these components. Nevertheless, no factor had a particularly weak output association level to warrant removal when the exploratory factor analysis was performed on the components, as shown in the table of results of their correlations. As a result, further analysis was performed and four factors were derived and rotated to an eigenvector of 1 or even greater, accounting for about 72% of the variance, as shown in the scree plot in Fig. 3.1.

Using the values of both the relationships between variables and their elements within the nonrotated variables, using the values summarized in Table 3.6, the procedure for determining the key metrics of SMEs' green business practices was determined.

The most important component analysis is the extraction technique.

Extract the constituent parts of A.

The first four factors have a causal relationship value greater than 0.7000, which constitutes the set of components found, according to Table 3.4, which also contains the coefficients of the correlations between variables and also their aspects within the factor rotated including the function.

A closer examination reveals that three components have correlation coefficients below 0.5. Components with a similarity value greater than 0.5000, found in the 12th place set, were retained using an extraction technique with a principal component analysis measure, while components with coefficients of correlation or less than 0.5000 were excluded. The table shows, in descending order of importance, the presence of support for green innovation, the growth of SME spending on green procurement, the presence of reputable green business consulting firms,

Table 3.4. Total Years in Business.

1–5 Years	5–10 Years	Over 10 Years	Total
66	18	24	108
62%	16%	22%	100%
62%	78%	100%	100%

Source: Research Data 2023.

Table 3.5. KMO and Also Bartlett's Test.

Kaiser-Meyer-Olkin Test for Sufficient Sample selection	0.688
Bartlett's Test of Approx. ChiSquare	1085.969
Sphericity Df Sig.	105.000

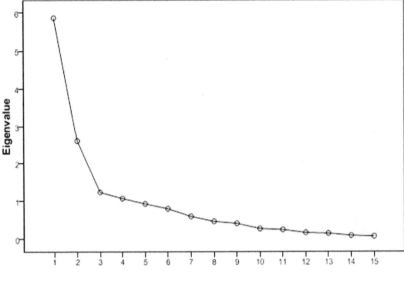

Fig. 3.1.   Scree Plot.

as well as the high percentage of SMEs providing access to green technologies, among the main factors behind the prevalence of environmentally friendly business practices in Karachi. You could say that these important variables are related to environmentally friendly manufacturing and advertising practices. And green practices that give SMEs a competitive advantage seemed to be among the most notable associated with the promotional aspects of green innovative products.

5.1 Factors Influencing Sustainable Business Practices

This section provides details on the variables believed to encourage SMEs in Karachi to engage in green entrepreneurship. Entrepreneurial skills, opportunities, access to finance, rewards, and inspiration for entrepreneurship were all variables for which effects were assessed.

5.2 Entrepreneurial Skills

To understand how entrepreneurial skills affect the green practices of SMEs, they started by assessing the impacts of the expected variables using a set of six propositions. The findings of the study are shown in Table 3.7.

According to the data in Table 3.7, the participants assigned an average score to the impact of business skills (mean of 2.66). This may be due to the fact that only a small percentage of participants (11.1%) admit that they have actually received training in environmentally friendly business practices, especially compared to those who have not yet i.e. only 19, 4% of the participants stated that

Table 3.6. Component Matrix.

Statement	Component			
	1	2	3	4
Sustainable new products are encouraged.	0.868	−0.177	−0.027	−0.050
You are spending more money on sustainable. Consumption.	0.796	−0.236	0.087	−0.030
I have direct connections to reputable consulting companies for green businesses.	0.769	−0.328	−0.190	0.101
Customers are increasingly requesting sustainable goods from you.	0.718	−0.285	0.119	−0.223
Customers are increasingly requesting sustainable goods from you.	0.625	0.542	0.245	0.165
Spending on non-green purchases is declining.	0.619	−0.442	−0.407	0.084
My business benefits from environmental sustainability.	0.614	−0.399	0.468	0.120
Recurring purchasers of sustainable products are increasing.	0.582	−0.158	0.247	0.256
The level of user satisfaction has increased.	0.550	0.463	0.213	0.044
I am capable of accessing international markets	0.545	−0.380	0.134	0.021
Pre-tax income for your company is increasing.	0.383	0.655	−0.262	0.309
Your reputation as a sustainable company is improving.	0.526	0.556	−0.167	0.491
Sustainable initiatives had also boosted sales.	0.491	0.553	−0.083	−0.473
There are more workers now.	0.634	−0.034	−0.652	−0.273
Production among relatives must have decreased.	0.466	0.487	0.288	−0.505

Source: Survey Data (2023).

they have skills in eco-friendly practices, while only 25.0% of the participants indicated that they have management skills in eco-friendly teams. Only 16.4% of respondents responded that they have the skills required for green promotional activities, and only a pitiful 19.4% of survey respondents said they have the skills required for a green planning process. However, 52.8% acknowledged that environmentally friendly business opportunities were visible to all. The findings

Table 3.7. Entrepreneurial Skill.

Statement	NE		LE		ME		GE		VGE		Total		Mean	STD
	F	%	F	%	F	%	F	%	f	%	f	%		
I've received training in eco-friendly business practices.	27	25.0	51	47.2	18	16.7	9	8.3	3	2.8	108	100	2.17	0.991
You're skilled in environmental management.	24	22.2	27	25.0	36	33.3	9	8.3	12	11.1	108	100	2.61	1.237
You are a skilled manager of a green team.	27	25.0	27	25.0	27	25.0	15	13.9	12	11.1	108	100	2.61	1.303
You are proficient in making plans ecofriendly businesses.	18	16.7	33	30.6	36	33.3	12	11.1	9	8.3	108	100	2.64	1.139
You are proficient in using ecofriendly advertising methods.	27	25.0	30	27.8	33	30.6	9	8.3	9	8.3	108	100	2.47	1.195
An possibility for a green business is obvious.	12	11.2	15	13.9	24	22.2	24	22.2	33	30.6	108	100	3.47	1.350
Grand Mean													2.66	1.203

Source: Survey Data (2023).

suggest that while SMEs in Karachi have had many opportunities to invest in environmentally friendly business practices, most small businesses have not been able to take advantage of the opportunities that already existed.

5.3 Possibilities for Green Entrepreneurship

The potential of green entrepreneurship was also assessed to determine its impact on SMEs. To determine the impact of different components of green entrepreneurship opportunities within their institutions, participants were interviewed. The results are shown in Table 3.8.

Participants indicated that green entrepreneurship opportunities are relatively influential, as specified in the weighted sum of 3.25 of Table 3.8, which also includes the results of influencing the components of green entrepreneurship opportunities. This may be due to the fact that, with the exception of very few study participants (30.6%), who were not market entry barriers for sustainable product development here, some other factors received significantly higher ratings by study participants. For example, 61.1% of respondents indicated that there are numerous green shopping opportunities, 44.5% said most people support green initiatives, and 52.7% said they have access to resources on the field in the field of renewable technologies. Only 25% of survey respondents disagree with the idea that there are countless huge markets for green products and services, leaving the rest of the respondents uncertain.

This supports the participants' previous claim that there are opportunities for SMEs in Karachi to invest in environmental initiatives.

5.4 Entrepreneur Motivation

The research also aimed to determine how entrepreneurial inspiration affects the operational areas of SMEs. The results are shown in Table 3.7.

The results of the strength of the influences of entrepreneurial motivational factors are presented in Table 3.9. The results show that entrepreneurial orientation has a strongly limited impact perimeter, as evidenced by the calculated average score of 3.91. Most of the members of this section agreed with a significant percentage of the study participants. First, 61.1% of respondents believe that entrepreneurial orientation has directly contributed to the growth of an organization. A similar percentage acknowledged the difficulty of starting and expanding a business, and 83.4% said they contribute to the welfare of their local community, while 86.1% also expressed a greater preference for a good efficiency. Participants indicated there were opportunities to gain knowledge, while 61.1% said they could find a solution or start a business and 61.2% said they could grow in the community by being pushed to invest. However, 61.1% of survey respondents said they had the freedom to change the way they approached their job and 72.3% said they were able to model their behaviour on someone they like looking up. The findings recognize the important role that inspiration can play in enabling

Table 3.8. Possibilities for Green Entrepreneurship.

Statement	SD		D		NS		A		SA		Total		Mean	STD
	F	%	F	%	F	%	F	%	F	%	F	%		
There aren't any obstacles to entering the marketplace I serve.	39	36.1	12	11.1	24	22.2	15	13.9	18	16.7	108	100	2.64	1.501
Demand for environmentally friendly products and services is very high.	12	11.1	15	13.9	27	25.0	36	33.3	18	16.7	108	100	3.31	1.226
There are numerous options for green purchasing.	6	5.6	12	11.1	24	22.2	42	38.9	24	22.2	108	100	3.61	1.118
The public is in favour of ecofriendly initiatives.	6	5.6	6	5.6	48	44.4	30	27.8	18	16.7	108	100	3.44	1.017
You can find out about green technology.	3	2.8	15	13.9	15	13.9	48	44.4	9	8.3	108	100	3.25	1.069
Grand Mean													3.25	1.186

Source: Survey Data (2023).

Table 3.9. Motivation of Entrepreneurs.

Statement	SD		D		NS		A		SA		Total		Mean	STD
	F	%	F	%	F	%	F	%	F	%	F	%		
Direct involvement in an organization's growth	15	13.9	3	2.8	24	22.2	42	38.9	24	22.2	108	100	3.53	1.264
The difficulty of launching and expanding a business	0	0	18	16.7	24	22.2	39	36.1	27	25.0	108	100	3.69	1.027
I want to earn a significant amount of money and contribute to the well-being of my community	0	0	3	2.8	15	13.9	57	52.8	33	30.6	108	100	4.11	0.740
An ambition to earn a lot of money	3	2.8	0	0	12	11.1	36	33.3	57	52.8	108	100	4.33	0.886
There are chances to continue learning.	0	0	3	2.8	21	19.4	42	38.9	42	38.9	108	100	4.14	0.826
Create a business and product idea.	3	2.8	6	5.6	33	30.6	27	25.0	39	36.1	108	100	3.86	1.063
Obtain a higher social standing	0	0	12	11.1	30	27.8	33	30.6	33	30.6	108	100	3.81	1.000
Freedom to modify my working style as I see fit	3	2.8	3	2.8	21	19.4	45	41.7	36	33.3	108	100	4.00	0.947
Take after a role model that I respect	0	0	3	2.8	33	30.6	45	41.7	27	25.0	108	100	3.89	0.813
Grand Mean													3.91	1.203

Source: Survey Data (2023).

Karachi SMEs to address the challenge of more open funding of environmentally friendly innovative ideas.

5.5 Green Rewards

Subsequently, to determine their appearance, the factors of green incentive systems were examined (Table 3.10). The results of the study are shown in Table 3.8.

Table 3.8s results demonstrated that the impacts of ecofriendly reward components was deemed towards being moderate as evidenced by it as a whole mean rating of 3.09.

The large percentage of the constituents had moderate or even higher average ratings than the median, demonstrating the real fact of their impact. This included the benefits of market diversification (3.46), the accessibility of commercially viable methods of doing green business (3.42), the development of green entrepreneurial skills (3.41), as well as the simplicity of the sector in relation to green businesses (3.20). Other factors include having an environmentally conscious leadership (3.14), anticipating the benefits of eco-friendly companies (3.14), adapting the product to green markets (3.06), and proximity to global markets that require durable goods (2.90). However, the government's tantalizing rewards (2.44) and the claim that the tax structure could promote environmentally friendly business practices (2.53) had a slightly lower overall average, indicating those with the least impact.

5.6 Access to Capital

The implications of capital accessibility on how well this goal's activities were coordinated were also investigated. The results are described in Table 3.11.

According to the data in Table 3.11, a slightly higher percentage of participants noted that funding was available for green businesses, giving the property an overall average rating of 2.87. This is because each of the study participants gave the components of this factor a low overall score. Also, for example, 27.6% of survey respondents thought the credit could be used for environmental initiatives, only 22.2% said a green entrepreneurship fund had been created, but only 27.8% said it took less paperwork to get green promotion aid from people who disputed the claims or were unsure. In addition, what is likely a slightly higher percentage of survey respondents – 36.1% – said the government was taking diligent action to encourage financial support for green entrepreneurship, and a higher proportion said confirmed the availability of incentives for green businesses. However, only 25.0% of participants responded that green entrepreneurs can get limited credit, and the other minority – 28.8% – indicated that there is a wider range of financial support available for business owners, green companies than those working in previous survey responses. This suggests that while the majority of participants recognized the importance of financial support for green entrepreneurship, it was difficult to secure funding for such activities.

Table 3.10. Green Rewards.

Statement	NE		LE		ME		GE		VGE		Total		Mean	STD
	F	%	F	%	F	%	F	%	F	%	F	%		
The tax system encourages green business operations	27	25.0	39	36.1	15	13.9	12	11.1	15	13.9	108	100	2.53	1.350
The government offers enticing incentives	15	13.9	48	44.4	30	27.8	9	8.3	6	5.6	108	100	2.44	1.018
Existence of environmentally conscious management	6	5.6	15	13.9	57	52.8	15	13.9	15	13.9	108	100	3.14	1.019
Green entrepreneurial endeavours are anticipated to have benefits	12	11.1	12	11.1	42	38.9	30	27.8	12	11.1	108	100	3.14	1.123
The advantages of market diversification	6	5.6	6	5.6	39	36.1	42	38.9	12	11.1	108	100	3.46	0.991
Gaining knowledge to enhance green business	3	2.8	12	11.1	39	36.1	42	38.9	12	11.1	108	100	3.41	0.931
There are successful green business practices available.	3	2.8	15	13.9	36	33.3	39	36.1	15	13.9	108	100	3.42	0.989
Simple product requirements for green business operation	6	5.6	24	22.2	30	27.8	36	33.3	12	11.1	108	100	3.20	1.088
Products are simple to adapt for markets focussed on sustainability	12	11.1	27	25.0	33	30.6	15	13.9	21	19.4	108	100	3.06	1.274
Proximity to international markets seeking sustainable goods	18	16.7	21	19.4	33	30.6	24	22.2	12	11.1	108	100	2.90	1.239
Grand Mean													3.09	1.102

Source: Survey Data (2023).

Table 3.11. Access to Capital.

Statement	SD F	SD %	D F	D %	NS F	NS %	A F	A %	SA F	SA %	Total F	Total %	Mean	STD
There are available loans for eco-friendly endeavours.	18	16.7	42	38.9	18	16.7	6	5.6	24	22.2	108	100	2.76	1.403
A fund has been established for green business.	12	11.1	48	44.4	24	22.2	21	19.4	3	2.8	108	100	2.58	1.015
Lowered administrative burden for receiving green funding.	6	5.6	24	22.2	48	44.4	15	13.9	15	13.9	108	100	3.08	1.069
To improve environmental entrepreneurship financing, the governing body is taking careful measures.	9	8.3	33	30.6	27	25.0	12	25.0	12	11.1	108	100	3.00	1.160
Green businesses receive financial assistance.	12	11.1	24	22.2	33	30.6	12	25.0	12	11.1	108	100	3.03	1.172
Green business owners can apply for low-interest loans.	12	11.1	48	44.4	21	19.4	9	16.7	9	8.3	108	100	2.67	1.136
Numerous financing options are available.	9	8.3	36	33.3	33	30.6	18	11.1	18	16.7	108	100	2.97	1.106
Grand Mean													2.87	1.166

6. Discussions

This study attempted to disclose more information about eco-friendly business practices collected from people in various management positions in SMEs in Karachi. Examination of data from distributed direct surveys revealed a number of issues. The overall positive average of the products used to determine the level of environmentally friendly business practices of SMEs was the first and most important means by which the research proved that SMEs had developed sustainable practices in their areas of activity. Participants provided an estimate higher than the average overall ranking than each of the statements used to assess the prevalence of green business practices among SMEs in Karachi, indicating a significant presence of the practices there. This could be explained by the seriousness with which SMEs are taking the notion of sustainable entrepreneurship as an unprecedented upsurge.

The variables influencing practice were found to produce a wide range of effects, as shown in Table 3.12.

According to the results of the multifactor average scores, Entrepreneur Inspiration (3.90) appears to have the greatest impact on sustainable business practices for SMEs, accompanied from highest to lowest by Green Entrepreneur Potentials (3.23) and Green Incentive Schemes (3.07), access to capital (2.85), and finally entrepreneurship (2.62). This could be explained by the importance of these variables for SMEs. This supports research by Kiss and Danis (2008) which showed how inspiration influenced the internationalization of the entrepreneurship ladder and also how proactive and reactive motivators influenced them differently. Adeyemi and Adeoti (2016) showed that business owners who were inspired from the outside were more likely than those who were inspired from the inside to achieve high levels of merit. In contrast, intrinsically motivated entrepreneurs were more likely to experience high levels of success than those who were externally constrained. Collins et al. (2004) showed a close relationship between motivation and the decision to become an entrepreneur and entrepreneurial self-efficacy.

Table 3.12. SMEs Green Entrepreneurs' Mean Affecting Factors ($N = 108$).

Factor	Mean Ranking	Standard Deviation
Entrepreneurial abilities	2.62	1.201
Possibilities for eco-entrepreneur	3.23	1.183
Entrepreneurial drive	3.90	0.936
Eco-friendly rewards	3.07	1.101
Access to capital	2.85	1.163

7. Conclusion

The connections developed from the various research objectives will be used to further the conclusions of the study. From the above overview, it can be concluded that the implementation of green practices as an emerging practice is steadily gaining popularity among the SMEs in Karachi and is being used by a significant proportion of them.

The results showed that a number of variables including business intent, opportunities for green entrepreneurs, benefits of going green, access to finance and finally business acumen impacted these practices. Entrepreneurship showed the highest degree of influence.

8. Recommendations

The results indicated that green business practices were still in their infancy among Karachi SMEs. It is therefore important that the authorities concerned take measures that encourage most businesses, including SMEs, to use and apply it. These initiatives, for example, can start with a widespread and repetitive exposure of all stakeholders to the importance of green business practices. This would therefore create opportunities for access to renewable technologies; accordingly, the government should increase support for eco-design practices in all relevant agencies. This can be achieved, among other things, by offering attractive incentive schemes e.g. B. Taxation that promotes environmentally friendly economic activities, creating an investment fund for green entrepreneurship and trying to negotiate with financial companies to propose investments in green businesses. Limited contractor loans. For pretty much this aspect, green entrepreneurship investors need to push for a broader and more powerful negotiation strategy with other interested parties. National and international markets and sometimes raw materials to increase production.

9. Limitations of the Study

A variety of participants engage with different business practices in the SME sector in Karachi, with green business practices emerging as a recent innovation. Only a small number of participants took part in the survey who demonstrated green business tendencies. The sample may not reflect all players in the Karachi market as the survey covered only a small number of industry stakeholders. Time and money constraints can also affect the study results.

10. Recommendations for Further Research

It is recommended that research be conducted to better understand what the people of Karachi think about the use of green technologies and to strengthen the city's initiatives in this area. It would be wise to invest in research on the elements that promote the sustainable growth of SMEs in Pakistan. A comparative analysis of the challenges faced by Pakistani SMEs engaging in green entrepreneurship is also important.

References

Adeyemi, S., & Adeoti, J. (2016). Motivation and business success. The relationship between entrepreneurs motivation and new business ventures success. *Journal of Arid Zone Economy*, *7*(1), 122–131.

Ahmed, Z. U., Julian, C. C., & Majar, A. J. (2016). Export incentives and international entrepreneurship in Malaysian firms. *The International Journal of Entrepreneurship and Innovation*, *7*(1), 49–57.

Akande, O. O. (2012). Strategic entrepreneurial skills influence on small businesses performance in Oyo and Osun Western States-Nigeria. *Research Journal in Organizational Psychology and Educational Studies*, *1*(6), 345–352.

Ambec, S., & Lanoie, P. (2018). *Does it pay to be green? A systematic overview* (pp. 45–62). The Academy of Management Perspectives.

Baum, J. R., Frese, M., & Baron, R. A. (2014). Born to be an entrepreneur? Revisiting the personality approach to entrepreneurship. In *The psychology of entrepreneurship* (pp. 73–98). Psychology Press.

Barle, G. (1993). *The green entrepreneur: Business opportunities that can save the Earth make you money*, *19*(2), 211–222.

Bennett, C. J. (1991). What is policy convergence and what causes it? *British Journal of Political Science*, *21*(2), 215–233.

Blue, J. (1990). *Ecopreneuring: Managing for results*. Scott Foresman.

CBS, Adetia, A., Budi, I., & Setiadi, F. (2020, August). Identification and analysis of factors affecting e-survey response rate at Central Bureau of Statistics. In *2020 international conference on information management and technology (ICIMTech)* (pp. 560–565). IEEE.

Collins, A. H., Bika, Z. L., & Swail, J. (2014). Gender and family business: New theoretical directions. *International Journal of Gender and Entrepreneurship*, *6*(3), 218–230.

Collins, C. J., Hanges, P. J., & Locke, E. A. (2004). The relationship of achievement motivation to entrepreneurial behavior: A meta-analysis. *Human Performance*, *17*(1), 95–117.

Giacomin, O., Janssen, F., Pruett, M., Shinnar, R. S., Llopis, F., & Toney, B. (2011). Entrepreneurial intentions, motivations and barriers: Differences among American, Asian and European students. *International Entrepreneurship and Management Journal*, *7*, 219–238.

Giddens, W. R. (1984). Giddens, structuration theory and strategy as practice. In *Cambridge handbook of strategy as practice* (pp. 109–126).

Gunasekaran, A., Forker, L., & Kobu, B. (2010). Improving operations performance in a small company: A case study. *International Journal of Operations & Production Management*, *20*(3), 316–336.

Hameed, I., Zaman, U., Waris, I., & Shafique, O. (2021). A serial-mediation model to link entrepreneurship education and green entrepreneurial behavior: Application of resource-based view and flow theory. *International Journal of Environmental Research and Public Health*, *18*(2), 550.

Harju, J., & Kosonen, T. (2012). *The impact of tax incentives on the economic activity of entrepreneurs (No. w18442)*. National Bureau of Economic Research.

Holt, D. (2011). Mainstreaming environmental enterprises–A strategic longitudinal analysis. International sustainable development research society newsletter, 2, pp. 23–24. *Journal of Business Venturing, 25*(5), 439–448.

Ho, Y. P., & Wong, P. K. (2017). Financing, regulatory costs and entrepreneurial propensity. *Small Business Economics, 28*(2), 187–204.

Ikram, M., Sroufe, R., Mohsin, M., Solangi, Y. A., Shah, S. Z. A., & Shahzad, F. (2019). Does CSR influence firm performance? A longitudinal study of SME sectors of Pakistan. *Journal of Global Responsibility, 11*(1), 27–53.

Jun, W., Ali, W., Bhutto, M. Y., Hussain, H., & Khan, N. A. (2019). Examining the determinants of green innovation adoption in SMEs: A PLS-SEM approach. *European Journal of Innovation Management, 24*(1), 67–87.

Karachi Metropolitan Corporation. (n.d.). http://www.kmc.gos.pk

Keter, J. (2012). Government regulations and procedures and the establishment of SMEs in the rural areas: A survey of SMEs in Kesses division, Uasin Gishu District, Kenya. *Journal of Emerging Trends in Educational Research and Policy Studies, 3*(6), 816–821.

Kim, P. H., Aldrich, H. E., & Keister, L. A. (2016). Access (not) denied: The impact of financial, human, and cultural capital on entrepreneurial entryin the United States. *Small Business Economics, 27*(1), 5–22.

Kiss, A. N., & Danis, W. M. (2008). Country institutional context, social networks, and new venture internationalization speed. *European Management Journal, 26*(6), 388–399.

Kiss, A. N., Fernhaber, S., & McDougall–Covin, P. P. (2018). Slack, innovation, and export intensity: Implications for small–and medium–sized enterprises. *Entrepreneurship Theory and Practice, 42*(5), 671–697.

Lacroix, D., Boucekkine, R., & Peeters, D. (2007). Early literacy achievements, population density, and the transition to modern growth. *Journal of the European Economic Association, 5*(1), 183–226.

Lee, S. M., Chang, D., & Lim, S. B. (2015). Impact of entrepreneurship education: A comparative study of the US and Korea. *The International Entrepreneurship and Management Journal, 1*(1), 27–43.

Mahmood, A., Ibrahim, M., Irshad, M. K., Quddusi, A. H. A., Bokhari, A.,... Show, P. L. (2022). Microplastics pollution from wastewater treatment plants: A critical review on challenges, detection, sustainable removal techniques and circular economy. *Environmental Technology & Innovation*, 102–146.

Mat, N. B., Ekpe, I., & Razak, R. C. (2010). The effect of microfinance factors on women entrepreneurs' performance in Nigeria: A conceptual framework. *International Journal of Business and Social Science, 1*(2).

Marshall, D. R., Meek, W. R., Swab, R. G., & Markin, E. (2016). Access to resources and entrepreneurial well-being: A self-efficacy approach. *Journal of Business Research, 120*, 203–212.

Mugenda, O. M., & Mugenda, A. G. (1999). *Research methods: Quantitative and qualitative approaches*. Acts Press.

Mungaya, M., Mbwambo, A. H., & Tripathi, S. K. (2012). Study of tax system impact on the growth of small and medium enterprises (SMEs): With reference to

Shinyanga municipality, Tanzania. *International Journal of Management and Business Studies, 2*(3), 99–105.

Nandanwar, M. V., Surnis, S. V., & Nandanwar, L. M. (2016). Incentives as a tool towards organizational success of entrepreneur business: A case study of small scale pharmaceutical manufacturing unit. *International Journal of Economics and Business Modeling, 1*(2), 15.

Omano, J. O. (2012). *Factors affecting adoption of green technology by firms in Kenya.* Doctoral dissertation, University of Nairobi.

Pearce, D., Barbier, E., & Markandya, A. (2013). *Sustainable development: Economics and environment in the Third World.* Routledge.

Penrose, E., & Penrose, E. T. (1959). *The theory of the growth of the firm.* Oxford University Press.

Pfeffer, J., & Pfeffer, J. (1981). *Power in organizations* (Vol. 33). Pitman.

Sakundarini, R., & Udin, K. (2021). Green manufacturing and sustainability of manufacturing firms in Malaysia: Literature based review. *Journal of Procurement & Supply Chain, 5*(1).

Sassetti, S., Marzi, G., Cavaliere, V., & Ciappei, C. (2018). Entrepreneurial cognition and socially situated approach: A systematic and bibliometric analysis. *Scientometrics, 116*(3), 1675–1718.

Stevenson, L., & St-Onge, A. (2015). *Support for growth-oriented women entrepreneurs in Kenya.* International Labour Organization.

Storey, D. J. (1994). New firm growth and bank financing. *Small Business Economics, 6,* 139–150.

Taylor, D. W., & Walley, E. E. (2013). *The green entrepreneur: Visionary, maverick or opportunist?, 28*(2), 111–121.

Thornton, P. H., Ribeiro-Soriano, D., & Urbano, D. (2011). Socio-cultural factors and entrepreneurial activity: An overview. *International Small Business Journal, 29*(2), 105–118.

Tripathi, R., Khatri, N., & Mamde, A. (2020). Sample size and sampling considerations in published clinical research articles. *Journal of the Association of Physicians of India, 68*(3), 14–18.

Ulijn, J. M., & Weggeman, M. C. D. P. (2011). Towards an innovation culture: What are its national, corporate, marketing and engineering aspects, some experimental evidence. In *Handbook of organizational culture and climate* (pp. 487–517). Wiley.

UNEP. (2019, July 5). *Pakistan's pathway to a Green Economy.* http://www.unep.org/greeneconomy/AdvisorySevices/Kenya

Walley, K., Custance, P., & Parsons, S. (2010). UK consumer attitudes concerning environmental issues impacting the agrifood industry. *Business Strategy and the Environment, 9*(6), 355–366.

Waweru, M. G. (2017, October). Addressing the different tax policy and tax administrative challenges of micro, small and medium businesses. In *A presentation at the international tax dialogue global conference from 17 the–19th October 2007 at Buenos Aires.*

Chapter 4

Green Practice Implementation Among SME's Logistic in Malaysia: A Conceptual Research Model of Determinants, Outcome, and Opportunities for Future Research

Sasidharan Raman Nair, Mohd Rushidi bin Mohd Amin, Vinesh Maran Sivakumaran and Shishi Kumar Piaralal

Abstract

In 2020, the logistics market in Malaysia was valued at USD 37.60 billion, and it is projected to grow to more than USD 55.0 billion by 2026 at a compound annual growth rate (CAGR) of more than 4%. However, more information is needed about the impact of green logistic practice determinants by the local SMEs on the market share. This study serves as a focal point by examining the factors involved by offering a conceptual framework of determinants and their potential outcomes. This study contributes by demonstrating a conceptual, theoretical framework derived from the synthesis of two theory such as the Resource-Based View theory and the Diffusion of Innovation Theory. At the same time, it offers a holistic approach with an in-depth understanding of the Technological and Organizational factors of SMEs. The relationship between the implementation of green practices and organizational performance is also explored.

Keywords: Green practice; technology–organization–environment; diffusion of innovation theory; CEO innovativeness; small–medium enterprise (SME); organizational performance

Entrepreneurship and Green Finance Practices, 77–89
doi:10.1108/978-1-80455-678-820231004

1. Introduction

Many nations' economies owe a significant amount of their overall expansion to the transport and logistics business, which is an essential element of commercial exchange. Logistics entails various activities and services that help connect buyers and sellers across international borders to support international trade (Ali et al., 2023). As a result, logistics has become a critical differentiator in today's business environment and an engine for economic expansion, wealth generation, and job creation worldwide, as demonstrated in South America, the Middle East, and East Asia (Khan et al., 2022; Wang et al., 2020). The globalization of businesses and the consequential competitive pressures have laid great emphasis on the capability of organizations to deliver products quickly and on time, as mentioned by Zowada (2021), Liu et al. (2020), and Zameer et al. (2020) in their study in Poland, United Kingdom, and China. Companies looking to save costs and improve value while distributing and transporting goods have little alternative but to outsource logistical activities to keep up with customer demand (Adebambo et al., 2015; Rozelin et al., 2020).

Demand for logistics services in Malaysia has been rising in recent years, reflecting the country's expanding economy (Lin et al., 2020). Many companies in Malaysia have outsourced most of their logistics functions to Third Party Logistics companies (3PLs), and the roles played by these logistics services providers (LSPs) are becoming increasingly important, as indicated by Ashok and Rajesh (2020) and Norkaew and Sureeyatanapas (2019). The deterioration of the natural environment is a major global problem today (Lin & Ho, 2008). According to the UN, Malaysia's carbon emissions increased to 7.7 tons per capita in 2020, compared to 5.9 tons per capita in 2010, which is in line with Al-Ogaili et al. (2021) that stated that Malaysia is a major contributor to environmental deterioration due to its rising emission levels, which have surpassed those of other developed countries. Although these outsourced logistics firms have been acknowledged to produce desired services, their activities are also known to have inflicted severe strain on the environment (Evangelista et al., 2011). Global warming, greenhouse gases, natural hazards, air and water pollution, landfills, and the energy crisis are all challenges that need to be addressed immediately (Salmona et al., 2010; Song-Turner et al., 2014). Abbasi and Hassan (2013) claimed that the success of Malaysian outsourced logistics firms in the perspective of sustainable practices adoption still needs to be clarified and supported by sufficient evidence. According to Zailani et al. (2017), 'green' is a relatively new concept in practice, particularly in Malaysia; only a few studies have been conducted on green adoption. Transportation is a significant component of the logistics industry and consumes a considerable amount of natural resources, and its operations negatively impact the natural environment substantially (Evangelista et al., 2017). The general focus of past studies emphasizes larger firms, and research on small firms should be more often addressed. This forms the primary justification for why this study should be conducted. While empirical evidence has shown that larger companies progressively incorporate environmental management practices into their corporate strategies, more is needed to know about small- and medium-sized enterprises (SMEs) (Goh & Zailani, 2010). This paper explores the determinants of green practice implementation in small- and medium-sized logistics firms and the impact of green practice implementation on organizational performance. This study aims to formulate a theoretical framework to determine the relationship between organizational, technological, and green practice implementation among SME logistics firms in Malaysia.

2. Literature Review and Hypotheses Formulation

2.1 Theoretical Foundation

This research provides a theoretical model focussing on green practice and organizational performance. The theoretical model was developed by combining the Resource-Based View (RBV) theory and the Diffusion of Innovation Theory (DOI). RBV has provided the theoretical underpinning to understand how innovation adoption is linked to firm performance (Oliveira & Martins, 2011; Sarkis et al., 2011). RBV focusses on green practice as a resource that can improve a firm's competitiveness. The resource-based view (RBV) is a theory that focusses on competitive advantage, which emphasizes the association between firm performance and firm-specific resources (Hitt et al., 2016). It describes how businesses can create a sustainable competitive advantage over their rivals by capitalizing and expanding upon resources that are difficult for them to replicate (Ali, 2021). In other words, a firm has a sustained competitive advantage when the competitor does not implement that advantage or when the competitive advantage cannot be implemented or duplicated by the competitor or competitors.

In the Diffusion of Innovation (DOI) Theory, Rogers (2003) defined diffusion as a process in which an innovation is communicated through specific channels over time among members of a social system. DOI theory explains how, why, and at what rate new technology or innovation spreads through cultures, operating at the individual or firm levels (Oliveira & Martins, 2011). In other words, the DOI theory concerns how a new technological idea moves from creation to use. Overall, this theory suggests several constructs and independent variables impact or determines the adoption rate of innovations, for example, individual (leader) characteristics, internal characteristics of organizational structure, and external characteristics of an organization. Many researchers used DOI to investigate innovation adoption (Hassen et al., 2021). In the adoption of the green practice, Sarkis et al. (2011) stated that DOI is a promising theory for adoption studies in many fields, such as health care, education, agriculture, and information technology, and it is used in various studies in several disciplines (Corrigan, 2012).

2.2 The Relationship Between Technological, Organizational, and Green Practice Implementation

2.2.1 Technological Factors

Ho and Lin (2012) stated that the technological factors of innovation are cognitive beliefs reflecting an attitude towards innovation. The technological elements represent potential technologies for business usage (Scupola, 2009). Technological factors have often been considered in the literature on technical innovation (Lin & Ho, 2011), which needs to be examined in green practice literature (Lin & Ho, 2008). It is only possible to investigate some of the determinants for adoption that have been found in the literature on technological innovation. This study focusses primarily on compatibility and relative advantage since previous research has shown that these two elements have a more significant impact on technological innovation's acceptance and implementation behaviour than any other aspects (Sia et al., 2004).

2.2.2 Compatibility

Compatibility refers to the extent to which an innovation is compatible with the firm's current beliefs, processes, and requirements (Rogers, 2003). A business will likely implement new technology or innovation if it is more congruent with how it already operates and its information (Sarooghi et al., 2015). Compatibility is also related to green innovation adoption, as green innovation is not disruptive but incremental. Green innovation is not just a single event but a process of assimilation and accumulation of knowledge (Weng & Lin, 2011). In other words, green innovation combines several innovations to the organization's current technologies and ongoing practices. Lin and Ho (2011) and Weng and Lin (2011) have found a positive relationship between compatibility and innovation adoption. A more significant environmental effect may emerge when environmental actions match previous experiences (Etzion, 2007). Prior studies provided evidence that organizations are more likely to adopt and use technology/innovation that is compatible with the organization's current practices, infrastructure, and value systems business process (Chau & Deng, 2021). In addition, Ho and Lin (2012), Weng and Lin (2011), and Ho et al. (2014) stated that there is a positive relationship between green practice adoption and compatibility of innovation. Therefore, the adoption of green practices for SMEs is expected to be positively associated with the compatibility of the innovations, and the following hypothesis is proposed:

H1. Compatibility has a positive relationship with Green Practice Implementation.

2.2.3 Relative Advantage

Relative advantage is the perception that innovation is more advantageous than its substitute idea (Rogers, 2003). From another perspective, Limthongchai and Speece (2003) and Lin and Ho (2008) defined relative advantage as the degree to which a new concept is seen as being more beneficial than the initial concept it replaces. Organizations will adopt and use new technology/innovation, such as environmental technologies, only when they perceive the innovation's potential benefits are better than that of the older technology it replaces. The perceived benefits of adopting an innovation may be measured in economic, social benefits, or satisfaction derived from adopting such innovations (Weng & Lin, 2011). Some potential benefits of environmental practices to an organization include lowering its consumption of energy and natural resources and its production of waste and pollution while raising its economic and environmental performance and receptivity to social and environmental exceptions. Ho et al. (2014) have found a positive relationship between relative advantage and technology/innovation adoption, and Lin et al. (2020) stated that there is strong evidence that some empirical studies support that relative advantage is one of the determinant factors to influence the organization's intention to adopt the green practice. Therefore, a positive relationship between green innovation adoption and relative advantage can be expected. Therefore, it is anticipated that:

H2. Relative Advantage has a positive relationship with Green Practice Implementation.

2.3 Organizational Factors

The support of top management is revealed to be the most critical component on the subject of the factors that influence the adoption of new technology or innovation by SMEs (Ulas, 2019), employees' knowledge, attitude towards the technology/innovation (Susanty et al., 2020), and size of the organization (Lin, 2014). Saunila et al. (2014) argued that having adequate organizational resources and capable organizational personnel is the two most critical organizational criteria for fostering innovation. Ibrahim and Jaafar (2016) hypothesized that competent human resources benefited from adopting innovations due to their capable learning and inventive capacities. Regarding innovation, the calibre of a company's human resources is one of the essential factors. This study will investigate the influence of top management support and the quality of human resources.

2.4 Top Management Support

The level of support from top management is crucial in determining whether or not an organization will successfully embrace new technology or innovation in its workforce (Taylor, 2015). According to Jeyaraj et al. (2006), to increase the rate at which innovations are adopted, it is vital to provide the required motivation for adoption/implementation by making available the necessary financial and technical resources. In addition, Bruque and Moyano (2007) discovered that the level of support from top management was a crucial determinant in the rate of information technology adoption by SMEs. When the resources necessary for implementing green innovation are made accessible, top-level support for environmental management will drive the employees to embrace other green practices

(Weng & Lin, 2011). Bengtsson et al. (2007) and Bharati and Chaudhury (2006) have found positive relations between top management support and innovation adoption. Ho et al. (2014) concluded that support from top management is necessary for the green practice to be successfully implemented. A small- or medium-sized organization's decision-maker needs to obtain top management's support when using cutting-edge technology (Chouki et al., 2020). Therefore, top management support for adopting green innovations by SMEs is expected to be positively associated with green innovation adoption.

H3. Top Management Support has a positive relationship with Green Practice Implementation.

2.4.1 Quality of Human Resources

The innovative capacities and the capable learning skills of knowledgeable human resources benefit the innovation's implementation (Ho & Lin, 2012). Adopting and implementing green innovation is intricate, requiring cooperation across academic disciplines and significant shifts in how businesses operate (Dabić et al., 2020). The green practice adoption process applies pressure and strain on the human resources and capabilities processed by the firm. The adoption process might be hampered by a lack of familiarity with emerging technologies or environmentally responsible practices. The lack of knowledge will be a stumbling block to adopting the green practice. In order to get beyond this obstacle and start implementing green practices, the employees need to undergo extensive and specialized training to get familiar with the core values that guide the green innovation process (Weng & Lin, 2011). Denicolai et al. (2021) contend that a company's propensity to adopt cutting-edge technologies is inversely proportional to the degree to which it is receptive to novel ideas and concepts. In addition, Lin and Ho (2008) have found a significant positive relationship between green adoption and knowledgeable human resources. Therefore, it is postulated that:

H4. Quality of Human Resources has a positive relationship with Green Practice Implementation.

2.5 Organizational Performance

Organizational performance was initially defined as a tool and metric used to analyze and assess an organization's ability to create and disperse value for its stakeholders (Antony & Bhattacharyya, 2010). Moullin (2007) described organizational performance as an indicator of an organization's ability to effectively manage its efficiency and provide value to its stakeholders and customers. Organizational performance has been discussed in many types of research from multiple perspectives (Alhadid & Abu-Rumman, 2014). Since this study is based on a developing economy in Malaysia, organizational performance measurements in the context of this research are identified as a combination of three criteria such as environmental, economic, and operational. The capacity of a logistics company to minimize its air emissions, solid waste, and consumption of hazardous and toxic products is directly related to the company's environmental performance (Montabon et al., 2007). The economic performance of a logistics company is measured by its success in lowering the prices of raw materials, energy, waste management, waste disposal, and penalties for environmental mishaps (Wagner, 2008). Operational performance relates to the capabilities of the organization to efficiently produce and deliver products and services to customers (Chien & Shih, 2007). Furthermore, incorporating green practices into these logistics-related activities will unquestionably mitigate some of the harmful effects on the environment. Waste minimization and prevention, efficient use of resources and energy, lowered emissions, removal of potentially harmful substances from the production process, and correct disposal of solid waste all contribute to financial savings (Tomar & Oza, 2015).

2.6 The Relationship Between Green Practice and Organization Performance

Green practices improve organizational performance, including financial and non-financial aspects (Khan et al., 2020). Many studies indicated that green practices could improve environmental performance (Judge & Elenkov, 2005). Zhu et al. (2010) have shown that green practice positively influences environmental performance. Furthermore, Balasubramanian et al. (2021)demonstrated a favourable correlation between environmental practice and organizational economic performance. Chien and Shih (2007) discovered that firms adopt green practices to reduce costs, promote market shares, and increase profits. At the company's level, adopting green practices may provide several benefits, for example, decreased use of energy and reductions in costs in general, and income increases (Mithas et al., 2010; Watson et al., 2010). Organizational performance may be boosted in several ways by businesses that have implemented green practices, including lower operational costs due to savings in energy and waste management expenses and improved resource use (Hedwig et al., 2009) and also by developing environmentally friendly goods that will help businesses to set themselves apart from rivals and even charge higher prices for their services, which will lead to an increase in income (Stefan & Paul, 2008). Numerous studies have shown a favourable, strong relationship between the implementation of green practices and operational productivity (González-Benito & González-Benito, 2006; Melnyk et al., 2003). Montabon et al. (2007) study comprising environmental and business performance data from 45 corporate reports demonstrated significant and positive relationships between environmental practices and measures of performance. Therefore, it is posited that

H5. Green Practice implementation has a positive relationship with Organization Performance.

3. Conceptual Research Framework

This study offers a holistic green practice and the organization performance model by incorporating resource-based (RBV) and DOI theories to establish the relationships, as shown in Fig. 4.1.

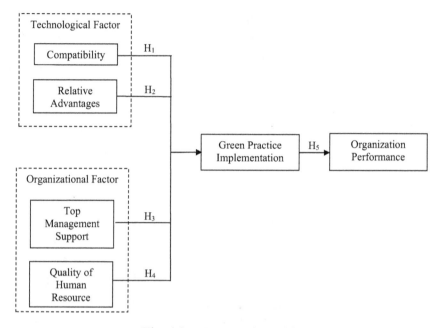

Fig. 4.1.   Proposed Model.

4. Conclusion

The implications of this research lead to a distinctive concept of green practice implementation by developing a conceptual framework synthesizing from the RBV and DOI theory. The findings would assist the managers in understanding the importance of each different factor contributing to the adoption of green practice implementation, especially in Malaysia. It adds value to the existing literature on green practice implementation as it studies a more complex three-way relationship (antecedent – green practice – organizational performance). The theoretical model is a unified framework that combines several distinct but interrelated ideas. This research has several important repercussions, particularly for the real world. To begin, a significant portion of the research that has been done on the topic of green adoption has focussed primarily on the adoption or implementation of environmentally responsible practices in manufacturing organizations.

Very few studies have been conducted on adopting service organizations such as logistics. The primary focus of this research was on adopting environmentally friendly business practices by small- and medium-sized enterprises (SMEs), particularly in logistics. This study expanded the understanding of green adoption in organizations to include small- and medium-sized enterprises (SMEs) in developing nations. Therefore, this study addresses the practical gap and contributes to improving current understanding while adding knowledge to the body of literature. This study would also have functional managerial implications for

SMEs. Malaysian SMEs can use the proposed model to evaluate the technological and organizational factors adopted by green logistic practices. The model could also be used as a guide for other small- and medium-sized businesses interested in going green. There is a great need for an intense and broader adoption and implementation of green innovation in the Malaysian logistics industry. These logistics firms must understand the green practice implementation. Adoption of environmentally responsible practices depends on the availability of appropriate government laws and regulations. The government may examine the regulations and incentives to encourage small- and medium-sized businesses to embrace environmentally friendly ideas for their expansion and development. Malaysia's government has implemented several reforms designed to streamline corporate operations and increase connections among smaller businesses. The proposed research model can assist in maximizing the benefits of the green implementation effort that the Malaysian government is making by understanding the factors influencing the adoption and implementation of green practices.

References

Abbasi, M. N., & Hassan, N. M. (2013). Sustainable logistic operations – Study of leading MNC from FMCG sector of Pakistan. *Journal of Social Sciences, 33*(2), 409–420.

Adebambo, S., Omolola, O., & Victor, D. (2015). Impact of logistics outsourcing services on company transport cost in selected manufacturing companies in south Western Nigeria European. *European Journal of Logistics, Purchasing and Supply Chain Management, 30*(4), 30–41.

Al-Ogaili, A. S., Al-Shetwi, A. Q., Babu, T. S., Hoon, Y., Abdullah, M. A., Alhasan, A., & Al-Sharaa, A. (2021). Electric buses in Malaysia: Policies, innovations, technologies and life cycle evaluations. *Sustainability, 13*(21), 1–22. https://doi.org/10.3390/su132111577

Alhadid, A., & Abu-Rumman, A. (2014). The impact of green innovation on organizational performance, environmental management behavior as a moderate variable: An analytical study on Nuqul Group in Jordan. *International Journal of Business and Management, 9*(7), 22–39.

Ali, M (2021). Imitation or innovation: To what extent do exploitative learning and exploratory learning foster imitation strategy and innovation strategy for sustained competitive advantage? *Technological Forecasting and Social Change, 165*, 1–18. https://doi.org/10.1016/j.techfore.2020.120527

Ali, A., Cao, M., Allen, J., Liu, Q., Ling, Y., & Cheng, L. (2023). Investigation of the drivers of logistics outsourcing in the United Kingdom's pharmaceutical manufacturing industry. *Multimodal Transportation, 2*(1), 1–14. https://doi.org/10.1016/j.multra.2022.100064

Antony, J. P., & Bhattacharyya, S. (2010). Measuring organizational performance and organizational excellence of SMEs-parts: An empirical study on SMEs in India. *Measuring Business Excellence, 14*(3), 4–28.

Ashok, R., & Rajesh, R. (2020). An analysis of third-party logistics market in the United Arab Emirates. *International Journal of Supply Chain Management, 9*(1), 888–901.

Balasubramanian, S., Shukla, V., Mangla, S., & Chanchaichujit, J. (2021). Do firm characteristics affect environmental sustainability? A literature review-based assessment. *Business Strategy and the Environment, 30*(2), 1389–1416. https://doi.org/10.1002/bse.2692

Bengtsson, M., Boter, H., & Vanyushyn, V. (2007). Integrating the internet and marketing operations: A study of antecedents in firms of different size. *International Small Business Journal, 25*(1), 27–48.

Bharati, P., & Chaudhury, A. (2006). Studying the current status of technology adoption. *Communications of the ACM, 49*(10), 88–93.

Bruque, S., & Moyano, J. (2007). Organizational determinants of information technology adoption and implementation in SMEs: The case of family and cooperative firms. *Technovation, 27*(5), 241–253.

Chau, N. T., & Deng, H. (2021). Conceptualization for mobile commerce adoption in SMEs: A perspective of developing countries. *International Journal of Business Information Systems, 38*(4), 449–488. https://doi.org/10.1504/IJBIS.2021.119835. PDF

Chien, M. K., & Shih, L. H. (2007). An empirical study of the implementation of green supply chain management practices in the electrical and electronic industry and their relation to organizational performances. *International Journal of Environmental Science and Technology, 4*(3), 383–394.

Chouki, M., Talea, M., Okar, C., & Chroqui, R. (2020). Barriers to information technology adoption within small and medium enterprises: A systematic literature review. *International Journal of Innovation and Technology Management, 17*(1), 1–32. https://doi.org/10.1142/S0219877020500078

Corrigan, J. A. (2012). The implementation of e-tutoring in secondary schools: A diffusion study. *Computers & Education, 59*(3), 925–936.

Dabić, M., Maley, J., Dana, L.-P., Novak, I., Pellegrini, M. M., & Caputo, A. (2020). Pathways of SME internationalization: A bibliometric and systematic review. *Small Business Economics, 55*, 705–725. https://doi.org/10.1007/s11187-019-00181-6

Denicolai, S., Zucchella, A., & Magnani, G. (2021). Internationalization, digitalization, and sustainability: Are SMEs ready? A survey on synergies and substituting effects among growth paths. *Technological Forecasting and Social Change, 166*(May), 1–15. https://doi.org/10.1016/j.techfore.2021.120650

Etzion, D. (2007). Research on organizations and the natural environment, 1992-present: A review. *Journal of Management, 33*(4), 637–664.

Evangelista, P., Colicchia, C., & Creazza, A. (2017). Is environmental sustainability a strategic priority for logistics service providers? *Journal of Environmental Management, 198*, 353–362.

Evangelista, P., Huge-Brodin, M., Isaksson, K., & Sweeney, E. (2011). The impact of 3PL's green initiatives on the purchasing of transport and logistics services: An exploratory study. *International Purchasing and Supply Education and Research Association (IPSERA) Conference, 1–15.*

Goh, C. W., & Zailani, S. (2010). Green supply chain initiatives: Investigation on the barriers in the context of SMEs in Malaysia. *International Business Management, 4*(1), 20–27.

González-Benito, J., & González-Benito, Ó. (2006). A review of determinant factors of environmental proactivity. *Business Strategy and the Environment, 15*(2), 87–102.

Hassen, H., Rahim, N. H. B. A., Othman, A. H. A., & Shah, A. (2021). A model for e-commerce adoption by SMEs in developing countries. In *The importance of new technologies and entrepreneurship in business development: In the context of economic diversity in developing countries. ICBT 2020. Lecture notes in networks and systems* (Vol. 194, pp. 516–529). https://doi.org/10.1007/978-3-030-69221-6_39

Hedwig, M., Malkowski, S., & Neumann, D. (2009). Taming energy costs of large enterprise systems through adaptive provisioning. *International Conference on Information Systems, 1–18.*

Hitt, M. A., Xu, K., & Carnes, C. M. (2016). Resource based theory in operations management research. *Journal of Operations Management, 41*, 77–94.

Ho, Y.-H., & Lin, C.-Y. (2012). An empirical study on Taiwanese logistics companies' attitudes toward environmental management practices. *Advances in Management and Applied Economics, 2*(4), 223–241.

Ho, Y.-H., Lin, C.-Y., & Tsai, J.-S. (2014). An empirical study on organizational infusion of green practices in Chinese logistics companies. *Journal of Economic and Social Studies, 4*(2), 159–189.

Ibrahim, I., & Jaafar, H. S. (2016). Adopting environment management practices for environment sustainability: A proposed model for logistics companies. *Asian Business Research, 1*(1), 70–75.

Jeyaraj, A., Rottman, J. W., & Lacity, M. C. (2006). A review of the predictors, linkages, and biases in IT innovation adoption research. *Journal of Information Technology, 21*(1), 1–23.

Judge, W. Q., & Elenkov, D. (2005). Organizational capacity for change and environmental performance: An empirical assessment of Bulgarian firms. *Journal of Business Research, 58*(7), 893–901.

Khan, S. A., Radi, R. M., Ali, S. M., Zahran, E. H., Al Sahtout, A. H., & Esam, S. A. (2022). An analysis of third party logistic selection criteria in oil and gas sector: An integrated SWOT-AHP approach. *International Journal of Logistics Systems and Management, 43*(1), 20–47. https://doi.org/10.1504/IJLSM.2022.125660

Khan, S. A. R., Yu, Z., Sharif, A., & Golpîra, H. (2020). Determinants of economic growth and environmental sustainability in South Asian association for regional cooperation: Evidence from panel ARDL. *Environmental Science and Pollution Research, 27*, 45675–45687. https://doi.org/10.1007/s11356-020-10410-1

Limthongchai, P., & Speece, M. (2003). The effect of perceived characteristics of innovation on ecommerce adoption by SMEs in Thailand. In *Proceedings of the seventh international conference on global business and economic development.*

Lin, H.-F. (2014). Understanding the determinants of electronic supply chain management system adoption: Using the technology–organization–environment framework. *Technological Forecasting and Social Change, 86*, 80–92.

Lin, C.-Y., Alam, S. S., Ho, Y.-H., Al-Shaikh, M. E., & Sultan, P. (2020). Adoption of green supply chain management among sMEs in Malaysia. *Sustainability, 12*, 1–15. https://doi.org/10.3390/su12166454

Lin, C.-Y., & Ho, Y.-H. (2008). An empirical study on logistics service providers' intention to adopt green innovations. *Journal of Technology Management and Innovation, 3*(1), 17–26.

Lin, C.-Y., & Ho, Y.-H. (2011). Determinants of green practice adoption for logistics companies in China. *Journal of Business Ethics, 98*(1), 67–83.

Liu, H., Purvis, L., Mason, R., & Wells, P. (2020). Developing logistics value propositions: Drawing insights from a distributed manufacturing solution. *Industrial Marketing Management, 89*(August), 517–527. https://doi.org/10.1016/j.indmarman.2020.03.011

Melnyk, S. A., Sroufe, R. P., & Calantone, R. (2003). Assessing the impact of environmental management systems on corporate and environmental performance. *Journal of Operations Management, 21*(3), 329–351.

Mithas, S., Khuntia, J., & Roy, P. K. (2010). Green information technology, energy efficiency, and profits: Evidence from an emerging economy. *Thirty First International Conference on Information Systems, 1*–20.

Montabon, F., Sroufe, R., & Narasimhan, R. (2007). An examination of corporate reporting, environmental management practices and firm performance. *Journal of Operations Management, 25*(5), 998–1014.

Moullin, M. (2007). Performance measurement definitions: Linking performance measurement and organizational excellence. *International Journal of Health Care Quality Assurance, 20*(3), 181–183.

Norkaew, K., & Sureeyatanapas, P. (2019). A survey of criteria for a selection of logistics service providers: A case of Thailand's automotive industry. *International Conference on Engineering, Applied Sciences and Technology, 1*–5. https://doi.org/10.1088/1757-899X/639/1/012002

Oliveira, T., & Martins, M. F. (2011). Literature review of information technology adoption models at firm level. *Electronic Journal of Information Systems Evaluation, 14*(1), 110–121.

Rogers, E. M. (2003). *Diffusion of innovations* (5th ed.). The Free Press.

Rozelin, A., Muhammad, Z. S., Suriani, M. D. M., Faradina, A., & Ramzi, M. N. (2020). A review on green logistics paradox. *International Journal of Advanced Trends in Computer Science and Engineering, 9*(1), 1–5. https://doi.org/10.30534/ijatcse/2020/0191.12020

Salmona, O. A., Selam, A., & Vayvay, O. (2010). Sustainable supply chain management: A literature review. In *International conference on value chain sustainability (ICOVACS 2010)* (pp. 1–10).

Sarkis, J., Zhu, Q., & Lai, K. (2011). An organizational theoretic review of green supply chain management literature. *International Journal of Production Economics, 130*(1), 1–15.

Sarooghi, H., Libaers, D., & Burkemper, A. (2015). Examining the relationship between creativity and innovation: A meta-analysis of organizational, cultural, and environmental factors. *Journal of Business Venturing, 30*(5), 714–731.

Saunila, M., Pekkola, S., & Ukko, J. (2014). The relationship between innovation capability and performance: The moderating effect of measurement. *International Journal of Productivity and Performance Management, 63*(2), 234–249.

Scupola, A. (2009). SMEs' e-commerce adoption: Perspectives from Denmark and Australia. *Journal of Enterprise Information Management, 22*(1/2), 152–166.

Sia, C.-L., Teo, H.-H., Tan, B. C. Y., & Wei, K.-K. (2004). Effects of environmental uncertainty on organizational intention to adopt distributed work arrangements. *IEEE Transactions on Engineering Management, 51*(3), 253–267.

Song-Turner, H., Courvisanos, J., & Zeegers, M. (2014). Green marketing the Chinese way: Insights from a medium-sized high-tech daily chemical firm. *Journal of Asia-Pacific Business*, *15*(2), 164–192. https://doi.org/10.1080/10599231.2014.904193

Stefan, A., & Paul, L. (2008). Does it pay to be green? A systematic overview. *Academy of Management Perspectives*, *22*(4), 45–62.

Susanty, A., Handoko, A., & Puspitasari, N. B. (2020). Push-pull-mooring framework for e-commerce adoption in small and medium enterprises. *Journal of Enterprise Information Management*, *33*(2), 381–406. https://doi.org/10.1108/JEIM-08-2019-0227

Taylor, P. (2015). The importance of information and communication technologies (ICTs): An integration of the extant literature on ICT adoption in small and medium enterprises. *International Journal of Economics, Commerce and Management*, *3*(5), 1–22.

Tomar, A., & Oza, H. (2015). Green supply chain management practices implementation and effect on organizational performance of ISO 14001 certified manufacturing companies of India. *Abhinav International Monthly Refereed Journal of Research in Management & Technology*, *4*(9), 21–26.

Ulas, D. (2019). Digital transformation process and SMEs. *Procedia Computer Science*, *158*, 662–671. https://doi.org/10.1016/j.procs.2019.09.101

Wagner, M. (2008). Empirical influence of environmental management on innovation: Evidence from Europe. *Ecological Economics*, *66*(2–3), 392–402.

Wang, Y., Jia, F., Schoenherr, T., Gong, Y., & Chen, L. (2020). Industrial marketing management. *Industrial Marketing Management*, *89*(August), 72–88. https://doi.org/10.1016/j.indmarman.2019.09.004

Watson, R. T., Boudreau, M.-C., & Chen, A. J. (2010). Information systems and environmentally sustainable development: Energy informatics and new directions for the IS community. *MIS Quarterly*, *34*(1), 23–38.

Weng, M.-H., & Lin, C.-Y. (2011). Determinants of green innovation adoption for small and medium-size enterprises (SMES). *African Journal of Business Management*, *5*(22), 9154–9163.

Zailani, S., Shaharudin, M. R., Razmi, K., & Iranmanesh, M. (2017). Influential factors and performance of logistics outsourcing practices: An evidence of Malaysian companies. *Review of Managerial Science*, *11*(1), 53–93.

Zameer, H., Wang, Y., & Yasmeen, H. (2020). Reinforcing green competitive advantage through green production, creativity and green brand image: Implications for cleaner production in China. *Journal of Cleaner Production*, *247*(February), 119–141. https://doi.org/10.1016/j.jclepro.2019.119119

Zhu, Q., Geng, Y., Fujita, T., & Hashimoto, S. (2010). Green supply chain management in leading manufacturers: Case studies in Japanese large companies. *Management Research Review*, *33*(4), 380–392.

Zowada, K. (2021). Going green in logistics: The case of small and medium-sized enterprises in Poland. *Journal of Economics & Management*, *43*, 52–69. https://doi.org/10.22367/jem.2021.43.03

Chapter 5

Green Management Execution at Malaysian Federal Seaports: Challenges and Opportunities

Prashanth Beleya and Geetha Veerappan

Abstract

Seaports are significant nodal points in any supply chain network. Accordingly, the need to consistently upgrade and further develop processes would bode well for the maritime industry and nations competitiveness. There has been a change in the pattern by which green issues have become significant themes to the global sea transportation players. Developed nations have been the leaders in pursuing green options for future development. This leads to developing nations pursuing the green agenda to stay competitive. As such, Malaysia's desire of being the preferred sea nodal point in Southeast Asia lies in its abilities of seeking innovative processes and business opportunities through green principles. This chapter will focus on:

- Introducing Malaysia's seaport industry.
- A review of green management at seaports.
- The current state of green management implementation at Malaysia's federal ports.
- Challenges and opportunities for Malaysia's federal ports in pursuing green management.

Keywords: Green management; Malaysia; port management; federal ports; sustainable development; case study

1. Background

Seaborne trade is a vital cog in the world economic system. Around 85% of world trade occurs via seaborne transportation, which is attributable to its economic benefits over different methods of transport. Owning to this, ports are imperative

Entrepreneurship and Green Finance Practices, 91–105

Copyright © 2024 Prashanth Beleya and Geetha Veerappan

Published under exclusive licence by Emerald Publishing Limited

doi:10.1108/978-1-80455-678-820231005

infrastructural essentials as far as their job as an integrator of the world economy is concerned. Ports influence the productive utilization of sea transportation. Moreover, to the specification of the foundation for global transportation, ports play an essential part in the logistics processes.

Sea cargo transport has experienced solid development and significant changes over the last two decades. Cargo volumes and container traffic specifically have developed with the escalation of global trade and the topographical scattering of economies. Modern organizations have advanced swiftly beyond borders seeking growth opportunities and new markets. These progressions have ensured the port business stays elevated in a competitive environment. Subsequently, ports are viewed as not just a vital piece of the transport framework, yet a significant sub-arrangement of the more extensive creation and logistics frameworks in the global supply chain.

Since the 11th Regional EST discussion in Mongolia in 2018, green cargo and management have been a theme of developing interest in ports. Populations are developing quickly, just as are Asian economies. Asia will be responsible for USD $148 trillion worth of trade by 2050, 51% of global GDP which implies more imports and products at seaports. Transportation contributes 3.7% each year to Asian nations (Wang et al., 2018). Cargo movements as of now make up 35% of the global energy utilization.

As seaports integrate supply chains, the impacts of green management are clearly noticeable through any drives executed from a seaport point of view. The significance of green management drives at seaports has been perceived positively by the government as the way forward for seaports in Malaysia. As a point of convergence of economic development, measures taken to present and upgrade green management at seaports are an unquestionable requirement to adapt to the consistently demanding economic scene and steady development of the essential players in the business. A variety of organizational characteristic variables such as quality of human resources, top management's leadership skills, organizational support, organizational culture, and organizational size have been discussed on their influences on green management. Growing number of organizations are under pressure from their partners to change their traditional management style, both operationally and organizationally, replacing them with integrated systems that help increase the speed and fluidity of physical and information flows. This is evident as ports have been noted to be labour-intensive in developing countries, while developed countries have progressed beyond and depend more on capital intensity (Cui, 2017).

Due to the impact of globalization, China, India, and SEA countries have become main exporters to many countries and therefore ports in the region have become vital nodes in the global supply chain (Notteboom & Lam, 2018). As a result of higher container volumes generated in Asian hinterlands, the size of vessels has grown and therefore many ports in Asia have been facing the challenge of limited capacity in port access and port terminals. For these reasons, a substantial amount of investment in port capacity expansion projects has been undertaken by governments in the region. At the same time, they have invested in advanced port technology, mainly in cargo handling, and striving to preserve their competitiveness amidst growing trade liberalizations. Malaysian ports have invested heavily in port infrastructure and port capacity expansion projects in anticipation of increasing cargo volumes. The location of major Malaysian ports along main trade lanes such as the Straits of Malacca has become a motivating factor for such positive approaches.

As seaports become supreme in any supply chain, the impacts of green management are clearly noticeable through any drives executed according to a port point of view. The significance of green management drives at seaports has properly been perceived by the government by holding fast to the way that it is the way forward for seaports in Malaysia. As a point of convergence of economic development, measures taken to present and upgrade green management at seaports are an unquestionable requirement to adapt to the consistently requesting economic scene and steady development of the essential players in the business.

As a developing nation, Malaysia has undoubtedly begun the process of incorporating green management in the transportation sector, particularly by focussing on the maritime business. This was highlighted in the United Nations Economic and Social Commission for Asia and The Pacific (ESCAP) Ministerial Conference on Transport in Moscow in December 2016 whereby Malaysia's representative mentioned that a strategy to guide Malaysian seaports towards green turns of events was in the pipeline (ESCAP, 2019). The approach being developed was known as green port management that especially centres around the ecological effects and steps to address such worries. The Malaysian federal ports had begun efforts to focus on landside developments that could spur growth prospects. Among the areas considered for green management according to the viewpoint of port authorities in Malaysia include green innovation and development processes in ports (Demsetz, 2019). As such, federal ports in Malaysia had begun to invest and strategize their focus towards green management, which has been considered as part of the transformation process in port operations.

2. Ports in Malaysia

Seaports in Malaysia are divided into two executives' control, namely Federal Government and State owned. The Federal ports were established under Port Authorities Act 1963 and subsequently were privatized under Port Privatization Act 1990. This move enabled the government to focus on providing governmental assistance and act as a regulatory body. The regulatory bodies have their own Board of Directors headed by a chairman. All federal ports fall under the jurisdiction of the Ministry of Transport within the Marine Division, while the State ports are directed by the respective State Ministries. The Federal Ports are further divided into major and minor ports. Finally, the smaller ports and jetties are controlled by the Marine Dept. At present, there are seven major federal ports, namely, Port Klang, Penang Port, Johor Port, Port of Tanjung Pelepas, Kuantan Port, Kemaman Port, and Bintulu Port. Tables 5.1 and 5.2 below depict the structure of Malaysian Federal seaports in terms of authority management, related port acts governing federal ports, and their operating structure.

Table 5.1. Federal Ports and Authorities (Ministry of Transport, Malaysia).

Major Ports	Local Authorities	Related Acts
Penang Port	Penang Port Commission	Penang Port Commission Act 1955
Port Klang	Port Klang Authority	Port Authorities Act 1963
Johor Port	Johor Port Authority	
Port of Tanjung Pelepas	Johor Port Authority (Tanjung Pelepas)	
Kuantan Port	Kuantan Port Authority	
Kemaman Port	Kemaman Port Authority	
Bintulu Port	Bintulu Port Authority	Bintulu Port Authority Act 1981

Table 5.2. Federal Port Operators (Ministry of Transport, Malaysia).

Major Ports	Ports Operator
Port Klang	
-North Port	North Port Sdn. Bhd.
-West Port	West Port Sdn. Bhd.
Johor Port	Johor Port Sdn. Bhd.
Kuantan Port	Kuantan Port Consortium Sdn. Bhd.
Bintulu Port	Bintulu Port Sdn. Bhd.
Tanjung Pelepas Port	Port of Tanjung Pelepas Sdn. Bhd.
Pulau Pinang Port	Penang Port Sdn. Bhd.

3. Green Management Evolution

Green management is characterized as the organization wide course of applying development to accomplish sustainability, waste decrease, social obligation, and a competitive advantage through ceaseless learning and improvement and by accepting ecological objectives and techniques and that are completely coordinated with the objectives and strategies of the organization (Haden et al., 2009). Accordingly, green supply chain management (GrSCM) is the strategic process for accomplishing the management aspect of green. Ref. Sarkis et al., 2018, stated GrSCM as coordinating not just environmental worries into the organization practices of supply chain management but include firm implementation and innovative strategies in functional aspects that could influence firm competitiveness. Considering this, GrSCM which especially incorporates development has been elevated to be coordinated with management responsibilities and their strategic processes to accomplish the much-needed sustainable competitive advantages. Global ports are starting to acknowledge such efforts by planning business possibilities connecting to the green management idea.

In the same manner, as numerous different spaces of human projects, greenness turned into a catchphrase in the transportation business during the late 1990s and into the millennium. This was due to the developing consciousness of ecological issues, specifically with widely acclaimed issues like corrosive downpour, chlorofluorocarbons (CFCs), and a dangerous atmospheric deviation. The United Nations through the establishment of its sustainable development goals in 2015 reiterated green as an important tool to focus in political and economic fields as part of its 17 goals.

Logistics is a significant contributor towards ecological disruption through its modes, frameworks, and deals. Accordingly, a seaport is considered the foundation of improvement which could lead to other positive outcomes related to logistics activities. Further improvements in logistics and their significance to the economy drew further investigations and strategy developments towards upgrading green management in this field (Yeo et al., 2014).

A report by United Nations Conference on Trade and Development (UNCTAD) in 2021 discussed green management at world seaports, specifically on creating awareness to seaports planning abilities and to implement sustainable changes. Additionally, the report covered different actions taken by worldwide seaports in implementing green efforts to improve their business. The study by the institute further revealed the need for port management to instil operations and performance enhancement tools to improve competitiveness of the overall port operations to further improve performances. This was a clear indicator of the importance for seaports around the world to pursue green management in their processes and strategy enhancements for future competitiveness.

4. Green Management at Malaysian Seaports

The present trend of supply chain management in Malaysia focusses on the outsourcing of logistics activities and the growth of 3rd Party Logistics (3PL) and 4th Party Logistics (4PL) providers. Consequently, the issue of cost appears to be the utmost important factor in the development of green issues where greater emphasis is placed on reducing cost and delivery lead time by outsourcing logistics activities. It is estimated that currently, there are about 22,000 firms in the logistics industry in Malaysia, undertaking various kinds of activities. The firms involved in the industry are constantly evolving and catering to the ever demanding and constantly changing consumer trends. Targets for the logistics industry as set by the Malaysian Logistics Council (MLC) are to achieve an overall growth of 8.6% during the planned period and contribute towards a 12.1% of GDP by 2025. On another note, MLC has also identified green initiatives from an operation's perspective as key towards competitiveness among supply chain players. All firms are one way or another connected to seaports as they are the nodal points of any movement of goods from and to a country. This elevates the importance of enhancing the seaports of the country to be equipped for future aspirations of industrial needs. However, apart from the ratification of very few policies on maritime matters, seaports in Malaysia have been slow in adopting green management to enhance competitiveness in line with global aspirations of shipping lines and other world logistics providers and manufacturers. There are policies which elevate the need for the green agenda in the logistics industry in Malaysia, with particular focus given to seaports. For instance, as stated in the Malaysian Investment Development Authority MIDA (2013) report, specific areas mentioned and needed due attention in enhancing the port business in Malaysia include:

- improving the productivity of port landside operations through green management;
- port privatization in enhancing competitiveness;
- development and improvement of ancillary services at ports; and
- development and improvement of land-side transportation (hinterland).

The improvements being tossed around have focussed on green management as a tool at the forefront of matters to achieve the desired results. The implementation of green management in port cities to achieve sustainable development in Malaysia is still in the early stages. Malaysian seaports, particularly the federal ports are perceived to be generally slow in terms of competitiveness in enhancing processes through green management tools. Further supporting this notion, Charan et al., 2018, mentioned that the Malaysian port policy aims to address challenges faced by ports that are lowering the efficiency levels which include:

- Utilize existing capacity.
- Enhancing green management agenda.
- Promoting the enhancement of technology through green management.
- Improving ancillary services within landside.

Green management adaptation in Malaysia must focus on port operations to achieve a more sustainable balance between the economic, environmental, and social elements related to the seaports and the stakeholders surrounding them. Nevertheless, only the Johor port authority has developed a green port policy as guidance for the future as of now. Westport and Northport have in their websites mentioned the need to focus on more green management implementations to spur the business forward.

Looking into the scenario in Malaysia, one of the major challenges highlighted in 2021 has been reported in the Malaysian Port Review. The review highlighted the need for new directions needed in port policy and development. Ports which are engaged in international trade and serving mainline shipping services are becoming under increasing pressure to meet the operational requirements and infrastructure needs of the ocean carriers which include new areas of business

Table 5.3. Port Competitive Values at Major Ports in Malaysia (Beleya et al., 2015).

RBV Principles	Penang Port	Port Klang		Johor	Port of Tanjung Pelepas
		Northport	Westport		
Rare	NCER (Growth Triangle) Northern Gateway	National Gateway 27% Import/Export	Deep Harbour Advanced technology Higher Productivity National Gateway 26%	Handling of non-ferrous metal/dangerous liquid	Sheltered bay/no tidal restriction
Valuable	Syariah Compliance FCZ	Comprehensive services /Facilities FCZ Margins >30% (EBITDA)	Advanced Tech Effective Linkages between 300 ports		FCZ/FIZ High Productivity (29 moves) Minimal diversion time
Inimitable	Syariah Compliance		Transhipment focus		Intermodalism FCZ/FIZ Transhipment rates < PSA
Non-Substitutable		Land Bank/Area	Land Bank/ development of area	Affiliation with ATP	Large clients (MAERSK, Evergreen)

expansion such as green innovations. Accordingly, ports must not only be innovative in meeting the further demands on terminal and yard capacities, highly efficient in service and productivity but also must link up with value added services that meet customer expectations and needs by enhancing new strategies of sustainability and green implementation to remain competitive.

Table 5.3 above highlights the current scenario of major ports competitiveness in Malaysia relative to the resource-based view theory by Beleya et al. (2015). It was noted that the federal ports have various strengths that many other world-renowned ports also possess, yet no new strategies or methods have been pursued yet to proactively seek new opportunities in the ever-changing green management environment. Such a strategy would be able to enhance the sustained competitive advantage as mentioned by the resource-based view theory. An example would be Qingdao port in China whereby their strategy applying green management has improved their rankings and business prospects. Port of Long Beach in the United States is another example where their ability in attracting shipping lines and other business clients due to the incentives and processes applied through green management elevated the port.

United Nations Conference on Trade and Development (UNCTAD) had mentioned in 2021 that environmental cost and its effect on overall port operations are an important tool from the perspective of port operators. The need to ensure customer satisfaction through constant cost cutting measures and profit slashing is no longer sustainable. This has been supported by strategies pursued by certain renowned ports in the world. Environmental strategies adopted by European ports in Sweden and the United Kingdom implemented differentiated port dues from a perspective of environmental issues can under certain conditions reduce the payback period of the investment and attract more clients Von Bahr et al. (2018). Environmentally differentiated port dues and fairways dues contributed to shipping companies' investment decision in abatement technologies. All the shipping companies stated that environmentally differentiated port dues are good incentives. Nevertheless, such strategies and environmental concerns are deeply lacking in the majority of Asian ports, thus leading to competitive losses.

5. Positive Outcomes of Going Green

The media notices companies that inhibit green aspirations into their business model. Port of Rotterdam and Qingdao port in China are highly recommended by positive publicity as current and future ports to be noticed and explored by businesses. Many corporations are scouting for seaports which adhere to green and sustainable efforts to cater for their own supply chain needs. For example, BMW is designing a vehicle whose parts will be entirely recyclable (Liu & Ge, 2018). Another example would be IKEA, which is transforming its entire supply chain operations towards sustainable and green innovation. Mc Donald's has pledged to ensure their supply chain operations are sustainable through various measures such as sustainable sourcing procedures. Several international ports have been strategizing using green management as a tool to spur growth and enhance competitiveness. Qingdao port in China is one such port whereby their strategy of applying green management has improved their rankings and business prospects. Port of Long Beach in the United States is an example of their ability to attract shipping lines and other business clients due to the incentives and processes applied through green management (Liu & Ge, 2018). To further prove the point, Table 5.4 below highlights the positive impact of Qingdao port pursuing green management in which cargo volumes had seen tremendous growth over a period of five years.

As such, the need for seaports and operators who adhere to principles of green management when conducting business is ever increasing. Apple seriously confronts their supply chain towards green innovation and practices especially at seaports to ensure a lean cost-effective manner of transporting goods (Fortune, 2019). It should be noted that international companies establishing regional bases are emphasizing on choosing their seaports with green capabilities to spur growth and have identified that aspect as their next growth strategy (Fortune, 2019).

Positive publicity from going green is not reserved for certain niche companies. Seaports taking voluntary steps to become greener will indeed gain visibility, earn credibility, and develop a reputation as global leaders. However, it should be noted that voluntary measures at present would ultimately change into mandatory measures over time as have been with so many policies and practices. Being in a conservative business or media shunned area does not stop the importance of being recognized. Seaports being gateways of national trade should be the focal

Table 5.4. Data for PPA – Port of Qingdao Port of Qingdao – Traffic Categories (×1,000 Twenty Foot Equivalent – TEUs or Tons).

2012–2018	CONT (TEUs)	CONT (Tonnes)	TOT (Tonnes)
Average Traffic	9,910	109,010	287,460
Share Traffic Category %	/	37.92%	100.00%
Average Market Share 2012–2018		6.21%	8.61%
Market Share 2012		6.85%	8.47%
Market Share 2013		6.99%	9.48%
Market Share 2014		6.99%	9.26%
Market Share 2015		7.50%	9.63%
Market Share 2016		7.72%	9.90%
Market Share 2017		7.82%	10.04%
Market Share 2018		8.19%	10.57%

point of changes as the after effects of changes or rather chain reactions would be positively enormous (Bouman et al., 2017).

6. Challenges for Malaysia's Seaports

Malaysia's federal ports have pursued the green agenda rather sporadically and at a slower pace due to various challenges present in implementing green management. Fig. 5.1 below is a graphical view of the challenges encountered by the ports in efficiently pursuing the green implementation on a full scale which is split into two broad themes, mainly internal and external challenges.

Firstly, the internal challenges identified elaborated on the difficulties encountered by factors associated internally by the federal ports in implementing green management. The theme is further broken down into three areas. Expertise within was related to the lack of internal employees from the administrative and operations divisions in developing and enhancing green management at the ports. This is related to the processes and also policy developments needed to strengthen green management initiatives at the ports. Secondly, internal views were on how the higher management perceived and supported green management at the respective federal ports. With the relevant support, ports are able to enhance green management initiatives within and further encourage employees to practice and innovatively find solutions pertaining to green management. The opposite by the higher management leads ports to focus on traditional competitive factors in driving port growth. Lastly, performance measures relate to the ability of ports to quantify and justify green management implementation. This is mostly done through financial measures and port productivity measures to justify the needs for green management.

Following this were external challenges which relate to factors beyond a port's control, yet affects the ability to implement green management at ports. Change of mindset was when customers, who are a diversified group from locals to

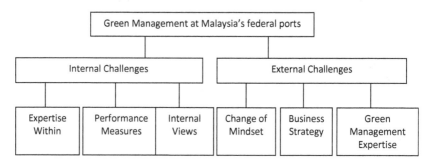

Fig. 5.1.   Challenges of Implementing Green Management at Malaysia's Federal Seaports.

multinational corporations at the ports portray differentiation. As their needs and demands change, the ports have no choice but to cater to and alter their operations to include green management to ensure customers stay loyal and engaged with the port. Next was business strategy, which was the ability of ports to raise the required investments needed for green management implementation. The lack of investment channels reduces the ability to implement such changes, which then reduces the ability of ports to enhance operations through green management. The final external factor was green management expertise that is severely lacking in the external environment from a Malaysian perspective. The federal ports are at a conundrum when acquiring technology as it requires foreign expertise if and when training and issues arise due to technicalities which lead to very high costs. On the other hand, training and development for internal employees face a backstep as the relevant expertise is not available locally and is very expensive to acquire from other developed countries.

7. Opportunities and the Future

The ability to identify the right talent and nurturing such personalities are clearly lacking in Malaysia's federal ports. Many developed countries have been at the forefront in developing talent and ensuring their availabilities to the necessary industries. Germany, Netherlands, and China are key examples of such practices. Having employees with the right mindset in an organization is key to ensuring competitiveness, then allows the development of sustained competitive advantages (Cui, 2017). Furthermore, the federal ports would need to better gauge customer requirements in terms of performance measurements to attract and retain customers over a sustained period of time. This will require a shift in internal policies and structure to enhance the port's competitiveness and remain an attractive destination for world class shippers and other customers alike.

The federal ports in Malaysia have been a labour-intensive industry for much of the last three decades. As such, the majority of employees working are either baby boomers or generation X categories. Mostly are nearing their retirement age while some are in their late 40s. The younger generation, or the generation Y employees are limited while the millennials are scarce. As green management has evolved and gained prominence over the past decade, employees of the ports have been left in a dilemma as they find it difficult to relate to the importance of implementing it into the business. This evidently delays the entire process, or worse in certain instances creates a lack of ideas for implementation. When compared to the developed countries, many ports there have employees in the generation Y category holding key positions. This is needed in Malaysia's federal ports to enhance new ideas, particularly related to green management.

Additionally, the hiring process of the federal ports needs to be revamped to include a talented younger generation to be able to mix into the experienced cohort currently at the port. The port management must not solely focus on experienced individuals of the older generation, yet find talent which is abundant in Malaysia. This could be done through a talent identification process. An agreement should be formed with the relevant educational institutes in Malaysia whereby courses related to maritime, logistics, and port management are being offered. As the logistics field, particularly maritime and port management are very niche areas in the industry, it is imperative that the ports are able to identify institutions offering such programmes. By associating with such institutions, the federal ports would be able to filter candidates with potential and hire them into the organization.

Several developed nations have taken various initiatives in addressing the gaps and issues faced by port operators in enhancing the green management agenda. Charan et al., 2018, have mentioned that countries such as United States of America, Netherlands, and also Canada have developed policies encouraging the financial institutions to provide appropriate fundings for businesses to pursue the green management agenda. Among the approaches include providing guarantees for loans taken to pursue green solutions. At the same time, the countries mentioned above provide matching grants for ports that have incorporated green management into their future business model. Port of Long Beach is a classic example of being able to pursue the sustainable and green management aspects through continuous government support. Ports in China have also been encouraged through government initiatives as mentioned above.

In Malaysia, financial institutions have various clauses before providing funding for green management. Another obstacle is the cost of funding as financial institutions are not keen on projects with long gestation periods. On another note, government funding has been second to none in Malaysia where green management is considered. Although technological funding is encouraged and provided, the amount and areas given is rather scarce. Often, such funding is given to technology companies pursuing high valued manufacturing. As the nation moves in tandem with the world towards the industry 4.0 revolution, the need to engage green management as a tool in enhancing the business functions and spurring productivity in the nation becomes imperative (Notteboom & Lam, 2018). Authorities need to work together in ensuring green management at ports is enhanced. This will involve the financial institutions and also the relevant government agencies such as the transport ministry, and the port authorities. Firstly, the government should be able to provide matching grants for any productive green management ideas brought forward by the individual ports, which are deemed economical. This will encourage more ideas to develop within the maritime industry. There has been consensus mentioning for government support not just through policy making but also through financial assistance. Seaport players have been commenting that port management could only support a minor portion financially due to resource allocation strategies. As such, by providing the needed financial assistance, the government would indirectly state the desire for industries to move towards green management and sustainability importance.

A clear green management and sustainability policy should be comprehensively developed. At present, there are various views and engagement policies stating the importance of going green and the effects of sustainability. There has been scarce evidence to relate environmental damage and cost related to operations by the federal ports in Malaysia as discussed in the earlier parts. This has been discussed through many avenues and the need to focus on environment costing has become prevalent from the policies being developed by the authorities (MIDA, 2018). Particularly in focus is the Green Technology Master Plan (GTMP) which was developed under the 11th Malaysia Plan. The GTMP creates a framework which facilitates the mainstreaming of green technology into the planned developments of Malaysia while encompassing the four pillars set in the National Green Technology Policy (NGTP) i.e. energy, environment, economy, and social. Additionally, the policy covers six areas from manufacturing to the service sectors. Transport-linked policy relates to the energy efficient vehicles and the need to focus more on public transportation efficiency. As such, there is no specific policy for port management or green management at present. Without a clear guideline or framework to work on, it would be near impossible to vision a green port for the foreseeable future. A clear guideline will provide the authorities and the port management to strategize and further enhance green management beyond the port operation areas. Supply chain operators have mentioned that port authorities were subjective as there were no clear guidelines to provide in support of green management at the federal ports. This slows the process as the federal ports have to look from within to develop such guidelines and policies. As previously discussed, the lack of talent and expertise further complicates the green management push whereby the ultimate aim is for ports to be identified as green ports. Research in developed countries has proven the importance of frameworks and guidelines in enhancing sustainability and green management. Notteboom and Lam (2018) reiterated the importance of structural changes through the development of green frameworks that have allowed certain ports to create niche advantages and quicken the green port agenda. Port of Long Beach and Rotterdam port are classic examples.

8. Conclusion

The importance of green management to the future of Malaysian federal ports has been well established. Addressing these concerns and developing appropriate strategies and measures would enable federal ports in Malaysia to gain competitive advantages and compete with other regional ports to stay ahead in this ever-demanding environment. The federal ports in Malaysia clearly understand the importance of green management and are working towards improvements. The next step would be to move towards smart port concepts, which is where developed country ports have strategized. All the relevant stakeholders need to work together to ensure green management is workable. For this to happen, regulatory frameworks need to be revamped focussing only on the seaports which will enable no contradictory rules and overlapping of policies. Additionally, the need to engage educational institutes and other policy makers in ensuring the development of green expertise is vital not just for seaports but for the nation as a whole. This is imperative as Malaysia may no longer depend on finite resources to power the nation's economy in the future. This will ensure ports in Malaysia would stay competitive and develop the necessary strategies and measures to stay ahead of our ever-improving neighbouring countries and regional ports alike.

References

Beleya, P., Raman, G., Chelliah, M. K., & Nodeson, S. (2015). Sustainability and green practices at Malaysian seaports: Contributors to the core competitiveness. *Journal of Business Management and Economics, 3*(3), 23–27.

Bouman, E. A., Lindstad, E., Rialland, A. I., & Strømman, A. H. (2017). State-of-the-art technologies, measures, and potential for reducing GHG emissions from shipping—A review. *Transportation Research Part D: Transport and Environment, 52*, 408–421.

Charan, R., Barton, D., & Carey, D. (2018). *Talent wins: The new playbook for putting people first.* Harvard Business Review Press.

Cui, Q. (2017). Environmental efficiency measures for ports: An application of RAM-Tobit-RAM with undesirable outputs. *Maritime Policy & Management, 44*(5), 551–564. https://doi.org/10.1080/03088839.2017.1319982

Demsetz, H. (2019). *The market concentration doctrine: An analysis of evidence and a discussion of policy.* American Enterprise Institute for Public Policy Research.

ESCAP. (2019). *The future of Asian & Pacific Cities: Transforming pathways towards sustainable urban development.* Bangkok: United Nations. www.unescap.org/sites/default/files/publications/Future%20of%20AP%20Cities%20Report%202019_0.pdf

Fortune, G. (2019). Determinants of corporate green investment practices in the Johannesburg Stock Exchange listed firms. *International Journal of Sustainable Economy, 9*(3), 250–279.

Haden, S. S. P., Oyler, J. D., & Humphreys, J. H. (2009). Historical, practical, and theoretical perspectives on green management. *An exploratory analysis Management Decision, 47*(7), 1041–1055.

Liu, D., & Ge, Y. E. (2018). Modelling assignment of quay cranes using queueing theory for minimizing CO2 emission at a container terminal. *Transportation Research Part D: Transport and Environment, 61*, 140–151.

MIDA Malaysia investment performance report. (2013). Malaysian Investment Development Authority. https://www.mida.gov.my/wp-content/uploads/2020/12/IPR2013.pdf

MIDA Malaysia economic corridors. (2018). http://www.mida.gov.my/home/malaysia-economic-corridors/posts/. Accessed on April 7, 2018.

Notteboom, T., & Lam, J. S. L. (2018). The greening of terminal concessions in seaports. *Sustainable Times, 10*, 3318.

Sarkis, J., Zhu, Q., & Lai, K. H. (2018). An organizational theoretic review of green supply chain management literature. *International Journal of Production Economics, 130*(1), 1–15.

UNCTAD. (2021). *Review of maritime transport 2020.* United Nations Conference on Trade and Development.

Von Bahr, J., Romson, Å., Sköld, S., & Winnes, H. (2018). Statlig styrning av hamnavgifter. *Report C, 370.* ISBN 978-91-7883-014-5. https://www.ivl.se/download/18.57581b9b167ee95ab998be/1548858877547/C370.pdf

Wang, J., Jiao, J., & Ma, L. (2018). An organizational model and border port hinterlands for the China-Europe Railway Express. *Journal of Geographical Sciences, 28*(9), 1275–1287.

Yeo, G. T., Ng, A. K., Lee, P. T. W., & Yang, Z. (2014). Modelling port choice in an uncertain environment. *Maritime Policy & Management, 41*(3), 251–267.

Chapter 6

Green Tourism Dependency Towards Promoting Tea Tour

Shuvasree Banerjee

Abstract

In conventional discourses on sustainability, the relationship between economics and ecology is central. A number of nations' economies benefited from responsible tourism following these conferences. By supporting local businesses and attractions, 'green' tourism helps communities achieve their natural and cultural objectives while also preserving their limited resources. In terms of sustainable travel, Kerala was an early leader. This study looks at RT initiatives in various stages, with an emphasis on green tourism's sustainable responsible travel practises. The green economic development bottom line method was used for this descriptive research. These results highlight the difficulties inherent with RT implementation. Our review of secondary data shows that the first rollout of RT was unsuccessful, but that subsequent stages showed great promise. In order to create sustainable tourism on a worldwide scale, the study also highlights the necessity for more research in other culturally distant places.

Keywords: Tourist; tea tourism; green tourism development; homestay; economy; sustainability

1. Introduction

Sustainable development requires coordinated efforts to address the negative impacts of mass tourism and overtourism (Korstanje & George., 2020). Economy-killing forms of greedy capitalism and externalities (Sarkar et al., 2020). When seasonal and occasional influxes of tourists impact the local population, it might become overcrowded. Negative effects on inhabitants' quality of life, access to services, and health might persist for quite some time (Milano et al., 2018). Harmful effects may be seen from mass tourism. Sustainable tourism development requires a wide range of approaches to addressing the economic, social, and

Entrepreneurship and Green Finance Practices, 107–128
Copyright © 2024 Shuvasree Banerjee
Published under exclusive licence by Emerald Publishing Limited
doi:10.1108/978-1-80455-678-820231006

environmental costs of the tourism industry. As the goal of environmental education is to usher in a low-carbon era, eco-tourism is the sector of the tourism industry that has the most promising future (Sarkar & George, 2018). Environmentally responsible tourism should be actively promoted by tour companies, travel brokers, hotels, guests, and hosts. Taking part in green tourism is a great way to show your support for environmentally responsible consumption. This aims for long-term stability in all spheres of society and the economy.

Nature-loving travellers from all over the globe have been captivated by the aromatic tea leaves, lush green tea fields, gorgeous valley with curling clouds, and trickling mountain streams for years. Whether it's served at a house or a restaurant, the world's most popular drink, tea, is a global symbol of hospitality (Walton, 2001). The oldest kind of tourism, tea, helps the hotel industry thrive. 'The art of travelling the world in quest of joy that develops from exposure to tracts of green tea farms', as it is defined in the literature, is what we mean when we talk about 'tea tourism'. Companies all around the globe have capitalized on this trend by creating tea-themed vacation packages. Guests stay in a quaint hut in a far-flung locale and spend several days harvesting, withering, rolling, and finishing teas. Indian, Nepalese, Chinese, Sri Lankan, and Japanese tea travel, both bespoke and commercial, is on the rise (Joliffe & Zhuang, 2007, pp. 133–144).

Fresh tea, cosy bungalows, and verdant tea gardens have long been attractions for tourists to these nations. They participated in native customs like preparing tea, which they observed. They have also observed the rich flora and animals, crystal-clear rivers, and hazy landscapes. Economic and social progress are aided by tea tourism, a 'alternative kind' of travel (Su Wall, & Wang, 2019; Su, Wall, Wang, & Jin, 2019). It has improved the prosperity of rural areas, the amount of money made, and the prestige of vacation spots. Cultural preservation and interpersonal bonds were also bolstered (Casalegno et al., 2020). Researchers acknowledge that the burgeoning tea tourism industry has boosted the regional economy, but they blame ineffective policymaking and administration for hindering long-term expansion (Bandara, 2003; Joliffe & Aslam, 2009).

We are all aware of the difficulties inherent in the tea plantation subsector in maintaining profitability and sustainability in the face of high costs of production and other industry-specific challenges, such as the need to increase land efficiency and labour productivity. This organization has put its focus on marketing and value addition, but it may not be able to solve the challenge facing the tea plantation industry. With a variety of tea-related activities, visitors may learn about local tea customs, businesses, and sights (Jolliffe, 2007). Because of these considerations, tea tourism presents a significant chance for the product and service sectors to diversify and maintain the national economy, particularly in tea-producing areas.

A sustainable way of life takes into account the goals, scope, and priorities of development. Improving our understanding of the lives of the poor and vulnerable and the significance of policies and institutions requires a focus on people's capacities, social networks, access to physical and financial resources, and influence over key institutions (Serrat, 2017, pp. 21–6). The research conducted by

Raja and Mithili indicates that the wages of tea workers have not changed as a result of the implementation of sustainability criteria (2019). Instead of relying only on wages or bonuses, the tea plantation community might benefit from more opportunities to diversify income sources and increase asset ownership (Su et al., 2019a). Sustainable livelihood strategies on a tea plantation may look to tourism as a way to learn more about the connections between local community growth and increased visitor numbers (Su et al., 2019a; Tao & Wall, 2009). With this method, we may evaluate the monetary, cultural, and environmental benefits of tea plantations. Culture and environment may be transported through tea. It is necessary to use these natural and cultural assets in conjunction with others to create novel means of sustenance. According to Jolliffe, 'curiosity in the history, culture, and use of tea' motivates tea tourists (2007). Each region's unique past, culture, and climate all play a role in shaping the beverage's production and popularity. Seeing the tea landscape, going to a tea store or museum, tasting tea, witnessing tea being manufactured, attending a tea ceremony or cultural event, staying in a hotel decorated with tea motifs, and eating tea-infused cuisine are all examples of tourist experiences that may appeal to a wide range of people (Cheng et al., 2010; Jolliffe, 2007; Jolliffe & Aslam, 2009).

In this chapter, we use this strategy to analyze tea tourism's potential and pinpoint its remaining concerns. As a result, the positive effects of travel and tea on the tea industry are highlighted in this section.

2. Background

The cultural significance of tea has deep historical roots that span across various societies and traditions. It has played a pivotal role in shaping social interactions, rituals, and daily routines in many cultures worldwide (Joliffe & Zhuang, 2007, pp. 133–144). Supporting local economies, the tourism industry has embraced tea production and consumption, recognizing its potential to attract tourists and enthusiasts alike (Su et al., 2019a, 2019b). This symbiotic relationship between tea and tourism not only stimulates economic growth but also fosters cross-cultural exchange and appreciation for the rich heritage associated with tea cultivation and preparation. The tea tourist industry is a sustainable and environmentally beneficial one (Cheng et al., 2012). Research on the tea tourist industry is scant (Cheng et al., 2010). Further research is needed to fully appreciate the value of tea to hospitality, customer happiness, and high-quality service, according to experts.

Hall et al. (2003), Boniface (2017), and Joliffe and Zhuang (2007, pp. 133–144) were the first to examine tea tourism, but 'Tea and Tourism: Visitors, Traditions, and Transformations' was the most influential. Joliffe and Zhuang defined 'tea tourism' in 2007. They said that tea tourists learn about the rich history, fascinating culture, and fascinating customs associated with the beverage. Their study also brought to light the many activities and attractions that tea can provide for tourists, such as seeing teahouses, participating in tea rituals, touring tea gardens and museums, and staying in one-of-a-kind bungalows on tea estates. The potential pitfalls of Sri Lanka's growing tea tourist business were investigated by

Joliffe and Aslam (2009). According to Cheng et al., visitors enjoy cultural activities like visiting tea gardens, picking their own tea leaves, and taking part in traditional ceremonies (2010). They looked at the experiences of Chinese tea tourists for the first time. According to Cheng et al. (2012), the main players in the tea tourism industry include tourists, tea garden owners, municipal authorities, tour operators, and the press. They also pointed out that despite having numerous attractions and services, tea tourism had failed in a few nations, demonstrating the need of careful planning, effective marketing, and collaboration amongst all relevant parties involved in the industry.

While Ranasinghe et al. (2017) investigated product-place co-branding with Ceylon Tea, Bennike (2017) highlighted Darjeeling, India's rising prominence on the global tea tourist map (Sri Lanka). Darjeeling's stunning scenery, high-quality tea, and fascinating colonial past all contribute to the city's popularity as a tourist destination. Exploration of the tea industry is thriving (Besky, 2014). Tea tourism was suggested by Fernando, Rajapaksha, et al. (2017) as a means to increase tourism in Sri Lanka. According to previous studies cited by Lin and Wen (2018), tea tourism may be leveraged to create economic growth in underdeveloped areas and alleviate poverty. Tourists who visit tea plantations may help improve the lives of those in the region's poorer communities, experts say. Weber (2018) observed that tea tourism protects national identity, promotes cultural heritage, and delivers sensory experiences in tourism, whereas Su et al. (2019a, 2019b) claimed that integrating tea with tourism achieved sustainable livelihood. Tea tourism in Darjeeling, India, is centred on a small number of farms, and Mondal and Samaddar have highlighted the importance of the local community in this industry (2020). There is a need for further research on the social and economic inequalities between tourists and locals (Su & Zhang, 2020, pp. 1–21).

3. Rise of Tea Tourism

The tea industry and travel are natural partners. The origins of tea tourism may be traced back to the ancient trade routes that connected the Mediterranean with China and Southeast Asia, such as the Silk Road (Hamel, 2001) and the Tea Horse Road (Freeman & Ahmed, 2011). Significant tea cultures have emerged in China, Japan, the United Kingdom, India, and Sri Lanka. Chinese culture is credited with the development of medicinal tea (Heiss & Heiss, 2007). China was the first to establish tea shops, museums, and services, while Japan popularized tea ceremonies as a means of attracting foreign tourists interested in its rich cultural heritage (Joliffe & Zhuang, 2007, pp. 133–144). The English tradition of afternoon tea is widely acknowledged as an integral component of the country's history and character. India has been in the forefront of encouraging people to visit its tea gardens and farms, which are a verdant green, for the sake of tourism (Cheng et al., 2012). Darjeeling, Assam, and Nilgiris have all contributed to a surge in tourism to India. Darjeeling Tea, available in a wide range of colours and flavours, is most well-known for its distinctive aroma (which is reminiscent of golden rum) and flavour profile. India is quickly becoming the go-to destination for tea connoisseurs on the alternative tourism circuit because to its picturesque tea fields and wide variety of tea brands (Mondal & Samaddar, 2020a; Shah & Pate, 2016). Indulge in a high-end treat with the ceremonial tea ice cream served at 'English afternoon tea' and 'Matcha', the most popular Japanese tea (Gupta, Sajnani, et al., 2020). Travellers have also been drawn to the 'apple tea' in Turkey, the 'floral tea' in Taiwan, and the 'Horse-milk tea' in Tibet (Joliffe & Zhuang, 2007, pp. 133–144). Several countries, including Kenya, Argentina, and the Middle East, grow tea for commercial purposes (Iran and Turkey). The growing popularity of tea and tea-related pursuits has made tea tourism a lucrative industry all around the globe. Conventions and workshops devoted to tea as a tourist attraction vary widely. To promote tea tourism among both domestic and foreign visitors, the Ministry of Tourism has organized festivals and seminars with local administrations, tourism professionals, and marketers.

4. Sustainability Strategies for the Growth of Green Tourism

Without proper protections, any fragile area where tourism is allowed to grow at an unregulated rate risk losing its unique character and its ability to sustain itself. The growth of the tourism sector in the area may threaten the environment and lead to its overexploitation. Growth that doesn't deplete the region's resources is crucial (Vazhakkatte Thazhathethil, 2020). There are several problems plaguing the tourism industry (Freya, 2017). Hence, the definition of tourism has to be widened to ensure its continued existence. Ecosystems are at danger unless sustainable tourism grows. Suddenly, it became public knowledge. To ensure long-term success in the tourism industry, it is essential that all parties involved, including political leadership, work together. For sustainable tourism to be a reality, it is essential to conduct impact assessments and preventive measures on a continuous basis. Sustaining tourism requires a high level of satisfaction amongst visitors. It's meant to wow guests. Sustainable tourism has to be promoted. Tourism that is environmentally responsible takes into account the needs of both the present and future generations of travellers, as well as the local community and economy. The 'green' concept may be applied to any specialized tourism company, no matter how big or little, rural or urban (Chin et al., 2018). Ecological sustainability is crucial to the reputation and future success of today's businesses. Business ethics requirements of customers evolve throughout time. Because of this, corporate social responsibility (CSR) agendas and CSR actions in responsible tourism have become essential (McWilliams & Siegel, 2001). To achieve sustainable success over the long term, CSR entails a dedication to the interests of all parties involved in an organization's activities and operations (Fatma et al., 2016). CSR is 'contextually relevant corporate activities and policies', according to the definition. 'Context-specific business activities and policies that meet stakeholder expectations while also taking into mind the triple underlying principles of economic, social, and environmental performance' is how it is defined (Coles et al., 2013). The travel industry, like many others, has adopted corporate social responsibility (CSR) initiatives to benefit local communities and the natural world (Bohdanowicz, 2006). Proponents argue that corporate social responsibility (CSR) initiatives make a location more desirable to tourists (Abaeian et al., 2019; Asadi et al., 2020; Blinova et al., 2018; Dodds & Kuehnel, 2010). As a result of its growth in several fields of study, responsible tourism has gained the open acceptance and support of many of the world's most popular tourist sites, marketers, decision-makers, and academic research organizations (Chan & Tay, 2016; Del Chiappa et al., 2016). Ethical travellers hope that their actions may lessen the strain that their industry has on the natural world. Responsible tourism seems to be more of a concept and a path than it is a sub-genre of travel writing (Clifton & Benson, 2006). In exploring and learning about the local culture and interacting with its people, tourists may practise responsible tourism that fosters a sense of reciprocity and participation for all parties involved (Stanford, 2008). This has led to the concept's widespread implementation.

5. Tea and Sustainable Tourism

If a significant number of locals can find work in tea tourism activities, it may help keep the economy afloat on tea estates. Green tourism in rural regions is a growing industry that has the potential to boost the local economy and aid in the battle against global warming [10] (Zeppel & Beaumont, 2011). With tea-green tourism, guests are invited to take part in every step of the process, from picking leaves to sealing tins (Chakraborty & Islam, 2020). Jobs in the tea tourist business encourage openness to guests. By luring tourists and satisfying their needs for amusement, rest, and new experiences like picking tea, sampling tea, erecting a glamping tent, setting up camp, and taking in the breathtaking view of a tea carpet while strolling, hospitality may boost commercial and economic interests. Financial and non-financial benefits to local communities may be increased through tea tourisms in the New Normal era, when people are more interested in ecotourism, or vacationing in a natural setting where they can breathe easy, feel healthy, and unwind while taking in breathtaking scenery, all while adhering to the COVID-19 protocol framework. It is also feasible to travel in a sustainable way.

6. Tea and Ecotourism

According to Mahanta (2014), ecotourism is defined as ethical travel to natural regions that helps the environment, the local community, and the social, eco-nomic, and environmental pillars of sustainable development (Devi, 2012). Due to the extensive geographic variety and different ecological diversity in the three research regions, in addition to tea eco-tours, diverse special cultivars can be developed into ecotourism objects as a genetic and in situ conservation measure (Zhouyiqi & Tao, 2012). If the government gives ecotourism development greater attention, it might become the foundation of the rural area's economy by, for example, supporting the construction of infrastructure.

7. Tea and Gastronomy Tourism

Culinary tourism focussed on tea is expanding. One kind of rural tourism that has recently gained popularity is gastronomy travel (Guzel & Apaydin, 2016). In addition to the obvious focus on food and drink, it also takes into account the origins of the cuisine, how it is prepared and served, and the local customs and traditions that may have an impact on the overall tea tourism experience and journey (Baran & Batman, 2013; Horng et al., 2012; Sukenti, 2014). While tea is more popular than coffee, coffee-based food is on the rise. Tourist interest in tea may increase if a tea shop or café is located close to a plantation. Young people nowadays have a penchant for custom tea products created by mixologists and blenders. The tourism industry and local environment of a tea resort may benefit from tea-themed sights and cuisine (Guzel & Apaydin, 2016). When visiting a tea farm, glampers have the option of making their own tea and presenting it in unique ways or dining on tea-themed dishes and drinks at nearby eateries. Traditional goods manufactured by smallholder tea farmers or tea enterprises, such 'teh gelang', green tea chocolates, tea chips, milk tea, etc., are often featured at local booths near tourist sites as part of tea gastronomy tourism experiences. The success of tea gourmet tourism in these two locations is highly dependent on the widespread distribution of advertising materials, especially on social media. Local tea houses in areas with established tea plantations tend to be as distinctive as the plants themselves. By encouraging visitors to choose eco-friendly and local attractions, culinary tourism might help keep businesses afloat (Sukenti, 2014).

8. Tourism and Tea Marketing

Attracting tourists may be a boon for the tea industry (Fernando, Rajapaksha, et al., 2017). More and more out-of-towners are spending their vacations at home in the country's many tea gardens, and they're all drinking tea because they're fascinated by tea's rich history, varied (Kaldeen, 2020). Travel destinations are promoted via social media, electronic word-of-mouth, blogs, and traditional media (Fernando, Kumari, et al., 2017).

9. Tourism and Tea Integration and Its Impacts on Sustainable Livelihood

Tourism related to tea has a positive effect on local economy (Su et al., 2019a). After the integrated tourist site in the tea plantation region was open, recognized, and running, the tourism community had many new ways to make a living. Businesses specializing in food and drink, agriculture (such strawberry farms or stores), tea and coffee, street sellers, parking lots, places to park, go to the bathroom, or relax at home; places where one may shop, park, or find other housing, retail, or transit options. The typical winners are the entertainers and sightseers. With friends and family at their side, 93% of vacationers said they felt better physically after spending time in nature. Most vacationers stay in a tent at least once. The money coming in every day went increased. The only jobs available to them were on tea plantations, in livestock care, and other rural settings (gardener, housekeeper, etc.). Those who lost their jobs as a result of the epidemic did not benefit from this raise in pay. There are now many more chances for people to make a living, thanks to the proliferation of temporary businesses catering to visitors, such as restaurants, bars, gift shops, souvenir shops, parking garages, and tour companies that provide activities like visiting a tea garden. An estimated 64% and 57% increases in living conditions and local pride as well as individual and collective skill development in areas crucial to the tourism industry (service, communication, and food), respectively, are attributable to the influx of visitors (Sita et al., 2021). Although the primary focus of the tea plantation sector is on tea production, tea tourism might help diversify revenue. It is important to acknowledge and include several aspects of tea tourism, such as tea production, history, culture, and traditions. In the tourism industry, the opening of a new venue or attraction is evaluated from both a financial and ecological perspective. Most popular tourist spots are located upstream, and as such have a duty to consider the welfare of those living and working in the river's downstream areas. In the same way that coffee cafes and coffee stores have been ingrained in millennial culture, tea mixology, and tea mixing goods may find a home in tea gastronomy tourism in popular tourist destinations. Green tourism and coffee production are conservation and development successes (Woyesa & Kumar, 2021). It's possible that agro-educational tourism, ecological tourism, gourmet tourism, and the preservation of traditional tea ceremonies and rituals may all coexist in a tea plantation's setting. Stronger ties and synergy between the government, tea businesses, and the local populace were required to empower and increase tea and tourist assets (natural, physical, human, financial, and social). As a result, the home, local/village, community, and tea plantation business have the potential to enhance quality of life in the long run. With a lack of workers in many tea-growing nations, the tea industry will have to compete with growing sectors like tourism for available workers. To make life more sustainable and responsive to local and global tea market demand, a new tea business model is required in the heart of the tea-producing area. One approach is encouraging people to go on tea-themed vacations.

In areas frequented by tea tourists, a wide range of family and community livelihoods is being supported by the local economy and available human resources. Environmental factors both within and outside of the tea plantation are taken into account by tea tourists. Tea estates that include ecotourism, agricultural tourism, culinary tourism, and cultural tourism into their offerings may give tourists with a more well-rounded tea experience, reap significant benefits for their local economy, and have a significant influence on their respective businesses. Eco-friendly tea travel is supported by companies with a strong commitment to CSR. Visitors' expectations of the service they get greatly influence whether or not they will return to the tea country. There may be a way to get around shortages in both materials and knowledge if the tourist and tea industries work together. Future practical consequences may be achieved by further tea and tourist integration, cooperation, local engagement, and local benefits as lifestyles.

10. Foreign Tourist's Tea Preferences

The importance of tourist food and drink to social, economic, and ecological sustainability has been highlighted in a number of worldwide tourism and hospitality studies (Gupta & Duggal, 2020; McKercher et al., 2004). Many research have shown that tourism is more than just photographic physiognomies of involvement; instead, it also involves taste, scent, colour, and touch (Davidson et al., 2005). Tourists increasingly place a high value on eating and drinking while abroad (Breakey & Breakey, 2015; Henderson, 2009). Scholars believe that a destination's food and drink may be used as a persuasive approach to increase the image and brand value of the location, as stated by Quan and Wang (2004) (Gupta et al., 2018; McKercher et al., 2004). A number of studies have shown that tourists are keen in trying out new pursuits and customs that emerge from an immersion in a destination's cultural norms and values (Gupta et al., 2019; Gupta, Roy, et al., 2020; McKercher et al., 2004). The contentment of tourists is also affected by what they eat and drink while on vacation (Breakey & Breakey, 2015; Gee et al., 1997; Zheng et al., 1996). It would be helpful, therefore, to have a better understanding of how the eating and drinking habits of visitors from other countries relate to the local cuisine. The focus of this study is on the tea preferences of foreign visitors to India. In both the United States and other countries, people regularly consume tea and coffee (Jolliffe, 2006). Most studies on tea have focussed on its qualitative attributes (Kyung et al., 2017), consumption patterns (Peck et al., 2017), hospitality sector (Jolliffe, 2006), tea tourism development, and heritage tourism despite the fact that it is the world's second most popular beverage after water (Jolliffe & Aslam, 2009) (2009). Several cultural practises centre on the act of brewing and drinking tea (Jolliffe, 2007). Research in the past has shown its significance as a means of communication and its use in learning about the customs and values of a particular group within a culture (Peck et al., 2017). Major shifts in Indian tea consumption and selection patterns have occurred due to changes in lifestyles, family structures, psychological concerns, and other social and cultural variables (Urala & Lähteenmäki, 2007). People looking for a cup of tea have many different tastes, so they look for tea vending machines that provide both good prices and convenient locations (Byun & Han, 2004; Gupta et al., 2018). This has resulted in the proliferation of tea shops, kiosks, gardens, and Chai spots around India, where foreigners may sample and learn about traditional Indian teas and customs (Lee et al., 2008; Timur & Getz, 2007; Yang, 2007). Taking into account the above, and the fact that India's tea culture is increasingly becoming a vital means for tourists to grasp ethnic Indian eating culture, tea may be seen as a technique to attract international visitors and a huge tourism destination in India. Tea is served during Indian celebrations and as a gesture of welcome to visitors. The widespread availability of tea vending machines is evidence of the widespread popularity of the beverage in India. Both locals and visitors alike may sip on a variety of teas, from traditional Kerala tea to exotic Kashmiri Kahwa. As a means of income generation, selling tea has become an important lifeline for many low-income households in India (Timur & Getz, 2007). Being the world's largest consumer and the second-largest producer of tea (behind China), India has a great deal to offer in terms of tea tourism (Yang, 2007). While there is a large and varied clientele in this subset of the tourist market, there is surprisingly little written about it (Sharples, 2008), particularly in India. Many chances to learn about and participate in regional tea rituals and cultures are made available to tourists by this niche sector of the travel business. Tea tourism and its influence on regional dining customs and tea consumption patterns have been the subject of recent research (Lee et al., 2008; Timur & Getz, 2007; Yang, 2007), albeit very little of this research has focussed on India. A small number of research (Ghosh & Ghosh, 2013; Varun et al., 2009) have looked at the tea tastes and purchasing patterns of foreign visitors to India. No consideration of what influences people's tea choices has been made by the researchers. The results of this research address a knowledge gap. It might provide valuable insight for the Indian tea industry, allowing its suppliers to better tailor their wares to the needs of tourists, as well as improve their cultivation techniques, market their wares, and boost India's standing as a travel destination.

Possible Tea Tourism in India and Current Sales Tendencies. The production and consumption of tea are inextricably related to the cultural, historical, and social aspects of a region, and so may give eye-catching and attractive tourist experiences to a wide range of viewers (Cheng et al., 2010; Jolliffe & Aslam, 2009). Jolliffe posits that people go to tea regions because of their fascination with history, cultural relations, and tea itself (2007). In addition, it may provide a variety of experiences for tea tourists, such as tours of tea farms and factories, classes for novice and expert tea tasters, sommelier training, and other tea-related educational opportunities. Activities such as taking online classes (Asian School of Tea, 2020), celebrating various regional ethnic festivals and customs, staying at tea-themed hotels, enjoying tea-infused treats, and engaging in tea-themed matchmaking sessions are all in the realm of possibility (Cheng et al., 2010; Jolliffe, 2007; Yang, 2007). By including tea harvesting and related social, cultural, and culinary activities, it may also be used to aid and stimulate the Indian tea industry, revitalize local ethnic culture, improve the destination's image, and strengthen the identities of rural areas (Kyung et al., 2017). The many varieties of tea available in India have become an integral part of the country's ethnic local culture, and as such, they present numerous opportunities, including bolstering the local tea vending industry, providing a significant revenue source for India's massive population, providing a fascinating introduction to India's tea tradition for foreign visitors, providing a platform for starting a new business with low overhead, and enhancing the country's reputation as a tourist destination (Calloni, 2013). This is also reflected in the proliferation and variety of Chaayos, Tea trails, Chai Point, Tea villas, and other themed tea businesses throughout a number of Indian cities (The Indian Wire, 2018). Organizations whose members grow, process, package, and sell tea as well as related items such as cups, saucers, kettles, and more may also play a role in attracting tourists (Lee et al., 2008; Su et al., 2019b). In this way, numerous opportunities for labour may be created and integrated with preexisting residential communities to sustain rural civilizations. Good reputations attract tourists from abroad (Kivela & Crotts, 2006; Morgan et al., 2011). Several studies have shown that a destination's positioning in the tourism market has an effect on the number and quality of visitors who choose to return (Gupta & Duggal, 2020; Gupta et al., 2019). Travellers are influenced by a variety of factors, including the food, drink, scenery, and locals they meet (Yuksel et al., 2010). Because of tea's positive effect on vacationers, the tourism industry must work together to create new items. To attract international visitors interested in experiencing and appreciating India's rich and varied tea traditions, the country may actively promote tea tourism. There is a significant information vacuum that has to be filled in this chapter, particularly when applied to the Indian context.

Below are some popular Indian teas amongst international drinkers. There are many variations in the way tea is prepared and served across the world. That's further evidence that the greatest tea in each country has its own character. As far back as one can trace records, kimono-clad women in Japan have been serving tea. Serving tea is more than just a ritual in China; it's also a way to connect with others, making it comparable to Japanese customs. Taking tea in the afternoon, often known as 'high tea' or 'afternoon tea', is a uniquely British tradition. The custom of drinking tea at four o'clock, started by Anna, Duchess of Bedford, in 1840, remains popular today. There are supposedly over a 1000 different kinds of tea. Only oolong, white, green, and black teas exist. Some of the most well-known varieties of tea are Turkish tea, Moroccan mint tea, Matcha tea, Ceylon tea, English morning tea, and Rooibos tea (a sweet and nutty flavoured tea from South Africa). Vacationers want to indulge their senses by enjoying the local cuisine and libations (Kivela & Crotts, 2006; Mill & Morrison, 2012). Trying the local libations is a great way to immerse yourself in the culture of your destination and have a memorable experience while on vacation (Khokhar & Magnusdottir, 2002; Morrison, 2012). To fully appreciate the exoticism and mystique of a destination, visitors should try a native alcoholic beverage (Gupta et al., 2019; Kivela & Crotts, 2006). Each host city should, therefore, take into account local beverage preferences (Byun & Han, 2004) and provide something exquisite or distinctive to give visitors really memorable experiences and improve the destination's reputation. France's tourism promotion links its wine industry with culinary traditions (Gupta & Sajnani, 2019). Local tourism businesses also need to study the drinks that tourists find most delightful on vacation in order to create effective marketing strategies (Gupta et al., 2019; Mill & Morrison, 2012). As a result, any venue that relies heavily on the sale of alcoholic beverages should give careful thought to the kind of beverages its guests like (Khokhar & Magnusdottir, 2002). To accommodate its international visitors, India offers a variety of teas. Teas from Darjeeling, Assam, Nilgiris, Munnar, Kangra, Sikkim, and Dooars Terai are among the most well-known in the world (Tea Board of India, 2019). Strong to medium flavours characterize Assam, Munnar, Darjeeling, and Kangra varieties, while floral notes distinguish Nilgiris and Sikkim teas. The origin of tea is a major factor in establishing its credibility, characteristics, and quality. Certain products, like tea, have a higher chance of being recognized as legitimate and of drawing tourists from other countries because of their geographical origin, hence the international community uses a term called 'geographical indications' to characterize this indicator (e.g. a town, region, or nation). A GI is able to attest to the quality of a product, the authenticity of its claims of utilizing traditional techniques of production, and the fame of its geographical origin. The logos for 'DARJEELING', 'ASSAM Orthodox', and 'NILGIRI Orthodox' are Geographical Indications in India (List of Geographical Indications in India, 2020). Darjeeling tea was India's first GI product in 2003, and in October 2011, the European Union officially acknowledged its country of origin. The designation as a GI for Orthodox Assam Tea in 2007 was good for both farmers and the industry. Green, oolong, and medicinal herbal teas are also produced in high quality in India. Masala, butter, and cold beverages are popular amongst foreign visitors. Cooperation among local actors in meeting the needs of tourists from outside calls for an accurate use of traditional tea preparation methods (Jolliffe, 2007; Morgan et al., 2011; Su et al., 2019b).

10.1 Factors Affecting the Tea Preferences of Foreign Tourists in India

There is evidence that tea consumption affects tourists' preference for diverse vacation spots (Jolliffe, 2007; Su et al., 2019a). Countries like China, Sri Lanka, South Korea, and Japan have marketed themselves as 'tea tourism meccas' by highlighting their unique traditions around the production, distribution, and consumption of tea (Shah et al., 2015). Examining travellers' tea preferences is crucial for maximizing their experience (Chaturvedula & Prakash, 2011; Gupta & Sajnani, 2019). Their lives will be better off because of this. It might also aid in the development of marketing campaigns aimed at tourists (Breakey & Breakey, 2015). Numerous studies of consumer behaviour look at vacationers' inclinations and habits. Favouritism is the act of selecting one item above another (Cheng et al., 2010). The term 'tea preference' is used in this chapter to refer to a foreign traveller's strong preference for one specific type of Indian tea over others. Visitors' preferences in food and drink have been the subject of much research (Gupta et al., 2018; Mak et al., 2012). Motivating factors, socio-demographics, religiousness, cultural norms, individual differences, and life experiences were all proposed by Mak et al. (2012). Demographic factors (such as gender, marital status, age, religion, and education level); physiological factors (such as neophilia (the desire to try new things) and nephobia (the fear of swallowing new things)); and motivational factors were the three categories Kim et al. (2009) used to classify these elements (intimacy, respect, status, sensual appeal, good experience, etc.). These features of Iranian urban consumers' tea drinking habits were validated by research conducted by Rezaee et al. (2016). As a result, many of these characteristics may be utilized to evaluate the teas that foreign visitors to India like to drink. To isolate the effects of demography on tea preferences, this study only surveys foreign visitors to India. The guests' top tea choices are determined using an AHP model and a Pairwise comparison matrix. This study looked at variables like country of origin, age, gender, level of education, income, religion, and marital status. The preferred tea of international visitors can vary by country. Coffee is a more popular choice among North and South American tourists than tea. They prefer iced tea to hot ones (Arab et al., 2009). Previous studies have found that Asian travellers, especially those from China, Sri Lanka, Korea, Taiwan, Indonesia, and Japan, favour and drink tea while on the road (Rezaee et al., 2016; Su et al., 2019a). Green teas and milk-based teas were the favourites of visitors from the United Kingdom, Turkey, Germany, France, and Poland (Rezaee et al., 2016). Tea is consumed by tourists from the Oceanic and Middle Eastern regions (Jolliffe, 2007). Tourists from Europe are more likely to order their tea with milk, while those from Asia are more likely to order herbal, green, or naturally flavoured teas without milk. Traveller's tea preferences decline with age (Lorenzo et al., 2003). Travellers' tastes in tea change as they mature (Arab et al., 2009; Kim et al., 2009). Those over the age of 45 and in the middle years were the most likely to drink tea (Rezaee et al., 2016). The tea consumption among children and teenagers was low. According to research by Chaturvedula and Prakash (2011), consumers under the age of 35 are more likely to drink black tea, herbal tea, and green tea without milk, while those over the age of 35 are more likely to drink black tea with milk. Customers aged 35 and up consume more tea than those aged 18–34. (Rezaee et al., 2016). Tourists' preferences in tea were also heavily influenced by their gender. Rozin (2006) found that there are differences in the food and drink preferences of American men and women. Women are more health-conscious and therefore prefer teas without sugar and milk but with flavour infusions, as shown by Yang (2007). Men, on the other hand, are more casual about their tea consumption (Cao et al., 2010).

The preferences for and the amount of money spent on tea are influenced by both income and education (Zheng et al., 1996). O'Donnell (1994) found that a person's level of education is significantly related to both their knowledge of nutrition and their propensity to purchase tea. Similar amounts of tea were consumed by all groups (whether less educated or highly educated). But those with more education favoured black tea without milk, while those with less did (O'Donnell, 1994). The results were the same for both high- and low-income groups. Tea was seen as a mixture of regional ethnic custom and culture, which made some well-travelled, affluent tourists uncomfortable (Zheng et al., 1996). Food and drink preferences are influenced by the newfound knowledge of local customs, traditions, and taboos gained by travellers (Cao et al., 2010). The religious beliefs of the consumer also affect their tea preferences (Grigg, 2002). Benn (2015) found that religious norms and practises have a momentary impact on how much tea people drink. Tea's rise to prominence in China, Taiwan, and the rest of southeast Asia can be traced back to the Buddhist value of sobriety. The production and distribution of tea were influenced by Buddhist and Taoist groups. The monks who lived in and around the monasteries enriched Asian tea culture by producing rare, unpredictable, and expensive teas (Benn, 2015). Subsequent research confirmed that religious leaders were a major factor in spreading the tea craze (Chieh et al., 2018; Grigg, 2002). In recent years, alcohol-free tea parties have become increasingly popular during Islamic and Hindu celebrations. Tea preferences were also influenced by respondents' marital status. Marriage is correlated with a rise in tea consumption (Shen et al., 2019).

10.2 Practical Implications

The tourist business operates in a dynamic environment that is always evolving. The moment has come to comprehend customer demands and preferences because travel has grown to be a vital source of self-expression. Tea tourism, along with other alternative types of travel, is slowly carving out a place for itself in the travel industry. The goal of this study is to draw attention to the important issues that require careful thought and evaluation. Every stakeholder must work together to promote tea tourism on social media and integrate it into mainstream business. The limited geographic reach of tea tourism up to this point supports its extension through marketing strategies like tea festivals, exhibits, seminars or cultural activities. When speaking with consumers or visitors in particular, the intersection between tea, travel and culture must be emphasized. For tea tourism to flourish sustainably, proper oversight must be provided since environmental preservation is of the highest importance. In addition to highlighting cultural characteristics, tea tourism has a good socio-economic aspect that has to be further investigated. In order to promote this type of tourism, it is necessary to train highly trained tea craftsmen who will not only impart superior information about tea farming but also effectively serve visitors to the tea estates. These modest actions will strengthen the community's identity while also strengthening the social capital and cultural diversity of the area. In light of this, this study significantly links tea tourism and sustainable development. The report will help destination tourist organizations and other service providers update their approach from a socio-economic standpoint. This chapter offers a variety of opportunities for policymakers and destination marketing organizations to implement appropriate legislative guidelines for making all stakeholders socially and ecologically responsible (Mondal & Samaddar, 2020b). This chapter aspires to develop a resilient and sustainable tea tourist industry that will not only thrive and flourish on its own but also foster an environment conducive to the survival and prosperity of future generations. This chapter will also serve as a point of reference in the field of tea tourist research, directing subsequent researchers in broadening the field and enhancing the literature with fresher discoveries.

10.3 Limitations and Future Research Agendas

The research presented in this chapter on tea tourism was carried out only inside India's borders. In the future, scholars may look into cross-sectional or cross-cultural research to better understand the tea tourism sector. India was selected as a case study because of the substantial amount of money it contributes to the global tea tourism business.

11. Conclusion

Based on the above study's in-depth look at tea travel, we can come to several important conclusions:

Tea tourism is a broad idea that includes cultural education, economic growth, protecting the environment and trying new foods. It gives visitors a chance to interact with local people, see the tea-making process for themselves and learn about the rich history and traditions of tea. Foreign tourists' tastes in different types of tea in India depend on many things, such as their age, gender, level of education, income, cultural norms, religious views and personal experiences. Different countries have different tastes, and different parts of the world like different kinds of tea and different ways to make it. Age, gender, school level and income are all important factors that affect how tourists choose their tea. Culture and religion also have an effect on the type of tea that tourists tend to choose. For the tea tourism business to be successful, it is important to meet the needs of people with different tastes. Sustainable methods and thinking about the environment are important for tea tourism to work. With a growing focus on responsible travel around the world, tea tourism places are becoming more popular by incorporating eco-friendly initiatives, preserving local ecosystems and preserving cultural traditions. Effective marketing tactics, such as using social media, doing cultural activities, going to tea festivals and going to seminars, are key to making tea tourism more popular. Tourists might be more interested in tea if they knew more about its culture and sensory aspects. Tea tourism has the ability to give local people more power by giving them jobs, keeping their cultural heritage alive and building social capital. Skilled tea craftsmen can improve tourists' experiences and help the region's economy by taking part in training programs and working together. This study focuses on tea tourism in India, but future research could look at tea tourism from a cross-cultural and cross-sectional viewpoint to learn more about tea tourism around the world. Also, this study shows that more research is needed to keep up with new trends, consumer tastes and the changing nature of the tea tourism business. Tea tourism is a unique way for tourists to not only try different kinds of tea but also learn about the culture of the places that make tea. Visitors can learn about the history, traditions and customs of growing and drinking tea. This gives them a better understanding of the drink and what it means in different cultures. This study shows how important it is for the different players in the tea tourism industry to work together. This includes people who make tea, run hotels, work for the government, live in small towns or work for tourist boards. When people work together well, they can make whole experiences that include lodging, guided trips, food and hands-on tea-related activities. Tea tourism has a lot of benefits, but it also has some problems, like being seasonal, having limited infrastructure and keeping the balance between commercialization and traditional preservation. Some ways to deal with these problems are to give more than just tea-related tourism, to invest in building up infrastructure and to use responsible tourism practices. In the modern world, technology is a key part of making tea travel more enjoyable. Tourists can use mobile apps, virtual reality experiences and web platforms to plan their trips, find out about tea varieties and learn about how tea is made before they even get to their destinations. Educating both tourists and locals is a key part of making tea tourism work. Tourists can learn about how tea is grown and processed through guided workshops and educational events. In turn, local communities gain from more people knowing how valuable their cultural heritage is and how much money tea tourism can bring in. Tea is a drink that is popular in many different places and countries. Because of this, tea tourism can help people from different cultures understand each other and feel more linked to the rest of the world through a shared love of this ancient drink. Tea tourism spots need to be flexible and open to new ideas so they can keep up with changing buyer tastes and market trends. This could be done by adding new kinds of tea, combining traditional ways of doing things with modern amenities and adding wellness and relaxation activities to the tea tourism offers. In the end, tea tourism stands out as a dynamic and multifaceted industry that includes history, sustainability and exchange between cultures. Its ability to boost economic growth, give communities more power and give travelers valuable experiences show how important it is in the changing world of tourism. By embracing the long history of tea, putting an emphasis on sustainability, encouraging collaboration and using technology, tea tourism can continue to grow as an enriching and memorable way for people all over the world to visit.

References

Abaeian, V., Kok Wei, K., Ken Kyid, Y., & Scott, McC. (2019). Motivations of undertaking CSR initiatives by independent hotels: A holistic approach. *International Journal of Contemporary Hospitality Management, 31*, 2468–2487.

Arab, L., Liu, W., & Elashoff, D. (2009). Green and black tea consumption and risk of stroke: A meta-analysis. *Stroke, 40*(1), 1786–1792. https://doi.org/10.1161/STROKEAHA.108.538470

Asadi, S., Seyedeh Om Salameh, P., Mehrbakhsh, N., Rusli, A., Sarminah, S., Elaheh, Y., & Nahla Aljojo Nor Shahidayah, R. (2020). Investigating influence of green innovation on sustainability performance: A case on Malaysian hotel industry. *Journal of Cleaner Production, 258*, 120860.

Asian School of Tea. (2020, August 19). *Using one tiny leaf to make one big difference.* https://asianschooloftea.org/

Bandara, H. M. (2003). *Tourism planning in Sri Lanka.* Stamford Lake (PVT).

Baran, Z., & Batman, O. (2013). Destinasyon pazarlamasında mutfak kültürünün rolü: Sakarya örneği. *14 Ulus. Tur. Kongresi Bildir. Kitabı, 5–8.*

Benn, J. (2015, July 2). *Tea in China: A religious and cultural History.* University of Hawai'i Press. www.jstor.org/stable/j.ctt13×1kn2

Bennike, R. (2017). Frontier commodification: Governing land, labour and leisure in Darjeeling, India. *South Asia: Journal of South Asian Studies, 40*(2), 256–271.

Besky, S. (2014). The labor of terroir and the terroir of labor: Geographical indication and Darjeeling tea plantations. *Agriculture and Human Values, 31*(1), 83–96.

Blinova, E., Gregoric, M., Elena, D., & Romanova, M. (2018). Corporate social responsibility in tourism: International practices. *European Research Studies Journal, 21*, 636–647.

Bohdanowicz, P. (2006). Environmental awareness and initiatives in the Swedish and Polish hotel industries—Survey results. *International Journal of Hospitality Management, 25*, 662–682.

Boniface, P. (2017). *Tasting tourism: Travelling for food and drink.* Routledge.

Breakey, N. M., & Breakey, H. E. (2015). Tourism and Aldo Leopold's 'cultural harvest': Creating virtuous tourists as agents of sustainability. *Journal of Sustainable Tourism, 23*(1), 85–103. https://doi.org/10.1080/09669582.2014.924954

Byun, J. O., & Han, J. S. (2004). A study on perception and actual status of utilization for green tea. *Journal of the Korean Society of Food Culture, 19*(2), 184–192.

Calloni, M. (2013). Street food on the move: A socio-philosophical approach. *Journal of the Science of Food and Agriculture, 93*(14), 3406–3413. https://doi.org/10.1002/jsfa.6353

Cao, H., Qiao, L., Zhang, H., & Chen, J. (2010). Exposure and risk assessment for aluminium and heavy metals in Puerh tea. *Science of the Total Environment, 408*(1), 2777–2784. https://doi.org/10.1016/j.scitotenv.2010.03.019

Casalegno, C., Candelo, E., Santoro, G., & Kitchen, P. (2020). The perception of tourism in coffee producing equatorial countries: An empirical analysis. *Psychology and Marketing, 37*(1), 154–166.

Chakraborty, A., & Islam, S. S. (2020). Impact of tea tourism in Dooars, North Bengal. *An Overview Mukt Shabd Journal, 9*, 5789–5804.

Chan Lian, K. J., & Xin Tay, K. (2016). Tour operator perspectives on responsible tourism practices: A case of Kinabalu National Park, Sabah. *International Journal of Culture, Tourism and Hospitality Research, 10*, 121–137.

Chaturvedula, V. S. P., & Prakash, I. (2011). The aroma, taste, color and bioactive constituents of tea. *Journal of Medicinal Plants Research, 5*(11), 2110–2124. https://doi.org/10.5897/JMPR

Cheng, S., Hu, J., Fox, D., & Zhang, Y. (2012). Tea tourism development in Xinyang, China: Stakeholders' view. *Tourism Management Perspectives, 2*(3), 28–34. https://doi.org/10.1016/j.tmp.2011.12.001

Cheng, S. W., Xu, F., Zhang, J., & Zhang, Y. T. (2010). Tourists' attitudes toward tea tourism: A case study in Xinyang. *Journal of Travel & Tourism Marketing, 27*(2), 211–220. https://doi.org/10.1080/10548401003590526

Chieh, H., Richard, H., Robinson, N. S., & Scott, N. (2018). Traditional food consumption behaviour: The case of Taiwan. *Tourism Recreation Research, 43*(4), 456–469. https://doi.org/10.1080/02508281.2018.1475879

Chin, C. H., Chee Ling, C., & Winnie Poh Ming, W. (2018). The Implementation of green marketing tools in rural tourism: The readiness of tourists? *Journal of Hospitality Marketing & Management, 27*, 261–280.

Clifton, J., & Benson, A. (2006). Planning for sustainable ecotourism: The case for research ecotourism in developing country destinations. *Journal of Sustainable Tourism, 14*, 238–254.

Coles, T., Fenclova, E., & Dinan, C. (2013). Tourism and corporate social responsibility: A critical review and research agenda. *Tourism Management Perspectives, 6*, 122–141.

Davidson, J., Bondi, L., & Smith, M. (2005). Emotional geographies. Ashgate. Eric, A. F., & Asafo-Adjei. R. (2013). Traditional food preferences of tourists in Ghana. *British Food Journal, 115*(7), 987–1002. https://doi.org/10.1108/BFJ-11-2010-0197

Del Chiappa, G., Grappi, S., & Romani, S. (2016). Attitudes toward responsible tourism and behavioural change to practice it: A demand-side perspective in the context of Italy. *Journal of Quality Assurance in Hospitality & Tourism, 17*, 191–208.

Devi, M. K. (2012). Ecotourism in Assam: A promising opportunity for development. *South Asian Journal of Tourism & Heritage*, *5*, 179–192.

Dodds, R., & Kuehnel, J. (2010). CSR among Canadian mass tour operators: Good awareness but little action. *International Journal of Contemporary Hospitality Management*, *22*, 221–244.

Fatma, M., Rahman, Z., & Khan, I. (2016). Measuring consumer perception of CSR in tourism industry: Scale development and validation. *Journal of Hospitality and Tourism Management*, *27*, 39–48.

Fernando, P. I. N., Kumari, K., & Rajapaksha, R. (2017). Destination marketing to promote tea tourism socio-economic approach on community development. *International Review of Management and Business Research*, *6*, 68–75.

Fernando, P. I. N., Rajapaksha, R. M. P. D. K., & Kumari, K. W. S. N. (2017). Tea-tourism as a marketing tool: A strategy to develop the image of Sri Lanka as an attractive tourism destination. *Kelaniya Journal of Management*, *5*(2), 64–79.

Freeman, M., & Ahmed, S. (2011). *Tea horse road: China's ancient trade road to Tibet.* River Books.

Freya, H. (2017). Sustainable tourism: Sustaining tourism or something more? *Tourism Management Perspectives*, *25*, 157–160.

Gee, Y. G., Maken, J. C., & Choy, D. J. (1997). *The travel industry*. Wiley.

Ghosh, M., & Ghosh, A. (2013). Consumer buying behaviour in relation to consumption of tea – A study of Pune city. *International Journal of Sales & Marketing Management Research and Development*, *3*(2), 47–54.

Grigg, D. (2002). The worlds of tea and coffee: Patterns of consumption. *Geojournal*, *57*(1), 283–294. https://doi.org/10. 1023/B:GEJO.0000007249.91153.c3

Gupta, V., & Duggal, S. (2020). How do the tourists' behavioural intentions influenced by their perceived food authenticity: A case of Delhi? *Journal of Culinary Science & Technology*. https://doi.org/10.1080/15428052.2020.1764430

Gupta, V., Khanna, K., & Gupta, R. K. (2018). A study on the street food dimensions and its effects on consumer attitude and behavioural intentions. *Tourism Review*, *73*(3), 374–388. https://doi.org/10.1108/TR-03-2018-0033

Gupta, V., Khanna, K., & Gupta, R. K. (2019). Preferential analysis of street food amongst the foreign tourists: A case of Delhi region. *International Journal of Tourism Cities*, *6*(3), 511–528. https://doi.org/10.1108/IJTC-07-2018-0054

Gupta, G., Roy, H., & Promsivapallop, P. (2020). Local cuisine image dimensions and its impact on foreign tourist's perceived food contentment in Delhi. *Tourism Recreation Research*. https://doi.org/10.1080/02508281.2020.1816762

Gupta, V., & Sajnani, M. (2019). Risk and benefit perceptions related to wine consumption and how it influences consumers' attitude and behavioural intentions in India. *British Food Journal*, *122*(8), 2569–2585. https://doi.org/10.1108/BFJ-06-2019-0464

Gupta, V., Sajnani, M., Dixit, S. K., & Khanna, K. (2020). Foreign tourist's tea preferences and relevance to destination attraction in India. *Tourism Recreation Research*, 1–15.

Guzel, B., & Apaydin, M. (2016). In N. T. Cevdet Avcıkurt, M. S. Dinu, N. Hacıoğlu, R. Efe, & S. Abdullah (Eds.), *Gastronomy in tourism global issues and trends in tourism* (pp. 394–404): St. Kliment Ohridski University Press.

Hall, C. M., Mitchell, R., & Sharples, L. (2003). *Consuming places: The role of food, wine and tourism in regional development*. Butterworth Heinemann.

Hamel, G. (2001). *Leading the revolution, strategy and leadership.* Harvard Business School Press.

Heiss, M. L., & Heiss, R. J. (2007). *The story of tea: A cultural history and drinking guide.* Random House Digital, Inc.

Henderson, J. C. (2009). Food tourism reviewed. *British Food Journal, 111*(4), 317–326. https://doi.org/10.1108/00070700 910951470

Horng, J. S., Liu, C. H., Chou, H. Y., & Tsai, C. Y. (2012). Understanding the impact of culinary brand equity and destination familiarity on travel intentions. *Tourism Management, 33*, 815–824.

Joliffe, L., & Aslam, M. S. (2009). Tea heritage tourism: Evidence from Sri Lanka. *Journal of Heritage Tourism, 4*(4), 331–344.

Joliffe, L., & Zhuang, P. (2007). *Tourism development and the tea gardens of funding, China, tea tourism: Global trends and development.* Channel View Publications.

Jolliffe, L. (2006). Tea and hospitality: More than a Cuppa. *International Journal of Contemporary Hospitality Management, 18*(1), 164–168. https://doi.org/10.1108/09596110610646718

Jolliffe, L. (2007). *Tea and tourism: Tourists, traditions and transformations* (Vol. 11). Channel View Publications.

Jolliffe, L., & Aslam, M. S. M. (2009). Tea heritage tourism: Evidence from Sri Lanka. *Journal of Heritage Tourism, 4*(4), 331–344. https://doi.org/10.1080/17438730903186607

Kaldeen, M. (2020). Marketing potentials to promote tea tourism in Sri Lanka. In *The 6th international tourism research conference and tourism leader's summit, 27th September 2020.*

Khokhar, S., & Magnusdottir, S. G. M. (2002). Total phenol, catechin, and caffeine contents of teas commonly consumed in the United Kingdom. *Journal of Agricultural and Food Chemistry, 50*(3), 565–570. https://doi.org/10.1021/jf0101531

Kim, Y. G., Eves, A., & Scarles, C. (2009). Building a model of local food consumption on trips and holidays: A grounded theory approach. *International Journal of Hospitality Management, 28*(3), 423–431. https://doi.org/10.1016/j.ijhm.2008.11.005

Kivela, J., & Crotts, J. (2006). Tourism and gastronomy: Gastronomy's influence on how tourists experience a destination. *Journal of Hospitality & Tourism Research, 30*(3), 354–377. https://doi.org/10.1177/1096348006286797

Korstanje, M. E., & George, B. P. (2020). Education as a strategy to tackle over tourism for overtourism and inclusive sustainability in the twenty-first century. In *Overtourism* (pp. 341–359). Palgrave Macmillan.

Kyung, H., Mark, A., & Meehee, C. (2017). Green tea quality attributes: A cross-cultural study of consumer perceptions using importance–Performance analysis (IPA). *Journal of Foodservice Business Research.* https://doi.org/10.1080/15378020.2017.1368809

Lin, Q., & Wen, J. J. (2018). Tea-tourism and its impacts on ethnic marriage and labor division. Journal of China Tourism Research, *14*(4), 461–483.

Lee, S. M., Chung, S. J., Lee, O. H., Lee, H. S., Kim, Y. K., & Kim, K. O. (2008). Development of sample preparation, presentation procedure and sensory descriptive analysis of green tea. *Journal of Sensory Studies, 23*(4), 450–467. https://doi.org/10.1111/j.1745-459X.2008.00165.x

List of geographical indications in India. (2020, July 16). In *Wikipedia*. https://en. wikipedia.org/wiki/List_of_geographical_indications_in_India

Lorenzo, M., Claudia, S., & Cannella, C. (2003). Eating habits and appetite control in the elderly: The anorexia of aging. *International Psychogeriatrics*, *15*(1), 73–87. https://doi.org/10.1017/S1041610203008779

Mahanta, M. G. D. (2014). Ecotourism and Dibru-Saikhowa national park. *Journal of Agriculture & Life Science*, *1*, 91–94.

Mak, A. H. N., Lumbers, M., Eves, A., & Chang, R. C. Y. (2012). Factors influencing tourist food consumption. *International Journal of Hospitality Management*, *31*(3), 928–936. https://doi.org/10.1016/j.ijhm.2011.10.012

McKercher, B., Ho, P. S., & du Cros, H. (2004). Attributes of popular cultural attractions in Hong Kong. Annals of Tourism Research, *31*(2), 393–407. https://doi.org/10.1016/j.annals.2003.12.008

McWilliams, A., & Siegel, D. (2001). Corporate social responsibility: A theory of the firm perspective. *Academy of Management Review*, *26*, 117–127.

Milano, C., Marina, N., & Cheer, M. J. (2018). Overtourism a growing global problem. *The Conversation*, *18*, 1–5.

Mill, R. C., & Morrison, A. M. (2012). *The tourism system* (7th ed.). Kendall/Hunt Publishing.

Mondal, S., & Samaddar, K. (2020b). Responsible tourism towards sustainable development: Literature review and research agenda. *Asia Pacific Business Review*, 1–38.

Mondal, S., & Samaddar, K. (2020a). Issues and challenges in implementing sharing economy in tourism: A triangulation study. *Management of Environmental Quality: An International Journal*, *32*(1), 64–81.

Morgan, N., Pritchard, A., & Pride, R. (2011). *Destination brands: Managing place reputation*. Elsevier Butterworth-Heinemann.

Morrison, A. M. (2012). *Marketing and managing tourism destinations*. Routledge.

O'Donnell, C. (1994). Food products for different age groups: Formulating for the ages. *Prepared Foods*, *3*(2), 39–44. https://doi.org/10.1375/jhtm.18.1.1

Peck Ting, G., Adeline, S., & Yien, T. (2017). Our tea-drinking habits: Effects of brewing cycles and infusion time on total phenol content and antioxidants of common teas. *Journal of Culinary Science & Technology*. https://doi.org/10.1080/15428052.2017.1409673

Quan, S., & Wang, N. (2004). Towards a structural model of the tourist experience: An illustration from food experience in tourism. *Tourism Management*, *25*(3), 297–305. https://doi.org/10.1016/S0261-5177(03)00130-4

Raja, M., & Mythili, C. (2019). Sustainable livelihood and economic status of tea labourers in the Nilgiris District. *IOSR Journal of Economics and Finance*, *10*, 33–38.

Ranasinghe, W. T., Thaichon, P., & Ranasinghe, M. (2017). An analysis of product-place co-branding: The case of Ceylon tea. *Asia Pacific Journal of Marketing and Logistics*, *29*(1), 200–214.

Rezaee, E., Mirlohi, M., Hassanzadeh, A., & Fallah, A. (2016). Factors affecting tea consumption pattern in an urban society in Isfahan, Iran. *Journal of Education and Health Promotion*, *5*, 13. https://doi.org/10.4103/2277-9531. 184568

Rozin, P. (2006). The integration of biological, social, cultural and psychological influences on food choice. In R. Shepherd & M. Raats (Eds.), *The psychology of food choice* (pp. 19–39). CABI.

Samaddar, K., & Menon, P. (2020). Non-deceptive counterfeit products: A morphological analysis of literature and future research agenda. *Journal of Strategic Marketing*, 1–24.

Sarkar, S. K., & George, B. (2018). Social media technologies in the tourism industry: An analysis with special reference to their role in sustainable tourism development. *International Journal of Tourism Sciences, 18*, 269–278.

Sarkar, S. K., Toanoglou, M., & George, B. (2020). The making of data-driven sustainable smart city communities in holiday destinations. In *Digital transformation in business and society* (pp. 273–296). Palgrave Macmillan.

Serrat, O. (2017). *The sustainable livelihoods approach knowledge solutions* (pp. 21–26). Springer.

Shah, S., Gani, A., Ahmad, M., Shah, A., Gani, A., & Massodi, F. A. (2015). In vitro antioxidant and antiproliferative activity of microwave-extracted green tea and black tea (Camellia sinensis): A comparative study. *Nutra Foods, 14*(4), 207–215. https://doi.org/10.1007/s13749-015-0050-9

Shah, S. K., & Pate, V. A. (2016). Tea production in India: Challenges and opportunities. *Journal of Tea Science Research, 6*(5), 1–6.

Sharples, L. (2008). Book reviews on 'Tea and tourism: Tourists, traditions and transformations'. Tourism Management, 29(4), 821–823.

Shen, K., Zhang, B., & Feng, Q. (2019). Association between tea consumption and depressive symptom among Chinese older adults. *BMC Geriatrics, 19*(1), 246–261. https://doi.org/10.1186/s12877-019-1259-z

Sita, K., Aji, T. M., & Hanim, W. (2021). Integrating tea and tourism: A potential sustainable livelihood approach for Indonesia tea producer central area. *IOP Conference Series: Earth and Environmental Science, 892*.

Stanford, D. (2008). 'Exceptional visitors': Dimensions of tourist responsibility in the context of New Zealand. *Journal of Sustainable Tourism, 16*, 258–275.

Sukenti, K. (2014). Gastronomy tourism in several neighbor countries of Indonesia: A brief review. *Journal of Indonesian Tourism and Development Studies, 2*, 55–63.

Su, M. M., Wall, G., & Wang, Y. (2019). Integrating tea and tourism: A sustainable livelihoods approach. *Journal of Sustainable Tourism, 27*(10), 1591–1608. https://doi.org/10.1080/09669582.2019.1648482

Su, M. M., Wall, G., Wang, Y., & Jin, M. (2019). Livelihood sustainability in a rural tourism destination Hetu town, Anhui province, China. *Tourism Management, 71*, 272–281.

Su, X., & Zhang, H. (2020). Tea drinking and the tastescapes of wellbeing in tourism. *Tourism Geographies.* https://doi.org/10.1080/14616688.2020.1750685.

Tao, T. C. H., & Wall, G. (2009). Tourism as a sustainable livelihood strategy. *Tourism Management, 30*, 90–98.

Tea Board of India. (2019, April 30). *Tea varieties in India.* http://www.teaboard.gov.in/TEABOARDCSM/MTA=

The Indian wire. (2018, April 30). *List of top 10 start ups in India that made it big selling Chai.* https://www.theindianwire.com/startups/top-tea-sellingstartups-india-74220/

Timur, S., & Getz, D. (2007). A network perspective on managing stakeholders for sustainable urban tourism. *International Journal of Contemporary Hospitality Management, 20*(4), 445–461. https://doi.org/10.1108/09596110810873543

Urala, N., & Lähteenmäki, L. (2007). Consumers' changing attitudes towards functional foods. *Food Quality and Preference, 18*(1), 1–12. https://doi.org/10.1016/j.foodqual.2005.06.007

Varun, T. C., Kerutagi, M. G., Kunnal, L. B., Basavaraja, H., Ashalatha, K. V., & Dodamani, M. T. (2009). Consumption patterns of coffee and tea in Karnataka. *Karnataka Journal of Agricultural Sciences, 22*(4), 824–827.

Vazhakkatte Thazhathethil, B. (2020). A study on factors influencing the visitor experience on eco tourism activities at Parambikulam Tiger Reserve. *International Journal of Hospitality & Tourism Systems, 13*, 81–89.

Walton, J. K. (2001). *The hospitality trades: A social history*. Butterworth-Heinemann.

Weber, I. (2018). Tea for tourists: Cultural capital, representation, and borrowing in the tea culture of mainland China and Taiwan. *Academica Turistica, 12*(2), 143–154.

Woyesa, T., & Kumar, S. (2021). Potential of coffee tourism for rural development in Ethiopia: A sustainable livelihood approach. *Environment, Development and Sustainability, 23*, 815–832.

Yang, Z. (2007). Tea culture and Sino-American Tea connections. *Chinese American Studies, 1*(2), 8–14.

Yuksel, A., Yuksel, F., & Bilim, Y. (2010). Destination attachment: Effects on customer satisfaction and cognitive, affective and conative loyalty. *Tourism Management, 31*(2), 274–284. https://doi.org/10.1016/j.tourman.2009.03.007

Zeppel, H., & Beaumont, N. (2011). *Green tourism futures: Climate change responses by Australian government tourism agencies* (Vol. 2): University of Southern Queensland, Australian Centre for Sustainable.

Zheng, W., Doyle, T. J., Kushi, L. H., Sellers, T. A., Hong, C. P., & Folsom, A. R. (1996). Tea consumption and cancer incidence in a prospective cohort study of postmenopausal women. *American Journal of Epidemiology, 144*(1), 175–182. https://doi.org/10.1093/oxfordjournals.aje.a008905

Zhouyiqi, C., & Tao, W. (2012). Application of special tea cultivars in landscape design of ecotourism tea gardens. *The Crop Journal, 2*.

Chapter 7

SMEs' Sustainability: Green Supply Chain Practices and Environmental Performance

Bak Aun Teoh, Yu Qing Soong and Jia Le Germaine Chee

Abstract

Purpose: This book chapter aimed to examine the relationships between green supply chain practices and environmental performance in Malaysian Small and Medium Enterprises (SMEs). The practices of green supply chain in achieving environmental performance have been one priority concerns in Malaysia. However, green supply chain practices adoption remains emergence.

Design/methodology/approach: This manuscript adopted the multiple regression analysis in investigating the green supply chain (GSC) practices and environmental performance's variables. The self-administered surveys were randomly disseminated to Malaysian SMEs and 59 responses were returned. The result theoretically ascertained the positive relationship between GSC practices and environmental performance measures.

Findings: The findings are in aligned with the Resource-Based View (RBV) theory that conceptualized the GSC practices and strategies to sustain the environmental performance within the SMEs. In a nutshell, these findings would serve as the research implications and recommendations to the scholars, industrial practitioners, and policymakers who are interested in these GSC practices and environmental performance. This would further serve as a guideline for companies that tend to implement these GSC practices for improving its environmental performance.

Originality/value: The research revealed that 'eco-design and packaging' and 'reverse logistics' are significant to environmental performance, but both 'green procurement' and 'investment recovery' are not significant to environmental performance. The literature gaps exhibited for this manuscript; hence, future studies should be carried out on supply chain practices and environmental performance since there is no prescriptive

Entrepreneurship and Green Finance Practices, 129–140

Copyright © 2024 Bak Aun Teoh, Yu Qing Soong and Jia Le Germaine Chee

Published under exclusive licence by Emerald Publishing Limited

doi:10.1108/978-1-80455-678-820231007

method in sustaining environmental performance that matches all conditions in Malaysian SMEs.

Keywords: GSCM; SME; environmental performance; sustainability; logistics

1. Malaysia SMEs' Sustainability: An Overview

Environmental issues have become a top priority for the nation in Malaysia. Natural resources depletion has resulted in a shortage of some raw materials as the world population grows while resources diminish. Companies are realizing that their supply chains need to be overhauled. The dynamic competitiveness in modern business environment forced organizations to adopt the concept of sustainability in improving the environmental and societal well-being, as well as effort of organizational cost reduction (Wong et al., 2018). In Malaysia, the capability in managing environmental wastes within different industries have always been a top concern in sustainability. For instances, based on MohdUzir (2021), industries that produced the most wastes in 2020 are power plant activity, metal refinery, chemical industry, electric and electronic, which contributed 24.2%, 12.2%, 10.7%, and 1 0.1% of wastes, respectively. These environmental concerns are being prioritized in aligned with the Environmental Quality Act, and it is applicable to the whole of Malaysian industries (Agamuthu & Barasarathi., 2021). It is an act that controls and regulates harmful environmental issues from the industrialization process to enhance environmental quality as part of the sustainability effort in Malaysian industries. Concept of sustainability complements the resource-based theory due to promoting the development and efficient used of environmental resources in sustaining competitive advantages (Khan et al., 2018).

Green supply chain management (GSCM) means reinforcing environmental approaches into supply chain that aims to reduce adverse environmental impacts along the product life cycle. The other objective of GSCM is to eliminate waste of resources from the raw ingredients to the final three green product (Iqbal et al., 2020). Nowadays, GSCM arises as a new environmental approach and innovation for most business organizations (Bag et al., 2022). In specific, Malaysian small and medium enterprises (SMEs) realize the importance of these GSCM practices and the adoption that could help the company to reduce environmental effects and enhance their environmental performance. Customers might boycott those companies with no proper green supply chain practices. Hence, consumers play an important role in the green supply chain as SMEs must respond actively to their customer demands. Consumer demands are known as an influential pressure for those companies. Consumers not only demand for product value and quality but they also seek environmental responsibility within the supply chain due to the increased environmental awareness (Kumar et al., 2013). Hence, the study would focus on green supply chain practices in achieving SME's environmental performance in Malaysia.

2. Environmental Performance

Environmental performance measures how well a company can reduce the negative impacts such as pollution and waste to the environment (Sezen & Çankaya, 2019). Environmental outcomes refer to the positive impacts of GSCM practices on the natural environment both within and outside of the businesses. Such examples include the reduction in wastes, emissions, and hazardous materials (Eltayeb et al., 2010). According to Incekara (2022), the adoption of green initiatives among SMEs have reduced the consumption of water, raw material, and wastes to the minimum. With the adoption of GSCM, environmental benefits include the replacement of primary resources with secondary resources in the green supply chain and the products diversion from landfill of the end-of-life waste. This helps in reducing the environmental burdens during the business processes (Rahman et al., 2014). Conclusively, studies suggest that by practicing green initiatives have positively impacted the environmental performance of a company.

3. Green Supply Chain Management

Implementation of environmental management practices into the entire supply chain management is critical for SMEs to sustain competitive advantage (Higgs & Hill, 2019). Based on Soliman and El-Kady (2020), GSCM is defined as the range from green procurement to integrated supply chain moving from suppliers to manufacturers to customers and closing the loop. According to Srivastava (2007), GSCM refers to 'incorporating environmental thinking into supply chain management which includes material sourcing, manufacturing operations, product delivery, material sourcing and the product's end-of-life management'. Adding the 'green' component into supply chain entails addressing the relationships and impacts of supply chain to the environment (Hervani et al., 2005). GSCM is a multi-dimensional variable, referring to green procurement, investment recovery, eco-design and packaging, reverse logistics (Soliman & El-Kady, 2020).

3.1 Green Procurement

Purchasing or procurement is the preliminary function in supply chain that could determine the organizational success in the capability to integrate procurement activities and the efforts and goals towards the environment. Green procurement is defined as environmentally oriented purchasing of materials and products that meet the environmental concerns such as waste reduction, materials substitution, and the reuse and recycle advocacy (Eltayeb et al., 2010). Green procurement is an important element in GSCM (Carter et al., 2000) to reinforce environmental performance; thus, Hypothesis 1 (*H1*): green procurement has a positive relationship with environmental performance was being developed.

3.2 Investment Recovery

Investment recovery is one of the green initiatives where excess or the used materials and inventories are resold (Zhu & Sarkis, 2004). Investment recovery (IR) is another most frequently mentioned dimension in the GSCM literature. Companies use IR as a strategic component to redeploy, resell, recycle, and other related approaches to recover more value from materials and products (Mehmood et al., 2021), that will improve environmental performance. Hence, Hypothesis 2 (*H2*): investment recovery has a positive relationship with environmental performance was being postulated.

3.3 Eco-Design and Packaging

Green packaging is defined as any packaging that uses safer and more reliable materials to produce and are recyclable and reusable to meet market requirements as in performance and costs (Rajendran et al., 2019). Green packaging intertwined with other value chain components and will directly impact the environmental performance (Sarkis, 2003). Examples for green packaging such as the excessive packaging elimination, biodegradability, polystyrene reduction, and simple packaging (Kung et al., 2013). Therefore, eco-design and packaging have a positive relationship with environmental performance was being hypothesized as Hypothesis 3 (*H3*).

3.4 Reverse Logistics

Reverse logistics is a logistics function that focusses on the product flow from customers to suppliers in a reverse direction (Hazen, 2011). It is considered as one of the important GSCM components since it helps to reduce waste generated by processing returned products through a range of disposal options (Hervani et al., 2005). Common disposal options of reverse logistics include reuse, remanufacturing, repair, recycling, and disposal (Pokharel & Mutha, 2009). Consequently, Hypothesis 4 (*H4*): reverse logistics has a positive relationship with environmental performance was being tested.

4. Data, Sample, and Analysis

This study adopted multiple regression analysis in studying the relationship between green supply chain practices and environmental performance among the SMEs in Penang. The organizations were used as the unit of analysis for the research. 120 questionnaires were distributed to small and medium enterprises' executives, managers, or supervisors (as they are the decision makers for GSCM-related practices towards environmental performance) and with the response rate of 49.1%. Next, the 59 responses were then used for subsequent analysis per indicated in Table 7.1.

Table 7.1. Demographic Profile.

Variables	Categories	Frequency	Percentage
Position in company	Executive	15	25.4
	Manager	19	32.2
	Supervisor	8	13.6
	Top management	17	28.8
Company establishment	Less than 10 years	26	44.1
	1–20 years	26	44.1
	21–30 years	7	11.9
Size of company	Less than 75 employees	26	44.1
	75–100 employees	15	25.4
	101–150 employees	10	16.9
	151–200 employees	8	13.6
Industry	Food	9	15.3
	Plastics manufacturing	5	8.5
	Electric and electronic	4	6.8
	Fabric and Leather	16	27.1
	Others	25	42.4
Sales Revenue (Estimated)	Less than RM 20 Million	35	59.3
	RM 20 Million–RM 50 Million	24	40.7

4.1 Reliability Analysis

Reliability is described as the stability and consistency of the measurement instruments. In general, Hair et al. (2019); Sekaran and Bougie (2016); Zikmund et al. (2013) commented the common statistical test of reliability score is Cronbach's Alpha. The alpha coefficient is considered good when the value is 0.80; acceptable when it is 0.70; and it is poor when the value is less than 0.60 (Sekaran & Bougie, 2016). Cronbach's Alpha coefficients indicate that all items used in the instruments are acceptable, with a range of 0.66–0.84 from Table 7.2. Consequently, the reliability of the items, as tested by the reliability test, provide a useful foundation for further hypothesis evaluation.

4.2 Pearson Correlation Analysis

Pearson Correlation Analysis identifies the relationship between independent variables and dependent variables. Generally, the correlation is strong if the absolute value or r is above 0.75 (Shrestha, 2020). Table 7.3 depicted the presence

Table 7.2. Reliability Analysis.

Variables	Number of Items Utilized	Cronbach's Alpha
GP	5	0.68
IR	5	0.66
EDP	6	0.79
RL	6	0.84
EP	5	0.74

Table 7.3. Pearson Correlation Analysis.

EP	
GP	0.34**
IR	0.51**
EDP	0.98**
RL	0.44**

Note: p**< 0.01 (one-tailed).

of the correlation between the independent variables and dependent variables. The eco-design and packaging (EDP) variable showed strongest relationship with environmental performance ($r = 0.98$), followed by investment recovery (IR) ($r = 0.51$) and reverse logistics (RL) ($r = 0.44$). Nonetheless, green procurement (GP) has the weakest relationship with environmental performance ($r = 0.34$). The correlation between all independent variables with environmental performance at significant level of 0.01. When correlation is higher than 0.80, it implies that multicollinearity might be a concern (Franke, 2010). In an unreported table, the value of variance inflation factor (VIF) for independent variables are less than 2. These low VIF indicate multicollinearity is not an issue in this study (Shrestha, 2020).

4.3 Multiple Regression Analysis

The R2 value is indicating that the GSCM practices yield 42.6% variations in environmental performance. Based on the F-value = 10.01 with p value <0.001, it can be said that the model is suitable for the data. Table 7.4 depicted that two out of four GSCM variables are positively related to environmental performance. If p value is more than 0.05, the hypothesis is not supported (Sardanelli & Leo, 2020). Therefore, the accepted variables were eco-design and packaging ($\beta = 0.94$, t value = 29.17, p value <0.05) and reverse logistics ($\beta = 0.08$, t value = 2.40, p value <0.05), showing that there is strong positive relationship with

Table 7.4. Regression Analysis for Environmental Performance.

Hypotheses	Standardized Beta (β)	t Value	p Value	Decision
H1: GP→EP	−0.05	−1.66	0.05	Not supported
H2: IR→EP	0.05	1.41	0.08	Not supported
H3: EDP→EP	0.94	29.17	0.00**	Supported
H4: RL→EP	0.08	2.40	0.01**	Supported

Note: p**<0.01 (one-tailed).

environmental performance of SMEs in Penang. Hence, *H3* and *H4* are supported. Meanwhile, there are no significant relationships for green procurement ($\beta = -0.05$, t value $= -1.66$, p value >0.05) and investment recovery ($\beta = 0.05$, t value $= 1.41$, p value >0.05) with environmental performance. Consequently, *H1* and *H2* are rejected.

5. Conclusions, Practical Implications, and Future Research

H1 is rejected. It shows that green procurement does not have a significant impact on environmental performance. Based on Sundram et al. (2017) and Green Jr et al. (2012), green procurement would only bring a positive impact towards operational performance compared to environmental concerns in the Malaysian manufacturing industry and Chinese companies, respectively. Moreover, Sezen and Çankaya (2019) also stated that green procurement practices have no significant relationship with environmental performance. One of the potential reasons why green procurement does not significantly impact environmental performance is because the concept of green procurement is still relatively new in Malaysia, causing a low awareness level among Malaysian firms (Rais et al., 2018). Moreover, company size may be one of the influence factors for companies to adopt green supply chain practices, larger size companies, particularly those with international markets or those export manufacturers or multinational companies (MNCs) typically have higher willingness to implement these eco-friendly practices (Eltayeb et al., 2010). SMEs often do not have sufficient information and expertise in dealing environmental issues (Lee, 2008). For example, the primary driver of green purchasing initiative is the establishment of the Responsible Business Alliance (RBA) in the Malaysian electronic industry. As an example, a Multinational Corporation, Sony has created its own code of conduct called Sony Group Code of Conduct which requires all its suppliers to follow the RBA standards, which including obtaining environmental registrations and permits from authorized organizations, minimizing and eliminating air and water emissions, and adhering to all applicable regulations and customer-specific hazardous substances restrictions (Eltayeb et al., 2010). Hence, it is important to increase green procurement awareness in Malaysia as environmental issues are becoming more prevalent. From the findings above, green procurement has a correlated but not significant relationship with environmental performance. *H2* rejected. This result is corresponding to previous related studies (e.g., Green Jr et al., 2012; Mehmood et al., 2021). It is because Malaysia clearly does not pay sufficient attention in investment recovery compared to developed countries such as China, Germany, and the United States. It is due to there being lesser waste management policies to support investment recovery and insufficient infrastructure for the closed-loop system in Malaysia (Yeoh et al., 2017). To prevent a resurgence of interest in investment recovery activities, the Malaysian government switched its focus away from subsidized resources to vital resources such as natural gas and coal (Mehmood et al., 2021). From these studies above, the results indicated that there is a correlated but not significant relationship between investment recovery and environmental performance.

H3 is supported. This outcome is consistent with the findings of previous research (e.g., Geng et al., 2017; Green et al., 2012; Rasit et al., 2019; Sezen & Çankaya, 2019; Sundram et al., 2017). Eco-design and packaging are the most crucial components throughout a product's life cycle as environmental consideration is already taken into during the design phase (Sundram et al., 2017). It is because negative environmental impacts are intended to be minimized throughout the production process (Rasit et al., 2019). Consequently, eco-design and packaging improve environmental performance and reduce energy, resources, and consumption. Examples for eco-design and packaging include reduced packaging material, reusable packaging, and recycling packaging (Sezen & Çankaya, 2019). As a result, eco-design and packaging is significantly related to environmental performance among SMEs in Malaysia. *H4* is supported. According to Azevedo et al. (2011), Geng et al. (2017), and Carter and Rogers (2008), the results of these studies are in line with this study. Implementing reverse logistics initiatives help companies to reduce the impact on the ecological system by reducing the environmental impact of end-of-life products (Waqas et al., 2021). Reverse logistics practices including recycling, reusing, reprocessing, waste management, and material recovery (Geng et al., 2017). These reverse logistics practices can improve environmental performance by reducing energy, water and waste consumption, better utilization of resources and materials, reducing packaging, and reducing pollutant emissions (Ali et al., 2018).

This study is not exempted from any limitations, and it is not a section for undermining the results, in fact, it shows that the study is aware of the limitations. Firstly, the sample selection only focussed on the small and medium enterprises in one of the Malaysian states in Penang. Consequently, the findings of this study are limited to only Penang SMEs and do not fully represent the entire population of the Malaysian SMEs. Moreover, the sample size is small as the unit of analysis in this research is one SME in Penang equivalent to one unit. Furthermore, the generalizability of this study is limited as only one representative from the company can answer the questionnaire and it is also time intensive as appointments are needed to be made in advance. It is because this study required respondents who only held high positions (e.g. executives or top management, manager, and supervisor) in the company to complete the questionnaires and normal staff are not required to answer the questionnaire. Thus, the response rate is low. The main purpose of the research is to examine the impact of GSCM practices towards the environmental performance among the SMEs in Penang. However, there is a lack of previous research studies on the topic as the concept of green initiatives is still relatively new and not many Malaysian companies have implemented it. Also, this study is unable to get in-depth understanding as only survey questionnaires were used. Thus, the environmental performance level could not be measured accurately based on their experience with implemented green initiatives in their company. It is because all designed items in the questionnaire are scale-type questions which caused the respondents to not further explain their perspectives. Besides, it restricted the findings to be compared with other data sources by using the questionnaire as the only data source. Lastly, there is a limitation in scope as only four GSCM practices were proposed.

Future research can expand the sample selection to other Malaysian states. This enables the researchers to obtain more responses and be able to further examine how GSCM practices impact environmental and operational performance among Malaysian companies in a bigger context with the considerations of different company size and industry. Moreover, future study may also use qualitative data collection methods by having interviews with experts to obtain in-depth understanding on the related research topic. Researchers may also conduct both quantitative and qualitative data collection methods, it allows the researchers to receive different perspectives and be able to compare the data collected. The researcher can also design the questionnaire items with a combination of open-ended questions and rating-scale questions. This enables the researchers to have a more in-depth understanding compared to only scale type questionnaires. Besides, further studies can include other potential green supply chain practices such as reducing energy consumption, green supply chain collaboration, green manufacturing, green distribution, and green transportation. This allows the researchers to further examine how other potential green practices could influence the environmental and operational performance and provide a comprehensive study to the readers.

Acknowledgements

The authors wish to thank all the respective respondents during the interviews and provide data throughout this study conducted. In addition, the authors acknowledge the support given by Universiti Teknikal Malaysia Melaka (UTeM), Fakulti Pengurusan Teknologi Dan Teknousahawanan (FPTT), Centre of Technopreneurship Development (CTeD), 75450 Ayer Keroh, Melaka, Malaysia for the financial support and facilities provided in completing this research. We will welcome any collaboration for this kind of research with an open arm.

References

Agamuthu, P., & Barasarathi, J. (2021). Clinical waste management under COVID-19 scenario in Malaysia. *Waste Management & Research*, *39*, 18–26.

Ali, A. H., Zalavadia, S., Barakat, M. R., & Eid, A. (2018). The role of sustainability in reverse logistics for returns and recycling. *Archives of Business Research*, *6*, 12–33.

Azevedo, S. G., Carvalho, H., & Machado, V. C. (2011). The influence of green practices on supply chain performance: A case study approach. *Transportation Research Part E: Logistics and Transportation Review*, *47*, 850–871.

Bag, S., Dhamija, P., Bryde, D. J., & Singh, R. K. (2022). Effect of eco-innovation on green supply chain management, circular economy capability, and performance of small and medium enterprises. *Journal of Business Research*, *141*, 60–72.

Carter, C. R., Kale, R., & Grimm, C. M. (2000). Environmental purchasing and firm performance: An empirical investigation. *Transportation Research Part E*, *36*, 219–228.

Carter, C. R., & Rogers, D. S. (2008). A framework of sustainable supply chain management: Moving toward new theory. *International Journal of Physical Distribution & Logistics Management*, *38*, 360–387.

Eltayeb, T. K., Zailani, S., & Jayaraman, K. (2010). The examination on the drivers for green purchasing adoption among EMS 14001 certified companies in Malaysia. *Journal of Manufacturing Technology Management*, *21*, 206–225.

Franke, G. R. (2010). *Multicollinearity*. Wiley International Encyclopedia of Marketing.

Geng, R., Mansouri, S. A., & Aktas, E. (2017). The relationship between green supply chain management and performance: A meta-analysis of empirical evidence in Asian emerging economies. *International Journal Production Economies*, *183*, 245–258.

Green, K. W., Jr, Zelbst, P. J., Meacham, J., & Bhadauria, V. S. (2012). Green supply chain management practices: Impact on performance. *Supply Chain Management: An International Journal*, *17*, 290–305.

Hair, J. F., Risher, J. J., Sarstedt, M., & Ringle, C. M. (2019). When to use and how to report the results of PLS-SEM. *European Business Review*, *31*, 2–24.

Hazen, B. T. (2011). Strategic reverse logistics disposition decisions: From theory to practice. *International Journal of Logistics Systems and Management*, *10*, 330–353.

Hervani, A. A., Sarkis, J., & Helms, M. M. (2005). Performance measurement for green supply chain management. *Benchmarking: An International Journal*, *12*, 330–353.

Higgs, C. J., & Hill, T. (2019). The role that small and medium-sized enterprises play in sustainable development and the green economy in the waste sector, South Africa. *Business Strategy & Development*, *2*, 25–31.

Incekara, M. (2022). Determinants of process reengineering and waste management as resource efficiency practices and their impact on production cost performance of small and medium enterprises in the manufacturing sector. *Journal of Cleaner Production*, *356*, 1–11.

Iqbal, M. W., Kang, Y., & Jeon, H. W. (2020). Zero waste strategy for green supply chain management with minimization of energy consumption. *Journal of Cleaner Production*, *245*, 1–17.

Khan, M. P., Talib, N. A., & Tan, K. O. (2018). Development of sustainability framework based on the theory of resource-based view. *International Journal of Academic Research in Business and Social Sciences*, *8*(7), 636–647.

Kumar, S., Luthra, S., & Haleem, A. (2013). Customer involvement in greening the supply chain: An interpretive structural modelling methodology. *Journal of Industrial Engineering International, 9,* 1–13.

Kung, F. H., Huang, C. L., & Cheng, C. L. (2013). Assessing the green value chain to improve environmental performance: Evidence from Taiwan's manufacturing industry. *International Journal of Development Issues, 11,* 111–128.

Lee, S. (2008). Drivers for the participation of small and medium-sized suppliers in green supply chain initiatives. *Supply Chain Management, 13,* 185–198.

Mehmood, T., Asim, M., & Manzoor, S. (2021). The relationship between green supply chain and logistics practices performance. *Electronic Research Journal of Behavioural Sciences, 4,* 69–87.

MohdUzir, M. (2021). *Environmental statistics 2020.* Department of Statistics Malaysia.

Pokharel, S., & Mutha, A. (2009). Perspective in reverse logistics: A review. *Resources, Conservation and Recycling, 53,* 175–182.

Rahman, A., Ho, J. A., & Rusli, K. A. (2014). Pressures, green supply chain management practices and performance of ISO 14001 certified manufacturers in Malaysia. *International Journal of Economics and Management, 8,* 1–24.

Rais, S. L. A., Bidin, Z. A., Bohari, A. A. M., & Saferi, M. M. (2018). The possible challenges of green procurement implementation. *International Conference on Advanced and Manufacturing and Industry Applications, 429,* 1–7.

Rajendran, S., Wahab, S. N., & Kaur, M. (2019). Malaysian consumers' preference for green packaging. *International Journal of Society Systems Science, 11,* 312–331.

Rasit, Z. A., Zakaria, M., Hashim, M., Ramli, A., & Mohamed, M. (2019). Green supply chain management (GSCM) practices for sustainability performance: An empirical evidence of Malaysian SMEs. *International Journal of Financial Research, 10,* 371–379.

Sardanelli, F., & Leo, G. D. (2020). Statistical significance: P value, 0.05 threshold, and applications to radiomics–Reasons for a conservative approach. *European Radiology Experimental, 4,* 1–8.

Sarkis, J. (2003). A strategic decision framework for green supply chain management. *Journal of Cleaner Production, 11,* 397–409.

Sekaran, U., & Bougie, R. (2016). *Research methods for business: A skill building approach.* John Wiley & Sons.

Sezen, B., & Çankaya, S. Y. (2019). Effects of green supply chain management practices on sustainability performance. *Journal of Manufacturing Technology Management, 30,* 98–121.

Shrestha, N. (2020). Detecting multicollinearity in regression analysis. *American Journal of Applied Mathematics and Statistics, 8,* 39–42.

Soliman, K., & El-Kady, G. (2020). Green supply chain practices framework for petrochemicals in Egypt. *Renewable Energy and Sustainable Development, 6,* 48–60.

Srivastava, S. K. (2007). Green supply-chain management: A state-of-the-art literature review. *International Journal of Management Reviews, 9,* 53–80.

Sundram, V. P. K., Bahrin, A. S., Othman, A. A., & Abdul Munir, Z. (2017). Green supply chain management practices in Malaysia manufacturing industry. *International Journal of Supply Chain Management, 6,* 89–95.

Waqas, M., Xue, H., Khan, S. A. R., Ahmad, N., Ullah, Z., & Iqbal, M. (2021). Impact of reverse logistics barriers on sustainable firm performance via reverse logistics practices. *Scientific Journal of Logistics, 17*, 213–230.

Wong, K. L., Chong, K. E., Chew, B. C., Tay, C. C., & Mohamed, S. B. (2018). Key performance indicators for measuring sustainability in health care industry in Malaysia. *Journal of Fundamental and Applied Sciences, 10*, 646–657.

Yeoh, B. G., Idrus, A. Z., & Ong, K. (2017). Technology research development for environmental management with specific reference to Malaysia. *ASEAN Journal on Science and Technology for Development, 5*(1), 1–13.

Zhu, Q., & Sarkis, J. (2004). Relationships between operational practices and performance among early adopters of green supply chain management practices in Chinese manufacturing enterprises. *Journal of Operations Management, 22*, 265–289.

Zikmund, W. G., Babin, B. J., Carr, J. C., & Griffin, M. (2013). *Business research methods*. Cengage Learning.

Chapter 8

Barriers and Challenges in Green Concepts Implementation

Naveed R. Khan, Muhammad Rahies Khan, Wasim Ahmad and Rana Muhammad Sohail Jafar

Abstract

The environmental performance of organizations has come under public policy limelight since the phenomenal increase of natural resource degradation and industrial waste. Thus, green concepts have been put forward, but the implementation of green practices faces many barriers and challenges. These barriers require attention as organizational practices are negatively affecting the environment leading to global warming and climate change. Therefore, this chapter systematically identifies four internal barriers including inadequate management commitment and support, insufficient technology competence and infrastructure, financial constraints, the uncertainty of economic benefits, and eight sub barriers within an organization concerning green concepts implementation. Moreover, this chapter also identifies four external barriers including lack of stakeholder's interest, inadequate environmental administrative support, scarce academic research, and lack of green collaborative practices, and eight sub barriers outside an organizational context concerning green concept implementation. The barriers in this research were identified by reviewing the existing literature on the topic. This chapter advances the green literature by identifying multiple barriers and challenges to the successful implementation of green concepts in organizations. This is of significance as if these barriers are tackled strategically, it would reduce environmental degradation problems and help make financial gains. Moreover, this research can help managers understand the key barriers to green concept implementation and provide guidance to them when attempting to implement green practices in their organizations. This research would also motivate researchers to extend further investigation on how to overcome such barriers and find out strategies to mitigate the barriers to green concept implementation to effectively address environmental issues.

Entrepreneurship and Green Finance Practices, 141–161
doi:10.1108/978-1-80455-678-820231008

Keywords: Internal barriers; external barriers; green concepts; environmental degradation; green initiatives; green practices

1. Introduction

The industrial revolution after World War II has brought massive economic gains but comprises environmental gains (Dhull & Narwal, 2016). The achievement of economic gain was gain attraction due to the conservative philosophy of Maslow's basic needs theory, however, philosophical thinking of sustainable performance has dramatically changed the business operations of organizations, especially in developed countries. Therefore, these countries have focussed on environmental legislation to address sustainable and competitive performance. Primarily, the developed countries have initiated legislation regarding the reduction of hazardous and electrical substances which include the Restriction of Hazardous Substances (RoHS) and waste electrical and electronic equipment (WEEE) (Yu et al., 2006). The implementation of these environmental concepts is brought into practice by initiating the ISO 14000 certification among the companies. The concept was initiated to overcome the industrial burden on the natural environment however, companies took a competitive advantage over their competitors by promoting the green slogan in their marketing strategies. Besides ISO 14000 certification, external bodies also played their role in the implementation of green initiatives among these organizations. These external bodies include environmental protection agencies, NGOs, and other government legalization bodies. In developed countries, the majority of the firms are implementing environmentally friendly practices however, the developing countries are in the transit phase.

To address the environmental concern, green initiatives including the GSCM practices are considered the true strategies among organizations. GSCM practices are an integration of internal business operations and external organizational practices. Organizations are addressing these initiatives to gain sustainable development. Therefore, this concept is gaining considerable importance because of global and national pressures, industrial demand, legislation, consumers awareness, environmental practices, and social concerns (Dallasega & Sarkis, 2018; Moktadir, Ali, et al., 2018; Moktadir, Rahman, et al., 2018). These pressures are focussing on these initiatives to minimize environmental damage and energy usage. Initially, these practices were incorporated into traditional supply chain operations (Batista et al., 2018; Kumar et al., 2016, 2019). These green initiatives help out the firms to reduce energy consumption, safeguard the biodiversity and eco-system, and also reduce environmental degradation (Alahmad et al., 2011, pp. 521–526; Carbone & Moatti, 2008; Colicchia et al., 2017; Sinaga et al., 2019). These green initiatives and especially the GSCM practices are gaining exponential attention and popularity during the current fragile and dynamic industrial environment. Therefore, the manufacturing sector is implementing these practices to ensure environmental protection, gain profitable growth, and enhance their production and manufacturing activities to achieve popularity, reliability, and access to national and international markets (Badi & Murtagh, 2019; Choudhary et al., 2019; Maditati et al., 2018; Rahmani & Yavari, 2019).

Green initiative and GSCM practices are defined as the mechanism of implementing eco-friendly processes and materials and converting the inputs into eco-friendlier products which can be retrieved after their end of life for possible reuse, recycling, remanufacturing, and proper disposal (Nasrollahi, 2018; Vivek & Sanjay Kumar, 2019; Zhang et al., 2017). Green initiatives are essential in addressing and reducing the adverse effects of business operations on the environment and fostering the firm's sustainable and competitive performance (Chin et al., 2015; Gunasekaran et al., 2015; Ninlawan et al., 2010). The implementation of these green initiatives is an integrated process that involves sourcing, transportation, logistics, product design, production, packaging, warehousing, and distribution (Ahi & Searcy, 2013). Practicing green initiatives brought enormous benefits, and competitive and sustainable growth to these organizations and also help them to promote their green image and reputation. Therefore, these green initiatives are very popular and implemented with true letter and spirit among the developed countries due to strong legislative and regulatory pressures (Chan et al., 2012; Dües et al., 2013; Sarkis, 2012). However, the developing and emerging economies are still struggling and are in the transit phase (Jakhar et al., 2018). Besides, the implementation of these green concepts, initiatives, and practices is found challenging and difficult among these nations due to their well-articulated and integrated approach. Therefore, the are numerous challenges and barriers involved in the implementation of green initiatives and strategies.

Identification and discussion of these barriers and challenges is an essential and crucial stage to optimize the business processes and gain competitive and sustainable organizational performance. Therefore, previous literature has discussed these barriers and challenges in different contexts, countries, and industries. In this regard, Jayant and Azhar (2014) discussed the adoption of these green concepts in the Indian manufacturing industry. On the other hand, Mehrabi et al. (2012) identified the barriers and challenges in the implementation of these concepts in the Iranian petrochemical industry. Among others, Rahman et al. (2020) also identified these barriers among emerging economies and also provide alternative strategies to mitigate these barriers and challenges. These studies showed that the identification of these barriers and challenges is only focussed at different industrial or sector levels and has not been discussed with true letter and spirit and in-depth at the macro level. Further, no research has been conducted to simultaneously identify and discuss the internal and external barriers and challenges among emerging and developing nations. Additionally, there exists gap in literature in identification and discussion of macro, micro, and meso level barriers and challenges in the implementation of these green initiatives, concepts, and practices. Therefore, this research gap has motivated the researcher to identify the internal, external, and sub-barriers and challenges in the adoption of these green initiatives among developing and emerging economies by evaluating the previous literature. More specifically, the major objectives of this chapter include:

(1) To identify the significant and potential internal barriers and challenges in the implementation of green initiatives, concepts, and practices.
(2) To identify the significant and potential external barriers and challenges in the implementation of green initiatives, concepts, and practices.
(3) To identify the significant and potential sub-dimensions of these barriers and challenges in the implementation of green initiatives, concepts, and practices.

This chapter contributed in various ways to GSCM literature as this chapter has identified, and summarized the internal, external, and sub-barriers of the green initiatives and practices implementation. Further, this study is of significance as if these barriers are tackled strategically, it would reduce environmental degradation problems and help make financial gains. Moreover, this research can help managers understand the key barriers to green concept implementation and provide guidance to them when attempting to implement green practices in their organizations. This research would also motivate researchers to extend further investigation on how to overcome such barriers and find out strategies to mitigate the barriers to green concept implementation to effectively address environmental issues.

This chapter is designed as the identification of internal barriers in the implementation of green initiatives, identification of external barriers and challenges, summarize the internal, external, and sub-barriers to green initiatives implementation, and finally providing alternative strategic plans to mitigate these barriers and challenges. Finally, future research avenues and implications are highlighted.

2. Identification of Internal and External Barriers

For the identification of internal and external barriers, the previous literature was evaluated and critically discussed. The majority of the business sectors are eager to implement these green initiatives however, certain barriers and challenges are confronted before, during, and even after the implementation of these green concepts and practices. The barriers and challenges might be a lack of infrastructure, government legislation, organizational commitment, and a lack of stakeholders' interests (Dhull & Narwal, 2016). Similarly, previous literature suggests that some of the external barriers like lack of customer knowledge and social consciousness regarding green products are a little lower (Min & Galle, 2001). Further, Walker et al. (2008) identified internal barriers and complications including disclosure of poor environmental performance measures, mistrust regarding confidentiality and information, etc. Similarly, Wang et al. (2008) also indicated both the external and internal barriers which include deficiency of adequate strategic planning, poor industrial environment, and structure, lack of IT knowledge and management commitment, deficiency of trained and skilled workforce, lack of social participation, huge capital and investment risk, deficiency of proper production technological tools, in appropriate energy sources, in adequate financial and other assets resources, inefficient data sources, and many more. Further, previous literature also indicated that there are various barriers faced by organization as per their organizational structure, sectors, and industry based regarding the implementation of green practices (Walker et al., 2008; Zhu & Sarkis, 2006).

Additionally, some of the previous studies also found some potential barriers like insufficient public pressures, lower societal interferences, and other stake-holders' lack of interest. Similarly, lack of social pressure from communities, media houses, NGOs, financial institutions, and or political parties are the key barriers to the implementation of these green practices (Carrillo-Hermosilla et al., 2009). Similarly, Massoud et al. (2010) identified some of the barriers that cause hindrance in the formation of the legislative and regulatory pressure like ISO 14000 certification. These barriers include the time required for certification, insufficiency of awareness, lack of management commitment, certification cost and long-term ambiguous benefits from these certifications and practices, and poor support from the government. Further, the lack of customer preferences, poor and standardized metrics criteria, and insufficient green ideas and concepts are some of the drivers identified by Koho et al. (2011). However, the major internal barriers include the lack of top-level management, lack of technological infrastructure and know-how, lack of financial resources, and ambiguous financial returns.

Similarly, a previous study conducted by Koho et al. (2011) has identified 12 internal and external barriers that inhibit the implementation of the green concept. These include lack of customers, suppliers, and stakeholders' knowledge, higher cost, lack of firm's interest and awareness, firms' management commitment, lack of IT tools, lack of inter-departmental coordination, weak government intervention and regulations, improper waste treatment, and lack of necessary analytical and measurement tools. Further, previous literature also suggested some similar barriers and challenges among emerging economies which comprises of insufficient information, lack of society and communities' involvement, in appropriate legislation, poor capacity building, scarce environmental resources, lack of awareness and approach to these resources, less government intervention and support, and lack of preferences and demands from customers (Abdullah et al., 2016; Khan et al., 2022; Muduli & Barve, 2013). Further, their study highlighted some of the potential barriers that include lower organizational attitude and perception, poor coordination with external parties, lack of customer demands, and inappropriate environmental information and returns. Besides these, some of the broad but crucial external barriers are summarized as the lack of stakeholders' interest, inadequate environmental administrative support, and information, scarce academic research, and lack of green collaborative practices.

3. Internal Barriers

For this chapter, green initiative barriers are divided into two major categories: internal and external barriers. The obstacles that prevent the implementation of green practices within the organizations are called internal barriers and the barriers and challenges that create obstacles from the external environment are called external barriers. Internal barriers include inappropriate understanding regarding green operations, lack of organizational structure, cost burden, and lack of management commitment. Further, lack of financial resources and long-term ambiguous returns regarding the implementation of green practices are the chief barriers to the implementation of green practices. A previous study by Min and Galle (2001) identified the cost and financial concern of organizations in the implementation of green initiatives and practices.

3.1 Management Commitment

Motivation, commitment, and initiative are driving tools of every organizational performance. Especially, the commitment of top-level management is essential to initiate any task or action as all the decisions are originated and directed from top to down in an organizational setting. Implementation of cost-centred and capital-intensive projects is of vital importance among the strategic level decisions. The implementation of green initiative and practices require capital resources, financial assistance, technological assistance, and well-trained human resource therefore, implementation of these practices need special concentration from these managerial levels. Further, previous literature also suggests that implementation and adoption of green and sustainable performance required strong and committed support from top-level management (Hamel et al., 1989). The initial phase in the initiation of a new cost-intensive initiative requires comprehensive organizational analysis. This analysis motives the management to initiate the green initiative and practice. Further, strategic level commitment can support and promote the newly strategic goals and initiatives by promoting the employee's role, motivating them through incentives and rewards, providing them advanced training, and enhancing inter-departmental communication that promotes teamwork and team spirit (Mathiyazhagan et al., 2013; Ravi & Shankar, 2005; Sarkis, 2012). However, all the mentioned tasks and strategies required strong managerial commitment therefore, previous literature has suggested that due to these hurdles and issues, a managerial level commitment was found to be the most primitive and crucial barrier in the implementation and adoption of green practices and concepts (Jayant & Azhar, 2014).

Sub-dimensions of top-level management commitment and motivation can be bifurcated into different but critical tasks. The very first initiative in implementing green strategies requires the allocation of resources. Previous literature suggested that organizational resources are scarce and their utilization requires strong and negotiated analysis (Andersén, 2021). Further, the literature also suggested that the successful implementation of green initiatives or any other capital-intensive project needs sound organizational resources (Andersén, 2021; Gavronski et al., 2011). More importantly, organizations facing severe and acute shortages of natural resources due to exponential population growth and massive industrialization. Therefore, this shortage of resources includes a deficiency of skilled professionals and employees, green infrastructure, green developers, green architects, and green contracts among firms (Andrews-Speed, 2004; Balasubramanian, 2012). The well-trained, flexible, and diverse workforce is one of the major organizational resources that guaranteed the successful implementation of any organizational objective. This type of men's power provides an organization with creative and core ideas, concepts, and practices that play an important role to shape the organization's sustainable development. Further, highly qualified men power help firms to create knowledge, share the knowledge, learn the advanced technologies, and develop the firms at some advanced level of sustainability (Lin & Ho, 2008; Wang et al., 2008). Unfortunately, acquiring such type of team needs sound capital which acts as a strong and intense financial barrier (Luthra et al., 2011). Further sub-dimensions of management commitment include a lack of IT infrastructure to implement these green practices. The successful implementation of green practices largely depends on the adequate availability of information technologies that are helpful in the proper disposal of waste, recycling, and reuse procedures (AlKhidir & Zailani, 2009; Mathiyazhagan et al., 2013; Ravi & Shankar, 2005). It is further highlighted that the information technology structure minimized the waste production, product design, online sourcing, and manufacturing processes (Luthra et al., 2011).

Implementation of green practices is not a one-man show and required strong teamwork and departmental coordination as different phases and strategies are segregated across organizational departments. For example, initialization of green practices starts from the top-level management and trim down to finance, marketing, and human resource departments to fulfill their requirements information technology and infrastructure is considered to be the crucial element. Therefore, critical and deep understanding, coordination, and teamwork of all stakeholders and departments are necessary for the successful implementation of green initiatives and practices. However, previous literature has indicated that a lack of coordination, communication, and information transfer among all stakeholders through IT resources acts as a strong barrier to the implementation and success of any green practices and initiatives (Balasubramanian, 2012).

3.2 Financial Constraints

Green initiative implementation requires sound financial support therefore, management critically analyzes the decisions regarding their implementation. For the implementation of environmentally friendly practices, direct and indirect transaction costs are involved. These two costs act as significant and critical barriers to the implementation of these practices (AlKhidir & Zailani, 2009). Further, green practices need strong support from other associated activities which also require a financial investment. These associated activities include the initiation of IT infrastructure, hiring of qualified and IT-friendly staff and training of existing staff, product green design, access to advanced technology tools, green procurement, green product manufacturing, green packaging, disposal of industrial waste, and recycling and reuse strategies development (Luthra et al., 2011). Additionally, the financial return from these practices is a long-term project therefore, firms feel reluctant to adopt these practices. Further, all the green initiatives require a heavy initial investment and long-term return on investment, and ambiguous profit margins. Hence, these financial constraints are the major barriers to the implementation of these green practices (Balasubramanian, 2012; Mathiyazhagan et al., 2013).

Green initiatives are eco-friendly practices and come under the firm's image-building activities. Further, firms most of the time cash eco-friendly practices under the CSR domain therefore, CSR activities required financial assistance from firms. Additionally, monitoring and analyzing the ongoing CSR and eco-friendly practices also need specialized teams and financial support. Therefore, organizations require the compliance and alignment of these practices with national and international standards for the betterment of the society and community at large (Henriques & Sadorsky, 1999; Mathiyazhagan et al., 2013; McWilliams & Siegel, 2001; Mudgal et al., 2010; Seuring, 2004).

3.3 Acceptance of Advanced Technology

Green initiatives are the drivers of change in associated departments. More importantly, these practices enhanced the digitalization of the organization and hence, promoted the development of technological infrastructure. Further, these practices also initiate the upgradation of the existing IT infrastructure (Holt & Ghobadian, 2009). Technological advancement promotes knowledge and information sharing among the departments and organizations resulting in transparent and accurate transactions among the partners (Grant, 1996; Khan et al., 2021). Additionally, organizations use this speedy, accurate, and transparent information sharing as a competitive tool in the marketplace (Akhtar et al., 2022; Tsai & Ghoshal, 1998). However, the adoption of technologically advanced tools requires not only the initial financial investment but also need a trained and well knowledgeable, and skilled workforce. Therefore, the decision to adopt these green and advanced technologies requires strong and critical managerial insight hence, act as a chief barrier to the implementation of these practices.

3.4 Ambiguous Economic Gains

The majority of organizations are reluctant to adopt green initiatives as it needs a sophisticated initial process of certification and adoption. Further, green practices are comprised of a series of interlinked activities and require joint efforts from all departments. One of the chief barriers in the initial phase of green practices is the massive initial cost. Therefore, organizations need an adequate number of financial resources to execute every green activity across the departments and outside the firms. More importantly, the return on investment from these practices is long term and organizations use to focus on short-term returns to compete in local markets. For organizations, the external environment is more fragile and dynamic, and unpredictable due to various disruptions and natural disasters. Hence, these factors create an ambiguous situation regarding the organization's profitability, therefore, organizations focus to concentrate on short-term goals consequently neglecting the long-term goals and initiatives like green initiatives and implementation of green practices.

4. External Barriers

Implementations of green initiatives are not only a game of organizational internal affairs but some of the external factors are also involved in the implementation of green practices. External barriers are more sophisticated and complicated for organizations to manage; therefore, these barriers are out of organizational control. These barriers include lack of stakeholder interest, inadequate environmental administrative support, scarce academic research, and lack of green collaborative practices.

4.1 Lack of Stakeholder's Interest

According to institutional theory, organizations are not only for profit generations but also held responsible for the external environment (DiMaggio & Powell, 1983). Further, organizations are surrounded by many stakeholders which include government, legislative bodies, institutions, NGOs, customers, and international bodies. Certain factors are key drivers among these organizations to implement some of the important initiatives. Literature has indicated that certain institutional forces compel firms to initiate green initiatives (DiMaggio & Powell, 1983). Similarly, resource acquisition and availability in the national and international markets are also affecting the firms to behave differently. It is also an important factor to share cooperation, communication, and information among organizational stakeholders (Balasubramanian, 2012).

Institutional forces and the interest of stakeholders are quite different among developed, developing, and emerging economies. Developed countries have already implemented green initiatives due to well awareness, knowledge, and keen interest of stakeholders. In this regard, European Union has already initiated certain legislations like Restriction of Hazardous Substances (RoHS), Waste Electrical and Electronic Equipment (WEEE), and End of Life Vehicles (ELV) (Yu et al., 2006). To promote the firms' green initiatives, however, the developing and emerging economies are still in the transit phase for such type of legislation. Further, among developing and emerging economies, environmental knowledge, awareness, and priority were found inadequate among the stakeholders. Moreover, the customers are the key stakeholders and more efficient drivers for firms to behave environmentally friendly but due to a lack of ecological knowledge and awareness.

Similarly, one of the most primitive and crucial barriers to stakeholders' lack of interest is inadequate knowledge and training of not only the employees of the organization but also the workforce available in the market. Most employees feel implementation of GSCM practices is a complicated and sophisticated process due to inadequate expertise and lack of green concepts knowledge (Balasubramanian,

2012). Further, investment in the training and professional development of employees discourages the stakeholders to adopt these green practices, especially the firm's internal stakeholders. To maintain and monitor these green practices implementation needs continuous training and professional development of these employees (Bowen et al., 2001; Holt & Ghobadian, 2009; Mathiyazhagan et al., 2013). Further stakeholders have to announce benefits, rewards, and incentives to those employees actively involved in the implementation of these green practices (Hsu & Hu, 2008).

Additionally, one of the crucial factors that discourages the stakeholders from the implementation of the green concept was the uncertain, ambiguous, dynamic, and fragile external environment and market competition. Further, customer fluctuating needs and preferences, market uncertainty, and the application of advanced technologies also hinder the stakeholder's decisions regarding the implementation of green initiatives (Lin & Ho, 2011). The innovation and adoption of these technologies enhanced the incorporation of new technological tools in production, manufacturing, operations, distribution, waste disposal, and other managerial activities which require trained, skilled, and professional staff and also needs financial and HR capital (Hosseini, 2007). In short, external barriers and uncertainties include intense competition in energy resources, ambiguous market conditions, project executions, global disruptions and crises, fluctuation in exchange rates, etc. (Balasubramanian, 2012; Mudgal et al., 2010).

4.2 Inadequate Environmental Administrative Support

Administrative support from the stakeholders played a critical role in the successful implementation of green practices. Administrative environmental support includes the support and incentives to firms in EMS certification, subsidies on different ecological projects, and installation of renewable energy sources. Previous literature indicated that the implementation of green practices is a cost-intensive initiative, therefore firms feel reluctant in approaching these practices (Waqas et al., 2018). Lack of environmental administrative support from stakeholders discourages the organizations from initiating green practices therefore, these non-supportive administrative behaviour act as a chief barrier to the implementation of green practices.

4.3 Lack of Green Collaborative Practices

Green practices are composed of several stages, steps, and collaborative initiatives. Besides, green practices engaged in knowledge collection regarding sustainable practices, organizational commitments, and training and development of the workforce (Balasubramanian, 2012; Lin & Ho, 2011). Green practices also involve proper disposal of waste, safeguarding of energy resources, processes of reusing, recycling and refurbishment of products, products green design, green procurement, and green production. Through these practices, firms obtain a green and positive image in the marketplace. However, the external market environment is competitive and fragile enough that firms need to struggle hard to reduce the cost of services and products. Green products need huge capital for their production and this cost acts as a strong barrier to their production (Ravi & Shankar, 2005).

Further, to remain competitive in the national and global market there needs a dire requirement for these companies to fulfil the customers' demands and preferences. Therefore, these interlinked activities are so sophisticated that need a strong and well-coordinated, and collaborative framework. These green collaborative practices include a lack of adequate knowledge and HR capacity building, lack of certifications like ISO 14000/14001, and lack of audits for sustainable practices among the trading partners (Balasubramanian, 2012; Luthra et al., 2011; Mathiyazhagan et al., 2013). The lack of this collaborative practice and coordination among trading partners reduces the sharing of knowledge and information.

4.4 Inadequate Academic Research

From the academic perspective, the majority of the research has been conducted to test the traditional issues and only focussed on the operational end of supply chains. The literature is saturated with traditional topics but failed to address the recent and more important environmental issues. Further, to research environmental issues and firms' perspectives, certain barriers inhibit the researchers to gauge and measure the implementation of green practices and their impact on organizational performance. Therefore, the lack of academic research in the environmental perspective left gaps in many operational areas which created further barriers to the implementation of green practices (Table 8.1).

5. Solutions to Barriers and Action Plans

One of the important barriers identified was a lack of organizational top management commitment and top-level managerial decisions based on the ground realities of organizational financial and HR capital. Organizations need to continuously monitor, promote, and inculcate the professional, ethical, and technological training and capacity building of their organization's financial, HR, and technological capital to meet the external environment. Through these initiatives, management would be capable to understand and identify the weak points and loopholes in the implementation of green initiatives. Upon identification of these weak points management could be in a better position to handle the initiation and implementation of green concepts, initiatives, and practices more successfully and fruitfully. Previous literature and this discussion also revealed that top-level management's continuous support and commitment played a significant role in the implementation of green practices. Further, a managerial initiative to launch different awareness programmes for green initiatives and green practices among stakeholders and customers can minimize the barriers (Gunasekaran et al., 2015; Luthra et al., 2011).

Table 8.1. Internal and External Barriers of Green Concept Implementation.

Barriers	Description of Barriers	Sources
Internal Barriers		
Higher operational costs	Green practices are capital intensive due to which the operational costs due to eco-design and manufacturing are too high.	Zhu and Geng (2013), Gangele and Verma (2011), Abdullah et al. (2016), Bey et al. (2013), Dhull and Narwal (2016), Jayant and Azhar (2014),
Lack of understanding in procuring	The organization feels reluctant and has lower knowledge and awareness regarding green procurement.	Luthra et al. (2011), Mathiyazhagan et al. (2013), Mehrabi et al. (2012) Mudgal et al. (2010), Muduli and Barve (2013), Quesada et al.
Inadequate organizational structure	Implementation of green practices is not supported due to inadequate organizational structure.	(2011), Rahman et al. (2020), Ravi and Shankar (2005), Walker et al. (2008), Wang et al. (2008), Zhang et al. (2009)
'Cost reduction at the cost of environment'	'Industries have the pressure of lowering the prices at the cost of environment for their survival'.	
Inadequate management commitment	Unsupported management commitment is a chief hurdle in executing the GSCM.	
Insufficient IT infrastructure	Deficiency of training is the foremost barrier to GSCM execution in industries.	
Lack of training/development	'The GSCM practices are too difficult/complex to implement'.	
Highly complex procedure	The majority of the small and medium-sized companies are reluctant in adapting to advancements in Technology.	

Table 8.1. *(Continued)*

Barriers	Description of Barriers	Sources
Ambiguous financial returns	'Low or no return from the investment is considered to be a major hurdle in implementing the GSCM'.	
External Barriers		
Cost of ecological packaging	The cost of adopting green packaging materials is quite high.	Balasubramanian (2012), Dashore and Sohani (2013), Dhull and Narwal (2016), Kumar et al. (2016), Luthra et al. (2011), Mudgal et al. (2010), Ravi and Shankar (2005), Wang et al. (2008)
Inadequate technology infrastructure	Lack of technological innovation is considered to be the GSCM barrier.	
Lack of innovation	Lack of technological innovation is considered to be the GSCM barrier.	
Deficient trained workforce in implementation of GSCM	SCM could not be effectively implemented till the industries get the skilled manpower for the same.	
Lack of supplier commitment	Suppliers do not show commitment to supplying the environment-friendly goods/services.	
Poor information sharing	The industries are reluctant to exchange their trade information with each other.	
Insufficient government support	Government regulation can discourage the adoption of innovation, as Government sets the environmental regulations for the industry.	
Inefficient IT infrastructure	Lack of IT implementation is an important barrier to achieving efficient GSCM.	

Table 8.1. *(Continued)*

Barriers	Description of Barriers	Sources
Poor ethical standards and CSR	Ethical values and social accountability are missing most in the business houses.	

Secondly, the adoption, incorporation, and development of IT infrastructure and tools were found to be the chief barriers to the implementation of green initiatives. Further, through the discussion, the researcher has analyzed that the availability, access, and purchasing of any IT tool and technology was a crucial factor in implementing green practices, therefore, organizations need to focus, alert, and be capable to acquire, instal and operate these technological tools to initiate, adopt, and implement the green initiatives.

Thirdly, the managerial decisions regarding the implementation of green initiatives and practices and acquiring trained HR and training of the existing workforce majorly depend on the availability of financial support. Therefore, proper planning, allocation of financial resources, and utilization are crucial phases in the initiation and implementation of green practices. It is recommended that top-level management should prioritize the sustainable performance of the organization and focus on the three pillars of sustainability equally while allocating financial resources to meet the competitive, national, and international market demands. Importantly, literature indicated that sound, dedicated, and prioritized allocation of financial resources played significant role in the implementation of organizational sustainable and competitive performance (Dhull & Narwal, 2016).

Fourth, today's business environment needs long-term goals orientation for survival and gaining sustainable performance. Previous literature and our discussion have revealed that the majority of organizations focus on and prioritize the short-term goals and objectives to gain immediate returns that cause hindrance in the implementation of green initiatives and green practices as these practices are based on long-term financial returns. Hence, strategic managers need to focus, prioritize, and formulate long-term goals and objectives to promote sustainable performance and long-term survival in the market.

Fifth, the role of stakeholders is very important in motivating, forcing, and appreciating the initiating and implementation of green practices. Previous literature indicated that stakeholders' interests, priorities, and motivations influence the implementation of green initiatives. Therefore, the government, political parties, NGOs, and the community has to enforce firms to initiate green practices to safeguard the environment and sustainable performance. Additionally, the legislative and environmental protection agencies need to focus on the implementation of green practices among the firms.

Sixth, environmental issues are considered to be the least priority among the stakeholders and organizations. Therefore, stakeholders and organizations do not bother to provide adequate environmental administrative support. Through adequate administrative environmental support, stakeholders and organizations could overcome the implementation issues. One of the chiefs and emerging barriers is the lack of environmental academic research. Further, the lack of industry and academic block cooperation deteriorated the scenario. This barrier can be overcome through enhanced collaboration among corporate and academic institutions regarding sustainable and environmental issues. Abundant quality research can minimize environmental issues more precisely.

Lastly, a lack of collaboration among trading partners was found potential barrier to the implementation of green practices. This is the most difficult barrier to address due to the imbalance of financial, HR, technological, and other resources among these partners. However, trading partners including suppliers, buyers, and third-party providers should collaborate on a more comprehensive and fruitful mechanism to counter this barrier. Therefore, the most adequate and competitive tool to enhance collaboration among these partners for the implementation of the green initiative is blockchain technology and other suitable industry 4.0 technologies (Bragazzi, 2020). Further, one of the important enablers of enhanced collaborations among the trading partners would be the acquisition, adoption, and incorporation of cleaner technologies in supply chain operations (Mutingi et al., 2014; Tachizawa et al., 2015; Wu et al., 2011).

6. Conclusion

Green initiatives provide companies a chance to survive in a dynamic marketplace through gaining sustainable and competitive performance. Therefore, these practices are an essential tool for firms however; implementation of these practices is a challenging job for organizations worldwide. Hence, this chapter has discussed the barriers to implement green practices and identified four major internal and four external drivers. These barriers include a lack of top-level management commitment, lack of financial resources, inadequate technological support, and ambiguous long-term financial returns. Further, four external barriers like lack of stakeholder interest, inadequate environmental administrative support, scarce academic research, and lack of green collaborative practices were identified. This chapter has also suggested some countermeasures to cope with these barriers. Finally, the research implications were provided for managerial and academic consultants.

7. Implications

This chapter has provided sound practical implications both for managerial and academic scholars. First, through critical analysis of previous literature, this chapter has identified and evaluated the broad barriers to the implementation of GSCM practices and green initiatives. The internal drivers identified implicate that managers need to address these barriers through provided solutions and action plans. Further, this chapter has also provided adequate solutions to four broad internal and external barriers that could help management in formulating adequate decisions regarding the implementation of green practices. This chapter also provides sound implications to external stakeholders like government, and national and international legislative bodies to behave more appropriately to counter the barriers in initiating the green practices regulations and policies.

8. Future Research Directions

Certain limitations are associated with this research. First, this chapter only discussed the barriers to the implementation of green initiatives and only identified four major external and internal barriers. Future research can be conducted to identify the most recent barriers to the implementation of these practices. Further, this chapter has also discussed the sub barriers in the implementation of GSCM practices. Future research direction can be conducted to evaluate the interlinked relationship of these barriers and provide action plans for these sub-barriers. Further, in-depth action plans to mitigate the sub barriers of all four external and internal general barriers should be discussed in future studies.

References

Abdullah, M., Zailani, S., Iranmanesh, M., & Jayaraman, K. (2016). Barriers to green innovation initiatives among manufacturers: The Malaysian case. *Review of Managerial Science, 10*(4), 683–709.

Ahi, P., & Searcy, C. (2013). A comparative literature analysis of definitions for green and sustainable supply chain management. *Journal of Cleaner Production, 52,* 329–341.

Akhtar, P., Ghouri, A. M., Saha, M., Khan, M. R., Shamim, S., & Nallaluthan, K. (2022). Industrial digitization, the use of real-time information, and operational agility: Digital and information perspectives for supply chain resilience. *IEEE Transactions on Engineering Management.* ahead of print. https://doi.org/10.1109/TEM.2022.3182479

Alahmad, M., Zulfiqar, M. F., Hasna, H., Sharif, H., Sordiashie, E., & Aljuhaishi, N. A. (2011). Green and sustainable technologies for the built environment. In *2011 developments e-systems engineering.*

AlKhidir, T., & Zailani, S. (2009). Going green in supply chain towards environmental sustainability. *Global Journal of Environmental Research, 3*(3), 246–251.

Andersén, J. (2021). A relational natural-resource-based view on product innovation: The influence of green product innovation and green suppliers on differentiation advantage in small manufacturing firms. *Technovation, 104,* 102254.

Andrews-Speed, C. P. (2004). *Energy policy and regulation in the People's Republic of China* (Vol. 19). Kluwer Law International BV.

Badi, S., & Murtagh, N. (2019). Green supply chain management in construction: A systematic literature review and future research agenda. *Journal of Cleaner Production, 223,* 312–322.

Balasubramanian, S. (2012). A hierarchiacal framework of barriers to green supply chain management in the construction sector. *Journal of Sustainable Development,* *5*(10)

Batista, L., Bourlakis, M., Smart, P., & Maull, R. (2018). In search of a circular supply chain archetype–A content-analysis-based literature review. *Production Planning & Control, 29*(6), 438–451.

Bey, N., Hauschild, M. Z., & McAloone, T. C. (2013). Drivers and barriers for implementation of environmental strategies in manufacturing companies. *Cirp Annals, 62*(1), 43–46.

Bowen, F. E., Cousins, P. D., Lamming, R. C., & Farukt, A. C. (2001). The role of supply management capabilities in green supply. *Production and Operations Management, 10*(2), 174–189.

Bragazzi, N. L. (2020). Digital technologies-enabled smart manufacturing and industry 4.0 in the post-COVID-19 era: Lessons learnt from a pandemic. *International Journal of Environmental Research and Public Health, 17*(13), 4785. https://doi.org/10.3390/ijerph17134785

Carbone, V., & Moatti, V. (2008). Greening the supply chain: Preliminary results of a global survey. *Supply Chain Forum: International Journal, 9*(2), 66–76.

Carrillo-Hermosilla, J., del González, P. R., & Könnölä, T. (2009). Policy strategies to promote eco-innovation. In *Eco-innovation* (pp. 51–91). Springer.

Chan, H. K., He, H., & Wang, W. Y. (2012). Green marketing and its impact on supply chain management in industrial markets. *Industrial Marketing Management, 41*(4), 557–562.

Chin, T. A., Tat, H. H., & Sulaiman, Z. (2015). Green supply chain management, environmental collaboration and sustainability performance. *Procedia Cirp, 26,* 695–699.

Choudhary, K., Sangwan, K. S., & Goyal, D. (2019). Environment and economic impacts assessment of PET waste recycling with conventional and renewable sources of energy. *Procedia CIRP, 80,* 422–427.

Colicchia, C., Creazza, A., & Dallari, F. (2017). Lean and green supply chain management through intermodal transport: Insights from the fast moving consumer goods industry. *Production Planning & Control, 28*(4), 321–334.

Dallasega, P., & Sarkis, J. (2018). Understanding greening supply chains: Proximity analysis can help. *Resources, Conservation and Recycling, 139,* 76–77.

Dashore, K., & Sohani, N. (2013). Green supply chain management-barriers and drivers: A review. *International Journal of Engineering Research and Technology, 2*(4), 2021–2030.

Dhull, S., & Narwal, M. (2016). Drivers and barriers in green supply chain management adaptation: A state-of-art review. *Uncertain Supply Chain Management, 4*(1), 61–76.

DiMaggio, P. J., & Powell, W. W. (1983). The iron cage revisited: Institutional isomorphism and collective rationality in organizational fields. *American Sociological Review,* 147–160.

Dües, C. M., Tan, K. H., & Lim, M. (2013). Green as the new Lean: How to use Lean practices as a catalyst to greening your supply chain. *Journal of Cleaner Production, 40,* 93–100.

Gangele, A., & Verma, A. (2011). The investigation of green supply chain management practices in pharmaceutical manufacturing industry through waste minimization. *International Journal of Industrial Engineering and Technology*, *3*(4), 403–415.

Gavronski, I., Klassen, R. D., Vachon, S., & do Nascimento, L. F. M. (2011). A resource-based view of green supply management. *Transportation Research Part E: Logistics and Transportation Review*, *47*(6), 872–885.

Grant, R. M. (1996). Prospering in dynamically-competitive environments: Organizational capability as knowledge integration. *Organization Science*, *7*(4), 375–387.

Gunasekaran, A., Subramanian, N., & Rahman, S. (2015). Green supply chain collaboration and incentives: Current trends and future directions. In *Transportation research part E: Logistics and transportation review* (Vol. 74, pp. 1–10). Elsevier.

Hamel, G., Doz, Y. L., & Prahalad, C. K. (1989). Collaborate with your competitors and win. *Harvard Business Review*, *67*(1), 133–139.

Henriques, I., & Sadorsky, P. (1999). The relationship between environmental commitment and managerial perceptions of stakeholder importance. *Academy of Management Journal*, *42*(1), 87–99.

Holt, D., & Ghobadian, A. (2009). An empirical study of green supply chain management practices amongst UK manufacturers. *Journal of Manufacturing Technology Management*, *20*(7), 933–956.

Hosseini, A. (2007). Identification of green management system's factors: A conceptualized model. *International Journal of Management Science and Engineering Management*, *2*(3), 221–228.

Hsu, C.-W., & Hu, A. H. (2008). Green supply chain management in the electronic industry. *International journal of Environmental Science and Technology*, *5*(2), 205–216.

Jakhar, S. K., Mangla, S. K., Luthra, S., & Kusi-Sarpong, S. (2018). When stakeholder pressure drives the circular economy: Measuring the mediating role of innovation capabilities. *Management Decision*, *57*(4), 904–920.

Jayant, A., & Azhar, M. (2014). Analysis of the barriers for implementing green supply chain management (GSCM) practices: An interpretive structural modeling (ISM) approach. *Procedia Engineering*, *97*, 2157–2166.

Khan, M. R., Khan, H. R., & Ghouri, A. M. (2022). Corporate social responsibility, sustainability governance and sustainable performance: A preliminary insight. *Asian Academy of Management Journal*, *27*(1), 1–28.

Khan, M. R., Khan, H. R., Vachkova, M., & Ghouri, A. M. (2021). The mediating role of real-time information between location-based user-generated content and tourist gift purchase intention. *Advances in Hospitality and Tourism Research*, *9*(1), 49–77.

Koho, M., Torvinen, S., & Romiguer, A. T. (2011). Objectives, enablers and challenges of sustainable development and sustainable manufacturing: Views and opinions of Spanish companies. In *2011 IEEE international symposium on assembly and manufacturing (ISAM)* (pp. 1–6).

Kumar, N., Brint, A., Shi, E., Upadhyay, A., & Ruan, X. (2019). Integrating sustainable supply chain practices with operational performance: An exploratory study of Chinese SMEs. *Production Planning & Control*, *30*(5–6), 464–478.

Kumar, S., Luthra, S., Govindan, K., Kumar, N., & Haleem, A. (2016). Barriers in green lean six sigma product development process: An ISM approach. *Production Planning & Control, 27*(7–8), 604–620.

Lin, C.-Y., & Ho, Y.-H. (2008). An empirical study on logistics service providers' intention to adopt green innovations. *Journal of Technology Management and Innovation, 3*(1), 17–26.

Lin, C.-Y., & Ho, Y.-H. (2011). Determinants of green practice adoption for logistics companies in China. *Journal of Business Ethics, 98*(1), 67–83.

Luthra, S., Kumar, V., Kumar, S., & Haleem, A. (2011). Barriers to implement green supply chain management in automobile industry using interpretive structural modeling technique: An Indian perspective. *Journal of Industrial Engineering and Management, 4*(2), 231–257.

Maditati, D. R., Munim, Z. H., Schramm, H.-J., & Kummer, S. (2018). A review of green supply chain management: From bibliometric analysis to a conceptual framework and future research directions. *Resources, Conservation and Recycling, 139*, 150–162.

Massoud, M. A., Fayad, R., Kamleh, R., & El-Fadel, M. (2010). *Environmental management system (ISO 14001) certification in developing countries: Challenges and implementation strategies.* ACS Publications.

Mathiyazhagan, K., Govindan, K., NoorulHaq, A., & Geng, Y. (2013). An ISM approach for the barrier analysis in implementing green supply chain management. *Journal of Cleaner Production, 47*, 283–297.

McWilliams, A., & Siegel, D. (2001). Profit maximizing corporate social responsibility. *Academy of Management Review, 26*(4), 504–505.

Mehrabi, J., Gharakhani, D., Jalalifar, S., & Rahmati, H. (2012). Barriers to green supply chain management in the petrochemical sector. *Life Science Journal, 9*(4), 3438–3442.

Min, H., & Galle, W. P. (2001). Green purchasing practices of US firms. *International Journal of Operations & Production Management, 21*(9), 1222–1238.

Moktadir, A., Rahman, T., Jabbour, C. J. C., Ali, S. M., & Kabir, G. (2018). Prioritization of drivers of corporate social responsibility in the footwear industry in an emerging economy: A fuzzy AHP approach. *Journal of Cleaner Production, 201*, 369–381.

Moktadir, M. A., Ali, S. M., Kusi-Sarpong, S., & Shaikh, M. A. A. (2018). Assessing challenges for implementing Industry 4.0: Implications for process safety and environmental protection. *Process Safety and Environmental Protection, 117*, 730 741.

Mudgal, R. K., Shankar, R., Talib, P., & Raj, T. (2010). Modelling the barriers of green supply chain practices: An Indian perspective. *International Journal of Logistics Systems and Management, 7*(1), 81–107.

Muduli, K., & Barve, A. (2013). Empirical investigation of the barriers of green supply chain management (GSCM) implementation in Indian mining industries. In *3rd international conference on business, economics, management and behavioral sciences (ICBEMBS'2013). April 29–30, 2013 Singapore.*

Mutingi, M., Mapfaira, H., & Monageng, R. (2014). Developing performance management systems for the green supply chain. *Journal of Remanufacturing, 4*(1), 1–20.

Nasrollahi, M. (2018). The impact of firm's social media applications on green supply chain management. *International Journal of Supply Chain Management, 7*(1), 16–24.

Ninlawan, C., Seksan, P., Tossapol, K., & Pilada, W. (2010). The implementation of green supply chain management practices in electronics industry. In *World congress on engineering 2012. July 4–6, 2012. London, UK., 2182* (pp. 1563–1568).

Quesada, G., Bailey, C., & Woodfin, B. (2011). An analysis of drivers and barriers to innovations in green supply chain practices in Mexico. In *Proceedings global business and social science research conference.*

Rahman, T., Ali, S. M., Moktadir, M. A., & Kusi-Sarpong, S. (2020). Evaluating barriers to implementing green supply chain management: An example from an emerging economy. *Production Planning & Control, 31*(8), 673–698.

Rahmani, K., & Yavari, M. (2019). Pricing policies for a dual-channel green supply chain under demand disruptions. *Computers & Industrial Engineering, 127,* 493–510.

Ravi, V., & Shankar, R. (2005). Analysis of interactions among the barriers of reverse logistics. *Technological Forecasting and Social Change, 72*(8), 1011–1029.

Sarkis, J. (2012). A boundaries and flows perspective of green supply chain management. *Supply Chain Management: An International Journal, 17*(2), 202–216.

Seuring, S. (2004). Industrial ecology, life cycles, supply chains: Differences and interrelations. *Business Strategy and the Environment, 13*(5), 306–319.

Sinaga, O., Mulyati, Y., Darrini, A., Galdeano, D. M., & Prasetya, A. R. (2019). Green supply chain management organizational performance. *International Journal of Supply Chain Management, 8,* 76–85.

Tachizawa, E. M., Gimenez, C., & Sierra, V. (2015). Green supply chain management approaches: Drivers and performance implications. *International Journal of Operations & Production Management, 35*(11), 1546–1566.

Tsai, W., & Ghoshal, S. (1998). Social capital and value creation: The role of intrafirm networks. *Academy of Management Journal, 41*(4), 464–476.

Vivek, P., & Sanjay Kumar, J. (2019). Analysis of green supply chain management enablers in FMCG sector using integrated ISM and MICMAC approach. In *Advances in industrial and production engineering* (pp. 69–75). Springer.

Walker, H., Di Sisto, L., & McBain, D. (2008). Drivers and barriers to environmental supply chain management practices: Lessons from the public and private sectors. *Journal of Purchasing and Supply Management, 14*(1), 69–85.

Wang, G., Wang, Y., & Zhao, T. (2008). Analysis of interactions among the barriers to energy saving in China. *Energy Policy, 36*(6), 1879–1889.

Waqas, M., Dong, Q., Ahmad, N., Zhu, Y., & Nadeem, M. (2018). Critical barriers to implementation of reverse logistics in the manufacturing industry: A case study of a developing country. *Sustainability, 10*(11), 4202. https://doi.org/10.3390/su10114202

Wu, K.-J., Tseng, M.-L., & Vy, T. (2011). Evaluation the drivers of green supply chain management practices in uncertainty. *Procedia-Social and Behavioral Sciences, 25,* 384–397.

Yu, J., Welford, R., & Hills, P. (2006). Industry responses to EU WEEE and ROHS directives: Perspectives from China. *Corporate Social Responsibility and Environmental Management, 13*(5), 286–299.

Zhang, B., Bi, J., & Liu, B. (2009). Drivers and barriers to engage enterprises in environmental management initiatives in Suzhou Industrial Park, China. *Frontiers of Environmental Science and Engineering in China, 3*(2), 210–220.

Zhang, M., Tse, Y. K., Dai, J., & Chan, H. K. (2017). Examining green supply chain management and financial performance: Roles of social control and environmental dynamism. *IEEE Transactions on Engineering Management, 66*(1), 20–34.

Zhu, Q., & Geng, Y. (2013). Drivers and barriers of extended supply chain practices for energy saving and emission reduction among Chinese manufacturers. *Journal of Cleaner Production, 40*, 6–12.

Zhu, Q., & Sarkis, J. (2006). An inter-sectoral comparison of green supply chain management in China: Drivers and practices. *Journal of Cleaner Production, 14*(5), 472–486.

Chapter 9

The Importance of Green Innovation and Technologies for Sustainable Business in Asia: Issues and Challenges of the Contemporary Sustainable Business Models

Eman Zameer Rahman and Syed Haider Ali Shah

Abstract

This chapter examines the significance of green innovation and technologies for sustainable business in Asia, focussing on the issues and challenges confronted by contemporary sustainable business models. The concept of sustainable development is introduced, which seeks to minimize negative impacts on ecosystems and preserve the environment for future generations. This chapter's methodology entails a comprehensive review of existing literature and research on green innovation, green technology, and sustainable business models in Asia. The expansion of 'green' energy is directly proportional to the global demand for energy resources. Understanding how green innovation influences a company's capacity for sustainable development is essential for identifying the factors that influence sustainable business models and their economic consequences. Green innovation practices encompass a variety of factors, including government regulations, preferences, supplier competence, and consumer concerns. Green technologies, such as green human resource management (HRM) practices and green innovation practices, play a crucial role in attaining sustainable development by conserving energy, protecting the environment, and enhancing business efficiency. Businesses that adopt green innovation acquire a competitive edge and enhance their performance. This chapter emphasizes the importance of green innovation research and application for business stability in Asia, where sustainability and green concepts are acquiring momentum. Customer, government, and societal pressures further emphasize the significance of green innovation in businesses. For the success of ecological innovation practices, collaboration and knowledge-sharing among various

Entrepreneurship and Green Finance Practices, 163–180
Copyright © 2024 Eman Zameer Rahman and Syed Haider Ali Shah
Published under exclusive licence by Emerald Publishing Limited
doi:10.1108/978-1-80455-678-820231009

stakeholders are crucial. The adoption of green innovation practices is influenced by external environmental impacts, stakeholder pressure, and organizational support. Green technology innovation, which concentrates on resource conservation, energy efficiency, and environmental protection, is crucial to the sustainability of a business. This chapter concludes by emphasizing the importance of business sustainability in achieving environmental and economic goals and assuring sustainable corporate development. Long-term success requires an understanding of the process of value creation, delivery, and capture within sustainable business models.

Keywords: Green innovation; green technology; sustainable business models; sustainable development; Asia; stakeholder pressure; environmental laws; business sustainability

1. Introduction

In the late 1980s, people started reevaluating the effects of humans on the planet. Many competing theories have been advanced in this area, each with its take on how to protect the environment while keeping the economy thriving. The term 'sustainable development' is used to describe these theories. Sustainable development focusses on minimizing negative impacts on ecosystems, using green technology as the foundation for green innovation and overall innovative growth, with an aim to safeguard the right of future generations to a quality environment. The growth of 'green' energy is directly related to the increasing demand for energy resources across nations (Mantaeva et al., 2021). Against the background of growing environmental concerns, studying how green innovation affects businesses' capacity for sustainable development can broaden our understanding of what factors affect businesses' capacity for sustainable development and what economic consequences stem from such innovations. The understanding of sustainable development can serve as a useful point of reference for publicly listed companies as they make important strategic choices (Liao et al., 2022).

The phrase 'go green' refers to an endeavour that is mostly used by businesses to address issues related to the environment. Over many years, the subfield of management sciences that is concerned with strategies to achieve environmentally friendly capabilities and newly emerging eco-friendly practices has been the centre of attention and discussion (Ullah, 2017). Businesses need to take into account the important aspects and predecessors in their operations to make it easier for consumers to adopt green innovation (GI) (Arfi et al., 2018). These considerations of GI practices include government regulatory bodies and their regulations (Kammerer, 2009), professional and owner preferences (Huang et al., 2009), supplier and partner competence (Chiou et al., 2011), and organizational, technological, and environmental aspects (Lin & Ho, 2011), and Consumer concerns (Zhu et al., 2017).

Green technologies comprise Green HRM practices that make up green technologies (e.g. green administrative support and culture, training and development, compensation, compensation, and benefits, recruitment, and selection), and green innovation practices (e.g. green process, product, marketing, and management). Green Innovation is a crucial strategic approach for achieving sustainable development since it employs measures to conserve energy, protect the environment, recycle waste, and lessen the effects of pollution (Albort-Morant et al., 2018). In addition, Green Innovation can be broken down into subfields like 'green management', 'green marketing', 'green processes', and 'green product', all of which aim to create a more sustainable environment by, respectively, reducing energy consumption, increasing resource efficiency, limiting pollution emissions, and recycling waste; boosting business efficiency; and giving people access to a cleaner, healthier environment (Seman et al., 2019).

Now more than ever, businesses are keen to attain a higher Green Innovation (GI). Thus, GI is a crucial tool for companies that want to take on the green consciousness challenges while gaining a competitive advantage (Chang, 2011; Chen & Chang, 2013; Chen et al., 2012). When the ecological needs of the company and its stakeholders (clients, business associates, governments, and society at large) can be met, GI can improve business performance. The ability of businesses to engage in sustainable development is greatly enhanced by the green innovation concept. Liao et al. (2022) stated that private companies benefit more from green innovation's capacity-building effects for sustainable development than do state-owned ones. Furthermore, only green innovation invention patents can significantly enhance a company's capacity for sustainable development. Green innovation may impede replication increasing barriers to other competitors and enabling developers to gain a competitive edge (Chang, 2011; Rennings, 2000). Literature has been conducted to determine the factors of green innovation practices that include environmental regulations, supply chains, ethics, and legal frameworks (Feng & Chen, 2018; Seman et al., 2019).

Sustainability in asset operations and pollution prevention have emerged as major global issues due to constrained resources and environmental concerns (Wang et al., 2021). Eco-friendly professionals are striking a balance between resource consumption of resources (Chan et al., 2012). In order to survive, many businesses have embraced strategies that generate and enhance economic value (Porter & Kramer, 2019). Rapid economic development has resulted in the excessive use of non-renewable resources, which has harmed the environment and resulted in several environmental concerns (Atlin & Gibson, 2017). In response, organizations have embraced environmentally friendly practices (Afridi et al., 2020) to boost productivity and get an edge over rivals (Claver et al., 2007; Rusinko, 2007), and to have a positive branding image (Chen, 2008; Hillestad et al., 2010). Hydropower, wind energy, solar and bioenergy, and geothermal energy are only a few examples of the 'green' technologies that the majority of developed nations are investing heavily in.

Concerning green innovation practices in Asia, China has lately committed to decreased emissions and increased energy efficiency to combat the effects of environmental impact on the manufacturing sector, manufacturing, logistic firms, and express firms (Chu et al., 2019; Song et al., 2020; Zhang et al., 2020). Due to the fact that Pakistan is a developing economy and in the early phases of green innovation practices adoption, the country looked into the service and manufacturing sectors to identify the problem of conducting and focussing on stakeholder demand for Green Innovative Practices (GIP) (Shahzad et al., 2020), and its impact on the organizational and environmental performance (Wang et al., 2021). There is still a huge gap in research and application of green innovation for business stability in Asia.

There is optimized pressure from customers, government, and society to practice green innovation in present and is increasing. Foo (2018) argued that companies need to be more proactive about the green environmental challenges of their supply chain execution because of rising stakeholder and public knowledge and pressure in this area. Customers, society, and government all put pressure on the sectors to reduce their carbon footprints, conserve energy, avoid damaging the environment, and ensure sustainability (Chang, 2011; Chen, 2008; Cordano et al., 2010; Lin & Ho, 2011). Therefore, it is essential to pay attention to the perspectives of stakeholders within an organization when developing and maintaining GI practices and abilities. The manufacturing industry is under more scrutiny from concerned parties because it is among the most waste-generating in the economy (Chang, 2011; Chen, 2008; Cordano et al., 2010; Lin & Ho, 2011). To learn how different groups of people can have an effect on GI procedures, it is helpful to take a broad look at the organization, as provided by the 'stakeholder theory' (Freeman, 2010). However, to respond to stakeholder pressure, planning is required for the corporate strategy that involves and satisfies all of its stakeholders (Bryson, 2018). Hence, sustainable businesses are required which in turn have developed the need of developing and implementing sustainable business models involving green concepts such as green innovation and green technology.

This chapter focusses and addresses this issue other than describing the concepts and importance of Green Innovation (GI) and green technology on sustainable businesses and issues and challenges of the contemporary sustainable business models (SBMs). The methodology employed in this chapter involves a comprehensive review of existing literature and research on the topic of green innovation, green technology, and sustainable business models in Asia.

2. Green Innovation

The prevalent definition of innovation is the introduction of new products, offerings, or procedures that involve some sort of transformation within an organization (Ashok et al., 2014). The term Green Innovation (GI) has emerged since the late 1990s (Sezen & Çankaya, 2013). GI is defined by Xie et al. (2019) as improved products, techniques, practices, processes, and systems that aim to prevent or reduce ecological harm and subsidize the sustainability of firms. Green product designs and configurations that render recycling of waste or business sustainable development is a strategic response to green innovation (Chen et al., 2014). Ilvitskaya and Prihodko (2018) defined GI as 'the new or modified products and processes, including technology, managerial, and organizational innovations, which help to sustain the surrounding environment'. There are generally two categories of GI research works; company's competencies (Gluch et al., 2009), and eco-friendly policies and procedures (Ho et al., 2009; Lin & Ho, 2008).

In the body of research that focusses on technological innovations, the terms 'product innovation' and 'process innovation' are frequently differentiated from one another (Chen et al., 2006). Therefore, green product innovations (providing new eco-friendly products to consumers) and green process innovations (or 'greening' business procedures) are the two main categories of GI (Tang et al., 2018). The negative environmental impacts of the products are minimized through green product innovation through changes to the product's design and features. Innovations that lessen their impact on the environment in any way, whether during the sourcing of raw materials, the actual making of the product, or its final distribution, are collectively known as 'green process innovation' (Klassen & Whybark, 1999). Green Innovation products and processes development is dependent not just on the availability of internal resources but also on a comprehensive set of knowledge-related competencies. There are positive and significant relationships between the organizations' efforts to foster collaboration and knowledge sharing among their employees and their efforts to develop proactive environmental strategies (Aragon-Correa et al., 2013).

GI performance ensures that sustainability is at the core of corporate innovation activities; and various strategies are implemented to achieve sustainability as firms may modify their activities to address environmental challenges (De Marchi & Grandinetti, 2013; Ghisetti et al., 2015). Research and development cooperation with suppliers encourages environmentally responsible innovation to a greater extent as this characteristic is a direct consequence of the extremely complex nature that is fundamental to environmental innovations (De Marchi, 2012). This level of complexity can only be overcome by combining the knowledge and skills of a diverse group of specialists, who must necessarily be based in different workplaces (De Marchi & Grandinetti, 2013). Given the complexity involved in taking a proactive, inventive strategy to achieve environmental effect minimization, businesses must develop and maintain limited cooperation ties with the diverse stakeholders within their value network.

Green and environmental concerns aren't typically at the core of a company's operations, which leads to the lack of the expertise and resources to effectively encourage GIs management (Cainelli et al., 2015). In addition, the environmental problems complexity necessitates that organizations build both a broad and extensive web of connections with the stakeholders (Ngai et al., 2008). External to the firm's sphere of influence, these stakeholders appear to be a resource of environmental expertise. The efficiency of the GIP will be aided by the collaboration and sharing of information with external stakeholders (Albort-Morant et al., 2016).

Improvements in environmental performance can be seen as a direct and indirect result of environmental management practices, demonstrating the importance of eco-friendly practices (Famiyeh et al., 2018). Correspondingly, emerging customer-centered concerns about environmental protection have made ecological management an integral aspect of many businesses' strategic policies (Chiou et al., 2011; Khan et al., 2019). Environmental regulations can perform dual tasks, increasing profits and reducing pollution (Kammerer, 2009). GI practices, both within and outside of companies, are essential for influencing economic and ecological performance objectives (Khan & Qianli, 2017; Saeed et al., 2018). There is a strong correlation between a company's internal and external environmental orientation and the adoption of GI practices, according to research conducted by Feng et al. (2018).

Furthermore, encouragement for practicing green innovation and responsible business practices is found to be influenced by stakeholder pressure, societal expectations, and organizational support (Lee et al., 2018; Shahzad et al., 2020). Sustainable performance is significantly impacted by green innovation technology, supplier intervention, and regulation all of which were mediated by service innovation capabilities (Fernando et al., 2019).

3. Green Technology

The term 'green technology innovation' refers to any new method of environmental management or technological development to protect the environment (Mengxin et al., 2021). Despite the potential of innovation practice to boost productivity, hardly consider the potential external environmental impacts; for instance, technological innovation often focusses solely on increasing output in energy-intensive industries. Consequently, businesses across sectors adhere to the green principle and devote increasing resources to addressing both economic growth and environmental issues (Gorelick et al., 2020). Green technology is the technological innovation that takes into account the conservation of resources and energy, which seeks to prevent or decrease pollution and other forms of environmental harm, ensuring the reduction of the ecological footprint in technological innovation.

As stated by Zhou et al. (2014) and Li et al. (2018), the goals of green technology innovation are long-term sustainable development, providing benefits in social, environmental, and economic, terms, the conservation of resources and energy, and the eradication of environmental and degradation. Since green technology innovation takes environmental effectiveness into account, it can be weakened when enterprises' self-interests and social benefits come into conflict during the process of implementing green technology innovation (Braun & Wield, 1994; Li et al., 2019).

4. Business Sustainability

Corporate sustainability management identifies business sustainability as one of its central components. Effects on environmental and economic performance dimensions from green human resource management activities are discussed by Singh et al., 2020. Business sustainability can be viewed as attaining environmental objectives while simultaneously achieving sustainable corporate development. According to Székely and Knirsch (2005), business sustainability is based on the processes of resulting in social and corporate sustainability, expanding sustainability and society's economic growth. Environmental pollution governance, market share, and corporate profits are all indicators of a company's performance and efficiency (Russo & Fouts, 1997; Sharma, 2000).

The value proposition and the ability to innovate serve as the logical foundation for long-term success in business (Molina-Castillo et al., 2021). However, for the sustainability dimensions, it is important to comprehend the process of value creation, delivery, and capture within the company. The social, economic, and environmental value creation (Evans et al., 2017) is what full sustainability aims for. Business is not sustainable if any one of the dimensions is not taken into account as presented in Fig. 9.1. The Brazilian cosmetics firm Natura serves as a model for how to create cutting-edge SBM. It competes with other major players like L'Oreal, P&G, and Unilever by providing high-quality cosmetics to consumers with value. Its value creation process is unique in that it seeks to protect the Amazonia's Forest while also enhancing the economic well-being of local families (Minatogawa et al., 2022).

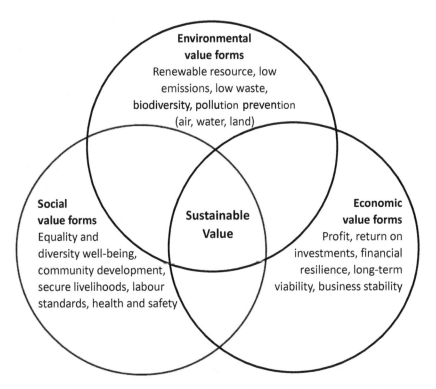

Fig. 9.1.   Sustainability Dimensions of the Triple Bottom Line for Business Stability (Evans et al., 2017).

Since the notion of sustainability was first introduced, several governments have implemented strict environmental regulations and established long-term sustainable goals to combat environmental change; many businesses have also adopted and developed green or environmentally friendly innovations. Insight into how environmental innovation influences the financial, environmental, and social outcomes of businesses is intriguing (Long et al., 2017; Singh et al., 2020). Sustainability measures take into account financial aspects, ecological factors, social performance, and environmental outcomes (Asadi et al., 2020).

In terms of business sustainability, environmental performance is often considered a crucial element. It may also be thought of as a company's efficiency in minimizing carbon dioxide emissions such as an increase in renewable materials, reducing environmental incidents and wastage. Corporate sustainability managers should prioritize green transformation, reduction of carbon emissions, and sustainable social, environmental, and economic development (Hoffman, 2018). Environmental performance can be improved through corporate green innovation (Lee & Min, 2015; Long et al., 2017). Corporate governance, the firm's size, and corporate reputation influence social performance (Aggarwal & Dow, 2012).

Social responsibility based on green innovation is seen as fundamental and is directly associated with the success of innovation (Wang & Berens, 2015). Javed et al. (2020) suggest that responsible leadership can enhance business reputation and performance and that CSR can play a role in boosting a company's financial performance (Javed et al., 2020). GI practices are influenced by a wide range of drivers, including Green supply chain management practices, corporate environmental ethics, and environmental law (El-Kassar & Singh, 2019; Feng & Chen, 2018; Gao et al., 2018; Seman et al., 2019). To investigate the second-order variables of green innovation and company sustainability, Li et al. (2020) used alternative models to examine the interaction between second-order variables such as green innovation and company sustainability (Fig. 9.2). They broke down green innovation into three distinct sub-categories: green product innovation, green publicity, and recycling, while business sustainability was sub-categories into social performance, financial performance, and environmental performance.

Business sustainability is significantly impacted by green innovation, and recycling had a greater effect on social performance than green publicity. Though green product innovation has a greater effect on financial performance than green publicity, green publicity has a significant impact on environmental performance. The outcomes of financial and social performance are enhanced by environmental performance.

5. Sustainable Business Model Innovation

According to Lazenby (2018), the key to maintaining a competitive edge is developing a groundbreaking innovation that rivals are simply not able to produce counterfeit. Daft (2011) argues similarly, noting that securing a company's

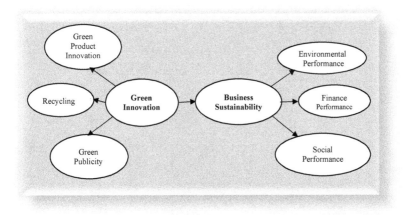

Fig. 9.2.   Model of Green Innovation and Business Sustainability
Factors (Li et al., 2020).

sustainable competitive advantage will set the organization apart providing it
with a distinguished position and reputation in the market. A sustainable business
aims at improving the lives of its customers, employees, and the community as a
whole, while also protecting the environment (Savitz & Weber, 2006). Taking into
account these arguments, we can conclude that sustainable businesses require a
Sustainable Business Model.

Changes in one aspect of sustainability will inevitably have effects on others
(Meza-Ruiz et al., 2017) due to the interconnected nature of business, their
models, and the environment in which they operate in. Sustainable businesses aim
to minimize their impact on the environment that relates to the term sustainable
development (Hart & Milstein, 2003). Conflicts between social, environmental,
and economic goals are common in sustainable development (Van der Byl &
Slawinski, 2015). The so-called 'triple bottom line' framework is defined by these
three criteria of social, environmental, and economic objectives. Therefore, to
meet current and future human needs and realize aspirations, a process of change
known as sustainable development is necessary. This change requires a delicate
balancing act between investment decisions, resource exploitation, institutional
transformations, and the direction of technological development. (Keeble, 1987).
Processes in SBMI include a quest for equilibrium through change, which is
necessary for meeting the triple bottom line (Minatogawa et al., 2022).

The concept of sustainable business model innovation (SBMI) is closely related
to that of business model innovation. Five important gaps or issues and challenges in SBMI management were identified by Minatogawa et al. (2022), who
developed a complete framework for SBMI management and identified areas
where future research might potentially contribute to sustainable development
(Fig. 9.3). There are five key challenges to systematic SBMI: (1) In order to solve

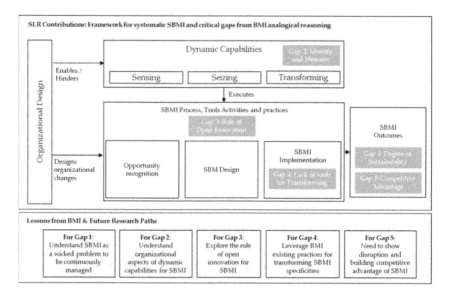

Fig. 9.3.   Framework for Systematic Sustainable Business Model
Innovation (Minatogawa et al., 2022).

the issue of the sustainable business model, a systematic approach to SBMI is
required; (2) the inability of defining dynamic capability dimensions for SBMI; (3)
due to a lack of research, we don't know how innovation process might help the
SBMI system; (4) lack of resources to aid in the implementation of SBMI; and (5)
the imperative to learn more about SBMI's potential advantages in the marketplace. Moreover, the gap is visible for green technology and green innovation
mentions though the innovation in SBMI points to Green Innovation that can be
further researched in these accurate phenomena.

6. Conclusion

In conclusion, this chapter discussed the concepts of green innovation (GI), and
green technology, and their importance in achieving sustainable business models
(SBMs). The creation of sustainable development ideas was a result of a change in
thinking about how human activity affects the environment in the late 1980s. To
protect the environment for future generations, sustainable development attempts
to reduce negative effects on ecosystems, and use green technology for innovation
and growth.

Sustainability can only be attained with the help of green innovation, which
includes green product and process improvements. Green process innovations
seek to cut back on energy use, boost resource efficiency, control pollutant
emissions, and encourage waste recycling, whereas green product innovations

concentrate on reducing environmental impacts through improvements in design and features. These innovations require collaboration and knowledge-sharing among diverse stakeholders, both internal and external to the organization. On the other hand, green technology innovation describes new approaches to environmental management or technological advancements that save the environment. It entails reducing ecological footprints and conserving energy and resources. Innovation in green technology promotes long-term sustainable development, as well as social, environmental, and economic advantages.

The fundamental elements of business sustainability management incorporate these ideas. Sustainable business models aim to advance company growth while achieving environmental goals. They consider business earnings, market share, and environmental pollution governance as measures of effectiveness. The key to long-term success in a sustainable firm is the capacity for innovation and value creation.

This chapter also focussed on the significance of organizational support, environmental laws, and stakeholder views in fostering green innovation and sustainable business practices. The adoption and application of green innovation and technology are influenced by stakeholder pressure, social expectations, and organizational collaboration. Businesses are facing increasing pressure from customers, governments, and society to address environmental concerns, reduce carbon footprints, and ensure sustainability.

The importance of green innovation and technology in developing sustainable business models was emphasized throughout this chapter. It brought attention to how the environmental, economic, and social factors interact and how firms must take into account all three in order to be sustainable. Businesses can improve their capacity for sustainable development, gain a competitive edge, and contribute to a cleaner, healthier environment by embracing green innovation and technology.

7. Recommendations

Encourage government support: Governments in Asia should play a proactive role in promoting green innovation and technologies by implementing supportive policies and regulations. This can include providing incentives such as tax benefits, grants, and subsidies for businesses that adopt and invest in green practices. Additionally, governments should establish clear environmental standards and regulations to ensure businesses adhere to sustainable practices.

Foster collaboration and knowledge sharing: Companies should actively collaborate with suppliers, customers, and other stakeholders to develop and share knowledge related to green innovation practices. This can be achieved through partnerships, joint research projects, and industry networks. By leveraging external expertise and resources, businesses can enhance their green innovation capabilities and improve environmental performance.

Embrace a holistic approach: Businesses should adopt a holistic approach to green innovation, considering not only product innovation but also process innovation. This involves integrating green principles into various aspects of the organization, including production processes, supply chains, and waste management. By taking a comprehensive approach, companies can minimize their environmental impact and maximize sustainable development.

Enhance employee awareness and training: Organizations should prioritize employee awareness and training programmes to foster a culture of sustainability and green innovation. This can include providing training on green practices, promoting environmental consciousness among employees, and incorporating sustainability goals into performance evaluations. By empowering employees with the necessary knowledge and skills, businesses can drive green innovation from within and create a sustainable workforce.

Business needs to address the issues and challenges to Sustainable Business Models: The gaps mentioned in this chapter need to be assessed in detail to counter these challenges in implementing a sustainable business model innovation systematically.

8. Future Directions

Investigate the impact of green innovation on different industries: Further research is needed to explore the specific effects of green innovation on various industries in Asia. Understanding how different sectors, such as manufacturing, services, and logistics, can benefit from and implement green innovation practices will provide valuable insights and help tailor strategies to specific industry needs.

Explore the role of technology in green innovation: The rapid advancement of technology offers new opportunities for green innovation and sustainable business practices. Future studies should investigate the potential of emerging technologies, such as artificial intelligence, blockchain, and renewable energy systems, in driving green innovation and enhancing sustainability in Asian businesses.

Assess the economic benefits of green innovation: While the environmental benefits of green innovation are well-documented, further research should focus on quantifying the economic advantages for businesses. This includes analyzing the cost savings, market opportunities, and competitive advantages that can be achieved through the adoption of green practices. Such assessments will help strengthen the business case for green innovation and encourage wider adoption.

Empirically assess the issues and challenges with SBM: There is a need to address the challenges and issues with the contemporary sustainable business models that are required to be examined in detail in order for businesses to apply them smoothly and attain their aimed SDGs (Sustainable Development Goals).

References

Afridi, S. A., Afsar, B., Shahjehan, A., Khan, W., Rehman, Z. U., & Khan, M. A. (2020). Impact of corporate social responsibility attributions on employee's extra role behaviors: Moderating role of ethical corporate identity and interpersonal trust. *Corporate Social Responsibility and Environmental Management, 114.*

Aggarwal, R., & Dow, S. (2012). Corporate governance and business strategies for climate change and environmental mitigation. *The European Journal of Finance, 18*, 311–331.

Albort-Morant, G., Leal-Millán, A., Cepeda-Carrion, G., & Henseler, J. (2018). Developing green innovation performance by fostering of organizational knowledge and coopetitive relations. *Review of Managerial Science, 12*, 499–517. https://doi.org/10.1007/s11846-017-0270-z

Albort-Morant, G., Leal, A., & Cepeda-Carrion, G. (2016). The antecedents of green innovation performance: A model of learning and capabilities. *Journal of Business Research, 69*, 4912–4917.

Aragón-Correa, J. A., Martín-Tapia, I., & Hurtado-Torres, N. E. (2013). Proactive environmental strategies and employee inclusion: The positive effects of information sharing and promoting collaboration and the influence of uncertainty. *Organization & Environment, 26*(2), 139–161. https://doi.org/10.1177/10860266 13489034

Arfi, W. B., Hikkerova, L., & Sahut, J. M. (2018). External knowledge sources, green innovation and performance. *Technological Forecasting and Social Change, 129*, 210–220. https://doi.org/10.1016/j.techfore.2017.09.017

Asadi, S., Pourhashemi, S., Nilashi, M., Abdullah, R., Samad, S., Yadegaridehkordi, E., & Razali, N. (2020). Investigating influence of green innovation on sustainability performance: A case on Malaysian hotel industry. *Journal of Cleaner Production, 258*, 120860.

Ashok, M., Narula, R., & Martinez-Noya, A. (2014). *End-user collaboration for process innovation in services: The role of internal resources.* Maastricht Economic and Social Research Institute on Innovation and Technology (UNU-MERIT) & Maastricht Graduate School of Governance (MGSoG).

Atlin, C., & Gibson, R. (2017). Lasting regional gains from non-renewable resource extraction: The role of sustainability-based cumulative effects assessment and regional planning for mining development in Canada. *The Extractive Industries and Society, 4*, 36–52. https://doi.org/10.1016/j.exis.2017.01.005

Braun, E., & Wield, D. (1994). Regulation as a means for the social control of technology. *Technology Analysis & Strategic Management, 6*(3), 259–272. https://doi.org/10.1080/09537329408524171å

Bryson, J. M. (2018). *Strategic planning for public and nonprofit organizations: A guide to strengthening and sustaining organizational achievement*: John Wiley & Sons.

Cainelli, G., De Marchi, V., & Grandinetti, R. (2015). Does the development of environmental innovation require different resources? Evidence from Spanish manufacturing firms. *Journal of Cleaner Production, 94*, 211–220.

Chang, C. H. (2011). The influence of corporate environmental ethics on competitive advantage: The mediation role of green innovation. *Journal of Business Ethics, 104*, 361–370. https://doi.org/10.1007/s10551-011-0914-x

Chan, H. K., He, H., & Wang, W. Y. (2012). Green marketing and its impact on supply chain management in industrial markets. *Industrial Marketing Management, 41*, 557–562. https://doi.org/10.1016/j.indmarman.2012.04.002

Chen, Y. S. (2008). The positive effect of green intellectual capital on competitive advantages of firms. *Journal of Business Ethics, 77*, 271–286. https://doi.org/10.1007/s10551-006-9349-1

Chen, Y.-S., & Chang, C.-H. (2013). Greenwash and green trust: The mediation effects of green consumer confusion and green perceived risk. *Journal of Business Ethics, 114*(3), 489–500. http://www.jstor.org/stable/23433794

Chen, Y., Chang, C., & Lin, Y. (2014). The determinants of green radical and incremental innovation performance: Green shared vision, green absorptive capacity, and green organizational ambidexterity. *Sustainability, 6*(11), 7787–7806.

Chen, Y. S., Chang, C. H., & Wu, F. S. (2012). Origins of green innovations: The differences between proactive and reactive green innovations. *Management Decision, 50*(3), 368–398. https://doi.org/10.1108/00251741211121619

Chen, Y. S., Lai, S. B., & Wen, C. T. (2006). The influence of green innovation performance on corporate advantage in Taiwan. *Journal of Business Ethics, 67*, 331–339. https://doi.org/10.1007/s10551-006-9025-5

Chiou, T. Y., Chan, H. K., Lettice, F., & Chung, S. H. (2011). The influence of greening the suppliers and green innovation on environmental performance and competitive advantage in Taiwan. *Transportation Research Part E: Logistics and Transportation Review, 47*, 822–836. https://doi.org/10.1016/j.tre.2011.05.016

Chu, Z., Wang, L., & Lai, F. (2019). Customer pressure and green innovations at third party logistics providers in China. *International Journal of Logistics Management, 30*, 57–75. https://doi.org/10.1108/ijlm-11-2017-0294

Claver, E., Lopez, M. D., Molina, J. F., & Tarí, J. J. (2007). Environmental management and firm performance: A case study. *Journal of Environmental Management, 84*, 606–619. https://doi.org/10.1016/j.jenvman.2006.09.012

Cordano, M., Marshall, R. S., & Silverman, M. (2010). How do small and medium enterprises go "green"? A study of environmental management programs in the US wine industry. *Journal of Business Ethics, 92*, 463–478. https://doi.org/10.1007/s10551-009-0168-z

Daft, R. (2011). *The leadership experience* (5th ed.). South-Western Cengage Learning.

De Marchi, V. (2012). Environmental innovation and R&D cooperation: Empirical evidence from Spanish manufacturing firms. *Research Policy, 41*(3), 614–623. https://doi.org/10.1016/j.respol.2011.10.002

De Marchi, V., & Grandinetti, R. (2013). Knowledge strategies for environmental innovations: The case of Italian manufacturing firms. *Journal of Knowledge Management, 17*(4), 569–582.

El-Kassar, A.-N., & Singh, S. K. (2019). Green innovation and organizational performance: The influence of big data and the moderating role of management commitment and HR practices. *Technological Forecasting. Social Change 144*, 483–498. https://doi.org/10.1016/j.techfore.2017.12.016

Evans, S., Vladimirova, D., Holgado, M., Fossen, K. V., Yang, M., Silva, E. A., & Barlow, C. Y. (2017). Business model innovation for sustainability: Towards a unified perspective for creation of sustainable business models. *Business Strategy and the Environment, 26*, 597–608. https://doi.org/10.1002/bse

Famiyeh, S., Adaku, E., Amoako-Gyampah, K., Asante-Darko, D., & Amoatey, C. T. (2018). Environmental management practices, operational competitiveness and environmental performance: Empirical evidence from a developing country. *Journal of Manufacturing Technology Management, 29*, 588–607. https://doi.org/10.1108/jmtm-06-2017-0124

Feng, Z., & Chen, W. (2018). Environmental regulation, green innovation, and industrial green development: An empirical analysis based on the spatial Durbin model. *Sustainability, 10,* 223. https://doi.org/10.3390/su10010223

Feng, L., Zhao, W., Li, H., & Song, Y. (2018). The effect of environmental orientation on green innovation: Do political ties matter? *Sustainability, 10.* https://doi.org/10.3390/su10124674

Fernando, Y., Jabbour, C. J. C., & Wah, W.-X. (2019). Pursuing green growth in technology firms through the connections between environmental innovation and sustainable business performance: Does service capability matter? *Resources, Conservation and Recycling, 141,* 8–20. https://doi.org/10.1016/j.resconrec.2018.09.031

Foo, M. Y. (2018). *Green purchasing capabilities and practices towards triple bottom line performance: Moderating effects of institutional pressure.* Phd Thesis, University of Malaya.

Freeman, R. E. (2010). *Strategic management: A stakeholder approach.* Cambridge University Press.

Gao, Y., Tsai, S. B., Xue, X., Ren, T., Du, X., Chen, Q., et al. (2018). An empirical study on green innovation efficiency in the green institutional environment. *Sustainability, 10,* 724. https://doi.org/10.3390/su10030724

Ghisetti, C., Marzucchi, A., & Montresor, S. (2015). The open eco-innovation mode. An empirical investigation of eleven European countries. *Research Policy, 44*(5), 1080–1093.

Gluch, P., Gustafsson, M., & Thuvander, L. (2009). An absorptive capacity model for green innovation and performance in the construction industry. *Construction Management & Economics, 27,* 451–464. https://doi.org/10.1080/01446190902896645

Gorelick, J., Walmsley, N., & Walmsley, N. (2020). The greening of municipal infrastructure investments: Technical assistance, instruments, and city champions. *Green Finance, 2,* 114–134. https://doi.org/10.3934/gf.2020007

Hart, S., & Milstein, M. (2003). Creating sustainable value. *Academy of Management Perspectives, 17,* 56–69.

Hillestad, T., Xie, C., & Haugland, S. A. (2010). Innovative corporate social responsibility: The founder's role in creating a trustworthy corporate brand through "green innovation". *Journal of Product & Brand Management, 19,* 440–451. https://doi.org/10.1108/10610421011085758

Hoffman, A. J. (2018). The next phase of business sustainability. *Stanford Social Innovation Review, 16,* 34–39.

Ho, Y., Lin, C. Y., & Chiang, S. H. (2009). Organizational determinants of green innovation implementation in the logistics industry. *International Journal of Organizational Innovation, 2,* 3.

Huang, Y. C., Ding, H. B., & Kao, M. R. (2009). Salient stakeholder voices: Family business and green innovation adoption. *Journal of Management and Organization.* https://doi.org/10.5172/jmo.2009.15.3.309

Ilvitskaya, S., & Prihodko, V. (2018). Innovative technologies in the field of topography, land management, territorial planning, construction and architecture. *IOP Conference Series: Materials Science and Engineering, 365.* https://doi.org/10.1088/1757-899x/365/2/022030.022030.

Javed, M., Rashid, M., Hussain, G., & Ali, H. (2020). The effects of corporate social responsibility on corporate reputation and firm financial performance: Moderating role of responsible leadership. *Corporate Social Responsibility and Environmental Management, 27,* 1395–1409.

Kammerer, D. (2009). The effects of customer benefit and regulation on environmental product innovation: Empirical evidence from appliance manufacturers in Germany. *Ecological Economy, 68,* 2285–2295. https://doi.org/10.1016/j.ecolecon.2009.02.016

Keeble, B. (1987). World commission on environment and development report of the world commission on environment and development: Our common future (the Brundtland report). *Medicine, Conflict and Survival, 4.*

Khan, M. A., Ali, M., Usman, M., Saleem, S., & Jianguo, D. (2019). Interrelationships between ethical leadership, green psychological climate, and organizational environmental citizenship behavior: The moderating role of gender. *Frontiers in Psychology, 10,* 1977. https://doi.org/10.3389/fpsyg.2019.01977

Khan, S. A. R., & Qianli, D. (2017). Impact of green supply chain management practices on firms' performance: An empirical study from the perspective of Pakistan. *Environmental Science and Pollution Research International, 24*(20), 16829–16844. https://doi.org/10.1007/s11356-017-9172-5

Klassen, R. D., & Whybark, D. C. (1999). The impact of environmental technologies on manufacturing performance. *Academy of Management Journal, 42,* 599–615. https://doi.org/10.5465/256982

Lazenby, K. (2018). *The strategic management process: A South African perspective.* Van Schaik.

Lee, J. W., Kim, Y. M., & Kim, Y. E. (2018). Antecedents of adopting corporate environmental responsibility and green practices. *Journal of Business Ethics, 148,* 397–409. https://doi.org/10.1007/s10551-016-3024-y

Lee, K., & Min, B. (2015). Green R&D for eco-innovation and its impact on carbon emissions and firm performance. *Journal of Cleaner Production, 108,* 534–542.

Liao, Y., Qiu, X., Wu, A., Sun, Q., Shen, H., & Li, P. (2022). Assessing the impact of green innovation on corporate sustainable development. *Frontiers in Energy Research, 9,* 800848. https://doi.org/10.3389/fenrg.2021.800848

Li, T., Huang, Z., Huang, Z., & Drakeford, B. M. (2019). Statistical measurement of total factor productivity under resource and environmental constraints. *National Accounting Review, 1*(16–27), 16–27. https://doi.org/10.3934/nar.2019.1.16

Li, Z., Liao, G., Wang, Z., & Huang, Z. (2018). Green loan and subsidy for promoting clean production innovation. *Journal of Cleaner Production, 187,* 421–431. https://doi.org/10.1016/j.jclepro.2018.03.066

Li, L., Msaad, H., Sun, H., Tan, M. X., & Lu, Y. (2020). Green innovation and business sustainability: New evidence from energy intensive industry in China. *International Journal of Environmental Research and Public Health, 17*(7826), 1–18. https://doi.org/10.3390/ijerph17217826

Lin, C., & Ho, Y. H. (2008). An empirical study on logistics service providers' intention to adopt green innovations. *Journal of Technology Management and Innovation, 3,* 17–26.

Lin, C. Y., & Ho, Y. H. (2011). Determinants of green practice adoption for logistics companies in China. *Journal of Business Ethics, 98,* 67–83. https://doi.org/10.1007/s10551-010-0535-9

Long, X., Chen, Y., Du, J., Oh, K., & Han, I. (2017). Environmental innovation and its impact on economic and environmental performance: Evidence from Korean-owned firms in China. *Energy Policy, 107*, 131–137.

Mantaeva, E. I., Slobodchikova, I. V., Goldenova, V. S., Avadaeva, I. V., & Nimgirov, A. G. (2021). Green technologies as a factor in the sustainable development of the national economy. *IOP Conference Series: Earth and Environmental Science, 848*, 012133. https://doi.org/10.1088/1755-1315/848/1/012133

Mengxin, W., Yanling, L., & Gaoke, L. (2021). Research on the impact of green technology innovation on energy total factor productivity. *Based on Provincial Data of China, 9*. https://doi.org/10.3389/fenvs.2021.710931

Meza-Ruiz, I., Rocha-Lona, L., del Rocío Soto-Flores, M., Garza-Reyes, J., Kumar, V., & Lopez-Torres, G. (2017). Measuring business sustainability maturity-levels and best practices. *Procedia Manufacturing, 11*, 751–759.

Minatogawa, V., Franco, M., Rampasso, I., Holgado, M., Garrido, D., Pinto, H., & Quadros, R. (2022). Towards systematic sustainable business model innovation: What can we learn from business model innovation. *Sustainability, 14*, 2939. https://doi.org/10.3390/su14052939

Molina-Castillo, F., Sinkovics, N., & Sinkovics, R. (2021). Sustainable business model innovation: Review, analysis and impact on society. *Sustainability, 13*, 8906.

Ngai, E., Jin, C., & Liang, T. (2008). A qualitative study of inter-organizational knowledge management in complex products and systems development. *R & D Management, 38*(4), 421–440.

Porter, M. E., & Kramer, M. R. (2019). Creating shared value. In *Managing sustainable business*. Springer.

Rennings, K. (2000). Redefining innovation – Eco-innovation research and the contribution from ecological economics. *Ecological Economics, 32*(2), 319–332. https://doi.org/10.1016/s0921-8009(99)00112-3

Rusinko, C. (2007). Green manufacturing: An evaluation of environmentally sustainable manufacturing practices and their impact on competitive outcomes. *IEEE Transactions on Engineering Management, 54*, 445–454. https://doi.org/10.1109/tem.2007.900806

Russo, M., & Fouts, P. (1997). A resource-based perspective on corporate environmental performance and profitability. *Academy of Management Journal, 40*, 534–559.

Saeed, A., Jun, Y., Nubuor, S., Priyankara, H., & Jayasuriya, M. (2018). Institutional pressures, green supply chain management practices on environmental and economic performance: A two theory view. *Sustainability, 10*, 1517. https://doi.org/10.3390/su10051517

Savitz, A., & Weber, K. (2006). *The triple bottom line: How today's best-run companies are achieving economic, social, and environmental success-and how you can too*. Jossey-Bass.

Seman, N. A., Govindan, K., Mardani, A., Zakuan, N., Saman, M. Z., Hooker, R. E., & Ozkul, S. (2019). The mediating effect of green innovation on the relationship between green supply chain management and environmental performance. *Journal of Cleaner Production, 229*, 115–127.

Sezen, B., & Çankaya, S. Y. (2013). Effects of green manufacturing and eco-innovation on sustainability performance. *Procedia – Social and Behavioral Sciences, 99*, 154–163.

Shahzad, M., Qu, Y., Javed, S. A., Zafar, A. U., & Rehman, S. U. (2020). Relation of environment sustainability to CSR and green innovation: A case of Pakistani manufacturing industry. *Journal of Cleaner Production, 253*, 119938. https://doi.org/10.1016/j.jclepro. 2019.119938

Sharma, S. (2000). Managerial interpretations and organizational context as predictors of corporate choice of environmental strategy. *Academy of Management Journal, 43*, 681–697.

Singh, S., Del Giudice, M., Chierici, R., & Graziano, D. (2020). Green innovation and environmental performance: The role of green transformational leadership and green human resource management. *Technological Forecasting and Social Change, 150*.

Song, M., Yang, M. X., Zeng, K. J., & Feng, W. (2020). Green knowledge sharing, stakeholder pressure, absorptive capacity, and green innovation: Evidence from Chinese manufacturing firms. *Business Strategy and the Environment, 29*, 1517–1531. https://doi.org/10.1002/bse.2450

Székely, F., & Knirsch, M. (2005). Responsible leadership and corporate social responsibility: Metrics for sustainable performance. *European Management Journal, 23*, 628–647.

Tang, M., Walsh, G., Lerner, D., Fitza, M. A., & Li, Q. (2018). Green innovation, managerial concern and firm performance: An empirical study. *Business Strategy and the Environment, 27*, 39–51. https://doi.org/10.1002/bse.1981

Ullah, M. (2017). Integrating environmental sustainability into human resource management: A comprehensive review on green human resource management. *Maghreb Review of Economics and Management, 4*(1), 6–22. https://platform.almanhal.com/Files/Articles/103460

Van der Byl, C., & Slawinski, N. (2015). Embracing tensions in corporate sustainability: A review of research from win-wins and trade-offs to paradoxes and beyond. *Organization & Environment, 28*, 54–79.

Wang, Y., & Berens, G. (2015). The impact of four types of corporate social performance on reputation and financial performance. *Journal of Business Ethics, 131*, 337–359.

Wang, H., Khan, M., Anwar, F., Shahzad, F., & Adu, D. M. (2021). Green innovation practices and its impacts on environmental and organizational performance. *Frontiers in Psychology, 11*, 553625. https://doi.org/10.3389/fpsyg.2020.553625

Xie, X., Huo, J., & Zou, H. (2019). Green process innovation, green product innovation, and corporate financial performance: A content analysis method. *Journal of Business Research, 101*, 697–706.

Zhang, H., He, J., Shi, X., Hong, Q., Bao, J., & Xue, S. (2020). Technology characteristics, stakeholder pressure, social influence, and green innovation: Empirical evidence from Chinese express companies. *Sustainability, 12*, 2891. https://doi.org/10.3390/su12072891

Zhu, Q., Feng, Y., & Choi, S. B. (2017). The role of customer relational governance in environmental and economic performance improvement through green supply chain management. *Journal of Cleaner Production, 155*, 46–53. https://doi.org/10.1016/j.jclepro.2016.02.124

Part 2
From Academic and Behavioural
Perspective

Chapter 10

Does Green Blogging Affect Consumer Green Behaviour? Moderating Role of Green Psychology Variable

Wasim Ahmad, Rana Muhammad Sohail Jafar, Naveed R. Khan, Irfan Hameed and Noshin Fatima

Abstract

The sources and platforms utilized for environmental communication have been significantly expanded by the emergence of social media. The validity, form, and content of environmental communication processes are particularly radical departures from conventional media, making personal green blogs important of study as areas of everyday culture politics where people make understanding of environmental challenges. There is currently a lack of research on how social media might encourage green behaviours. This research reveals the impact of social media use and green blogging on green purchasing behaviour, which is supported by the social learning theory. Present study shows that social media use and green blogging have a substantial positive connection, drawing on a sample of 580 respondents from Pakistan examined using structural equation modelling. Both notions have a considerable impact on consumers' intentions to make green purchases, and social media trust plays a moderating role in this relationship. Furthermore, social media trust considerably modifies the connections between green blogging and social media use that is related to green behaviour. The current study is novel and offers important information to understand how social media might promote eco-friendly habits and behaviour.

Keywords: Green blogging; Social media usage; green behaviour; trust in social media; green products; green psychology

Entrepreneurship and Green Finance Practices, 183–192
doi:10.1108/978-1-80455-678-820231010

1. Introduction

In July 2022, 4.70 billion social media users spend an average two and half hours daily on social media platforms (Tao & Fisher, 2022). Social media plays a key role in influencing the behaviours of individuals and societies (Lee & Hsieh, 2022) Social media holds the capacity to alter sustainable purchase decisions that affect sustainable consumption. Therefore, organizations are making use of social media to disseminate information regarding green products and enhance public awareness regarding green consumption. In the field of sustainability, green consumption offers consumers with the opportunity to avert environmental issues, and an effective way to protect nature lies in purchasing green products (Ahmad & Zhang, 2020).

Therefore, many bloggers also share their blogs on social media for the knowledge sharing about the sustainability and green purchases. Blogging has emerged as the most reliable source for green information in recent years (Pop et al., 2020). The source of information and social media for environmental communication have been dramatically expanded as a result of the blogosphere's expansion and the introduction of other social media. Traditional news sources no longer have ways that demonstrate to the public's attention, like newspapers or radio stations. As an alternative, every business or individual can, in theory, engage with publics that are significantly broader than their own direct and intimate social networks. Blogs, Twitter, and Facebook are just a few of the places where new environmental viewpoints can be voiced (Enke & Borchers, 2021). Various perspectives have been presented regarding the effects of these new platforms and sources for education and learning (Joosse & Brydges, 2018).

Further, the Paris agreement of 2015 concentrates on accomplishing sustainable development (e.g. controlling the global temperature by 2030 and promoting sustainable consumption) (Junsheng et al., 2019). Undoubtedly, these measures are also engrained in green purchase behaviour; consequently, driving the consumers towards sustainable shopping is of prime concern for the respective stakeholders for which they are making considerable efforts. For instance, 82% of organizations are more likely to spend on green marketing, and 74% of such organizations employ the Internet to provoke the users to buy environmentally friendly products (Szabo & Webster, 2021). The efforts of the green advocates are paying off as people are changing their consumption patterns and consequently, many green products are available in the market belonging to different sectors (Cerri et al., 2018). The environmental issues and their unpleasant effects are considered a domineering problem among academicians, businesses, and governments. United Nations is accentuating to positively alter the ecosystem's structure to solve the environmental problems embedded in every individual's action. It cannot be achieved without appropriate awareness, which can play a significant part in inducing a sustainable behaviour and, eventually, sustainable development (Zafar et al., 2021).

The current research argues that social media's contemporary environment may be a vital element in this context, since people have trust and spend a lot of time on such platforms (Zafar et al., 2020). Social media sites increase users' knowledge, reliance, and concern, but its impact is still underexplored in sustainability. Therefore, the current study explicitly concentrates on green purchase behaviour triggered by green blogging in the social media framework in Pakistan. Considering the scope of these constructs, this research tried to explore the impact of social media usage and green blogging on the consumer's green behaviour. Joshi and Rahman (2019) and Feng et al. (2022) posited that individuals must have proper knowledge and awareness ensuring them that they are capable of changing the environment. Thus, this study incorporates the information published on the social media and green blogs to address the under-consideration phenomenon and provide in-depth insights. It is worth mentioning that despite majority of the research being conducted in the developed countries, the awareness regarding green purchase behaviour is growing in developing countries (Cerri et al., 2018; Zaremohzzabieh et al., 2021).

This study aims to close a critical research gap by studying about the social media usage, social media trust, and green blogging that serve as the underlying pathologies and major determinants of green purchase intention in the setting of social media. Current study proposed a conceptual framework based on the social learning theory, which holds that human behaviour can be learnt by witnessing other people's behaviour and is reproduced over time (Bandura & McCelland, 1977). The current study contends, in line with the social learning theory, that material posted on various social media platforms improves users' environmental knowledge, awareness, and confidence. As a result, individuals are inspired by the eco-friendly actions of other social media users, developing a desire for environmental responsibility, and encouraging sustainable purchasing habits. This study specifically focusses on social media-based green purchase behaviours motivated by green blogging. Leong et al. (2018) theorized the effect of social media on users' inclinations and behaviours for shopping by theorizing usage and browsing as antecedents.

2. Literature Review

2.1 Green Purchase Intention

The term 'green purchase intention' refers to customers' declared eagerness to buy environmentally friendly items. Such consumers' willingness also serves as a driving force for buying green products (Wei et al., 2018). Ecological or environmentally friendly items are other names for 'green' goods. Compared to green products, traditional goods are known to be less hazardous to the environment or to human health. Low-pollution, recyclable, and resource-efficient are the three tenets of the green movement (Ali et al., 2021; Can et al., 2021). Because it satisfies their needs, attitudes, and perceptions of the product, a consumer's purchasing intention is related to how they choose to acquire a good or service (Ahmad & Zhang, 2020). Some recent research also demonstrated the direct association of green purchasing intention (GPI) with green purchase behaviour from various contexts, in addition to the underlying relationship of green purchase intention with social media use and green blogging (GB) for green items

(Pittman et al., 2022; Pop et al., 2020). However, these connections weren't given much attention in the social media environment, especially since researchers are less drawn to green blogging and green information sharing (Zafar et al., 2021).

2.2 Influence of Social Media Usage

A collection of websites and software applications together referred to as 'social media' place a focus on communication, information sharing, teamwork, and crowdsourced input. Social networking websites can be used by people to build relationships in order to overcome social isolation or to have a feeling of belonging (Hwang & Zhang, 2018). People are more conscious of their environmental responsibility as a result of the knowledge they have gained from social media (Chung et al., 2020). The popularity of social networking sites can be a good indicator of a user's surfing behaviour because their pervasiveness has made it possible for people to engage in online blogging with convenience (Zhang et al., 2018). Despite the fact that social media use can have a substantial impact on blogging, previous studies have not examined this topic. As a result, social media usage volume has been made a focus point of this study and is thought to have the following potential effects on user blogging behaviour. The following hypotheses are developed as a result of the aforementioned assertions.

H1. Social media usage has a positive associate with green blogging.

Gonzales and Hancock (2011) claim that utilizing social networking sites can increase one's self-esteem and make the user more eager to brag regarding themselves to their peers. Such encouraging information typically results in a favourable response, which may lead to advantageous social benefits, well-being, and environmental views (Ellison et al., 2011; Junsheng et al., 2019; Sujata et al., 2019). Social media is essential for developing a green mindset because both are concerned with social qualities and users of social media participate in numerous communities. Likewise, some studies have demonstrated that social media use affects environmental views, standard of living, and consumerism (Sujata et al., 2019; Zhou, 2019). Thus:

H2. Social media usage has a positive and significant associate with green purchase intentions.

2.3 Green Blogging

Green bloggers on social media have revolutionized consumer–company communication, including green products, and enabling consumers to have a more engaged purchase experience (Fatma et al., 2020). In comparison to traditional information sources, the blogosphere has expanded in prominence. Green blogs have resulted in a significant shift in information access, how individuals interact with information, and 'whose information counts'. Numerous perspectives have underlined the importance of social media and its psychological consequences on sustainability (Simeone & Scarpato, 2020); however, green blogging and browsing behaviour is an essential part of all social media activities. Social media bloggers are better informed about the activities of their social relation-ships. In order to obtain more environmental data, we expect that social media and green blogs will be used more frequently. This will affect consumers' green behaviour in the following ways:

H3. Green blogging has a positive influence on users' green purchase intention.

2.4 Moderating Role of Perceived Trust in Social Media

The basis for people's trust in others is truthfulness, reliability in behaviour and attitude, and honouring commitments (Zafar et al., 2021). According to earlier studies, it is crucial for groups, societies, or organizations to evoke people's social reactions for green behaviours in the societies (Maon et al., 2019). In relation to the trust transfer theory, diverse sources can convey trust both physically and digitally. Trust had played a key role when the transaction or other activities occurred in an online environment (Sun et al., 2016). Furthermore, individuals had a varying degree of confidence in virtual communities. Individuals that sense high social trust in social networking sites continue to use them, influencing their interactive and purchase behaviour (Zafar et al., 2020). Ventre et al. (2021) stated that the amount of trust that people have in social media platforms may vary. This is due to the fact that strong user views of social media trust may serve to better draw users' attention to posts, comments, or videos that are environmen-tally friendly.

H4. Perceived social media trust positively moderates the association between social media usage and green purchase behaviour.

H5. Perceived social media trust positively moderates the association between green blogging and green purchase behaviour.

3. Research Methodology

A questionnaire was used for data collection to validate the theoretical model. The measurement items were borrowed from the previous literature and modified according to the context of this study. Five-point Likert scale was used to measure the instruments which were anchored from 'strongly disagree' to 'strongly agree'. The use of social media (SMU) was evaluated using seven questions suggested by earlier research (Ellison et al., 2007; Leong et al., 2018). Four items were used to assess green blogging (GB) (Biswas & Roy, 2015). Furthermore, three items were used to measure the trust in social media (TSM) (Hajli, 2014; Ventre et al., 2021). Lastly, green behaviour measured are borrowed from (Ahmad & Zhang, 2020) study. A survey was conducted in Pakistan to get the data during December 2021 to March 2022. Only those respondents were included in the final sample who came across the environmental posts while using social media. Out of 750 distributed surveys, 645 were received, and 65 were found incomplete and therefore they were rejected. There are no restrictions that we were collected data only from these organization. We just mentioned where we have collected the data. The majority of responders (53.7%) were female and between the ages of 18 and 30 (43.6%). A bachelor's degree is obtained by 48.1% of respondents, while between 30,000 and 50,000 rupees is the range of income for 34.6% of respondents. Furthermore, 93.5% of respondents said they used social networking sites on a regular basis. The final valid sample comprised of 580 responses. Table 10.1 lists the organizations that took part in the survey.

4. Results and Conclusion

The structural model was estimated to test the hypotheses once the measurement model was confirmed. The model's findings supported the hypotheses *H1*, *H2*, and *H3*, showing a positive and significant relationship between social media use and green blogging (*H1*: beta = 0.295; $p > 0.005$), social media use and green purchase intentions (*H2*: beta = 0.261; $p > 0.005$), and green blogging and green behaviour (*H3*: beta = 0.222; $p > 0.005$). The hypotheses *H1*, *H2*, and *H3* are acceptable in light of the current results. The current study examines how social media usage, green-blogging, and green behaviour are moderated by perceived social media trust. The relationship between social media use and plans to make green behaviour is moderated by perceived trust in social media (*H4*: beta = 0.307; $p > 0.005$). The association between green blogging and green behaviour is also positively moderated by perceived trust (*H5*: beta = 0.121; $p > 0.005$).

The current research examines the effect of social media in green behaviour. The results show that using social media encouraged people to blog about sustainability. Leong et al. (2018) emphasized the significance of social media use and the intensity of green blogging in the e-commerce context. Users' intents to make green purchases are also highly influenced by social media use and green blogging. These outcomes resemble the general scenario in which (Sujata et al., 2019). They emphasized how social media use shapes people's intentions to recycle. The research reveals that social media use and green blogging encourage consumers to purchase eco-friendly goods. These results are consistent with the

Table 10.1. Organizations That Participated in the Survey.

Sr. #.	Types and Number of Organizations	Surveys Distributed	Respondents	Percentage (%)
1	Banks (10)	100	87	87
2	Colleges and Universities (12)	200	139	69.5
3	IT and Telecommunication Companies (7)	100	80	80
4	Media Channels (10)	150	116	77.3
5	Hospitals (6)	100	75	75
6	Hotels (5)	100	83	83
		T = 750	RB = 580	

viewpoint of Chung et al. (2020), who showed that social media serves as an essential forum for fostering environmental discourse and motivating individuals to live more sustainably. *H1*, *H2*, and *H3* are therefore supported. However, the current study also reveals how green blogging functions as a mediator in the social media space. The level of consumption that social media users engage in differs from the behaviour of green bloggers, which might change depending on the situation. Additionally, it denotes how the conceptual uniqueness of usage and blogging through the use of social media led to green intention through green blogging. Therefore, *H4* and *H5* were therefore supported.

When compared to those with less education, it was shown that those with professional and master's degrees demonstrated better knowledge of green blogging. According to a survey performed in Pakistan, people's knowledge of environmental issues was comparable regardless of their professions or educational backgrounds. They concurred that, regardless of their educational background, the majority of Pakistan's populace utilized information from international and governmental media to stay informed. In a recent poll conducted in Pakistan, those with higher salaries, spouses, and educational levels scored better on knowledge tests about green buying. Younger participants were more supportive of eco-friendly practices than subjects who were older in age. It was comforting to see that the majority of people in Pakistan. Despite having low levels of awareness, it was gratifying to see that the majority of Pakistanis (95%) had good habits and favourable attitudes towards the green purchasing initiatives. A thorough comprehension of the material accessible in books and the media can be shown in the fact that only two thirds of the research participants had adequate awareness about green activities.

As a result, we can affirm that social media use and blogging have an impact on forecasting long-term green purchase behaviour when combined with a moderate level of perceived social media trust. The results of the empirical study show that social media use and green blogging have a significant impact on users' green behaviour and to take responsibility for the environment.

5. Research Implications and Limitations

First, a conceptual model is suggested to understand social media's impact on consumers' intents to make green purchases, and various additional correlates are offered. To the best of our knowledge, this is one of the earliest studies examining the effects of social media usage, green blogging, and the interactions among contextual social media aspects to address the entire topic in an original and effective manner. Although the majority of earlier studies Gupta and Syed (2021), Khan et al. (2021), and Zhao et al. (2019) used the theory of planned behaviour or theory of reasoned action to examine the green behaviour, the structure of the proposed psychological model may be supported by social learning theory.

Secondly, present study enriches the literature of social media by operationalizing blogging and social media use from a green perspective. For these constructs, significant predictors of users' intentions to make green purchases behaviour have been discovered. Social media's pervasive virtual world has been influencing people's perceptions of and behaviour towards green development, but results have been conflicting because these studies primarily focus on the influence of social media usage (Pittman et al., 2022; Zhao et al., 2019).

It emphasizes the moderating function of social media trust. Prior research has shown a strong connection between using social media, blogging about the environment, and making green purchases (Joshi & Rahman, 2019). The current study made a point of highlighting green blogging as a potential link in fresh contexts with the interaction of social media platform trust. Last but not least, it is essential to argue that encouraging people's perceptions of social media environments as trustworthy is essential to advancing green behaviour (Alzubaidi et al., 2021).

References

Ahmad, W., & Zhang, Q. (2020). Green purchase intention: Effects of electronic service quality and customer green psychology. *Journal of Cleaner Production, 267,* 122053.

Ali, M., Puah, C. H., Ali, A., Raza, S. A., & Ayob, N. (2021). Green intellectual capital, green HRM and green social identity toward sustainable environment: A new integrated framework for Islamic banks. *International Journal of Manpower, 43*(3), 614–638.

Alzubaidi, H., Slade, E. L., & Dwivedi, Y. K. (2021). Examining antecedents of consumers' pro-environmental behaviours: TPB extended with materialism and innovativeness. *Journal of Business Research, 122,* 685–699.

Bandura, A., & McClelland, D. C. (1977). *Social learning theory* (First Published). Grneral Learning Press.

Biswas, A., & Roy, M. (2015). Green products: An exploratory study on the consumer behaviour in emerging economies of the East. *Journal of Cleaner Production, 87,* 463–468.

Can, M., Ahmed, Z., Mercan, M., & Kalugina, O. A. (2021). The role of trading environment-friendly goods in environmental sustainability: Does green openness matter for OECD countries? *Journal of Environmental Management, 295,* 113038.

Cerri, J., Testa, F., & Rizzi, F. (2018). The more I care, the less I will listen to you: How information, environmental concern and ethical production influence consumers' attitudes and the purchasing of sustainable products. *Journal of Cleaner Production, 175,* 343–353.

Chung, C. H., Chiu, D. K., Ho, K. K., & Au, C. H. (2020). Applying social media to environmental education: Is it more impactful than traditional media? *Information Discovery and Delivery, 48*(4), 255–266.

Ellison, N. B., Steinfield, C., & Lampe, C. (2007). The benefits of Facebook "friends:" Social capital and college students' use of online social network sites. *Journal of Computer-Mediated Communication, 12*(4), 1143–1168.

Ellison, N. B., Steinfield, C., & Lampe, C. (2011). Connection strategies: Social capital implications of Facebook-enabled communication practices. *New Media & Society, 13*(6), 873–892.

Enke, N., & Borchers, N. S. (2021). Social media influencers in strategic communication: A conceptual framework for strategic social media influencer communication. In *Social media influencers in strategic communication* (pp. 7–23). Routledge.

Fatma, M., Ruiz, A. P., Khan, I., & Rahman, Z. (2020). The effect of CSR engagement on eWOM on social media. *International Journal of Organizational Analysis, 28*(4), 941–956.

Feng, H., Liu, Z., Wu, J., Iqbal, W., Ahmad, W., & Marie, M. (2022). Nexus between government spending's and green economic performance: Role of green finance and structure effect. *Environmental Technology & Innovation, 27*, 102461.

Gonzales, A. L., & Hancock, J. T. (2011). Mirror, mirror on my Facebook wall: Effects of exposure to Facebook on self-esteem. *Cyberpsychology, Behavior, and Social Networking, 14*(1–2), 79–83.

Gupta, M., & Syed, A. A. (2021). Impact of online social media activities on marketing of green products. *International Journal of Organizational Analysis, 30*(3), 679–698.

Hajli, M. N. (2014). A study of the impact of social media on consumers. *International Journal of Market Research, 56*(3), 387–404.

Hwang, K., & Zhang, Q. (2018). Influence of parasocial relationship between digital celebrities and their followers on followers' purchase and electronic word-of-mouth intentions, and persuasion knowledge. *Computers in Human Behavior, 87*, 155–173.

Joosse, S., & Brydges, T. (2018). Blogging for sustainability: The intermediary role of personal green blogs in promoting sustainability. *Environmental communication, 12*(5), 686–700.

Joshi, Y., & Rahman, Z. (2019). Consumers' sustainable purchase behaviour: Modeling the impact of psychological factors. *Ecological Economics, 159*, 235–243.

Junsheng, H., Akhtar, R., Masud, M. M., Rana, M. S., & Banna, H. (2019). The role of mass media in communicating climate science: An empirical evidence. *Journal of Cleaner Production, 238*, 117934.

Khan, M. R., Khan, H. R., Vachkova, M., & Ghouri, A. (2021). The mediating role of real-time information between location-based user-generated content and tourist gift purchase intention. *Advances in Hospitality and Tourism Research, 9*(1), 49–77.

Lee, C. T., & Hsieh, S. H. (2022). Can social media-based brand communities build brand relationships? Examining the effect of community engagement on brand love. *Behaviour & Information Technology, 41*(6), 1270–1285.

Leong, L. Y., Jaafar, N. I., & Ainin, S. (2018). The effects of Facebook browsing and usage intensity on impulse purchase in f-commerce. *Computers in Human Behavior, 78*, 160–173.

Maon, F., Vanhamme, J., De Roeck, K., Lindgreen, A., & Swaen, V. (2019). The dark side of stakeholder reactions to corporate social responsibility: Tensions and micro-level undesirable outcomes. *International Journal of Management Reviews, 21*(2), 209–230.

Pittman, M., Oeldorf-Hirsch, A., & Brannan, A. (2022). Green advertising on social media: Brand authenticity mediates the effect of different appeals on purchase intent and digital engagement. *Journal of Current Issues and Research in Advertising, 43*(1), 106–121.

Pop, R. A., Săplăcan, Z., & Alt, M. A. (2020). Social media goes green—The impact of social media on green cosmetics purchase motivation and intention. *Information, 11*(9), 447.

Simeone, M., & Scarpato, D. (2020). Sustainable consumption: How does social media affect food choices? *Journal of Cleaner Production, 277,* 124036.

Sujata, M., Khor, K. S., Ramayah, T., & Teoh, A. P. (2019). The role of social media on recycling behaviour. *Sustainable Production and Consumption, 20,* 365–374.

Sun, Y., Wei, K. K., Fan, C., Lu, Y., & Gupta, S. (2016). Does social climate matter? On friendship groups in social commerce. *Electronic Commerce Research and Applications, 18,* 37–47.

Szabo, S., & Webster, J. (2021). Perceived greenwashing: The effects of green marketing on environmental and product perceptions. *Journal of Business Ethics, 171*(4), 719–739.

Tao, X., & Fisher, C. B. (2022). Exposure to social media racial discrimination and mental health among adolescents of color. *Journal of Youth and Adolescence, 51*(1), 30–44.

Ventre, I., Mollá-Descals, A., & Frasquet, M. (2021). Drivers of social commerce usage: A multi-group analysis comparing Facebook and Instagram. *Economic Research-Ekonomska Istraživanja, 34*(1), 570–589.

Wei, S., Ang, T., & Jancenelle, V. E. (2018). Willingness to pay more for green products: The interplay of consumer characteristics and customer participation. *Journal of Retailing and Consumer Services, 45,* 230–238.

Zafar, A. U., Qiu, J., & Shahzad, M. (2020). Do digital celebrities' relationships and social climate matter? Impulse buying in f-commerce. *Internet Research, 30*(6), 1731–1762.

Zafar, A. U., Shen, J., Shahzad, M., & Islam, T. (2021). Relation of impulsive urges and sustainable purchase decisions in the personalized environment of social media. *Sustainable Production and Consumption, 25,* 591–603.

Zaremohzzabieh, Z., Ismail, N., Ahrari, S., & Samah, A. A. (2021). The effects of consumer attitude on green purchase intention: A meta-analytic path analysis. *Journal of Business Research, 132,* 732–743.

Zhang, K. Z., Xu, H., Zhao, S., & Yu, Y. (2018). Online reviews and impulse buying behavior: The role of browsing and impulsiveness. *Internet Research, 28*(3), 522–543.

Zhao, L., Lee, S. H., & Copeland, L. R. (2019). Social media and Chinese consumers' environmentally sustainable apparel purchase intentions. *Asia Pacific Journal of Marketing and Logistics, 31*(4), 855–874.

Zhou, T. (2019). Understanding user social commerce usage intention: A stimulus-organism-response perspective. *Information Resources Management Journal, 32*(4), 56–71.

Chapter 11

Are Knowledge Management and Green Entrepreneurial Knowledge the Rescuer of Sustainable Tourism Post COVID-19 Pandemic?

Mcxin Tee, Lee-Yen Chaw and Sadia Mehfooz Khan

Abstract

Sustainable tourism will be an appropriate strategy to be promoted during the post COVID-19 pandemic, as this is a turning point for the tourism industry to grab the unique chance to have a true reset by focussing on achieving long-term sustainability and a shift from a 'me to we' economy. To support sustainable tourism and foster future success in the tourism industry, the process of integrating green knowledge and knowledge management can begin with entrepreneurial education in higher education institutions (HEIs). However, empirical research on university students' green entrepreneurial intention in sustainable tourism has not been exhaustively studied. Additionally, there is a need to further explore knowledge management process and entrepreneurial learning in HEIs. Hence, the aim of this study is to analyze knowledge management as a technique to explore the green entrepreneurial intention of students in HEIs in sustaining Malaysia's tourism post COVID-19 pandemic. Exploratory research with quantitative analysis was conducted through partial least squares structural equation modelling (PLS-SEM). The findings reveal that there is a positive and significant relationship between green entrepreneurial knowledge and green entrepreneurial intention in sustainable tourism among university business students. Additionally, knowledge revision and conceptual change positively and significantly influence green entrepreneurial knowledge and green entrepreneurial intention in sustainable tourism. However, knowledge application has no impact on green entrepreneurial knowledge and green entrepreneurial intention. The results of this study also reveal that green entrepreneurial knowledge does not have a

Entrepreneurship and Green Finance Practices, 193–217

Copyright © 2024 Mcxin Tee, Lee-Yen Chaw and Sadia Mehfooz Khan

Published under exclusive licence by Emerald Publishing Limited

doi:10.1108/978-1-80455-678-820231011

mediation effect on green entrepreneurial intention. The present work contributes by going beyond the study of entrepreneurial intention, as the research focusses on interconnection among these three major areas: knowledge management, sustainable tourism, and entrepreneurship education post COVID-19 pandemic. Hence, the combination of these diverse aspects in this study provides insights to educators and policy makers to investigate the importance of green entrepreneurial knowledge and benefits of knowledge management that can be integrated into entrepreneurship education for current and future sustainable tourism development.

Keywords: Entrepreneurial intention; green entrepreneurial knowledge; knowledge management; sustainable tourism; university business students; COVID-19 pandemic

1. Introduction

The global pandemic, COVID-19 caused economic shocks across all industries worldwide. Although some industries could transform their business into digital platforms, others kept struggling for survival during the outbreak (Mehrolia et al., 2021). One industry that faced extreme consequences in surviving during the pandemic was the tourism industry due to health hazards and travel bans (Sharma et al., 2021; Yan et al., 2021). The United Nation World Tourism Organization (UNWTO) reported a drop of 22% international tourist arrivals during the first-quarter of 2020 arising from COVID-19 pandemic and the trend continued to worsen to an annual decline in the range of 60% and 80% when compared to the previous years (UNWTO, 2021). Similarly, Statista (2022) reported approximately 62 million tourism jobs and related activities which suffered losses or got in danger because of the pandemic. Hence, sustainable tourism will be the most appropriate strategy to be promoted during COVID-19 pandemic as this is a turning point for tourism industry to grab the unique chance to have a true reset by focussing on environmental and social justice, ethics of care, racial healing, and a shift from 'me to we' economy, which means working together towards sustainable development and green economy (Benjamin et al., 2020). It is imperative to set up a balanced, sustainable tourism industry and abandon the 'dark sides' of tourism development of many years, such as congestion, unsustainable tourism products, high resources consumption, economic abuse, or environmental deprivation (Gössling et al., 2020; Niewiadomski, 2020). Sustainability may be one of the best solutions for the tourism industry as it supports everyone's advantage and achieves positive outcomes by changing people's awareness and beliefs (Galvani et al., 2020; Stankov et al., 2020). Furthermore, it is important to call for local belongingness as domestic tourism will come to the rescue and resume before the resumption of international tourism (Brouder et al., 2020; Haywood, 2020). Local belongingness will be one of the pathways for transformation in tourism businesses and to revive from the COVID-19 repercussions (Sharma et al., 2021).

The current tourism industry is required to be included as part of education as tourism during crisis must bring into both corporate and academic interests (Sharma et al., 2021). It is crucial to explore how transformative innovation solutions can be used for the recovery of tourism businesses. Hence, it is essential for higher education institutions (HEIs) to promote entrepreneurship education relevant to business development from theoretical to practical training with the aim of addressing the negative impacts of COVID-19 pandemic (Liguori & Winkler, 2020). There are a few prior scholars who have studied on green entrepreneurial intentions of university students during COVID-19 outbreak. Alvarez-Risco et al. (2021) have explored factors affecting green entrepreneurial intentions among business university students during COVID-19 pandemic. Similarly, Zulfiqar et al. (2021) evaluated the entrepreneurial intent of university students by using business simulation games during the same period. Hence, to the best of authors' knowledge, there are no researches which specifically explore university students' green entrepreneurial intention in sustainable tourism industry post COVID-19.

Moreover, entrepreneurial education is different from other aspects of business education as it requires real-world engagement, experiential approaches, and deliberated practices for the university students. However, many HEIs are facing criticism due to focussing more on theoretical and academic knowledge but fail to deliver practical business knowledge, entrepreneurial mindset, and competencies of the students (Ameer & Khan, 2022; Cheah et al., 2022; Zulfiqar et al., 2021). Hence, this research will focus specifically on the perspective of business students in HEIs to explore effective approaches to enhance green entrepreneurial knowledge of students.

HEIs are the centre for creation and distribution of knowledge to society (Dhamdhere, 2015). Thus, knowledge to integrate sustainability should start from HEIs as the societal role to generate proactive and transformative ways for positive change for the betterment of the world (Ruiz-Mallén & Heras, 2020). In the current modern knowledge-based economy, knowledge management (KM) plays an important role in HEIs to produce knowledge workers through various techniques in KM, such as knowledge transmission and knowledge sharing (Gamlath & Wilson, 2017; Paudel, 2019). KM is an instrument to incorporate collaborate learning with the support of Internet-based tools and technologies (Pattnayak et al., 2017). Hence, KM is the technique that suits perfectly to current HEIs during post-pandemic period that promotes online learning, hybrid learning, or distance learning approaches (Neş;tian et al., 2021). However, Secundo et al. (2019) have highlighted that there is a need to have further study on knowledge creation and entrepreneurial learning within universities.

Based on the above-mentioned research gaps and interference during post COVID-19 pandemic, we concluded that the main research question of the study is: How KM can be used as a technique to explore the green entrepreneurial intention of business students in HEIs in sustaining Malaysia's tourism post COVID-19 pandemic? Furthermore, this research goes beyond the study of entrepreneurial intention as the research focusses on interconnection among three major areas: KM, sustainable tourism, and entrepreneurship education post the pandemic. Hence, the results of this study can contribute to the green entrepreneurship education literature. The green entrepreneurial knowledge integration and KM process should begin with HEIs to support sustainable tourism and promote future success in the tourism industry. The most up-to-date green entrepreneurial knowledge in the curriculum offered by entrepreneurial education is likely to produce significant and sustainable ideas that will engage the universities' business students' interests and prepare them for the continuing and unpredictable future post the pandemic. Hence, the combination of diverse aspects in this study can provide insights to educators and policy makers to investigate the importance of green entrepreneurial knowledge and the benefits of KM that can be integrated into entrepreneurship education in current and future sustainable tourism development.

The paper is arranged as follows. We commence with an introduction followed by a literature review on Sustainable Tourism, Green Entrepreneurship, Green Entrepreneurial Knowledge, and Knowledge Management. Next, the research method is reported. The findings and discussion are then presented, followed by the main conclusions drawn from the study.

2. Literature Review

2.1 Sustainable Tourism

The term sustainable tourism was first introduced in the late 1980s to combat the negative issues related to environmental damage that led to serious impacts on society (Zolfani et al., 2015). Although many different definitions have been given to sustainability, most scholars will adopt this definition for sustainable tourism as 'tourism that takes full account of its current and future economic, social, and environmental impacts, addressing the needs of visitors, the industry, the environment, and host communities' Burgoyne and Mearns (2020 cited UNWTO, 2013, p. 10). Sustainable tourism exists to make a balance between protecting the environment, promoting economic benefits, and enhancing the standard of living of the local communities at the same time providing travelling pleasures to tourists (Zolfani et al., 2015). As a result, terms such as green, sustainable, and eco-friendly are frequently appeared in the tourism and social science-related academic research.

Viglia and Acuti (2022) urged all stakeholders such as entrepreneurs, education providers, higher education students, tourism operators, and policy makers to work together to stop any possible barriers that prevent the development of sustainable traveller's behaviour. The cooperation among these stakeholders enables tourism of the future to be more sustainable. In this study's context, we focus on green entrepreneurial knowledge and how it can affect green entrepreneurial intention.

2.2 Green Entrepreneurship

Green entrepreneurship is about addressing the current environmental issues and implementing innovations relevant to sustainability, for instance the implementation of eco-friendly inputs and processes (Alvarez-Risco et al., 2021). Therefore, green entrepreneurship acts as the solution to environmental and social problems (Qazi et al., 2020). Crnogaj et al. (2014) pointed out that tourism industry is highly dependent on entrepreneurship and thus it requires both important ingredients: sustainability and entrepreneurship at the same time to survive in the long run.

2.2.1 Green Entrepreneurial Knowledge and Green Entrepreneurial Intention

Previous studies (Nabi et al., 2018; Souitaris et al., 2007) reported that entrepreneurial knowledge influences the entrepreneurial intention of students by means of learning, training, and inspiration from business leaders. In the same vein, a study conducted by Karyaningsih et al. (2020) revealed that entrepreneurial knowledge obtained from entrepreneurship education has positively influenced students' intention to be entrepreneurs. It is important to note that entrepreneurial knowledge is closely associated with several business activities, such as firm formation, marketing, finance, and resource management. Wang et al. (2021) assert that students equipped with entrepreneurship knowledge represent an important reserve force for the nations' development, with great potential for green entrepreneurship. Muo and Azeez (2019) has mentioned that entrepreneurial knowledge stockpile and spillover is important for further green entrepreneurship development. Furthermore, the researchers have identified that entrepreneurial knowledge is one of the concepts in green entrepreneurship that needs to be further studied.

In 2017, a total of 79 Green Economy Indicators Malaysia has been established to monitor the performance of various industries in Malaysia towards achieving a green economy (Green Economy Indicators, 2018). Then, the Green Technology Master Plan Malaysia 2017–2030 was launched to drive Malaysia's key economic sectors towards a more sustainable growth and achieving green economy (Green Technology Master Plan, 2017). Green entrepreneurship is needed for the development of a green economy. Some researchers (Nordin & Hassan, 2019; Soomro et al., 2020; Wei et al., 2023) have emphasized the importance of green entrepreneurial intention as it is valuable mechanism to support the development of green economy in a nation. Particularly, few past studies (Qazi et al., 2020; Soomro et al., 2020; Yi, 2021) have highlighted the significance of green entrepreneurial intention of university students to support the growth of green economy.

Hence, studying the intentions of university students to start green tourism business ventures in times of the post-pandemic environment is deemed crucial to the country's economic recovery which will help to achieve sustainable tourism. Thus, we theorize that green entrepreneurial knowledge is associated with green entrepreneurial intention in sustainable tourism. Therefore, our first hypothesis was formulated:

H1. Green entrepreneurial knowledge is positively associated with green entrepreneurial intention in sustainable tourism among university business students.

2.3 Knowledge Management

A well-known KM theory is the Knowledge Spiral SECI Model introduced by Nonaka and Takeuchi that emphasizes on the importance of knowledge creation and conversion (Nonaka & Toyama, 2008). Subsequently, different models of KM have been introduced by many researchers, commonly focussed on knowledge acquisition, knowledge sharing, knowledge innovation, and knowledge application (Bashir & Farooq, 2019; Costa & Monteiro, 2016; Migdadi, 2020; Pacharapha & Ractham, 2012; Wu & Hu, 2018; Zia, 2020). Capabilities of KM in enhancing organizational effectiveness and value creation in knowledge-intensive environment are proven by existing scholars (Campanella et al., 2018; Carrillo et al., 2019; Farooq, 2018). Besides, there are a few recent studies focussing on exploring KM implications in universities during COVID-19 global pandemic (Sharma et al., 2022; Velásquez & Lara, 2021). Additionally, KM has also shown positive effect on achieving sustainability from environmental, economic, and societal perspectives (de Souza Moraes et al., 2018; Liu & Dong, 2021; Shahzad et al., 2020), and positive influence on supporting the attainment of United Nations Sustainable Development Goals for 2030 (Briceño & Santos, 2019).

Evidently, universities act as the central actor to shape, influence, and inspire the entrepreneurial ecosystems (Miller et al., 2018). In the past decade, there is an emerging trend on the studies of relationship between KM and entrepreneurial education. Based on the systematic literature review conducted by Secundo et al. (2019), one of the main areas which has received growing attention is about the knowledge creation in entrepreneurship education, by preparing entrepreneurially equipped university students in business schools to develop entrepreneurial competencies for the society. Besides, there are some recent studies which have explored the importance of KM processes in higher educations, such as to achieve HEIs' competitive goals through KM (Nair & Munusami, 2019; Ramjeawon & Rowley, 2018), attain organizational innovation in HEIs through KM (Boroujerdi et al., 2019), and provide equal opportunities in distance education through KM (Adeinat & Abdulfatah, 2019). Moreover, few recent scholars have presented the importance of entrepreneurial knowledge and KM in affecting students' entrepreneurial intention (Karyaningsih et al., 2020; Zulfiqar et al., 2021).

2.3.1 Knowledge Revision and Conceptual Change

KM implications are unique to any given context or organization and need to be tailored to meet the current needs (Bhatt, 2000). In this study's context, firstly, we will focus on the main KM element: knowledge innovation, to show the significance of transforming conceptual understandings that are learnt in classroom to new knowledge. Stored entrepreneurial knowledge can be converted to innovative ideas generation to emanate green business advantages and opportunities (Muo & Azeez, 2019). We adapt and rename knowledge innovation as knowledge revision and conceptual change (Neştian et al., 2021) to represent the importance of revising process of past knowledge and existing understandings to bring conceptual change to individual's knowledge management, which ultimately, brings new innovations. Moreover, recent findings have presented KM is important for attaining service excellence in tourism industry (Tee & Chaw, 2021). Hence, the following hypotheses relevant to KM were formulated:

H2a. Knowledge revision and conceptual change is positively associated with green entrepreneurial intention in sustainable tourism among university business students.

H2b. Knowledge revision and conceptual change is positively associated with green entrepreneurial knowledge.

2.3.2 Knowledge Application

Secondly, we will focus on the main KM element of knowledge application that is to apply the stored knowledge in practice. Among the few KM elements of knowledge generation, storage, and application, Ode and Ayavoo (2020) have proved that knowledge application has the greatest impact on innovation in the context of service's sector in developing countries. Moreover, few past studies (Anand et al., 2022; Horng et al., 2020) have found out that knowledge application is highly crucial for students to become tourism entrepreneurs. Therefore, based on the above-mentioned statements, we proposed the following hypotheses:

H3a. Knowledge application is positively associated with green entrepreneurial intention in sustainable tourism among university business students.

H3b. Knowledge application is positively associated with green entrepreneurial knowledge.

2.3.3 Entrepreneurial Knowledge as Mediator

Entrepreneurs explore opportunities from the external environment and apply different types of knowledge to create innovative products or services to meet the market demands. Hussain et al. (2021), Ikhram and Novadjaja (2020), and Roxas (2014) have proved that entrepreneurial knowledge positively influences Asian students' entrepreneurial intention. In addition, Saptono et al. (2020), Karyaningsih et al. (2020), and Ni and Ye (2018) have confirmed that entrepreneurial knowledge plays a significant mediating role in influencing Asian students' entrepreneurial intention. However, findings of Alkhalaf et al. (2022) have shown that there is no significant relationship between entrepreneurial knowledge and French students' entrepreneurial intention. Based on the Entrepreneurial Human Capital concept, people who are equipped with entrepreneurial knowledge are more likely to become an entrepreneur (Ni & Ye, 2018). Therefore, based on the aforesaid statements, we theorize that green entrepreneurial knowledge can act as a mediator in this study. The following hypotheses were formulated:

H4. Green entrepreneurial knowledge mediates the impact of knowledge revision and conceptual change on the green entrepreneurial intention in sustainable tourism among university business students.

H5. Green entrepreneurial knowledge mediates the impact of knowledge application on the green entrepreneurial intention in sustainable tourism among university business students.

3. Research Methodology

3.1 Research Design and Sample

This study aims to explore the determining factor of KM elements on green entrepreneurial intention in sustainable tourism among university business students. Cross-sectional survey-based research with quantitative approach was conducted with the aim of testing the proposed hypotheses about relationships between variables. The reason of choosing this research design is that it is more suitable for deductive reasoning with hypotheses clearly defined before the data collection. This method was widely applied in entrepreneurial intention research

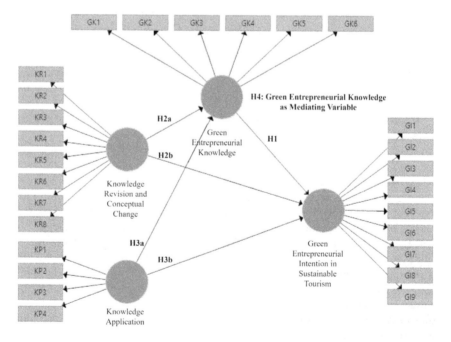

Fig. 11.1.   Proposed Framework.

as it created valid and reliable results (Anwar et al., 2020; Hassan et al., 2021; Karyaningsih et al., 2020). Fig. 11.1 depicts the proposed research framework with hypothesized relationships. Data were collected and analyzed empirically. As inclusion criteria, university students who are studying business and management programmes at universities in Malaysia were considered for the research. We relied on convenience sampling for this exploratory study as time- and cost-savings can be achieved.

This research is an exploratory study. The reason is that although there are some prior scholars who have studied green entrepreneurial intention of university students during the COVID-19 outbreak (Alvarez-Risco et al., 2021; Liguori & Winkler, 2020; Zulfiqar et al., 2021), KM implication in HEIs during the pandemic (Neş;tian et al., 2021; Sharma et al., 2022; Velásquez & Lara, 2021), KM implication to integrate sustainability and green movement (Briceño & Santos, 2019; de Souza Moraes et al., 2018; Liu & Dong, 2021; Shahzad et al., 2020), and KM integration in entrepreneurial education (Karyaningsih et al., 2020; Secundo et al., 2019; Zulfiqar et al., 2021), however, to the best of the authors' knowledge, there are no such prior studies focussing on KM's implications on green entrepreneurial intention of university students post COVID-19 pandemic. Therefore, this research is an exploratory study as the goal of the analysis is to extend the KM concept being tested, to explore the relationships in the data, and how the variables are related (Hair et al., 2016). Sample size was calculated through G*Power software for a minimum sample size as recommended by Hair et al. (2017). Fig. 11.2 presents the G*Power analysis, which had shown the minimum sample size was 74 samples. Hence, the final sample size of 99 collected was more than the required threshold.

3.2 Measurement Development

Table 11.1 presents measurement items of the four constructs, for which the items are adapted from existing literature. Close-ended online questionnaire with 5-point Likert scale (strongly disagree, disagree, neutral, agree, and strongly agree) was applied.

3.3 Data Collection and Analysis Methods

Data was collected via an online questionnaire through Microsoft Form. Data analysis was conducted with Partial Least Squares Structural Equation Modelling (PLS-SEM) and by following thresholds suggested by Ramayah et al. (2018) and Hair et al. (2016). The reason of choosing PLS-SEM for analysis follows the rules of thumb explained by Ramayah et al. (2018) which is that the goal of this study is about to predict key target constructs and to maximize the explained variance of the dependent variable of green entrepreneurial intention in sustainable tourism.

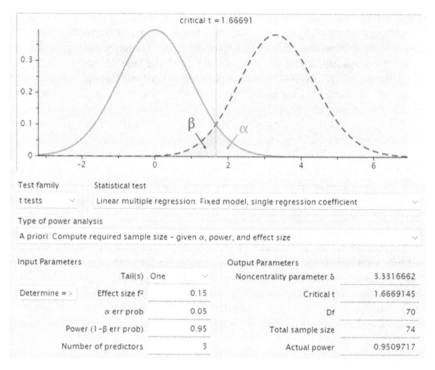

Fig. 11.2.   G*Power Analysis for Minimum Sample Size.

Table 11.1. Measurement Instrument.

Constructs	Items	Adapted From
Knowledge revision and conceptual change	8 items	Neştian et al. (2021); Chang et al. (2013)
Knowledge application	4 items	
Green entrepreneurial knowledge	6 items	Karyaningsih et al. (2020); Roxas (2014)
Green entrepreneurial intention in sustainable tourism	9 items	Alvarez-Risco et al. (2021)

4. Findings and Discussion

4.1 Demographic Characteristics

The respondents' demographic characteristics are shown in Table 11.2. Total collected and useable responses are 99. All the respondents were university students studying business and management relevant programmes at universities in Malaysia. There are 50 male respondents and 49 female respondents who voluntarily participated in the study. Most of them were from the following three programmes: 26 respondents from business administration programme, 25 respondents from business management programme, and 16 respondents from international business programme. Out of the total sample 63 students are from urban areas, and the remaining 36 students are from rural areas. Furthermore, a total of 75 students were 18–20 years old, while the second highest range of age is 21–23 years old which consists of 17 students. Consecutively, 49 students are from a diploma degree, while the remaining 46 students are from the bachelor's degree programmes. Lastly, there were four respondents who were from the Master of Business Administration.

Table 11.2. Demographic Characteristics of Respondents ($N = 99$).

Gender	Percent	Area of Staying	Percent
Male	50.5	Urban area	63.6
Female	49.5	Rural area	36.4
Total	*100*	*Total*	*100*
Major of Business Programme	*Percent*	*Age*	*Percent*
Business Administration	26.3	18–20 years old	75.8
Business Management	25.3	21–23 years old	17.2
International Business	16.2	24–26 years old	4.0
Banking & Finance	9.1	27–29 years old	1.0
Business in Psychology	7.1	30 years old and above	2.0
Accountancy	5.0	*Total*	*100*
Human Resource Management	3.0		
Marketing	3.0	*Current Student Category*	*Percent*
Operations Management	3.0	Diploma student	49.5
Business Information Technology	2.0	Bachelor's degree student	46.5
Total	*100*	Master's degree student	4.0
		Total	*100*

4.2 Measurement Model Evaluation

As shown in Table 11.3, measurement model evaluation was performed for verifying validity and reliability of the measurement instrument by following threshold of Ramayah et al. (2018) and Hair et al. (2016). Table 11.3 presents two items: GI4 and GI5 which were deleted to achieve satisfactory value of Average Variance Extracted (AVE). As mentioned by Hair et al. (2017), not more than 20% of items in the model can be deleted. Hence, the deletion of GI4 and GI5 is

Table 11.3. Measurement Model Evaluation.

Construct	Items	Loadings	CR	AVE	VIF →GK	→GI
Knowledge Revision and Conceptual Change (KR)	KR1	0.735	0.924	0.605	1.708	1.826
	KR2	0.855				
	KR3	0.808				
	KR4	0.781				
	KR5	0.810				
	KR6	0.737				
	KR7	0.835				
	KR8	0.643				
Knowledge Application (KA)	KA1	0.843	0.903	0.701	1.708	1.709
	KA2	0.814				
	KA3	0.866				
	KA4	0.824				
Green Entrepreneurial Knowledge (GK)	GK1	0.793	0.924	0.671	–	1.133
	GK2	0.887				
	GK3	0.863				
	GK4	0.771				
	GK5	0.730				
	GK6	0.860				
Green Entrepreneurial Intention in Sustainable Tourism (GI)	GI1	0.589	0.885	0.527	–	–
	GI2	0.645				
	GI5	0.773				
	GI6	0.809				
	GI7	0.784				
	GI8	0.720				
	GI9	0.734				

acceptable. After deleting the two items, all values of AVE are more than the threshold of 0.5 suggested by Ramayah et al. (2018). Moreover, all values of Variance Inflation Factor (VIF) are less than the threshold of 3.3 as suggested by Diamantopoulos and Siguaw (2006), and all values of Cronbach's Alpha (CR) are more than the threshold of 0.7 suggested by Ramayah et al. (2018). Moreover, all loadings for items are more than the threshold of 0.708 as suggested by Ramayah et al. (2018) except KR8 (0.643), GI1 (0.589), and GI2 (0.645). Ramayah et al. (2018) have pointed out that loadings can still be kept if AVE of the construct is more than the value of 0.5. Hence, we decided to keep the items of KR8, GI1, and GI2. In summary, Table 11.3 represents the reliability and validity of the measurement instrument which is achieved in this study (Chaw et al., 2022; Hair et al., 2016; Ramayah et al., 2018).

Next, discriminant validity was examined through Heterotrait-Monotrait (HTMT) Criterion, Fornell-Larcker's Criterion, and Cross Loading. As shown in Table 11.4, the values of HTMT Criterion are lower than the threshold of 0.85 as suggested by Kline (2011). Subsequently, Table 11.5 shows all the variables achieve sufficient discriminant validity as the square root of AVE is greater than the correlations for all variables (Fornell & Larcker, 1981). Then, Table 11.6 presents discriminant analysis through comparison of cross loadings between the variables. The results show that all items load high on its own variable and low on the other variables, which depicts satisfactory discriminant validity (Ramayah et al., 2018). Therefore, all the three methods of evaluating discriminant validity indicate that it is achieved for the variables of this study.

4.3 Path Analysis

As presented in Table 11.7, results of path analysis indicate that hypotheses of *H1*, *H2a*, and *H2b* are supported by following the threshold t-value >1.645; p-value <0.05 (Hair et al., 2016; Johan et al., 2022; Sun et al., 2022). Green entrepreneurial knowledge positively influences green entrepreneurial intention in sustainable tourism. Besides, knowledge revision and conceptual change positively influences green entrepreneurial knowledge and green entrepreneurial intention in sustainable tourism among university business students. However, the results show that knowledge application has no impact on green entrepreneurial knowledge and green entrepreneurial intention.

Table 11.4. HTMT Criterion.

	GI	GK	KA	KR
GI				
GK	0.678			
KA	0.408	0.259		
KR	0.586	0.364	0.729	

Table 11.5. Fornell-Larcker's Criterion.

	GI	GK	KA	KR
GI	**0.726**			
GK	0.604	**0.819**		
KA	0.356	0.237	**0.837**	
KR	0.532	0.341	0.644	**0.778**

Table 11.6. Loadings and Cross Loadings.

Items	GI	GK	KA	KR
GI1	**0.589**	0.263	0.154	0.280
GI2	**0.645**	0.360	0.405	0.417
GI5	**0.773**	0.460	0.276	0.488
GI6	**0.809**	0.468	0.238	0.388
GI7	**0.784**	0.504	0.259	0.415
GI8	**0.720**	0.417	0.167	0.294
GI9	**0.734**	0.530	0.284	0.381
GK1	0.499	**0.793**	0.170	0.184
GK2	0.524	**0.887**	0.150	0.237
GK3	0.513	**0.863**	0.203	0.313
GK4	0.467	**0.771**	0.304	0.326
GK5	0.437	**0.730**	0.178	0.317
GK6	0.522	**0.860**	0.158	0.293
KA1	0.329	0.232	**0.843**	0.600
KA2	0.259	0.103	**0.814**	0.490
KA3	0.317	0.243	**0.866**	0.554
KA4	0.273	0.185	**0.824**	0.494
KR1	0.456	0.265	0.460	**0.735**
KR2	0.412	0.264	0.453	**0.855**
KR3	0.449	0.339	0.533	**0.808**
KR4	0.291	0.102	0.604	**0.781**
KR5	0.449	0.321	0.542	**0.810**
KR6	0.339	0.243	0.482	**0.737**
KR7	0.452	0.235	0.516	**0.835**
KR8	0.385	0.272	0.442	**0.643**

Table 11.7. Path Analysis Results.

Hypothesis	Std. Beta	Std. Error	*t-* Value	*p* Value	Confidence Interval		Result
					LL (2.5%)	UL (97.5%)	
H1: GK→GI	0.477	0.065	7.395	0.000	0.365	0.579	Supported
H2a: KR→GK	0.323	0.156	2.065	0.020	0.049	0.566	Supported
H2b: KR→GI	0.363	0.085	4.255	0.000	0.204	0.480	Supported
H3a: KA→GK	0.029	0.132	0.222	0.412	−0.214	0.219	Not supported
H3b: KA→GI	0.010	0.096	0.099	0.460	−0.148	0.155	Not supported

4.4 Mediation Analysis

Mediation effect of green entrepreneurial knowledge between the construct of knowledge revision and conceptual change and the construct of green entrepreneurial intention was tested. However, based on results in Table 11.8, green entrepreneurial knowledge does not mediate the influence of knowledge revision and conceptual change on green entrepreneurial intention in sustainable tourism. Consequently, the mediation effect of green entrepreneurial knowledge between the construct of knowledge application and the construct of green entrepreneurial intention was tested, and the mediation effect is not supported too. After conducting the mediation analysis, the results have shown that there is no indirect effect between the constructs. *H4* and *H5* are not supported in this study.

Table 11.8. Mediation Analysis Results.

Hypothesis	Std. Beta	Std. Error	*t-* Value	*p* Value	Confidence Interval		Result
					LL (2.5%)	UL (97.5%)	
H4: KR→GK→GI	0.154	0.082	1.888	0.060	−0.022	0.300	Not supported
H5: KA→GK→GI	0.014	0.066	0.212	0.832	−0.100	0.117	Not supported

4.5 Discussion

The positive association between green entrepreneurial knowledge and green entrepreneurial intention in sustainable tourism among university business students has shown to be significant. This result is consistent with earlier studies (Karyaningsih et al., 2020; Nabi et al., 2018; Souitaris et al., 2007) which shows that students' intentions to become entrepreneurs are positively influenced by the entrepreneurial knowledge they acquire through entrepreneurship education. Additionally, students who are knowledgeable about green entrepreneurship have great potential to be a valuable reserve force for the growth of their countries. During COVID-19 pandemic, entrepreneurship has confronted new obstacles such as strained supply chains and increased online shopping. The global pandemic is a unique opportunity for educators and policymakers to rethink education systems and reimagine what is important, necessary, and desirable for future generations. Green entrepreneurial knowledge can be incorporated into entrepreneurship education to recognize how opportunities with consideration to environmental preservation can be addressed, to deal with climate change, carbon footprint, and pollution issues; and to satisfy the growing demand from customers for goods and services with responsibly sourced materials (Rieckmann, 2020).

Besides, it has been demonstrated that knowledge revision and conceptual change among university business students have positive and significant association with green entrepreneurial knowledge and green entrepreneurial intention in sustainable tourism. This finding is consistent with the findings of Neş;tian et al. (2021). Through the processes of analyzing, integrating, and revising their current understanding, university business students can undergo knowledge revision and conceptual change and ultimately produce new innovations in knowledge, such as thoughts, viewpoints, or solutions to issues in sustainable tourism.

However, findings from this study revealed that knowledge application has no direct impact on green entrepreneurial knowledge and green entrepreneurial intention in sustainable tourism. This result is inconsistent with previous studies (Anand et al., 2022; Horng et al., 2020). There is one possible explanation to support this result which is based on Brînză et al. (2020) study that students' perception of the success of educational process relevant to tourism industry must consist of collaboration with the companies of the industry, in which the collaboration is far more important than just depending on the resources offered by universities. Hence, knowledge application relevant to university students' entrepreneurial activities should be highly linked to the partnerships with companies in the tourism industry. Collaboration between the tourism industry and universities is essential, particularly post the COVID-19 pandemic (Wassler & Fan, 2021). During the post COVID-19 pandemic, the universities can consult entrepreneurship experts, seek role models from local businesses, and utilize community networks for collaboration with local entrepreneurs to ensure entrepreneurship education is incorporated with business activities, financial literacy, and learning in the real-world context (Hardie et al., 2022). Academic and corporate interests must be aligned in the post-pandemic tourism study (Sharma et al., 2021).

Furthermore, the results of mediation analysis have discovered that green entrepreneurial knowledge does not have mediation effect on green entrepreneurial intention. It means that there is only direct effect between the variable of knowledge revision and conceptual change and variable of green entrepreneurial knowledge, and direct effect between the variable of knowledge revision and conceptual change and variable of green entrepreneurial intention in sustainable tourism. The KM element of knowledge revision and conceptual change positively and directly influence green entrepreneurial knowledge as it is important to convert the knowledge gained to become innovative ideas for emanating advantages and opportunities (Muo & Azeez, 2019). However, this pattern of result does not necessarily imply that the direct relationships between the variable of knowledge revision and conceptual change and variable of green entrepreneurial knowledge, and direct relationship between the variable of green entrepreneurial knowledge and variable of green entrepreneurial intention are the total effect. The lack of significance in indirect effect implies this study does not have enough information on the absence of the effect. There are other elements in KM concept which can be explored further in future study to find out the plausible constructs that are able to extend the existing results.

5. Conclusion

The aim of this study is to analyze KM as a technique to explore the green entrepreneurial intention of students in HEIs in sustaining Malaysia's tourism post COVID-19 pandemic. The study was based on quantitative analysis, and the respondents were university business students. The path analysis indicates that a positive relationship between green entrepreneurial knowledge and green entrepreneurial intention in sustainable tourism among university business students has been found to be significant. The result presents the importance of incorporating green entrepreneurial knowledge in entrepreneurship education to recognize and address climate change, carbon footprint, and pollution issues; and to satisfy the growing demand from customers for goods and services with responsibly sourced materials. Subsequently, evidence shows that only knowledge revision and conceptual change have a significant impact on green entrepreneurial knowledge and green entrepreneurial intention in sustainable tourism among students. The revising process of students' current understanding can produce new innovations in knowledge, such as thoughts, viewpoints, or solutions to issues in sustainable tourism.

Surprisingly, the path analysis indicates that knowledge application has no impact on green entrepreneurial knowledge and green entrepreneurial intention. We can think of one possible reason that knowledge application relevant to tourism must consist of industry collaborations, in which the collaboration is far more important than just depending on the resources offered by universities. Students need to apply their knowledge in the real world. Additionally, green entrepreneurial knowledge does not have a mediation effect on green entrepreneurial intention. This could be because of the conceptual or theoretical support which is not strong enough for us to explore the significant mediation impact of green entrepreneurial knowledge.

The findings contribute to the entrepreneurship education literature by concentrating on KM elements. Knowledge revision and conceptual change can improve the capabilities of green entrepreneurship education in HEIs. The present work goes beyond the study of entrepreneurial intention as the research focusses on interconnection among three major areas: KM, sustainable tourism, and entrepreneurship education post COVID-19 pandemic. Tourism industry has confronted extreme difficulties in surviving during the pandemic. While we are in the post-pandemic phase, sustainable tourism will be the most appropriate strategy to be promoted as this is a turning point for the tourism industry to grab the unique chance to have a true reset by focussing on sustainability and a shift from a 'me to we' economy, which means working together towards sustainable development and green economy. The green knowledge integration and KM process should begin with HEIs to support sustainable tourism and promote future success in the industry. The most up-to-date green knowledge in the curriculum offered by entrepreneurial education is likely to produce significant and sustainable ideas that will engage the university business students' interests and prepare them for the continuing and unpredictable future in the post pandemic era. Hence, the combination of diverse aspects in this study can provide insights to educators and policy makers to investigate the importance of green entrepreneurial knowledge and the benefits of KM that can be integrated into entrepreneurship education in current and future sustainable tourism development. Besides, in the highly competitive and challenging tourism industry post pandemic, rather than pedagogy focussing on abstract theoretical concepts, HEIs should focus on assisting students to transform conceptual understandings that are learnt in classrooms to new entrepreneurial knowledge that can be converted to innovative ideas to grab green entrepreneurship advantages and opportunities in sustainable tourism industry. Lastly, due to the 'dark sides' of tourism development of many years and the current unique chance for tourism industry to realize sustainable tourism as the turning point, it is important for all the stakeholders (the government, HEIs and the private sector) to generate public programmes that will showcase on how sustainable tourism can rebuild tourism and support tourism businesses to adapt to the post COVID-19 period and survive for sustained period of time.

Considering the results obtained in the study, universities should emphasize incorporating green entrepreneurial knowledge and KM elements into entrepreneurship education to promote sustainable tourism. However, there are some limitations to this study. Firstly, due to restricted time and resources, we did not explore other KM elements such as Community of Practice to enhance collaboration between universities and local entrepreneurs in the tourism industry, recent tools, and technologies to enhance the effectiveness of KM. Secondly, there are other possible factors which may influence the students' green entrepreneurial intention, but they were not included in this study. Besides, the research only studied the students' perspective with a limited number of respondents. We recommend a future study to investigate a comprehensive resilience-based and community-centred KM framework to foster green entrepreneurship education for university students to reset the tourism industry in order to achieve long-term sustainability during the dynamic and unpredictable post-pandemic phase. Additionally, diverse perspectives from educators and industries should be collected to complete the unfinished puzzle of exploring green entrepreneurship education.

References

Adeinat, I. M., & Abdulfatah, F. H. (2019). Organizational culture and knowledge management processes: Case study in a public university. *VINE Journal of Information and Knowledge Management Systems, 49*(1), 35–53.

Alkhalaf, T., Durrah, O., Almohammad, D., & Ahmed, F. (2022). Can entrepreneurial knowledge boost the entrepreneurial intent of French students? The mediation role of behavioral antecedents. *Management Research Review.* ahead-of-print. https://doi.org/10.1108/MRR-06-2021-0432

Alvarez-Risco, A., Mlodzianowska, S., García-Ibarra, V., Rosen, M. A., & Del-Aguila-Arcentales, S. (2021). Factors affecting green entrepreneurship intentions in business university students in COVID-19 pandemic times: Case of Ecuador. *Sustainability, 13*(11), 6447. https://doi.org/10.3390/su13116447

Ameer, F., & Khan, N. R. (2022). Green entrepreneurial orientation and corporate environmental performance: A systematic literature review. *European Management Journal.* https://doi.org/10.1016/j.emj.2022.04.003

Anand, A., Shantakumar, V. P., Muskat, B., Singh, S. K., Dumazert, J.-P., & Riahi, Y. (2022). The role of knowledge management in the tourism sector: A synthesis and way forward. *Journal of Knowledge Management.* ahead-ofprint. https://doi.org/10.1108/JKM-02-2022-0083

Anwar, I., Saleem, I., Islam, K. B., Thoudam, P., & Khan, R. (2020). Entrepreneurial intention among female university students: Examining the moderating role of entrepreneurial education. *Journal for International Business and Entrepreneurship Development, 12*(4), 217–234. https://doi.org/10.1504/JIBED.2020.10032497

Bashir, M., & Farooq, R. (2019). The synergetic effect of knowledge management and business model innovation on firm competence: A systematic review. *International Journal of Innovation Science, 11*(3), 362–387. https://doi.org/10.1108/IJIS-10-2018-0103

Benjamin, S., Dillette, A., & Alderman, D. H. (2020). We can't return to normal: Committing to tourism equity in the post-pandemic age. *Tourism Geographies, 22*(3), 476–483. https://doi.org/10.1080/14616688.2020.1759130

Bhatt, D. (2000). *EFQM excellence model and knowledge management implications* (p. 8). EFQM Organization.

Boroujerdi, S. S., Hasani, K., & Delshab, V. (2019). Investigating the influence of knowledge management on organizational innovation in higher educational institutions. *Kybernetes, 49*(2), 442–459. https://doi.org/10.1108/K-09-2018-0492

Briceño, C. E. B., & Santos, F. C. A. (2019). Knowledge management, the missing piece in the 2030 agenda and SDGs puzzle. *International Journal of Sustainability in Higher Education, 20*(5), 901–916. https://doi.org/10.1108/IJSHE-01-2019-0019

Brînză, G., Anichiti, A., & Butnaru, G. I. (2020). Perceptions of the students in the tourism specialisations regarding the effectiveness of the educational process and their preparation for the tourism sector. *New Trends in Sustainable Business and Consumption, 137.*

Brouder, P., Teoh, S., Salazar, N. B., Mostafanezhad, M., Pung, J. M., Lapointe, D., & Clausen, H. B. (2020). Reflections and discussions: Tourism matters in the new normal post COVID-19. *Tourism Geographies, 22*(3), 735–746. https://doi.org/10.1080/14616688.2020.1770325

Burgoyne, C., & Mearns, K. (2020). Sustainable tourism/ecotourism. In W. Leal Filho, A. M. Azul, L. Brandli, P. G. özuyar, & T. Wall (Eds.), *Responsible consumption and production. Encyclopedia of the UN sustainable development goals.* Springer. https://doi.org/10.1007/978-3-319-95726-5_22

Campanella, F., Derhy, A., & Gangi, F. (2018). Knowledge management and value creation in the post-crisis banking system. *Journal of Knowledge Management, 23*(2), 263–278. https://doi.org/10.1108/JKM-11-2017-0506

Carrillo, F. J., Edvardsson, B., Reynoso, J., & Maravillo, E. (2019). Alignment of resources, actors and contexts for value creation: Bringing knowledge management into service-dominant logic. *International Journal of Quality and Service Sciences, 11*(3), 424–438. https://doi.org/10.1108/IJQSS-08-2018-0077

Chang, C. C., Tseng, K. H., Liang, C., & Chen, T. Y. (2013). Using e-portfolios to facilitate university students' knowledge management performance: E-portfolio vs. non-portfolio. *Computers & Education, 69*, 216–224. https://doi.org/10.1016/j.compedu.2013.07.017

Chaw, L. Y., Chu, A., Thong, C. L., & Tee, M. (2022). Technology acceptance before and after covid pandemic. In *International conference on human-computer interaction* (pp. 119–132). Springer. https://doi.org/10.1007/978-3-031-05014-5_10

Cheah, X. T., Chen, L. Y., Tee, M., Al Mamun, A., & Salamah, A. A. (2022). Investigating the intention to use social media as online business platform among female University students in Malaysia. In *International conference on business and technology* (pp. 969–981). Springer. https://doi.org/10.1007/978-3-031-08087-6_67

Costa, V., & Monteiro, S. (2016). Key knowledge management processes for innovation: A systematic literature review. *VINE Journal of Information and Knowledge Management Systems, 46*(3), 386–410. https://doi.org/10.1108/VJIKMS-02-2015-0017

Crnogaj, K., Rebernik, M., Hojnik, B. B., & Gomezelj, D. O. (2014). Building a model of researching the sustainable entrepreneurship in the tourism sector. *Kybernetes, 43*(3), 377–393. https://doi.org/10.1108/K-07-2013-0155

de Souza Moraes, S., Jabbour, C. J. C., Battistelle, R. A., Rodrigues, J. M., Renwick, D. S., Foropon, C., & Roubaud, D. (2018). When knowledge management matters: Interplay between green human resources and eco-efficiency in the financial service industry. *Journal of Knowledge Management, 23*(9), 1691–1707.

Dhamdhere, S. N. (2015). Knowledge management model for higher educational institutes. *Journal of Commerce and Management Thought, 6*, 130–161. https://doi.org/10.5958/0976-478x.2015.00010.5

Diamantopoulos, A., & Siguaw, A. (2006). Formative versus reflective indicators in organizational measure development: A comparison and empirical illustration. *British Journal of Management, 17*(4), 263–282. https://doi.org/10.1111/j.1467-8551.2006.00500.x

Farooq, R. (2018). Developing a conceptual framework of knowledge management. *International Journal of Innovation Science, 11*(1), 139–160. https://doi.org/10.1108/IJIS-07-2018-0068

Fornell, C., & Larcker, D. F. (1981). Evaluating structural equation models with unobservable variables and measurement error. *Journal of Marketing Research, 18*(1), 39–50. https://doi.org/10.1177/002224378101800104

Galvani, A., Lew, A. A., & Perez, M. S. (2020). COVID-19 is expanding global consciousness and the sustainability of travel and tourism. *Tourism Geographies, 22*(3), 567–576. https://doi.org/10.1080/14616688.2020.1760924

Gamlath, S., & Wilson, T. (2017). *Knowledge sharing among university students: A review of current practices*. Available at SSRN 2962616. https://doi.org/10.2139/ssrn.2962616

Gössling, S., Scott, D., & Hall, C. M. (2020). Pandemics, tourism and global change: A rapid assessment of COVID-19. *Journal of Sustainable Tourism, 29*(1), 1–20. https://doi.org/10.1080/09669582.2020.1758708

Green Economy Indicators Malaysia. (2018, March 9). Department of Statistics Malaysia. https://www.dosm.gov.my/v1/index.php?r=column/cone&menu_id=ZDU2TmFuYzYzMTVpa2R5YzI1citFZz09

Green Technology Master Plan Malaysia 2017–2030. (2017). Ministry of Energy, Green Technology and Water. https://www.pmo.gov.my/wp-content/uploads/2019/07/Green-Technology-Master-Plan-Malaysia-2017-2030.pdf

Hair, J. F., Jr, Babin, B. J., & Krey, N. (2017). Covariance-based structural equation modeling in the journal of advertising: Review and recommendations. *Journal of Advertising, 46*(1), 163–177. https://doi.org/10.1080/00913367.2017.1281777

Hair, J. F., Jr., Hult, G. T. M., Ringle, C., & Sarstedt, M. (2016). *A primer on partial least squares structural equation modeling (PLS-SEM)*. SAGE Publications.

Hardie, B., Lee, K., & Highfield, C. (2022). Characteristics of effective entrepreneurship education post-COVID-19 in New Zealand primary and secondary schools: A Delphi study. *Entrepreneurship Education, 5*(2), 199–218. https://doi.org/10.1007/s41959-022-00074-y

Hassan, A., Anwar, I., Saleem, I., Islam, K. B., & Hussain, S. A. (2021). Individual entrepreneurial orientation, entrepreneurship education and entrepreneurial intention: The mediating role of entrepreneurial motivations. *Industry and Higher Education, 35*(4), 403–418. https://doi.org/10.1177/09504222211007051

Haywood, K. M. (2020). A post COVID-19 future-tourism re-imagined and re-enabled. *Tourism Geographies, 22*(3), 599–609. https://doi.org/10.1080/14616688.2020.1762120

Horng, J. S., Liu, C. H., Chou, S. F., & Huang, Y. C. (2020). The roles of university education in promoting students' passion for learning, knowledge management and entrepreneurialism. *Journal of Hospitality and Tourism Management, 44*, 162–170. https://doi.org/10.1016/j.jhtm.2020.06.005

Hussain, T., Zia-Ur-Rehman, M., & Abbas, S. (2021). Role of entrepreneurial knowledge and personal attitude in developing entrepreneurial intentions in business graduates: A case of Pakistan. *Journal of Global Entrepreneurship Research*, 1–11. https://doi.org/10.1007/s40497-021-00283-0

Ikhram, A. D., & Novadjaja, L. H. (2020). The effect of entrepreneurial knowledge on entrepreneurial intention with the moderation of family support (a case study on university students in Indonesia). *APMBA (Asia Pacific Management and Business Application)*, *8*(3), 169–180. https://doi.org/10.21776/ub.apmba.2020.008.03.2

Johan, M. R. M., Zain, E. M. Y. L. M., Miura, T., Mcxin, T., & Annuar, N. (2022). Assessing consumer consumption behaviour through social media marketing: A survey among youths in Malaysia. *Jurnal Intelek*, *17*(1), 140–150. https://doi.org/10.24191/ji.v17i1.15918

Karyaningsih, R. P. D., Wibowo, A., Saptono, A., & Narmaditya, B. S. (2020). Does entrepreneurial knowledge influence vocational students' intention? Lessons from Indonesia. *Entrepreneurial Business and Economics Review*, *8*(4), 138–155. https://doi.org/10.15678/EBER.2020.080408

Kline, R. B. (2011). Convergence of structural equation modeling and multilevel modeling. In *The SAGE handbook of innovation in social research methods* (pp. 562–589). Sage Publications Ltd.

Liguori, E., & Winkler, C. (2020). From offline to online: Challenges and opportunities for entrepreneurship education following the COVID-19 pandemic. *Entrepreneurship Education and Pedagogy*, *3*(4), 346–351. https://doi.org/10.1177%2F2515127420916738

Liu, C. H. S., & Dong, T. P. (2021). Discovering the relationship among knowledge management, sustainability marketing and service improvement: The moderating role of consumer interest. *International Journal of Contemporary Hospitality Management*, *33*(8), 2799–2816. https://doi.org/10.1108/IJCHM-12-2020-1468

Mehrolia, S., Alagarsamy, S., & Solaikutty, V. M. (2021). Customers response to online food delivery services during COVID-19 outbreak using binary logistic regression. *International Journal of Consumer Studies*, *45*(3), 396–408. https://doi.org/10.1111/ijcs.12630

Migdadi, M. M. (2020). Knowledge management, customer relationship management and innovation capabilities. *Journal of Business & Industrial Marketing*, *36*(1), 111–124. https://doi.org/10.1108/JBIM-12-2019-0504

Miller, K., Alexander, A., Cunningham, J. A., & Albats, E. (2018). Entrepreneurial academics and academic entrepreneurs: A systematic literature review. *International Journal of Technology Management*, *77*(1–3), 9–37. https://doi.org/10.1504/IJTM.2018.091710

Muo, I., & Azeez, A. A. (2019). Green entrepreneurship: Literature review and agenda for future research. *International Journal of Entrepreneurial Knowledge*, *7*(2), 17–29. https://doi.org/10.37335/ijek.v7i2.90

Nabi, G., Walmsley, A., Liñán, F., Akhtar, I., & Neame, C. (2018). Does entrepreneurship education in the first year of higher education develop entrepreneurial intentions? The role of learning and inspiration. *Studies in Higher Education*, *43*(3), 452–467. https://doi.org/10.1080/03075079.2016.1177716

Nair, B. V., & Munusami, C. (2019). Knowledge management practices: An exploratory study at the Malaysian higher education institutions. *Journal of Research in Innovative Teaching & Learning*, *13*(2), 174–190. https://doi.org/10.1108/JRIT-01-2019-0008

Neștian, Ș. A., Vodă, A. I., Tiță, S. M., Guță, A. L., & Turnea, E. S. (2021). Does individual knowledge management in online education prepare business students for employability in online businesses? *Sustainability*, *13*(4), 2091. https://doi.org/10.3390/su13042091

Niewiadomski, P. (2020). COVID-19: From temporary de-globalisation to a re-discovery of tourism? *Tourism Geographies*, *22*(3), 651–656. https://doi.org/10.1080/14616688.2020.1757749

Ni, H., & Ye, Y. (2018). Entrepreneurship education matters: Exploring secondary vocational school students' entrepreneurial intention in China. *The Asia-Pacific Education Researcher*, *27*(5), 409–418. https://doi.org/10.1007/s40299-018-0399-9

Nonaka, I., & Toyama, R. (2008). Teoria da criação do conhecimento organizacional. In I. Nonaka & H. Takeuchi (Eds.), *Gestão Do Conhecimento*. Bookman, Porto Alegre.

Nordin, R., & Hassan, R. A. (2019). The role of opportunities for green entrepreneurship towards investigating the practice of green entrepreneurship among SMEs in Malaysia. *Review of Integrative Business and Economics Research*, *8*, 99–116. https://sibresearch.org/uploads/3/4/0/9/34097180/riber_8-s1_08_s18-156_99-116.pdf

Ode, E., & Ayavoo, R. (2020). The mediating role of knowledge application in the relationship between knowledge management practices and firm innovation. *Journal of Innovation & Knowledge*, *5*(3), 210–218. https://doi.org/10.1016/j.jik.2019.08.002

Pacharapha, T., & Ractham, V. V. (2012). Knowledge acquisition: The roles of perceived value of knowledge content and source. *Journal of Knowledge Management*, *16*(5), 724–739. https://doi.org/10.1108/13673271211262772

Pattnayak, J., Pattnaik, S., & Dash, P. (2017). Knowledge management in e-learning a critical analysis. *International Journal of Engineering and Computer Science*, *6*(5), 21528–21533. https://doi.org/10.18535/ijecs/v6i5.56

Paudel, K. P. (2019). Expectations and realities of knowledge management: Experiences from higher education in developing countries. *Education and Development*, *29*, 89–102. https://doi.org/10.3126/ed.v29i0.32574

Qazi, W., Qureshi, J. A., Raza, S. A., Khan, K. A., & Qureshi, M. A. (2020). Impact of personality traits and university green entrepreneurial support on students' green entrepreneurial intentions: The moderating role of environmental values. *Journal of Applied Research in Higher Education*. https://doi.org/10.1108/JARHE-05-2020-0130

Ramayah, T., Cheah, J., Chuah, F., Ting, H., & Memon, M. A. (2018). Partial least squares structural equation modeling (PLS-SEM) using smartPLS 3.0. In *An updated guide and practical guide to statistical analysis*. Pearson.

Ramjeawon, P. V., & Rowley, J. (2018). Knowledge management in higher education institutions in Mauritius. *International Journal of Educational Management*, *32*(7), 1319–1332. https://doi.org/10.1108/IJEM-05-2017-0129

Rieckmann, M. (2020). *Innovative learning approaches to foster sustainable entrepreneurship competencies with regard to the SDGs in Higher Education* [Webinar]. Intrinsic project. https://www.intrinsic.eu/_media/rieckmann-innovative-learning-approaches-to-foster-sustainable-entrepreneurship-competencies.pdf

Roxas, B. (2014). Effects of entrepreneurial knowledge on entrepreneurial intentions: A longitudinal study of selected South-east Asian business students. *Journal of Education and Work*, *27*(4), 432–453. https://doi.org/10.1080/13639080.2012.760191

Ruiz-Mallén, I., & Heras, M. (2020). What sustainability? Higher education institutions' pathways to reach the Agenda 2030 goals. *Sustainability*, *12*(4), 1290. https://doi.org/10.3390/su12041290

Saptono, A., Wibowo, A., Narmaditya, B. S., Karyaningsih, R. P. D., & Yanto, H. (2020). Does entrepreneurial education matter for Indonesian students' entrepreneurial preparation: The mediating role of entrepreneurial mindset and knowledge. *Cogent Education, 7*(1), 1836728. https://doi.org/10.1080/2331186X.2020.1836728

Secundo, G., Ndou, V., Del Vecchio, P., & De Pascale, G. (2019). Knowledge management in entrepreneurial universities: A structured literature review and avenue for future research agenda. *Management Decision, 57*(12), 3226–3257. https://doi.org/10.1108/MD-11-2018-1266

Shahzad, M., Qu, Y., Zafar, A. U., Rehman, S. U., & Islam, T. (2020). Exploring the influence of knowledge management process on corporate sustainable performance through green innovation. *Journal of Knowledge Management, 24*(9), 2079–2106. https://doi.org/10.1108/JKM-11-2019-0624

Sharma, G. V. S. S., Prasad, C. L. V. R. S. V., & Rambabu, V. (2022). Online machine drawing pedagogy—A knowledge management perspective through maker education in the COVID-19 pandemic era. *Knowledge and Process Management, 29*(3), 231–241. https://doi.org/10.1002/kpm.1684

Sharma, G. D., Thomas, A., & Paul, J. (2021). Reviving tourism industry post-COVID-19: A resilience-based framework. *Tourism Management Perspectives, 37*, 100786.

Soomro, B. A., Ghumro, I. A., & Shah, N. (2020). Green entrepreneurship inclination among the younger generation: An avenue towards a green economy. *Sustainable Development, 28*(4), 585–594. https://doi.org/10.1002/sd.2010

Souitaris, V., Zerbinati, S., & Al-Laham, S. (2007). Do Entrepreneurship programs raise entrepreneurial intention of science and engineering students? The effect of learning, inspiration and resources. *Journal of Business Venturing, 22*, 566–591. https://doi.org/10.1016/j.jbusvent.2006.05.002

Stankov, U., Filimonau, V., & Vujičić, M. D. (2020). A mindful shift: An opportunity for mindfulness-driven tourism in a post-pandemic world. *Tourism Geographies, 22*(3), 703–712. https://doi.org/10.1080/14616688.2020.1768432. https://www.statista.com/statistics/1104835/coronavirus-travel-tourism-employment-loss/

Sun, G., Tee, M., Al Mamun, A., & Salamah, A. A. (2022). Strategic orientation, ser-vice innovation capability and financial performance among Chinese service-oriented SMEs. In *International conference on business and technology* (pp. 725–736). Springer. https://doi.org/10.1007/978-3-031-08087-6_50

Tee, M., & Chaw, L. Y. (2021). Generation Z's perspective on tourists' knowledge sharing and service excellence in tourism. In *Service excellence in tourism and hospitality* (pp. 89–107). Springer. https://doi.org/10.1007/978-3-030-57694-3_7

UNWTO. https://www.unwto.org/news/covid-19-international-tourist-numbers-could-fall-60-80-in-2020

Velásquez, R. M. A., & Lara, J. V. M. (2021). Knowledge management in two universities before and during the COVID-19 effect in Peru. *Technology in Society, 64*, 101479. https://doi.org/10.1016/j.techsoc.2020.101479

Viglia, G., & Acuti, D. (2022). How to overcome the intention–Behavior gap in sustainable tourism: Tourism agenda 2030 perspective article. *Tourism Review*. https://doi.org/10.1108/TR-07-2022-0326

Wang, W., Cao, Q., Zhuo, C., Mou, Y., Pu, Z., & Zhou, Y. (2021). COVID-19 to green entrepreneurial intention: Role of green entrepreneurial self-efficacy, optimism, ecological values, social responsibility, and green entrepreneurial

motivation. *Frontiers in Psychology*, *12*(October). https://doi.org/10.3389/fpsyg.
2021.732904

Wassler, P., & Fan, D. X. (2021). A tale of four futures: Tourism academia and
COVID-19. *Tourism Management Perspectives*, *38*, 100818. https://doi.org/10.
1016/j.tmp.2021.100818

Wei, X., Ren, H., Ullah, S., & Bozkurt, C. (2023). Does environmental entrepreneurship play a role in sustainable green development? Evidence from emerging
Asian economies. *Economic Research-Ekonomska Istraživanja*, *36*(1), 73–85.
https://doi.org/10.1080/1331677X.2022.2067887

Wu, L., & Hu, Y. P. (2018). Open innovation based knowledge management implementation: A mediating role of knowledge management design. *Journal of
Knowledge Management*, *22*(8), 1736–1756. https://doi.org/10.1108/JKM-06-2016-
0238

Yan, J., Kim, S., Zhang, S. X., Foo, M. D., Alvarez-Risco, A., Del-Aguila-Arcentales, S., & Yáñez, J. A. (2021). Hospitality workers' COVID-19 risk perception
and depression: A contingent model based on transactional theory of stress model.
International Journal of Hospitality Management, *95*, 102935. https://doi.org/10.
1016/j.ijhm.2021.102935

Yi, G. (2021). From green entrepreneurial intentions to green entrepreneurial
behaviors: The role of university entrepreneurial support and external institutional
support. *The International Entrepreneurship and Management Journal*, *17*(2),
963–979. https://doi.org/10.1007/s11365-020-00649-y

Zia, N. U. (2020). Knowledge-oriented leadership, knowledge management behaviour
and innovation performance in project-based SMEs. The moderating role of goal
orientations. *Journal of Knowledge Management*, *24*(8), 1819–1839. https://doi.org/
10.1108/JKM-02-2020-0127

Zolfani, S. H., Sedaghat, M., Maknoon, R., & Zavadskas, E. K. (2015). Sustainable
tourism: A comprehensive literature review on frameworks and applications.
Economic Research-Ekonomska Istrazivanja, *28*(1), 1–30. https://doi.org/10.1080/
1331677X.2014.995895

Zulfiqar, S., Al-reshidi, H. A., Al Moteri, M. A., Feroz, H. M. B., Yahya, N., &
Al-Rahmi, W. M. (2021). Understanding and predicting students' entrepreneurial
intention through business simulation games: A perspective of covid-19.
Sustainability, *13*(4), 1838.

Chapter 12

Green Marketing Strategies and CSR: Are They Relevant to Consumer Willingness to Purchase Green Products?

Jagathiswary Ravichandran, Choi-Meng Leong, Tze-Yin Lim, Eva Lim and Lee-Yen Chaw

Abstract

The purpose of the study is to conceptualize the model of the predictors of consumer willingness to purchase green products. This study used the underpinning theories related to consumer willingness by integrating the green concept in deriving the consumer willingness to purchase green products. Based on the underpinning theories of marketing strategies, it was found that marketing mix was still fundamental in business. Therefore, green marketing mix was proposed to describe the consumer's green purchase willingness. Furthermore, corporate social responsibility (CSR) plays an important role as the key to organizational strategy. Thus, CSR is also included in the proposed framework. As this is a conceptual paper, further empirical study needs to carry out to verify the proposed hypotheses. This study contributes to the market practitioners or entrepreneurs in terms of re-considering marketing mix and CSR in deriving customer willingness to purchase green products. This study extends the literature of behavioural intention by integrating green marketing strategies with CSR in determining consumer willingness to purchase.

Keywords: Consumer willingness; green marketing strategies; corporate social responsibilities; green product; consumer trust; green purchase

1. Introduction

Increasing population and industrialization have a detrimental impact on the environment, as well as on infrastructure and natural resources already in

Entrepreneurship and Green Finance Practices, 219–238

Copyright © 2024 Jagathiswary Ravichandran, Choi-Meng Leong, Tze-Yin Lim, Eva Lim and Lee-Yen Chaw

Published under exclusive licence by Emerald Publishing Limited

doi:10.1108/978-1-80455-678-820231012

existence (Garg, 2015; Mishra et al., 2019). The transfer of toxic waste, the consumption of ozone, global warming, the destruction of forests, and the depletion of resources are just some examples of the environmental concerns that have become mainstream lifestyle highlights (Cheung et al., 2015; Dangelico & Vocalelli, 2017). Concern for the planet's ecosystems has entered the limelight. Numerous initiatives, some of which include 'green revolt', 'environmental safety', 'sustainable developments', 'going green', and 'protecting our earth', were created. All these initiatives to raise public consciousness about the deteriorating state of the environment are supported by both government and non-government organizations (Mahmoud, 2018). The concept of 'sustainability' has gained traction in recent research. It's a given that companies should provide for people's wants and needs while also safeguarding the environment (Awan et al., 2016). The current environmental challenges necessitate the development of strategies for the management of pollution and the preservation of natural resources. As a corollary, a growing number of businesses and organizations around the world have begun engaging in green marketing strategies (Al-dmour et al., 2021). Therefore, businesses should cater to widespread preferences by offering products and services that appeal to the masses.

There has been an uptick in discussions about environmental issues, and people's pro-environmental attitudes and actions have been shown to be correlated with a higher emphasis on environmental values. This study focusses on the strategy formulation of a business in terms of the marketing strategies as well as the organization strategies. Green marketing, which focusses on protecting the environment, is an important part of this phenomenon. There are many spheres of influence touched favourably by green marketing, including nature, consumers, society at large, and economies. Increasing environmental awareness has resulted in a shift in consumer preferences towards 'green' products that are safer for the planet. This has resulted in a rise in the popularity of green marketing.

Today's environmentally conscious policies are directly attributable to the success of green marketing campaigns. In this vein, the marketing industry has taken note of the ever-increasing emphasis on corporate social responsibility (CSR) (Lenz et al., 2017). CSR functions as one of the main organizational strategies that are related in economic, ethical, as well as communicative concepts (Karmasin & Litschka, 2017). According to Brown and Dacin (1997), marketing managers are obligated to consider how consumers evaluate the company's capabilities and social responsibility commitment. The influence of corporate social responsibility (CSR) on consumers has been the subject of a small number of studies, the vast majority of which have been conducted in industrialized countries such as the United States, the United Kingdom, and Spain (Du et al., 2010). In spite of this, the findings from developed nations cannot be extrapolated to developing markets because they lack empirical support. In light of this, Fatma and Rahman (2015) stress the importance of conducting CSR research on consumer points in emerging markets to determine the impact of CSR on consumers' willingness. In addition, consumers' trust in green products plays a significant role in their decision to purchase green products, and products are distinguished by their green qualities, indicating that they belong to the trust category (Li et al., 2021). Additionally, it is essential for marketers to have a solid understanding of how to modify CSR programmes for different markets. When it comes to issues of corporate social responsibility, Steg et al. (2011) state that it is essential to differentiate between the developed market and the developing market. According to the findings of the research that was published, the studies that have already been carried out on the positive effects that CSR has on consumer willingness are merely a starting point for further research (Li et al., 2021). It is essential for marketers to understand whether and how customers' willingness is influenced by a company's public image of CSR.

2. Literature Review

2.1 The Green Marketing Perspective

2.1.1 Consumer Intention

2.1.1.1 Theory of Value-Belief-Norm. Schwartz's (1977) moral norm-activation theory of altruistic behaviour and Dunlap and Van Liere's (1978) New Environmental Paradigm (NEP) used to foresee environmental activism are both expanded upon in the value-belief-norm model (VBN) (Putrawan, 2020). In order to better understand environmentally critical behaviour, the NEP (Dunlap & Van Liere, 1978) and moral norm-activation theory (Schwartz, 1977) have both been widely applied and have proven to be useful. Values, normative environmental preferences (NEP), awareness of consequences (AC), ascription of responsibility (AR) to self-beliefs, and personal norms (PN) are the five pillars of Stern's VBN theory of environmentalism (Stern, 2000). It is hypothesized that people's value orientation, which is defined as a guiding principle on what constitutes desirable or appropriate states or outcomes, directly influences their environmental beliefs (Stern, 2000).

Egoistic, altruistic, and biospheric value orientations are distinguished by the model of value orientations provided by VBN theory. The NEP (Dunlap & Van Liere, 1978; Dunlap et al., 2000) is a research measure on ecological worldviews that captures people's beliefs towards the ability of humanity to disturb the balance of nature, the existence of limits to the growth of human societies, as well as humanity's right to rule over the rest of nature. The NEP is widely used as a research measure on ecological worldviews. Whether a person is aware of the detrimental effects that acting unsocially has on other people or on other things that they value is referred to as AC; a person's sense of moral obligation to carry out or abstain from particular behaviours is referred to as PN; while AR refers to their sense of responsibility for the unfavourable effects that their lack of pro-social behaviour has created (Van Liere & Dunlap, 1978). To successfully explain a wide range of environmental behaviours, one of the most well-known and widely used paradigm models in environmental psychology is the VBN theory model, which was first proposed by Stern in the year 2000 (de Groot & Steg, 2008).

2.1.1.2 Theory of Planned Behaviour (TPB). Ajzen came up with the idea for the TPB in 1985 in order to address the most significant shortcoming of the TRA, which was that it ignored an individual's ability to voluntarily control his or her behaviour patterns. This model is an extension of the TRA model that incorporates perceived behavioural control as another determinant of intention (Ajzen, 1991). The capabilities, resources, and opportunities that are available to accomplish the desired result are the factors that determine how much behavioural control is felt to be exercised. According to Ajzen's research from 1991, it has a strong connection to the concept of efficacy beliefs. This idea focusses on the beliefs that people hold and how those beliefs affect their capacity to produce outcomes (Sniehotta, 2009). In his TPB framework, Ajzen (1991) posited that behaviour comes before actual behaviour, and that a person's intention to behave in a certain way can be influenced by any or all of attitudes, normative beliefs, or perceived behaviour control. Ajzen also suggested that behaviour predates actual behaviour (Ajzen, 1991). TPB is widely acknowledged to be one of the most significant models that are utilized in the attempt to explain user behaviour (Ajzen, 1991). In addition, the formation of behavioural intention is caused by the interaction of attitude towards behaviour, social norm, and behavioural control (Yadav & Pathak, 2017).

2.1.2 Behavioural Intention

2.1.2.1 Consumer Variety Seeking Behaviour. Changing one's consumption habits at different points in time without noticing a shift in the characteristics of available alternatives is an example of what is known as 'variety seeking behaviour' among consumers (Kahn, 1995). The research on consumer behaviour reveals that customers in a wide range of consumption situations actively seek out novelty (Kahn, 1995). For example, Seetharaman and Chintagunta (1998) postulate that repeat exposure to a brand makes consumers less enthusiastic about that brand, which could explain why consumers like to switch things up. Several statistical models of novelty-seeking behaviour have been developed in light of this theory (Desai & Trivedi, 2014). McAlister and Pessemier (1982) propose an alternate explanation for consumers' desire for diversity by positing that, after being exposed to one set of features, they feel satiated and start looking for options that feature a different set of features. In contrast to Jeuland (1978), this theory can accurately predict not only that a consumer will abandon the most recently consumed brand but also to which brand they will migrate. Several statistical models of variety seeking have been developed based on this hypothesis (McAlister & Pessemier, 1982; Seetharaman & Chintagunta, 1998).

A variety of behaviours were categorized by McAlister and Pessemier (1982) as either derived or direct. This variety-seeking behaviour was not intrinsically motivated by a craving for novelty, but rather was the byproduct of some other driving force. The phrase 'multiple needs, multiple users, or multiple situations' perfectly describes the conditions that led to this quest for variety. Direct variety-seeking behaviour was defined as stemming from internal motivations, including the need for change and/or novelty and the feeling of dissatisfaction with product attributes. Preference uncertainty or taste misprediction (Simonson, 1990) has been proposed as an additional motivation for variety-seeking behaviour in recent years, implying the need for a further expansion of the classification scheme. As we have seen, there are three primary drives behind people's desire for novelty that have been identified in the existing literature. The first factor is analogous to direct variety-seeking, as described by McAlister and Pessemier (1982), in which consumers actively seek out novelty for its own sake. As a way of pinpointing the precise cause of the urge to seek novelty, we refer to this type of motivation for variety seeking as satiation/stimulation. External circumstances, such as the variety-seeking motivation hypothesized by McAlister and Pessemier (1982), are the second element. Consumers in these situations are looking for variety more as a result of external pressures than any strong, intrinsic desire for change. Finally, we have what we call future preference uncertainty as a third motivation that is absent from the McAlister and Pessemier's (1982) framework. Here, buyers want selection so they can protect their interest in tried-and-true choices while also having a safety net against unknown future events.

Research over the past decade has refined our understanding of the factors that drive customers to seek out new products, and it has also yielded several new models of variety-seeking that can be used by retailers to quantify customer behaviour and foretell their preferences for the future. Although not a novel idea (panel data in supermarket categories have existed for some time), retailers of other categories or services have not always made it a top priority to look at variety measures within a customer's choice history. In the health club industry, for instance, members may be given membership cards that can be used to track their purchasing habits over time. It's possible that frequent diners' meal preferences are tracked by their favourite restaurants. Nearly all businesses that provide services also have the means to issue membership cards or frequent user cards, allowing them to track the preferences of their most devoted customers over time. This is essentially the purpose of the 'check-cashing' or 'bonus' cards that some supermarkets have started giving out in exchange for continued patronage. It is only possible to quantify and model individuals' desires for novelty once we have access to their complete choice histories over time. The models also fall into one of three categories that correspond to the proposed reasons for seeking novelty. Some models of variety-seeking postulate that consumers make a switch because they are bored or bored with their current options (Kahn, 1995). Different models of change-seeking behaviour are developed to assess the extent to which people change jobs in response to exogenous factors like promotions. Last but not least, there are portfolio-based models of variety, which consider the decisions consumers make during a single purchase occasion for consumption at a later time, raising questions of future preference uncertainty.

2.1.2.2 Diffusion of Innovation Theory. In 1962, Rogers created the concept of differential optical interference, or DOI theory (Dibra, 2015). According to the Diffusion of Innovations (DOI) theory, early adopters of a new technology or practise may be reluctant to join the bandwagon until the trend becomes more widespread. The theory of diffusion of innovations (DOI) postulates that, depending on the social context, those who adopt innovations may face a range of outcomes, some of which may be desirable while others may be less so. In light of this ambiguity, people may be quick to dismiss or eagerly embrace new ideas and methods. An innovation has the following five qualities, as seen by its users: relative advantage, compatibility, complexity, trialability, and observability (Bhola, 1966). The relative advantage of an innovation is how much of an improvement it is in the eyes of the user over the prior state of the art. The level of compatibility captures how well an innovation fits into the current technological and social framework. Generally speaking, an innovation's chances of spreading and being adopted improve the more it is compatible with existing values, prior experience, and the needs of potential adopters. Complexity is a metric used to evaluate how challenging a new idea is seen to be in terms of comprehension, application, and use. It's more likely that consumers will embrace a simple innovation. The trialability of an innovation is its potential to be tested with minimal outlay of resources. An improvement's trialability affects how likely it is that people will adopt it. The observability of an innovation's benefits is the degree to which they are readily apparent to prospective users. An innovation is unlikely to be adopted unless its benefits are widely recognized.

According to Rogers, innovators have the capacity to comprehend and implement the complex technical knowledge that is necessary for bringing innovation from outside the existing social system (Bhola, 1966). The early adopters are the next group, and they are a more ingrained component of the social system than the innovators were. They have a greater propensity to be economically successful, well-connected with new technologies, and well-informed regarding the latest innovations. In any given social system, 16% of the population is comprised of the first two groups of adopters. The next two groups are the earlier majority adopters and the later majority adopters, and together they make up 68% of the population of the social system. The individuals who make up the remaining 16% of the social system are referred to as laggards. They are the staunchest opponents of the introduction of a new innovation, and it is highly likely that they will not adopt the innovation at all. This is likely due to their limited resources as well as their lack of awareness or knowledge regarding the innovation.

2.1.2.3 Rational Choice Theory. A rule for determining utility is rational choice theory, which claims that, within certain limitations, how organisms behave is based on maximizing utility (Herrnstein, 1990). A normative application of rational choice theory is to determine whether behaviour is, in fact, best achieving desired goals and, if not, how it should be changed (Herrnstein, 1990). When social actors simply select the outcomes that are optimal for them given the constraints they are forced to deal with, the rational choice theory's explanations are more straightforward than when, for instance, the outcomes are the unintended and potentially undesirable by products of attempts to optimize in this way (Lovett, 2006).

In sociology, the rational choice theory is widely used, especially in the Netherlands and Germany. Explaining social phenomena in terms of the rational actions of individuals is the common thread running through all rational choice theorizing. Coleman's (1986) law can be used to describe this underlying structure. The premise of rational choice theory, which has its roots in classical criminology, is that people are free to choose the kinds of criminal behaviour they want to engage in; this is so even though their motivation is primarily driven by a desire to maximize pleasure and minimize/avoid pain. To be more precise, people voluntarily partake in criminal activity because they find it to be pleasurable, simple, and advantageous. However, if people are 'rational' by definition, as rational choice theory assumes, then it follows that they can be coerced into changing their behaviour if they're threatened with negative consequences. The utilitarian principle, which is central to rational choice theory, holds that people make decisions based on the perceived value of the outcomes of their actions (Coleman, 1986). To put it another way, if a person commits a crime, it will be because of a well-thought-out plan to achieve a specific goal while minimizing negative consequences. Thus, according to rational choice theory, an individual will commit an illegal act only if they have carefully considered the potential consequences of their actions and have concluded that the benefits outweigh the risks (Bentham, 1948). The rational choice theory argues that criminals should bear the consequences of their actions because they consciously made the decision to engage in criminal behaviour.

2.1.2.4 Consumer Choice Theory. Consumer demand curves and the theory of consumer choice are two important concepts in the study of microeconomics. It examines the ways in which consumers maximize utility within a consumer budget constraint, taking into account their preferences as a measure of what they should spend their money on. In other words, consumers' perception of value is a trade-off between cost and benefit (Wong et al., 2019). Consumers' perceptions of a product's value are affected by a variety of factors, including their income, their culture, and their biology and psychology (Gowdy & Mayumi, 2001).

Consumption and production are not synonymous with one another for logical reasons due to the involvement of two distinct economic agents. In the first scenario, consumption is done by the primary individual, and the amount of pleasure that people derive from the goods and services they consume is determined by the individual tastes or preferences of those individuals. In the second scenario, a producer may make something that he would not consume himself but sell it to other people. As a result, individuals bring their own unique set of capabilities and motivations to the table. On the basis of the hypothesis of constrained optimization, the models that constitute consumer theory are put to use to represent prospectively observable demand patterns for an individual purchaser. The price of the good per unit, the price of related goods, and the wealth of the consumer are three important variables that are considered when attempting to explain the rate at which the good is purchased (demanded) (Gowdy & Mayumi, 2001).

Even if the consumer is monetarily compensated for the effect of the higher price, according to the law of demand, the rate of consumption will still decrease when the price of the good increases. This phenomenon, which is known as the substitution effect, is predicted by the law of demand. When the price of a good goes up, customers will buy less of that good and more of the alternatives as a result of their purchasing decisions. If, as is typical, there is no compensation for the price increase, then the decrease in overall purchasing power brought on by the price increase will, for the most part, lead to a further decrease in the quantity demanded; this phenomenon is known as the income effect (Levin & Milgrom, 2004). The demand for almost all products goes up when an individual's wealth increases, which pushes the demand curve in an upward direction at any possible price.

2.1.2.5 The Norm Activation Theory. Individuals' prosocial intentions and actions are sought to be explained by the norm activation theory (Chen, 2015; Cordano et al., 2011). The norm activation theory has not been proven to adequately explain why and how people make environmentally responsible choices. It has been lauded by numerous previous research efforts in the fields of pro-environmental behaviour and consumer behaviour for its ability to accurately portray the complex procedure involved in the selection of environmentally friendly products and services (Bamberg & Möser, 2007; Stern, 2000). Existing theories with altruistic and environmentally conscious goals do not take into account all of the factors that affect green purchase behaviour. In particular, the attitudinal process (Han & Hyun, 2017), social norm (Bamberg & Möser, 2007), and image (Shin et al., 2018) all have been shown to play an important role in explaining why consumers have eco-friendly intentions when purchasing green products. The importance of these ideas in making environmentally responsible choices was emphasized by the researchers. Current prosocial and pro-environmental theories, however, fail to adequately outline any of these components.

Taking a qualitative approach, the Theory of green purchase behaviour (TGPB) directly addresses this problem by fusing the framework of existing theories with prosocial/pro-environmental motivations and such critical factors as attitude, social norm, image, and past behaviour. The theory posits that environmental value, an ecological worldview, and a virtuous image of green consumption all contribute to a heightened awareness of potential consequences. It is hypothesized that one's perspective on environmentally conscious purchases follows naturally from one's mental picture of such purchases and one's knowledge of their potential impacts. The authors propose that personal nom is directly activated by one's attitude towards environmentally friendly purchases, one's willingness to take responsibility, and one's exposure to the prevailing social norm. The most immediate direct antecedents of environmentally conscious purchasing behaviour are assumed to be the individual's past everyday behaviour and personal norm.

2.1.3 Green Product

Products that are considered green meet both the criteria of user and environmental safety and friendliness (Fraccascia et al., 2018; Tsai et al., 2020). Processes that are less harmful to the natural environment are typically used to manufacture green products (Davari & Strutton, 2014). Green products, according to Shamdasani et al. (1993), do not pollute the environment or deplete natural resources; they can be recycled or conserved; and they make use of eco-friendly ingredients and packaging (Nuttavuthisit & Thøgersen, 2017; Sreen et al., 2018).

Green products, as Ottman (2017) points out, are commonly used in business to refer to items that are environmentally friendly in terms of their materials, production methods, distribution channels, end-of-life care, or basic functionality (e.g. low energy consumption). Environmental sustainability is a product benefit, but it is not a benefit to the individual consumer in the same way that other product benefits, like quality attributes, are (Ottman, 2017). 'Green' or 'environmentally friendly' products are those that 'respect the principles of being recyclable, resource-saving, and low polluting during the raw material acquisition, manufacturing, distribution, consumption, and disposal processes', according to the Executive Yuan of Taiwan's Environmental Protection Administration (EPAT – 1995) (Ottman, 2017). According to this definition, eco-friendly goods are those that minimize their impact on the environment over the course of their full lifespan while maximizing resource efficiency. Other green goods are those that make efficient use of resources and minimize environmental damage across their entire product life cycle, or implement environmental safeguards. The introduction of environmentally friendly products has prompted businesses to take environmental responsibility more seriously and has created new market opportunities (Mukonza & Swarts, 2020). Related to this, enterprises' operational performance and profits can be boosted by investing time and resources into civic engagement and other CSR activities (Xie et al., 2019; Zameer et al., 2022; Zhang et al., 2019). As part of their corporate social responsibility efforts, businesses can also introduce environmentally friendly products (Zhang et al., 2019).

2.1.4 The Corporate Social Responsibility Perspective

2.1.4.1 Stakeholder Theory. Stakeholders are 'any group or individual who can affect or is affected by the achievement of the firm's objectives', as defined by Freeman and Reed (1983). Stakeholder theory proposes that a company's success hinges on how well it manages its relationships with its various constituencies (Freeman & Reed, 1983). Because the firm is seen as a nexus of explicit and implicit contracts (Jensen & Meckling, 1976), the traditional view that success is dependent solely on maximizing shareholder wealth is insufficient. Both a corporate planning and business policy model and a corporate social responsibility model of stakeholder management have emerged since Freeman and Reed's (1983) initial definition of stakeholders. The stakeholder concept is a model for corporate planning and business policy that emphasizes the creation and evaluation of corporate strategic decisions supported by groups essential to the corporation's survival. Users, owners, suppliers, and public interest groups are all considered stakeholders in this model; they do not act as competitors. By including potentially conflicting external influences on the company, the CSR model of stakeholder analysis broadens the scope of the corporate planning model. The antagonistic parties are typically portrayed as social-issue-focussed regulatory or special-interest groups. As the needs of society shift, the corporate social responsibility model can be adapted to meet them. Although these groups are not inherently hostile, their potentially contradictory behaviour is viewed as a limitation on the strategy created by management to optimally align the firm's resources with the environment. Stakeholder theory suggests that in light of this heightened environmental consciousness, businesses will need to broaden their corporate planning to include non-traditional stakeholders such as regulatory adversarial groups.

Stakeholder theory 'highlights organizational accountability beyond simple economic or financial performance', meaning that a company must fulfil the needs of more than just its shareholders if it is to succeed from a stakeholder perspective. According to stakeholder theory, a company's leadership must demonstrate responsibility to its constituents by carrying out the functions that these people have identified as crucial to the company's success. The literature examines how a central organization provides accountability to its various stakeholders (Smith & Rönnegard, 2016), and the term 'accountability' is frequently used in relation to this theory.

2.1.4.2 Ethical and Managerial Perspective of Stakeholder Theory. According to the ethical side of stakeholder theory, all stakeholders deserve to be treated fairly by a company, regardless of their relative strength (Deegan et al., 2002). The ethical stance requires taking into account all of an organization's stakeholders, rather than just a select few, such as the privileged parties who are in charge of providing crucial resources to the business (Deegan et al., 2002). From this vantage point, the organization is not seen as a means to maximize profits for its shareholders but rather as a means to satisfy the needs of all of its constituents, 'may require that the economic motive of organizations – to be profitable – be tempered to take account of the moral role of organizations and their enormous social effects on people's lives', write Atkin and Skitmore (2008), explaining the ethical branch of stakeholder theory. The accountability model of stakeholder theory put forth by Gray et al. (1988) has a direct bearing on this moral stance. It can be difficult for managers to treat all stakeholders fairly from an ethical standpoint, especially if those stakeholders' interests are at odds with one another. The ethical perspective of stakeholder theory or the normative approach to accountability has limited descriptive and explanatory power in a social accounting context, according to Gray et al. (1988).

In contrast, the managerial (positive) perspective of stakeholder theory holds that managers make an effort to satisfy the expectations of stakeholders who have control over the most important resources that the organization needs to function. To the extent that a stakeholder's resources are crucial to an organization (and thus highly relevant to the organization) the management of that organization should make every effort to fulfil the needs of that stakeholder (Deegan et al., 2002). Unlike the ethical perspective, which holds organizations accountable to all of their stakeholders, the managerial perspective holds them only to account for the most economically powerful of those stakeholders. According to this school of management thought, the firm's success or failure hinges on the level of activism and involvement from its various stakeholder groups (Murray & Vogel, 1997). Responsibility to whom and how far lies at the heart of this difficulty (O'Riordan & Fairbrass, 2008). Because of this, the managerial perspective of stakeholder theory is concerned primarily with the management of the connection between an organization and its most important stakeholders. Stakeholder theory from a managerial perspective, rather than an ethical perspective, can and is often subjected to empirical testing (Deegan et al., 2002).

2.1.4.3 Linking Stakeholder Theory to CSR Practice. In stakeholder theory, both the organization's responsibility and the stakeholders' rights are emphasized. Gray et al. (1988) stress that the disclosure of information should be responsibility-driven as opposed to demand-driven considering the stakeholders' rights to know. According to Gray et al. (1988) application of the accountability model to CSR reporting, 'the role of corporate social reporting is to provide society at large (the principal) with details (accountability) about the extent to which an organization (the agent) has met the responsibilities imposed on it'. Unlike the ethical perspective of stakeholder theory, which is rarely tested by empirical studies, the managerial perspective is the focus of many CSR empirical studies related to stakeholder theory. Some explanations for the levels and types of CSR disclosures can be found in the information needs of stakeholders and their measures of power, as demonstrated by Roberts (1992) in his application of stakeholder theory to the topic of corporate social responsibility disclosures. Capriotti and Moreno's (2007) study, which analyzed annual reports of publicly trading ecologically sensitive Canadian companies, came to similar conclusions. The findings suggest that companies cared more about the opinions of influential stakeholders like financiers and government regulators than they did about the views of less influential groups like environmentalists. Capriotti and Moreno (2007) conducted an interview-based study of corporate social responsibility (CSR) reporting in Bangladesh, using stakeholder theory to analyze data from 23 companies. These businesses represented a range of domestic, international, private, and public sectors. Findings suggest that managing the most influential stakeholder groups is the primary driver of CSR disclosure. By analyzing the CSR reporting practises of Bangladesh, Azizul Islam and Deegan (2008) looked into the ways in which the influence of stakeholder groups affects managerial decisions regarding CSR disclosures. According to their research, the foreign buyers of its member firms in the garment industry were the most influential stakeholders, and as such, they were the ones who largely shaped the CSR disclosure policies and practises of the industry as a whole.

In keeping with stakeholder theory, a company may partake in CSR activities and report on them so as to fulfil its responsibility to its various constituencies, both from an ethical and managerial point of view. To disclose corporate social responsibility (CSR) information is a clear acceptance by a company that its stakeholders have a right to know about certain aspects of the company's operations. CSR reporting helps level the playing field for various stakeholders by eliminating information gaps between them. A company that invests in its reputation and build relationships with its stakeholders stands to gain the support and approval of these groups, as well as improve the company's image and reputation, attract investors, reduce its cost of capital, retain and recruit top talent, and more (Gray et al., 1988). All these advantages may serve as a rationale for CSR reporting. CSR disclosure is motivated by the desire to manage powerful stakeholders, according to the managerial branch of stakeholder theory, while, according to the ethical branch, it is motivated by the desire to be accountable to all stakeholders regardless of their economic power.

3. Proposed Constructs of Customer Willingness

When evaluating people's decision-making processes, behavioural intentions are the closest precursors to actual behaviour (de Leaniz et al., 2019). Three crucial aspects have been used to study behavioural intentions: desire to suggest a company or make complimentary comments about its products, willingness to pay a premium price for these things, and willingness to repurchase goods or services from them (Zeithaml et al., 1996). This study investigates the behavioural intention using willingness to purchase. Morgan and Hunt demonstrated that the practise of 'relationship marketing', or the art of fostering and maintaining positive customer relationships, represents a significant departure from traditional approaches to marketing. Morgan and Hunt's (1994) KMV model of relationship marketing is grounded in the commitment-trust theory. The KMV model hypothesized that five antecedents (relationship termination cost, relationship benefits, shared value, communication, and opportunistic behaviour) were linked to five outcomes (trust, commitment, and honesty in relationships, shared values, and commitment) (acquiescence, propensity to leave, co-operation, functional conflict, and decision-making uncertainty). Morgan and Hunt (1994) hypothesized that their theory would apply to all relational exchanges, including those between suppliers, customers, and employees, and conducted tests in the context of the retail sale of automobile tyres. 'Further replication, extension, application, and critical evaluation' of their theory and model was something they felt was crucial. Trust, according to Morgan and Hunt (1994), exists when one party has faith in another's dependability and integrity as an exchange partner. Fostering trust between parties allows for the assessment of the predictability of future behaviour based on past interaction and promises, the mitigation of risk perception associated with opportunistic behaviour (Morgan & Hunt, 1994), the promotion of cooperative intention (Yoon & Rolland, 2012), the manipulation of parties' long-term orientation, and the development of relationship communication (Hashim & Tan, 2015). In the research, numerous trust factors have been isolated. In business, trustworthiness is crucial because it influences consumers' willingness to take risks (Humphrey & Schmitz, 1998). Morgan and Hunt (1994) assert that commitment is an essential complement to trust in economic exchange relationships. According to Moorman et al. (1993), relationship commitment is the 'enduring desire to maintain valued relationships'. Partners in business place a premium on maintaining strong bonds of trust among themselves (Hrebiniak, 1974). Morgan and Hunt (1994) also showed the trust-commitment interaction. Both trust and willingness lead to what we call 'behavioural intention'.

3.1 Direct Effect of CSR Image

Because it influences customers' behavioural decisions, the idea of a company's image has drawn significant attention from academics and practitioners (Martínez et al., 2017). Since CSR is an ethical standard for modern society and because it has implications for consumer behaviour and corporate financial performance, businesses across different industries are coming under increasing pressure to improve their socially responsible behaviour (Inoue & Lee, 2011). Consumer perceptions of environmental CSR programmes in restaurants lead to positive attitudes and intentions to patronize these businesses (Kim, 2017). CSR and corporate social irresponsibility (CSIR) are found to have an impact on customer behaviour, notably on willingness to pay and purchase intention (Ferreira & Ribeiro, 2017). As a result, we propose the following hypothesis:

H1. CSR image has positive impact on consumer willingness to purchase.

3.2 Direct Effect of Trust

Trust is essential to successful relationship marketing because it encourages marketers to work at sustaining relationships investments by collaborating with exchange partners (Morgan & Hunt, 1994). The propensity of a customer to believe that a company meets its promises about green performance can be used to define customer trust based on environmental factors (Chaudhuri & Holbrook, 2001). The intended behaviour will be aligned favourably if one side trusts the other (de Leaniz et al., 2019). Another study found that fair trade trust affects both self-reported and observed purchasing behaviour for fair trade products (Andorfer & Liebe, 2015). Based on the discussion, it is proposed that:

H2. Trust has positive impact on consumer willingness to purchase.

3.3 Indirect Effect of CSR Image

Trust is referred to as the expectation of ethical behaviour by one individual, group, or firm (Hosmer, 1994). Businesses should understand that CSR plays a crucial role in corporate reputation management and make the necessary investments, in which a good business reputation is regarded as the element that encourages partner companies to develop trust in managing business relations (Han & Lee, 2021). Companies may increase the trust of all stakeholders, including customers, by incorporating moral and responsible concepts into their strategic decision-making processes (Hosmer, 1994). Customers' trust can be increased by perceptions of CSR image (Lacey & Kennett-Hensel, 2010). CSR affects consumer attitudes and behaviours through trust (Vlachos et al., 2009). Thus, the following hypothesis is proposed:

H3. CSR image has positive impact on trust.

3.4 Indirect Effect of Green Marketing Mix

The creation of products with low energy use as well as possible pricing structures, outreach plans, and distribution networks were emphasized by Grove et al. (1996), in which all four P's of the traditional marketing mix should be green and take into account a wide range of various marketing choices that make up

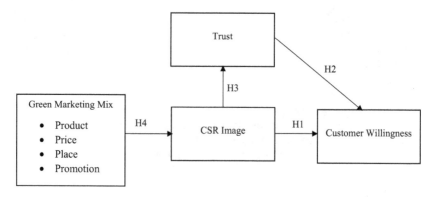

Fig. 12.1.   Preliminary Research Model.

green marketing. Evangelinos et al. (2009) revealed that banks' environmental performance and reputation are enhanced via green financial products and environmental tactics, such as loans to fund greener technology. Growing importance of social responsibility in marketing strategies is explained by the advent of the greening of marketing mix (Leonidou et al., 2013). Hanaysha (2020) found that advertising, price, store location, and store environment have an impact on store image. Therefore, we proposed that:

H4. Green marketing mix (product, price, promotion, and place) has positive impact on CSR image (see Fig. 12.1).

4. Conclusion

This study emphasizes on the development of the companies' strategies from the marketing mix and organization strategies. In view of the growing importance of the concept of sustainability, green marketing mix has been highlighted in this study. For organizational strategies development, CSR emerges as a critical aspect in relationship building among the stakeholders via trust. This study contributes to the strategies development of the green products business, which is significant to the success of entrepreneurs in this industry.

References

Ajzen, I. (1991). The theory of planned behavior. *Organizational Behavior and Human Decision Processes*, *50*(2), 179–211. https://doi.org/10.1016/0749-5978(91)90020-t

Al-dmour, H., Hadad, H., & Al-dmour, R. (2021). The impact of the adoption of green marketing on corporate performance of non-profitable organizations: Empirical study. *Social Responsibility Journal*, *19*(1), 1–19. https://doi.org/10.1108/srj-03-2021-0114

Andorfer, V. A., & Liebe, U. (2015). Do information, price, or morals influence ethical consumption? A natural field experiment and customer survey on the purchase of fair trade coffee. *Social Science Research, 52*, 330–350. https://doi.org/ 10.1016/j.ssresearch.2015.02.007

Atkin, B., & Skitmore, M. (2008). Editorial: Stakeholder management in construction. *Construction Management & Economics, 26*(6), 549–552. https://doi.org/10.1080/ 01446190802142405

Awan, A., Wamiq, S., & Ghafoor, A. (2016), Relationship between environmental awareness and green marketing. *Science International*, [online], *28*(3), 2959–2963. http://www.sci-int.com/pdf/636303798541729310.pdf

Azizul, I., & Deegan, M. (2008). Motivations for an organisation within a developing country to report social responsibility information. *Accounting, Auditing & Accountability Journal, 21*(6), 850–874. https://doi.org/10.1108/09513570810893272

Bamberg, S., & Möser, G. (2007). Why are work travel plans effective? Comparing conclusions from narrative and meta-analytical research synthesis. *Transportation, 34*(6), 647–666. https://doi.org/10.1007/s11116-007-9121-0

Bentham, J. (1948). *An introduction to the principles of morals and legislation (1789)*. Hafner.

Bhola, H. S. (1966). The configurational theory of innovation diffusion. *Public Opinion Quarterly, 30*(4), 668. https://doi.org/10.1086/267465

Brown, T. J., & Dacin, P. A. (1997). The company and the product: Corporate associations and consumer product responses. *Journal of Marketing, 61*(1), 68–84. https://doi.org/10.1177/002224299706100106

Capriotti, P., & Moreno, Á. (2007). Corporate citizenship and public relations: The importance and interactivity of social responsibility issues on corporate websites. *Public Relations Review, 33*(1), 84–91. https://doi.org/10.1016/j.pubrev.2006.11.012

Chaudhuri, A., & Holbrook, M. B. (2001). The chain of effects from brand trust and brand affect to brand performance: The role of brand loyalty. *Journal of Marketing, 65*(2), 81–93. https://doi.org/10.1509/jmkg.65.2.81.18255

Chen, M.-F. (2015). An examination of the value-belief-norm theory model in predicting pro-environmental behaviour in Taiwan: The value-belief-norm (VBN) theory model in predicting pro-environmental behaviour. *Asian Journal of Social Psychology, 18*(2), 145–151. https://doi.org/10.1111/ajsp.12096

Cheung, R., Lam, A. Y. C., & Lau, M. M. (2015). Drivers of green product adoption: The role of green perceived value, green trust and perceived quality. *Journal of Global Scholars of Marketing Science, 25*(3), 232–245. https://doi.org/10.1080/ 21639159.2015.1041781

Coleman, J. S. (1986). Social theory, social research, and a theory of action. *American Journal of Sociology, 91*(6), 1309–1335. https://doi.org/10.1086/228423

Cordano, M., et al. (2011). A cross-cultural assessment of three theories of pro-environmental behavior: A comparison between business students of Chile and the United States. *Environment and Behavior, 43*(5), 634–657. https://doi.org/10. 1177/0013916510378528

Dangelico, R. M., & Vocalelli, D. (2017). 'Green marketing': An Analysis of definitions, strategy steps, and tools through a systematic review of the literature. *Journal of Cleaner Production, 165*, 1263–1279. https://doi.org/10.1016/j.jclepro.2017.07. 184

Davari, A., & Strutton, D. (2014). Marketing mix strategies for closing the gap between green consumers' pro-environmental beliefs and behaviors. *Journal of Strategic Marketing, 22*(7), 563–586. https://doi.org/10.1080/0965254x.2014.914059

De Leaniz, P. M. G., Crespo, Á. H., & Gómez-López, R. (2019). The role of environmental CSR practices on the formation of behavioral intentions in a certified hotel context: Exploring the moderating effect of customer involvement in the buying process. *Spanish Journal of Marketing-ESIC, 23*(2), 205–226.

Deegan, C., Rankin, M., & Tobin, J. (2002). An examination of the corporate social and environmental disclosures of BHP from 1983–1997. *Accounting Auditing & Accountability Journal, 15*(3), 312–343. https://doi.org/10.1108/09513570210435861

de Groot, J. I. M., & Steg, L. (2008). Value orientations to explain beliefs related to environmental significant behavior: How to measure egoistic, altruistic, and biospheric value orientations. *Environment and Behavior, 40*(3), 330–354. https://doi.org/10.1177/0013916506297831

Desai, K. K., & Trivedi, M. (2014). Do consumer perceptions matter in measuring choice variety and variety seeking? *Journal of Business Research, 67*(1), 2786–2792. https://doi.org/10.1016/j.jbusres.2012.08.019

Dibra, M. (2015). Rogers theory on diffusion of innovation-the most appropriate theoretical model in the study of factors influencing the integration of sustainability in tourism businesses. *Procedia, Social and Behavioral Sciences, 195*, 1453–1462. https://doi.org/10.1016/j.sbspro.2015.06.443f

Du, S., Bhattacharya, C. B., & Sen, S. (2010). Maximizing business returns to corporate social responsibility (CSR): The role of CSR communication. *International Journal of Management Reviews, 12*(1), 8–19. https://doi.org/10.1111/j.1468-2370.2009.00276.x

Dunlap, R. E., et al. (2000). New trends in measuring environmental attitudes: Measuring endorsement of the new ecological paradigm: A revised NEP scale. *Journal of Social Issues, 56*(3), 425–442. https://doi.org/10.1111/0022-4537.00176

Dunlap, R. E., & Van Liere, K. D. (1978). The new environmental paradigm. *The Journal of Environmental Education, 9*(4), 10–19. https://doi.org/10.1080/00958964.1978.10801875

Evangelinos, K. I., Skouloudis, A., & Nikolaou, I. E. (2009). An analysis of corporate social responsibility (CSR) and sustainability reporting assessment in the Greek banking sector. In *Professionals' perspectives of corporate social responsibility* (pp. 157–173). Springer. https://doi.org/10.1007/978-3-642-02630-0_9

Fatma, M., & Rahman, Z. (2015). Consumer perspective on CSR literature review and future research agenda. *Management Research Review, 38*(2), 195–216. https://doi.org/10.1108/mrr-09-2013-0223

Ferreira, A. I., & Ribeiro, I. (2017). Are you willing to pay the price? The impact of corporate social (ir)responsibility on consumer behavior towards national and foreign brands: The CSR and COO effects on consumer behavior. *Journal of Consumer Behaviour, 16*(1), 63–71. https://doi.org/10.1002/cb.1603

Fraccascia, L., Giannoccaro, I., & Albino, V. (2018). Green product development: What does the country product space imply? *Journal of Cleaner Production, 170*, 1076–1088. https://doi.org/10.1016/j.jclepro.2017.09.190

Freeman, R. E., & Reed, D. L. (1983). Stockholders and stakeholders: A new perspective on corporate governance. *California Management Review, 25*(3), 88–106. https://doi.org/10.2307/41165018

Garg, A. (2015). Green marketing for sustainable development: An industry perspective: Green marketing for sustainable development: An industry perspective. *Sustainable Development, 23*(5), 301–316. https://doi.org/10.1002/sd.1592

Gowdy, J. M., & Mayumi, K. (2001). Reformulating the foundations of consumer choice theory and environmental valuation. *Ecological Economics: The Journal of the International Society for Ecological Economics, 39*(2), 223–237. https://doi.org/10.1016/s0921-8009(01)00197-5

Gray, R., Owen, D., & Maunders, K. (1988). Corporate social reporting: Emerging trends in accountability and the social contract. *Accounting Auditing & Accountability, 1*(1), 6–20. https://doi.org/10.1108/eum0000000004617

Grove, S. J., et al. (1996). Going green in the service sector: Social responsibility issues, implications and implementation. *European Journal of Marketing, 30*(5), 56–66. https://doi.org/10.1108/03090569610118777

Hanaysha, J. R. (2020). Marketing mix elements and corporate social responsibility: Do they really matter to store image? *Jindal Journal of Business Research, 9*(1), 56–71. https://doi.org/10.1177/2278682120908563

Han, H., & Hyun, S. S. (2017). Drivers of customer decision to visit an environmentally responsible museum: Merging the theory of planned behavior and norm activation theory. *Journal of Travel & Tourism Marketing, 34*(9), 1155–1168. https://doi.org/10.1080/10548408.2017.1304317

Han, S. L., & Lee, J. W. (2021). Does corporate social responsibility matter even in the B2B market?: Effect of B2B CSR on customer trust. *Industrial Marketing Management, 93*, 115–123.

Hashim, K. F., & Tan, F. B. (2015). The mediating role of trust and commitment on members' continuous knowledge sharing intention: A commitment-trust theory perspective. *International Journal of Information Management, 35*(2), 145–151. https://doi.org/10.1016/j.ijinfomgt.2014.11.001

Herrnstein, R. J. (1990). Rational choice theory: Necessary but not sufficient. *American Psychologist, 45*(3), 356–367. https://doi.org/10.1037/0003-066x.45.3.356

Hosmer, L. T. (1994). Strategic planning as if ethics mattered. *Strategic Management Journal, 15*, 20–32.

Hrebiniak, L. G. (1974). Effects of job level and participation on employee attitudes and perceptions of influence. *Academy of Management Journal, 17*(4), 649–662. https://doi.org/10.5465/255644

Humphrey, J., & Schmitz, H. (1998). Trust and inter-firm relations in developing and transition economies. *Journal of Development Studies, 34*(4), 32–61. https://doi.org/10.1080/00220389808422528

Inoue, Y., & Lee, S. (2011). Effects of different dimensions of corporate social responsibility on corporate financial performance in tourism-related industries. *Tourism Management, 32*(4), 790–804. https://doi.org/10.1016/j.tourman.2010.06.019

Jensen, M. C., & Meckling, W. H. (1976). Theory of the firm: Managerial behavior, agency costs and ownership structure. *Journal of Financial Economics, 3*(4), 305–360. https://doi.org/10.1016/0304-405x(76)90026-x

Jeuland, A. P. (1978). *Brand preference over time: A partially deterministic operationalization of the notion of variety seeking.* University of Chicago, Center for Research Marketing.

Kahn, B. E. (1995). Consumer variety-seeking among goods and services. *Journal of Retailing and Consumer Services, 2*(3), 139–148. https://doi.org/10.1016/0969-6989(95)00038-0

Karmasin, M., & Litschka, M. (2017). CSR as an economic, ethical, and communicative concept. In *Handbook of integrated CSR communication* (pp. 37–50). Springer International Publishing.

Kim, Y. (2017). Consumer responses to the food industry's proactive and passive environmental CSR, factoring in price as CSR tradeoff. *Journal of Business Ethics, 140*(2), 307–321. https://doi.org/10.1007/s10551-015-2671-8

Lacey, R., & Kennett-Hensel, P. A. (2010). Longitudinal effects of corporate social responsibility on customer relationships. *Journal of Business Ethics, 97*(4), 581–597. https://doi.org/10.1007/s10551-010-0526-x

Lenz, I., Wetzel, H. A., & Hammerschmidt, M. (2017). Can doing good lead to doing poorly? Firm value implications of CSR in the face of CSI. *Journal of the Academy of Marketing Science, 45*(5), 677–697. https://doi.org/10.1007/s11747-016-0510-9

Leonidou, C. N., Katsikeas, C. S., & Morgan, N. A. (2013). Greening' the marketing mix: Do firms do it and does it pay off? *Journal of the Academy of Marketing Science, 41*(2), 151–170.

Levin, J., & Milgrom, P. (2004). *Consumer theory.* [online]. https://web.stanford.edu/~jdlevin/Econ%20202/Consumer%20Theory.pdf

Li, Z., Zou, F., & Mo, B. (2021). Does mandatory CSR disclosure affect enterprise total factor productivity? *Economic Research-Ekonomska Istraživanja*, 1–20. https://doi.org/10.1080/1331677x.2021.2019596

Lovett, F. (2006). Rational choice theory and explanation. *Rationality and Society, 18*(2), 237–272. https://doi.org/10.1177/1043463106060155

Mahmoud, T. O. (2018). Impact of green marketing mix on purchase intention. *International Journal of Advanced and Applied Sciences, 5*(2), 127–135. https://doi.org/10.21833/ijaas.2018.02.020

Martínez García de Leaniz, P. M., Herrero Crespo, P., & Gómez López, Á. (2017). Customer responses to environmentally certified hotels: The moderating effect of environmental consciousness on the formation of behavioral intentions. *Journal of Sustainable Tourism, 26*(7), 1160–1177. https://doi.org/10.1080/09669582.2017.1349775

McAlister, L., & Pessemier, E. (1982). Variety seeking behavior: An interdisciplinary review. *Journal of Consumer Research, 9*(3), 311. https://doi.org/10.1086/208926

Mishra, M. K., Choudhury, D., & Rao, K. S. V. G. (2019). Impact of strategic and tactical green marketing orientation on SMEs performance. *Theoretical Economics Letters, 09*(05), 1633–1650. https://doi.org/10.4236/tel.2019.95104

Moorman, C., Deshpandé, R., & Zaltman, G. (1993). Factors affecting trust in market research relationships. *Journal of Marketing, 57*(1), 81–101. https://doi.org/10.1177/002224299305700106

Morgan, R. M., & Hunt, S. D. (1994). The commitment-trust theory of relationship marketing. *Journal of Marketing, 58*(3), 20–38. https://doi.org/10.1177/002224299405800302

Mukonza, C., & Swarts, I. (2020). The influence of green marketing strategies on business performance and corporate image in the retail sector. *Business Strategy and the Environment, 29*(3), 838–845. https://doi.org/10.1002/bse.2401

Murray, K. B., & Vogel, C. M. (1997). Using a hierarchy-of-effects approach to gauge the effectiveness of corporate social responsibility to generate goodwill toward the firm: Financial versus nonfinancial impacts. *Journal of Business Research, 38*(2), 141–159. https://doi.org/10.1016/s0148-2963(96)00061-6

Nuttavuthisit, K., & Thøgersen, J. (2017). The importance of consumer trust for the emergence of a market for green products: The case of organic food. *Journal of Business Ethics, 140*(2), 323–337. https://doi.org/10.1007/s10551-015-2690-5

O'Riordan, L., & Fairbrass, J. (2008). Corporate social responsibility (CSR): Models and theories in stakeholder dialogue. *Journal of Business Ethics, 83*(4), 745–758. https://doi.org/10.1007/s10551-008-9662-y

Ottman, J. A. (2017). *The new rules of green marketing,* [online]. Routledge. https://doi.org/10.4324/9781351278683

Putrawan, M. (2020). Students' value-belief-norm (VBN) model interfered by environmental big-five personality. *Journal of Advanced Research in Dynamical and Control Systems, 12*(SP8), 197–202. https://doi.org/10.5373/jardcs/v12sp8/20202515

Roberts, R. W. (1992). Determinants of corporate social responsibility disclosure: An application of stakeholder theory. *Accounting, Organizations and Society, 17*(6), 595–612. https://doi.org/10.1016/0361-3682(92)90015-k

Schwartz, S. H. (1977). Normative Influences on Altruism. In *Advances in experimental social psychology* (pp. 221–279). Elsevier.

Seetharaman, P. B., & Chintagunta, P. (1998). A model of inertia and variety-seeking with marketing variables. *International Journal of Research in Marketing, 15*(1), 1–17. https://doi.org/10.1016/s0167-8116(97)00015-3

Shamdasani, P., Chon-Lin, G. O., & Richmond, D. (1993). *Exploring green consumers in an oriental culture: Role of personal and marketing mix factors.* ACR North American Advances, NA-20. https://www.acrwebsite.org/volumes/7504/volumes/v20/NA-20/full. Accessed on January 14, 2023.

Shin, Y. H., et al. (2018). The theory of planned behavior and the norm activation model approach to consumer behavior regarding organic menus. *International Journal of Hospitality Management, 69*, 21–29. https://doi.org/10.1016/j.ijhm.2017.10.011

Simonson, I. (1990). The effect of purchase quantity and timing on variety-seeking behavior. *Journal of Marketing Research, 27*(2), 150. https://doi.org/10.2307/3172842

Smith, N. C., & Rönnegard, D. (2016). Shareholder primacy, corporate social responsibility, and the role of business schools. *Journal of Business Ethics, 134*(3), 463–478. https://doi.org/10.1007/s10551-014-2427-x

Sniehotta, F. (2009). An experimental test of the theory of planned behavior. *Applied Psychology. Health and Well-Being, 1*(2), 257–270. https://doi.org/10.1111/j.1758-0854.2009.01013.x

Sreen, N., Purbey, S., & Sadarangani, P. (2018). Impact of culture, behavior and gender on green purchase intention. *Journal of Retailing and Consumer Services, 41*, 177–189. https://doi.org/10.1016/j.jretconser.2017.12.002

Steg, L., De Groot, J. I. M., Dreijerink, L., Abrahamse, W., & Siero, F. (2011). General antecedents of personal norms, policy acceptability, and intentions: The role of values, worldviews, and environmental concern. *Society & Natural Resources, 24*(4), 349–367. https://doi.org/10.1080/08941920903214116

Stern, P. C. (2000). New environmental theories: Toward a coherent theory of environmentally significant behavior. *Journal of Social Issues, 56*(3), 407–424. https://doi.org/10.1111/0022-4537.00175

Tsai, P.-H., Lin, G.-Y., Zheng, Y.-L., Chen, Y.-C., Chen, P.-Z., & Su, Z.-C. (2020). Exploring the effect of Starbucks' green marketing on consumers' purchase decisions from consumers' perspective. *Journal of Retailing and Consumer Services, 56*, 102162. https://doi.org/10.1016/j.jretconser.2020.102162

Van Liere, K. D., & Dunlap, R. E. (1978). Moral norms and environmental behavior: An application of Schwartz's norm-activation model to yard burning 1. *Journal of Applied Social Psychology, 8*(2), 174–188.

Vlachos, P. A., Tsamakos, A., Vrechopoulos, A. P., & Avramidis, P. K. (2009). Corporate social responsibility: Attributions, loyalty, and the mediating role of trust. *Journal of the Academy of Marketing Science, 37*(2), 170–180. https://doi.org/10.1007/s11747-008-0117-x

Wong, T. Y., Iris, T., & Lim, W. (2019). Consumers purchase intention towards organic food in Malaysia. In *Proceedings of the 2nd international conference on big data technologies* (pp. 306–309). ACM Digital Library.

Xie, X., Huo, J., & Zou, H. (2019). Green process innovation, green product innovation, and corporate financial performance: A content analysis method. *Journal of Business Research, 101*, 697–706. https://doi.org/10.1016/j.jbusres.2019.01.010

Yadav, R., & Pathak, G. S. (2017). Determinants of consumers' green purchase behavior in a developing nation: Applying and extending the theory of planned behavior. *Ecological Economics: The Journal of the International Society for Ecological Economics, 134*, 114–122. https://doi.org/10.1016/j.ecolecon.2016.12.019

Yoon, C., & Rolland, E. (2012). Knowledge-sharing in virtual communities: Familiarity, anonymity and self-determination theory. *Behaviour & Information Technology, 31*(11), 1133–1143. https://doi.org/10.1080/0144929x.2012.702355

Zameer, H., Wang, Y., Yasmeen, H., & Mubarak, S. (2022). Green innovation as a mediator in the impact of business analytics and environmental orientation on green competitive advantage. *Management Decision, 60*(2), 488–507.

Zeithaml, V. A., Berry, L. L., & Parasuraman, A. (1996). The behavioral consequences of service quality. *Journal of Marketing, 60*(2), 31–46. https://doi.org/10.1177/002224299606000203

Zhang, L., et al. (2019). Extending the theory of planned behavior to explain the effects of cognitive factors across different kinds of green products. *Sustainability, 11*(15), 4222. https://doi.org/10.3390/su11154222

Chapter 13

Green Organizational Practices for Green Product Development: The Green Influence of Transformational Leadership

Abdul Samad, Salman Bashir and Sumaiya Syed

Abstract

Growing environmental challenge awareness among consumers is today's business reality that pushes for sustainable product development. Governments, industries, and consumers' attention are significantly moved from traditional products to eco-friendly product development. Green product development is the future for manufacturing businesses' survival in most markets. Green product development is an emerging phenomenon and, unfortunately, lacks theoretical and empirical research regarding effective organizational policies and practices for green product development. This study aims at filling research gaps towards green product development by highlighting green employee aspects influenced by leadership for sustainable business growth. The study hypothesized relations between the green effect of transformational leadership on green product development as an outcome through green behaviour, green climate, and green innovative creativity. Data was collected from small and medium enterprises (SMEs) of Karachi through a self-administered survey questionnaire. Results revealed significant support for hypothesized relations through the partial least square statistical tool. This study contributes theoretical and empirical advancement in past literature wherein leadership style influences employee behaviour that leads to predict product development from an environmental perspective. Study inferences suggest for visionary green leadership style for sustainable business growth. Limitations of this study regarding other variable inclusiveness, sampling, and geography are potential extensions for further scholarly investigation.

Keywords: Green Transformational leadership; green behaviour; green innovative climate; green creativity; green product development; SMEs

Entrepreneurship and Green Finance Practices, 239–265
Copyright © 2024 Abdul Samad, Salman Bashir and Sumaiya Syed
Published under exclusive licence by Emerald Publishing Limited
doi:10.1108/978-1-80455-678-820231013

1. Introduction

Human beings have evolved and changed over time, so has the environment. Unfortunately, environmental degradation reached exponentially to a threatening level to our environments, such as ozone layer depletion, global warming issues, and excessive use of earth's natural resources. These drastic changes have moved the global economy, governments, and businesses to realize that environmental challenges are critical for both economic development and organizational performance (Huang et al., 2016). Thus, natural environment and resource protection are inevitable for future generation viability (Dyllick & Hockerts, 2002), which urgently calls for an introduction to the notions of sustainable development (Bombiak & Marciniuk-Kluska, 2018) and formulation of policies and practices specifically on Asian developing countries to deal with this global problem (Mohsin et al., 2021).

Likewise, human activities over 50 years are reported to have sharply expanded demands for fish, freshwater, timber, fibre, and fuel, altering the ecosystem resulting in a loss to earth resources on which both industry and society depend (UNEP World Conservation Monitoring Centre, 2010). Besides the literary meaning of the word green as a colour, the environmental sustainability concept is now a global challenge related to human activities both in developed and developing countries. Adding to the graveness of the issue, the below Fig. 13.1 by Global Footprint Network shows how human activities have endangered the planet beyond sustainable thresholds.

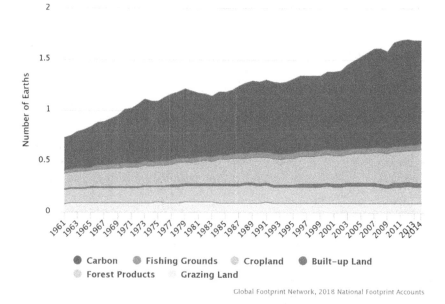

Global Footprint Network, 2018 National Footprint Accounts

Fig. 13.1.   World Ecological Footprint by Land Type.

In Fig. 13.1, the green line represents the earth's natural productive area available for human beings, while the coloured lines, since the 1980s, show footprint hype clearly beyond earth's bio-regenerative capacity to support human needs in terms of agriculture, fishing, and grazing. Accordingly, in an urgent call of General Assembly by United Nations, A global agenda for change, the chairman asked to formulate long-term environmental strategies by the year 2000 and beyond for sustainable development. And to recommend ways of cooperation, particularly among developing countries for mutual objective to achieve people, resources, and environmental development, figure out effective ways for the international community regarding the environment, and define courses to deal with environmental problems for years to come for the international community, without risking next-generation ability to satisfy their needs the greenway (WCED, 2018). Thus, contemporary organizations must effectively deliver and implement green HRM policies to track relevant eco-friendly behaviours, attitudes, and employees' motivations (Dumont et al., 2017).

Natural resources are being utilized lavishly to create different merchandise and facilities required by individuals who want to advance their lives. The environmentally ruinous nature of organizational activities and consequence (Shrivastava, 1994) has influenced global environmental problems. According to Rugman and Verbeke (1998), environmental problems are the critical and most complex executive challenges of the modern era. It includes environmental transformation, scarcity of resources, and natural disturbance. The rapid disaster of natural resources is becoming a critical issue in the current era. Consequently, organizations are accountable for the ecological weakening (Alshuwaikhat & Abubakar, 2008; Haden et al., 2009). Thus, it should be the goal of every organization to build a greener society. Unfortunately, few organizations step above the status quo to fulfil more significant societal needs, for example, *Google* data centres need energy for which solar panels are deployed, reducing 50% of energy consumption and bike-to-work programmes that help to reduce 10,000 tons of CO_2 each year. Likewise, *Ford* contributes by adopting electrified vehicles as an alternative to conventional fuel-based transport such as hybrid and electric vehicles that reduce CO_2 emissions (Ford Motor Company). *Toyota* has reduced the environmental impact of the vehicle at the cars' all stages of life cycle by establishing recycling-based society 'Eco-driving', from design to sales waste and promotes environmental management (Environmental Responsibility).

Similarly, in the context Pakistan, deterioration of global climate change was witnessed in Pakistan's heavy rains and flood of 2022. According to World bank report (2022), Pakistan has suffered heavy loss of over USD 300 billion, where total damages were USD 14.9 billion, economic loss USD 15.2 billion, while rehabilitation and reconstruction needs at least USD 16.3 billion. Along with that according to USAID report 2022 fact sheet # 3 estimated 33 million people estimated as flood affected, 6.4 people need humanitarian assistance, 1.7 million people houses were destroyed, 634,749 people located at flood affected cites, and more than 1,355 unfortunate people lost their lives.

2. Literature Review

The importance of effective production is widely acceptable for long-term corporate success (Cooper, 1979). Ceres is leading an organization comprising of business leaders, investors, public interest groups, and policymakers, and other critical economic players stressed the efforts for long-run sustainable environment and societal risks integration rather than short-term business profitability (Douglas, 2012). However, few researchers and practitioners are defining ways and means to follow clean and green operations. For example, the impact of consumers by consuming green products environment is more prevalent with strict environmental regulations in the world (Jain & Kaur, 2004).

Likewise, the public is aware of purchasing green products that are eco-friendly (Chen, 2010). Since consumers pay more attention to environmental issues making consumer environmentalism more popular (Murga-Menoyo, 2014), contemporary firms must incorporate green image and ideas into product developmental processes to ascertain competitive advantage (Chen, 2008). As evident that companies that have firm green policies are generally benefiting in terms of growing sales and brand recognition (Yang et al., 2011) and desirable employee outcomes (Salem et al., 2012). For example, 56% of Americans in the USA are more likely to pay for a product that is low at carbon emission (Roe et al., 2001), while another study by Makower (2009) reported that 53% of Americans, 83% Brazilians, and 93% of Thai consumers are ready to pay more for green products.

According to the UK Green Building council, the environment is adversely affected by construction companies that use more than 400 million tons of earthly materials for construction purposes. While US-based construction companies expel 160 million tons of construction industry trash that is 25% of non-industrial waste is added to the environment. Likewise, according to construction research blog Bimhow, the construction sector alone is responsible for 23% of air pollution, 40% drinking water pollution, and 50% global climate change. In another investigation conducted by US Green Building Council (USGBC), 40% of global energy is consumed by the construction industry, with an estimated increase of commercial carbon emission up to 1.8% by 2030 (Snook, 2017).

Asia is a dynamic region with a 45% global consumer market share by 2020, according to Forbs-custom report (2018). For example, Singapore is one of the emerging economies and hub for global innovation thriving from the book, food, and buildings to smartphones. It has recently stepped to go green in every sector of production. According to the Singapore business review report (2018), 88% of Singaporeans businesses should be responsible for corporate social responsibility. One of the leading examples is City Development Limited (CDL) existing for the last seven years. Based in Singapore was enlisted in 2016 among the 10 most sustainable companies in Global 100 by Canadian firm corporate Knights. In line with the United Nations' Sustainable Development Goals (SDGs), CDL is the first company that matched these goals related to their construction materials and is the only Singapore firm enlisted in Global Compact 100 Index.

CDL is a construction company in Singapore leading environmental, social, and economic aspects of development. CDL's tree-house project in Chestnut Avenue in Singapore, set for Guinness record, is expected to save 15%–30% of air-conditioning energy due to its eco-friendly material and structures. Moreover, between 2008 and 2015 CDL's green-certified buildings saved worth S$31 million of the energy a significant portion was passed to its residents and home buyers. Thus, sustainable development is not an option rather an essential component of economic and corporate success.

Unfortunately, in a similar context, Pakistan is entirely out of sight, which this empirical effort attempts to highlight. Pakistan Green Building Council (PGDC) is a member of the World Green Building Council, working as a non-profit organization and educating concerned authorities at all platforms such as through conferences and expo events. PGDC currently has 70-member organizations, and some of them are related to developing green products under the construction sector scope. Such as energy-saving lightings, electric appliances for a building material that is less costly and environmentally friendly.

While Pakistan is among developing countries where most organizations are still working on the traditional method, leading to misuse and waste of resources such as energy, transport, water, paper, and they hardly only focus on environmental issues. However, it falls against sustainable development goals 12 (SDG12) by the government of Pakistan through the National Action Plan (NAP) regarding sustainable consumption and production goals to follow the World Agenda 2030 as reported in the ministry of climate change 2017.

In Pakistan, the idea of green construction began in 2005, after an earthquake of 7.8 Richter scale. Followed by the 2010 floods, which resulted in collapse at a large scale, but no serious action was taken. Therefore, it is high time to bring attention back to sustainable construction (Ahmed & Asad, 2016). Contrary to conventional buildings, which add to environmental degradation, green buildings are one of the possible solutions to cope with energy and water shortage in the country (Ahmed & Asad, 2016).

Critically, Pakistan is running in an energy crisis state (Qasim & Kotani, 2014), and inefficient contemporary advancements are making it worse. Thus, energy-efficient equipment for buildings is inevitable for higher business operational costs. Luckily, the retail industry shares worth $ 8.4 billion in the green market in 2018–2025. These direct towards the adoption of green infrastructures and energy sufficient solutions for developing countries like Pakistan.

Further, Ramasamy et al. (2010), while categorizing for measuring social responsibility by any organization, identified a 'Green management system' that includes environmental practices which depend on the presence of environmental practice department in the organization based mainly on the person (leader, manager, or supervisor) that implements environmental practices. Similarly, from the past 10 years, there is a shift from thinking green to green housings and now to green buildings by companies as a strategy. Importantly, CEOs are stepping in to achieve corporate social goals through building green. Whereas increased environmentalism and green products are more prevalent in the market (Chen & Chang, 2012). Making it is compulsory for the companies to go green (Sheu, 2014) and establish management philosophies to compete and meet with green era challenges (Zhao & Guo, 2014).

The theory and literature have addressed this issue less yet, sustainability is a strategically future corporate asset (Weinberg, 1998), hence, sustainable business is not an option rather an essential component of social and business success. Similarly, it should be the goal of every contemporary organization to effectively deliver and implement green HRM policies to track relevant green environment in the organization (Chou, 2014; Dravigne et al., 2008), green behaviours, attitudes, and motivations of employees (Dumont et al., 2017; Mandip, 2012); employee green job satisfaction (DeHart-Davis et al., 2014); green creativity among employees (Chen & Chang, 2013); influenced by green transformational leadership (Jia et al., 2018). Since all the green technologies, products, and services are yet to be explored, similarly, most businesses and companies have not developed a green leadership to influence the green employee mindset. According to Dunst et al. (2018), professional development is the result of policies adopted and implemented by the leaders.

Though it is true that leadership sometimes is a mere perception of the individuals (Janda, 1960). Since leadership is at the core of any management system, this seems to be the most endeavoured and enriched topic in social science, while adjusted as per interest and requirement with time. Similarly, Voon et al. (2011) different leaders had different influence on subordinates. According to Silva (2016), many scholars argue that there are more than 1,000 definitions of leadership. This leads researchers to fill the gap for direct and indirect effect green transformational leadership on green product development.

For businesses to succeed in the future, they must think about developing products that are environmentally friendly and meet the demands of consumers related to environmental protection. In this respect, SMEs are essential for viable productivity, delivering more inclusive growth, and adapting to megatrends.

Globally, informal and formal SMEs makeup over 95% of all firms, account for approximately 50% of GDP and 60%–70% of total employment. Which equates to worth between 420 million and 510 million SMEs, 310 million of which are in emerging markets. Considering the impact and vitality, promoting financing to SMEs has been on the global reforms' agenda since the global financial crisis (Elasrag, 2016). In addition, SMEs' growth has a considerable impact on employment creation, innovations, productivity, and competitiveness (Cusmano et al., 2018). For example, with an unemployment rate of 2.1% and per capita GDP of nearly $53,000, Singapore's economy is one of the world's strongest economies. This vibrant economy is powered by SMEs, which make up 99% of all enterprises and 65% of all employed workforce (Hoffman, 2018).

As far as the role of SMEs in Pakistan is concerned (Shah & Syed, 2018, pp. 21–23) the support of SMEs to Pakistan's economy is revealed in Fig. 13.2. According to the Chairman of a Regional Trade Association '. . .. SME sector has the potential to turn around Pakistan's economy. . .' Although numerous

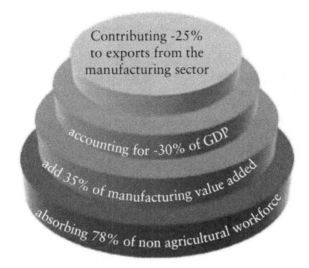

Fig. 13.2.   SMEs Contribution to Pakistan Economy.

researches have established that the development of the green product is the need of the day. In contrast, considerable gaps are still there to examine the effects of green innovations in green product performance development (e.g. Kawai et al., 2018). Hence, besides potential profitability, going green in terms of building equipped with energy-efficient appliances, energy-saving lightings, and air conditioning will contribute to cost efficiency and environmental quality, directing colossal potential for research and development in the manufacturing industry for green product development. Unfortunately, there is scarcity regarding green product development research in-depth and its implementation and application in organizations daily.

Consequently, this study aims at filling the theoretical and empirical gap by examining what influence green transformational leadership has on green product development through both green creativity and green behaviour.

3. Hypothesis Development

The following sections detail the development of a conceptual model for business through transformational leadership with green effects on important organizational aspects towards the development of green product development.

3.1 The Green Perspective of Transformational Leadership

According to Conger (1999), the past empirical and theoretical scholarly work mainly focussed on leader's behaviour and their effect areas, while Bass and Avolio (1994); Conger and Kanungo (1998); Shamir et al. (1993) provided extensive exploration which paved the common grounds to understand the transformational leadership phenomenon. Similarly, scholars indicated environmental aspects of transformational leadership (e.g. Chen & Chang, 2013). From the theoretical perspectives, the integration of transformational leadership to execute successful green practice and the contemporary organization achieve desired green goals for the sustainable environment through influencing followers, based on well-known Leader–Member–Exchange theory (Graen & Uhl-Bien, 1995). The latest development of LMX theory explains the green influence integration over followers and performance of team members based on informal association with leaders (Graen & Canedo, 2016). Those followers who accept the influence that results in a robust leader–follower association share mutual respect, trust, and goodwill (Graen & Schiemann, 2013). Further, these followers are more collaborative, helpful team members, and engage well with the team, and contribute towards organizational prosperity. This seems a win-win situation for leader–follower, team members, and overall organization (Nier, 2013). Therefore, based on firm literature, transformational leadership is contended to have a green impact on environment sustainable productions and services (Huang et al., 2023), and to positively execute new greener practices in an organization which will effectively reduce environmental problem faced by developed and developing nations at present and in the long run.

3.2 Green Transformational Leadership and Follower Green Behaviour

Employees are the main force that makes feasible the execution of green organizational policies. Thus, organizations need to align green organizational policies with their green goals through the change in employee behaviour (Daily et al., 2009; Ones & Dilchert, 2012). For instance, employee behaviours are at the discretion of different factors which determine when and how to exhibit these behaviours (Hoffman & Dilchert, 2012). Whereas green behaviours are influenced by antecedents in the organization, leadership style is one (Andersson, 2013). The employee's green behaviour is pro-social (Chou, 2014). Accordingly, transformational leaders promote collective identity (Conger, 1999), which is the extent to which people see themselves as pro-environmental and act accordingly (Werff et al., 2014) resulting in employee green behaviour (Hu et al., 2023). Therefore, from a practical perspective, green behaviour at the workplace daily should involve both in-role and extra-role green behaviour (Ramus & Killmer, 2007). Where in-role green behaviour is job described role that the organization expects from employees (Paillé & Boiral, 2013). While extra-role green behaviour is rather a pro-environmental act not encrypted in job description such as turning off computers while leaving the office or simple suggestions to improve green organizational ambiance (Paillé & Boiral, 2013). Both in-role and extra-role green behaviours are essential to achieve organizational green goals (Norton et al., 2014). Based on integrated discussion following hypothesis is developed;

H1: Green transformational leadership positively affect green employee behaviour.

3.3 Green Transformational Leadership and Innovative Climate

Past literature on organizational climate suggests that employees' behavior is the reflection of collective perception about the organization (Schneider et al., 2013). Rupp et al. (2006) contended on theoretical bases that employees' behavior, attitude, and emotional response are the perception of an organizational social programme, for example, corporate social responsibility initiatives. Hence, employees will not take productive initiatives if the organization is not highly concerned with innovation; even employees are given complete autonomy (Yukl, 2001). Moreover, Mumford and Gustafson (1988) argued that organizational innovation capacity depends on the climate supporting innovation. While integrating leadership, Mumford et al. (2002) found that organizational climate and culture signify the collective social construction embarked on under leaders' control. As leaders or managers play a crucial role in developing, transform, and institutionalize organizational culture (Schein, 1992), leaders communicate what is right and what is wrong to practice, which becomes the norms of the organizational climate (Jung, 2001).

Transformational leaders have features that motivate and change follower's long-term inventive perspectives. Further, transformational leaders trigger employee innovation efforts by interrogating their problems, assumptions, and approaches in different ways that induce establishing a culture that creates value through innovative work approaches by the employees. Once achieved, this innovative organizational climate develops sense and guides principles that ultimately innovative products and services (Scott & Bruce, 1994). Followed by Begum et al. (2022) found that transformational leadership induces green innovation.

Based on literature and empirical evidence following hypothesis:

H2: Transformational leadership has a positive effect on innovative organizational climate.

3.4 Transformational Leadership on Green Creativity

Leaders with the appropriate feature have an important effect on organizational creativity (Andriopoulos, 2001; Halbesleben et al., 2003). A leader may influence employee creativity in both direct and indirect ways. For example, addressing followers' intrinsic motivation and higher-level needs is an important source of creativity (Gong et al., 2009; Tierney et al., 1999). While transformational leaders indirectly may provide a work environment from punishment worry on trying creative ideas (Amabile et al., 1996), which will foster employee creativity (Keller, 2006). Accordingly, Gardner and Avolio (1998) define a transformational leader that motivates followers to achieve environmental goals and inspires followers beyond expected levels of environmental performance through their behaviour.

Similarly, transformational leadership possesses behaviour that makes followers think about new beliefs, ideas, and vision (Bass & Avolio, 1990; Conger & Kanungo, 1998; Keller, 1992) which energizes and establishes generation of members to abstract problems from different viewpoints enhancing environmental performance (Andriopoulos, 2001), employee creativity (Avolio et al., 1999; Elkins & Keller, 2003), and creative thinking (Mittal & Dhar, 2016). Moreover, transformational leaders enhance collective identity (Conger, 1999) and fulfil self-actualization among followers that generates strong leader–follower personal identification (Rosenbach, 2018), which helps green creativity among followers (Jia et al., 2018). This argument has been reflected by Chen and Chang (2013) in the electronic industry and Wang (2014) in the hotel industry, as they found that transformational leadership was associated with employee green creativity. It is, therefore, based on literature (Avolio et al., 1999; Gong et al., 2009; Shin & Zhou, 2003), green transformational leadership is highly correlated with green employee creativity leading to hypothesize the following relationship:

H3: Green transformational leadership is positively associated with green creativity.

3.5 Transformational Leadership, Green Behaviour, Green Innovative Climate, Green Creativity, and Green Product Development

Environmental sustainability will get no benefit from organizational productivity unless organizational production involves green product choices for consumers (Pujari et al., 2003). Chen (2010) argued that public awareness and companies' attention are more focussed on environmental issues. Further, if a company needs to excel in green products, it must incorporate the mind-set with activities of green production. With the resource-based theory, basic assumptions revisited in the natural resource-based theory by Hart and Dowell (2011) argued that organizations actively seek to improve the natural internal and external environment by pursuing environmental strategies of pollution reduction, product stewardship, and sustainable development. Based on these arguments, this study builds understanding between the relationships of internal and external natural environment activities, where green transformational leadership plays a strategic role to stimulate internal activities such as green behaviour, green innovative climate, and green creativity. These internal natural factors lead towards product stewardship in terms of green product development. This ultimately enhances the sustainable organizational development goal.

The due rise in organizational environment sustainability goals has been observed (Wensen et al., 2011). Where management is focussed to change the attitudes and behaviours of employees have a significant impact. Once employees are aware of their pro-environmental activities, they are more likely to contribute towards organizational eco-friendly activities through their attitude and behaviour (Iqbal et al., 2018). Accordingly, green product development is a product stewardship gesture of any organization towards a sustainable environment. Here employees play a vital role and without their contribution, it is difficult to achieve organizational environmental goals (Kolk et al., 2008). Thus, green employee behaviour is directly linked with green product development.

Similarly, new product, service, or procedure development is considered as organizational creativity (Anderson et al., 2014). This argument is also based on the creativity theory that green product, process, or service development is the outcome of green creativity. Likewise, green creativity is assumed directly linked with green product development. Research shows that new products or services such as green product development are influenced by the overall organizational competitiveness and culture that supports such outcomes (Przychodzen et al., 2016). Where culture is a set of shared values, believes and assumptions and the perception of such a culture is also known as the climate of any organization (Stolp & Smith, 1995). Thus, innovative climate leads to the development of innovative products such as green products and contributes to a sustainable environment (Ar, 2012). Moreover, green innovative climate assists the successful application of green product developmental strategies (Chang, 2015). Based on these arguments, the green innovative climate is likely responsible for green product development by generating situations and stimulate innovative product efforts.

Based on literary arguments, the following relations are hypothesized:

H4: Green behaviour, *H5*: Green innovative climate, and *H6*: Green creativity, positively influences green product development.

As leaders play the primary strategic role in the production of new product development based on their knowledge, ability, and leadership features to persuade followers to achieve desired organizational outcomes (Edmondson & Nembhard, 2009). Similarly, transformational leadership operating under leader–member exchange bases turns psychology of followers with the green environment to extract desired green behaviour (Zhou et al., 2018) to enhance productivity (Gumusluoglu & Ilsev, 2009) by creativity as a primary input for innovative solutions (Halbesleben et al., 2003) that facilitates green products development (Zhou et al., 2018) that can effectively respond to consumer needs (Cooper, 1979).

Transformational leadership contends strongly to enhance new product development in terms of vision and high-performance expectations by inspiring followers to set clear goals, integration, and caring followers through individual support (Podsakoff et al., 1990; Sarros et al., 2008). Similarly, the literature shows transformational leadership could foster successful innovative organizational performance (Howell & Avolio, 1993; Jung et al., 2003; Waldman & Bass, 1991). Thus, transformational leadership is beneficial for green product development with creativity, innovativeness, green behaviour, and enabling a sustainable working environment that inspires followers to consider problems in innovative ways (Keller, 1992; Waldman & Bass, 1991).

According to established arguments, the author asserts the following hypothesis:

Green transformational leadership positively influences green product development through *H4*: Green behaviour, *H5*: Green Innovative climate, and *H6* Green creativity.

Fig. 13.3 below depicts the conceptual framework for the relationship among variables.

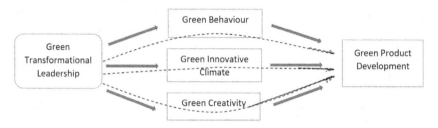

Fig. 13.3.   Conceptual Framework. *Note*: Bold lines show direct relations and doted lines show mediating relations.

4. Material and Methods

4.1 Population and Sample

The research population was manufacturing SMEs in the capital city and financial hub of Pakistan located in the eastern side of the country. Karachi was chosen being the largest business hub and 40% of total SMEs open in Karachi (Ibrahim & Mahmood, 2022). Moreover, the chamber of commerce and industries (KCCI) has 23,520 listed SMEs as their members (KCCI, 2021). Since Karachi holds the most variety of manufacturing SMEs, CEOs or Owners were randomly approached for data collection through a self-administered questionnaire.

4.2 Measures

All the measures used in this study were adapted from a western context. Therefore, the reliability and validity of measures were also checked. The language was kept in the standard English, and gender was encoded as 1 for male and 2 for female. Education was coded from 1 to 4, and the response was taken on a 1–5 point Likert scale ranging from 1 – strongly disagree to 5 – strongly agreeing to provide standard anchoring to measure a subjective character or attitude (Sekaran & Bougie, 2016).

4.2.1 Green Transformational Leadership

The measure for green transformational leadership is 6 items scale anchored on a 5-point Likert scale developed by Chen and Chang (2013) in Taiwan and includes sample items:

- The leader of the green development project inspires project members with the environmental plans.
- Provides an environmental vision for project members.
- Gets project members to work together.
- Encourages the member to achieve environmental goals.

– Acts with considering environmental beliefs of the member.
– Stimulates project members to think of green ideas.

4.2.2 Employee Green Behaviour
The measure of Employee Green Behaviour is 6 items scale anchored on a 5-point Likert scale developed by Robertson and Barling (2013) includes sample items:

– I print double side page whenever possible,
– I put recyclable materials (cans, paper, water bottles),
– I take part in environmentally friendly programmes,
– I make environmentally friendly suggestions to concerned authorities,
– I turn off the light after office hours, and
– I use the bin for trash.

4.2.3 Green Creativity
Green Creativity scale comprised of 6 items anchored on a 5-point Likert scale developed by Amabile (1988) and Rego et al. (2007) include sample items:

– Members of the green product development project suggest new green ideas to promote environmental performance,
– Members suggest new green goals,
– Promote new green ideas,
– Member develop adequate plans to implement new green ideas,
– Members would re-think new green ideas, and
– Members would think of creative solutions to the environmental problems.

4.2.4 Green Innovation Climate
The Green innovation climate scale comprised of 6 items anchored on a 5-point Likert scale developed by Amabile (1988) and Rego et al. (2007) includes sample items:

– The company chooses the material that produces less amount of pollution to conduct product development or design,
– The company chooses material that requires the least amount of energy and resource for product development or design,
– The company uses the fewest materials that comprise the product, and
– The company is conscious of whether the product is easy to recycle, reuse, and decompose.

4.2.5 Green Product Development
The Green product development scale comprised of 5 items anchored on a 5-point Likert scale developed by Marsh and Stock (2006) includes sample items:

- The green product development project contributes the key source to the company's revenue.
- The project develops excellent green products.
- The project continuously improves over time.
- Is more innovative than competitors' green products.
- The green product project can meet its environmental goals in green product development.

5. Analysis and Results

The analysis started with the initial screening of data collected for outliers and incomplete questionnaires from 150 responses. In response, 135 questionnaires were collected back and were screened with a response rate of 90%, out of which 120 were found useable. Demographics were composed of 89% male and 11% female staff. The respondent's average experience of work in the current job was 3.5 years. While, at an average, minimum education was the graduation of both genders. The screened responses were moved for further analysis through Smart-PLS 3.2.8 version. Following Hair et al. (2012) guidelines, structural equation modelling has produced robust results in the testing and development towards theoretical concept evaluations. The following section elaborated the validity of the measurement model and assessment of the structural model.

5.1 Validation of Measurement Model

Hair et al. (2016) suggested assessing measurement models that include item reliability: in terms of factor loadings above 0.5, convergent validity shows how much constructs resample to others. As suggested by Fornell et al. (1996), to measure composite reliability (CR) at or above 0.7 and average variance extracted (AVE) at or above 0.5 must be achieved for convergent validity. Further, the measurement model is assessed by discriminant validity that shows how much each construct differs from the other (Duarte & Raposo, 2010). The Fornell-Larcker method is widely used for discriminant validity (Fornell et al., 1996). The square root of AVE of one construct should be higher than the other construct squares AVE. Table 13.1 reveals cross-loadings, AVE, and CR values at or above acceptable levels. Whereas Table 13.2 reveals the discriminant validity of the measurement model ranging from 0.827 to 0.885, which holds the discriminant validity assumption acceptable.

5.2 Assessment of Structural Model

The assessment aims to validate the structured frame of this research comprised of green transformational leadership (GTL) influence on green behaviour of employees (GB), green climate (GClim), green innovation (GInn), green crea-tivity (GC), and ultimately resulting in green product development (GPD) under

Table 13.1. Convergent Validity.

Item	GB	GC	GIC	GPD	GTL	CR	AVE
GB							
1	**0.857**	0.76	0.736	0.722	0.746	**0.935**	**0.705**
2	**0.84**	0.753	0.716	0.754	0.736		
3	**0.844**	0.752	0.755	0.725	0.727		
4	**0.86**	0.797	0.786	0.783	0.761		
5	**0.815**	0.777	0.726	0.742	0.745		
6	**0.822**	0.756	0.7	0.783	0.799		
GIC							
1	0.727	**0.715**	0.842	0.738	0.7	**0.909**	**0.714**
2	0.76	**0.78**	0.858	0.757	0.732		
3	0.764	**0.775**	0.857	0.765	0.754		
4	0.713	**0.733**	0.822	0.735	0.723		
GC							
1	0.778	0.837	**0.752**	0.767	0.748	**0.929**	**0.684**
2	0.795	0.837	**0.775**	0.78	0.749		
3	0.732	0.799	**0.71**	0.72	0.698		
4	0.785	0.832	**0.756**	0.744	0.743		
5	0.707	0.819	**0.772**	0.711	0.688		
6	0.728	0.838	**0.742**	0.753	0.731		
GPD							
1	0.768	0.79	0.766	**0.881**	0.843	**0.937**	**0.75**
2	0.754	0.762	0.743	**0.86**	0.777		
3	0.762	0.773	0.777	**0.871**	0.754		
4	0.778	0.798	0.788	**0.879**	0.823		
5	0.815	0.782	0.761	**0.839**	0.77		
GTL							
1	0.762	0.724	0.657	0.772	**0.838**	**0.956**	**0.784**
2	0.812	0.78	0.806	0.823	**0.917**		
3	0.775	0.777	0.768	0.803	**0.878**		
4	0.766	0.769	0.747	0.775	**0.863**		
5	0.816	0.783	0.765	0.822	**0.912**		
6	0.83	0.83	0.821	0.869	**0.9**		

Note: GB, Green behaviour; *GIC*, Green innovative climate; *GC*, Green creativity; *GPD*, Green product development; *GTL*, Green transformational leadership.

Table 13.2. Discriminant Validity.

Construct	GB	GC	GIC	GPD	GTL
GB	**0.84**				
GC	0.811	**0.827**			
GIC	0.825	0.839	**0.845**		
GPD	0.836	0.848	0.854	**0.866**	
GTL	0.857	0.861	0.871	0.878	**0.885**

Leader–member–exchange theory. The respective hypothesis were tested through PLS model measures for R^2, beta values, t-values, the effect size f^2, and Q^2 on 5,000 sample resampling by bootstrapping process following the Hair et al. (2014) recommendations.

Table 13.3 below reveals that GTL has significantly influenced GB ($\beta = 0.293$, $t = 2.79$, $p < 0.01$) which supported *H1*. Further, GTL is positively related to GIC ($\beta = 0.225$, $t = 2.33$, $p < 0.01$) supporting *H2*, and GTL is positively related to GC ($\beta = 0.299$, $t = 2.531$, $p < 0.01$) supporting *H3*. Moreover, GB was positively related to GPD ($\beta = 0.25$, $t = 2.93$, $p < 0.05$), GIC was positively related to GPD ($\beta = 0.21$, $t = 2.44$, $p < 0.05$), and GC was positively related to GPD ($\beta = 0.297$, $t = 2.89$, $p < 0.05$) supporting *H4*, *H5*, and *H6*, respectively. Similarly, mediating effect (see Table 13.3) was observed for the relationships and hypothesis *H7*, *H8*, and *H9* were supported and values, respectively, for *H7* (GTL-> GB-> GPD) were ($\beta = 0.281$, $t = 3.832$, $p < 0.01$), *H8* (GTL-> GIC-> GPD) were ($\beta = 0.261$, $t = 3.251$, $p < 0.01$), and *H9* (GTL-> GC-> GPD) were ($\beta = 0.305$, $t = 3.174$, $p < 0$).

Table 13.3. Structural Model.

Relationship	Beta	*t* Stat.	*p* Value
GB -> GPD	0.25	2.93	0.004
GC -> GPD	0.297	2.89	0.004
GIC -> GPD	0.21	2.44	0.015
GTL -> GB	0.293	2.79	0.001
GTL -> GC	0.299	2.531	0.001
GTL -> GIC	0.225	2.33	0.001
Indirect effect (Mediation)			
GTL -> GB -> GPD	0.281	3.832	0.001
GTL -> GC -> GPD	0.305	3.174	0.002
GTL-> GIC-> GPD	0.261	3.251	0.010

Hair et al. (2014) suggested evaluating the change in R^2 values to find the effect size. Finally, the R^2 value for GB is 0.804 (80.4%), GIC is 0.742 (74.2%), GC is 0.772 (77.2%), and GPD is 0.862 (86.2%). The values for R^2 vitally explained the large variance brought by the predictor on predicted variables. GTL direct effect sizes on GB, GIC, and GC were 4.112, 2.871, and 3.389, respectively. In comparison, f^2 values of GB, GIC, and GC on GPD were medium as 0.105, 0.122, and 0.117, respectively. These effect sizes are quite considerable according to Cohen's (1988) guidelines.

Finally, model predictiveness was assessed by Q^2 values through blindfolding procedure as suggested by Hair et al. (2014). The Q^2 value for GB is 0.528, GIC is 0.498, GC is 0.492, and GPD is 0.604, which suggests that the model has large predictive relevance.

6. Discussion and Conclusion

6.1 Summary of Findings

This study aimed to investigate the relationship between green transformational leadership and green product development through the green behaviour of employees, green innovation climate, and green creativity in the organization. The hypothesized relationships were built on the basic assumptions of the leader–member–exchange theory, creativity theory, and natural resource-based-view theory. The path analysis affirmed the LMX effect on green product development which assures the natural resource-based view theory through the employee green behaviour, innovative green climate, and green creativity which links with creativity theory.

Accordingly, the mediating effect of these variables had high variance and mediated the positive effect of green transformational leadership on the green product development of the organization. In addition to that, the structural model also predicts a vital occurrence for the model of this study. These findings have important practical and theoretical implications of green transformational leadership on green product development for various organizations.

6.2 Theoretical Research and Research Implications

This study adds to the theoretical contribution by extending empirical evidence on basic assumptions of natural resource-based-view theory that contends for natural resource allocation towards sustainable service, processes, or product development, through creativity theory that suggests innovativeness directs employee behaviours and attitudes towards the development of green product development, and finally led by leadership style by integrating the leader–member exchange assumptions.

Supporting theories and results demonstrate the green effect of transformational leadership on green product development underpinned by leader–member–exchange theory. Further, this study adds in the green aspects of transformational leadership in the green production of firms. Moreover, previous studies took the internal motivation aspect of employee behaviour (Graves et al., 2013), while this study adds green aspects of employee behaviour to the literature. Another addition to the theoretical perspective is that the individual and organizational measures were taken together, expanding the view towards a complete picture of green product development under the green influence of transformational leadership.

In past literature, the green transformational leadership samples were taken from western countries (Kura, 2016). Whereas this study brought Pakistan from the Asian context with a green product development perspective which is barely focussed. Specifically, this study brings developing countries into the green light through green transformational leadership, where culture and perception towards green product development are quite different from developed countries. Thus, this study sets a strong theoretical ground for future research.

6.3 Practical Implications

For the development of developing countries, the performance of SMEs is as important as any other critical sector as they make up 78% of employment, 35% of GDP, 30% of manufacturing, and 20% of exports (Shah et al., 2018). Similarly, management environmental aspects are at the core for SMEs (Del Brio & Junquera, 2003). Where leader mainly cascade their effect the organizational strategies outcome through management in Asian context (Koo & Park, 2018). Supported by leader–member exchange theory, the green influence of green transformational leadership on their member shows more significant implications regarding the green behaviour of employees. This green behaviour later helps achieve green product development targets for the organizations specifically SMEs. Accordingly, it was observed in this study that providing a green climate and green innovative climate within the organization is more feasible than mere training and rewards to motivate employees towards achieving green goals. This practically suggests improving the green quality aspects of the organization and efficient use of resources through leadership.

For efficient green resource utilization and sustainable product development, this study emphasizes the important role played by the leadership. Where management must initiate training for both employee and team leaders to improve close coordination for the process of eco-friendly product development. Moreover, innovation influenced by leaders through integrating technology and production methods may also reduce per unit cost, increase profitability, and help achieve sustainable competitive advantage.

6.4 Limitations and Future Research

This study has expanded the green zone for the scholars regarding the green effect of transformational leadership on green product development for the organizations. The findings of this study signal green light for future studies, and hope for green transformational leadership can make a difference for governments, industries, and manufacturing industries towards green product development.

Since limitations are inevitable in the real world. Most apparent is the limited scope of generalizability because the data was collected from the sample of a single major city SMEs rather than multiple cities or organizations. Thus, scholars may replicate this study in different fields and industries. Longitudinal studies are also considered to evaluate the formation of leader–member relations in the long run as cross-sectional data is a snapshot at a given time. Further, leader–member relations may be evaluated from an individual or team perspective as the green behaviour of individual employees may vary from team to team. Finally, green transformational leadership influence may differ concerning employees' green behaviour and their green output due to certain factors such as performance appraisal system, organizational political influence, organizational vision, organizational culture, government initiatives, or organizational support which may be explored in the future studies.

7. Conclusion

The present study has provided initial ground on the role of green transformational leadership in facilitating green behaviour, green innovative climate, and green creativity, which leads towards green product development. The empirical results have supported the hypothesized model with high structural model predictiveness in the field. Theoretical findings also added new knowledge in the literature with specific recommendations, which will stimulate theoretical and practical research towards green transformational leadership and greener product development literature.

The green effect of transformational leadership is practically essential to consider for a greener productive environment with green work settings. The results also reveal that green features of transformational leadership encourage a green attitude to overall target achievement, which would improve organization profitability and sustainable competitive advantage. Results also reveal Asian perspectives and transformational leaders have great potential for developing nations to be green in productivity which is essential for a sustainable future for the organization as well as the nation.

References

Ahmed, & Asad. (2016). *A need to minimise the impacts on water resources and health. A need to minimise the impacts on water resources and health.* Retrieved from DAWN on April 24, 2021.

Alshuwaikhat, H. M., & Abubakar, I. (2008). An integrated approach to achieving campus sustainability: Assessment of the current campus environmental management practices. *Journal of Cleaner Production, 16*(16), 1777–1785.

Amabile, T. M. (1988). A model of creativity and innovation in organization. *Behavior, 10*, 123–167.

Amabile, T. M., Conti, R., Coon, H., Lazenby, J., & Herron, M. (1996). Assessing the work environment for creativity. *Academy of Management Journal, 39*(5), 1154–1184.

Anderson, N., Potočnik, K., & Zhou, J. (2014). Innovation and creativity in organizations: A state-of-the-science review, prospective commentary, and guiding framework. *Journal of Management, 40*(5), 1297–1333.

Andersson, E. (2013). Det politiska rummet: Villkor för situationspolitisk socialisation i en nätgemenskap av och för ungdomar (Doctoral dissertation, Örebro universitet).

Andriopoulos, C. (2001). Determinants of organizational creativity: A literature review. *Management Decision, 39*(10), 834–840.

Ar, I. M. (2012). The impact of green product innovation on firm performance and competitive capability: The moderating role of managerial environmental concern. *Procedia-Social and Behavioral Sciences, 62*, 854–864.

Avolio, B. J., Bass, B. M., & Jung, D. I. (1999). Re-examining the components of transformational and transactional leadership using the multifactor leadership questionnaire. *Journal of Occupational and Organizational Psychology, 72*, 441–462.

Bass, B. M., & Avolio, B. J. (1990). The implications of transactional and transformational leadership for individual, team, and organizational development. *Research in Organizational Change and Development, 4*, 231–272.

Bass, B. M., & Avolio, B. J. (1994). Transformational leadership and organizational culture. *The International Journal of Public Administration, 17*(3–4), 541–554.

Begum, S., Ashfaq, M., Xia, E., & Awan, U. (2022). Does green transformational leadership lead to green innovation? The role of green thinking and creative process engagement. *Business Strategy and the Environment, 31*(1), 580–597.

Bombiak, E., & Marciniuk-Kluska, A. (2018). Green human resource management as a tool for the sustainable development of enterprises: Polish young company experience. *Sustainability, 10*(6), 1739.

Chang, C. H. (2015). Proactive and reactive corporate social responsibility: Antecedent and consequence. *Management Decision, 53*(2), 451–468.

Chen, Y. S. (2008). The driver of green innovation and green image–Green core competence. *Journal of Business Ethics, 81*(3), 531–543.

Chen, Y.-S. (2010). The drivers of green brand equity: Green brand image, green satisfaction, and green trust. *Journal of Business Ethics, 93*(2), 307–319.

Chen, Y. S., & Chang, C. H. (2002). Enhance green purchase intentions: The roles of green perceived value, green perceived risk, and green trust. *Management Decision, 50*, 502–520.

Chen, Y. S., & Chang, C. H. (2012). Enhance green purchase intentions: The roles of green perceived value, green perceived risk, and green trust. *Management Decision, 50*(3), 502–520.

Chen, Y. S., & Chang, C. H. (2013). The determinants of green product development performance: Green dynamic capabilities, green transformational leadership, and green creativity. *Journal of Business Ethics, 116107–116119*. https://doi.org/10.1007/s10551-012-1452-x

Chou, C.-J. (2014). Hotels' environmental policies and employee personal environmental beliefs: Interactions and outcomes. *Tourism Management, 40*, 436–446.

Cohen, J. (1988). *Statistical power analysis for the behavioural sciences.* Lawrence Erlbaum Associates.

Conger, J. A. (1999). Charismatic and transformational leadership in organizations: An insider's perspective on these developing streams of research. *The Leadership Quarterly, 10*(2), 145–179.

Conger, J. A., & Kanungo, R. N. (1998). *Charismatic leadership in organizations.* SAGE Publications.

Cooper, R. G. (1979). The dimensions of industrial new product success and failure. *Journal of Marketing, 43,* 93–103.

Cusmano, L., Koreen, M., & Pissareva, L. (2018). 2018 OECD ministerial conference on SMEs: Key issues paper.

Daily, B. F., Bishop, J. W., & Govindarajulu, N. (2009). A conceptual model for organizational citizenship behaviour directed toward the environment. *Business & Society, 48*(2), 243–256.

DeHart-Davis, L., Davis, R. S., & Mohr, Z. (2014). Green tape and job satisfaction: Can organizational rules make employees happy? *Journal of Public Administration Research and Theory, 25*(3), 849–876.

Del Brio, J. A., & Junquera, B. (2003). A review of the literature on environmental innovation management in SMEs: Implications for public policies. *Technovation, 23*(12), 939–948.

Douglas, L. (2012, September 19). *Green leadership—What is it?* https://www.huffingtonpost.com/douglas-labier/green-leadership-what-is-_b_1689916.html

Dravigne, A., Waliczek, T. M., Lineberger, R. D., & Zajicek, J. M. (2008). The effect of live plants and window views of green spaces on employee perceptions of job satisfaction. *HortScience, 43*(1), 183–187.

Duarte, P. A. O., & Raposo, M. L. B. (2010). A PLS model to study brand preference: An application to the mobile phone market. In V. Esposito Vinzi, W. Chin, J. Henseler, & H. Wang (Eds.), *Handbook of partial least squares: Concepts, methods and applications* (pp. 449–485). Springer.

Dumont, J., Shen, J., & Deng, X. (2017). Effects of green HRM practices on employee workplace green behavior: The role of psychological green climate and employee green values. *Human Resource Management, 56*(4), 613–627.

Dunst, C. J., Bruther, M. B., Hamby, D. W., Howse, R., & Wilkie, H. (2018). Meta-analysis of the relationships between different leadership practices and organizational, teaming, leader, and employee outcomes. *Journal of International Economic Law, 8*(2), n2.

Dyllick, T., & Hockerts, K. (2002). Beyond the business case for corporate sustainability. *Business Strategy and the Environment, 11,* 130–141.

Edmondson, A. C., & Nembhard, I. M. (2009). Product development and learning in project teams: The challenges are the benefits. *Journal of Product Innovation Management, 26,* 123–138.

Elasrag, H. (2016). *Islamic finance for SMES.* Hussein Elasrag.

Elkins, T., & Keller, R. T. (2003). Leadership in research and development organizations: A literature review and conceptual framework. *The Leadership Quarterly, 14,* 587–606.

Environmental Responsibility. (n.d.). toyota global.com. http://www.toyotaglobal.com/sustainability/environmental_responsibility/

ForbsCustom. (2018, August 1). *Singapore: A global hub for innovation.* https:// custom.forbes.com/2018/08/13/singapore-a-global-hub-for-innovation/

Ford Motor Company. (n.d.). Retrieved from corporate.ford.com on April 25, 2021.

Fornell, C., Johnson, M. D., Anderson, E. W., Cha, J., & Bryant, B. E. (1996). The American customer satisfaction index: Nature, purpose, and findings. *Journal of Marketing, 60*(4), 7–18.

Gardner, W. L., & Avolio, B. J. (1998). The charismatic relationship: A dramaturgical perspective. *Academy of Management Review, 23,* 32–58.

Gong, Y., Huang, J.-C., & Farh, J.-L. (2009). Employee learning orientation, trans-formational leadership, and employee creativity: The mediating role of employee creative self-efficacy. *Academy of Management Journal, 52*(4), 765–778.

Google. (n.d.). Retrieved from Google Inc. on April 25, 2021.

Graen, G. B., & Canedo, J. (2016). *The new workplace leadership development.* Oxford Bibliography on Management. Oxford University Press.

Graen, G. B., & Schiemann, W. (2013). Leadership-motivated excellence theory: An extension of LMX. *Journal of Managerial Psychology, 28*(5), 452–469

Graen, G. B., & Uhl-Bien, M. (1995). The relationship-based approach to leadership: Development of LMX theory of leadership over 25 years: Applying a multi-level, multi-domain perspective. *The Leadership Quarterly, 6*(2), 219–247. https://doi.org/ 10.1016/1048-9843(95)90036-5

Graves, L. M., Sarkis, J., & Zhu, Q. (2013). How transformational leadership and employee motivation combine to predict employee proenvironmental behaviors in China. *Journal of Environmental Psychology, 35,* 81–91.

Gumusluoglu, L., & Ilsev, A. (2009). Transformational leadership, creativity, and organizational innovation. *Journal of Business Research, 62*(4), 461–473. http:// www.google.com/green/bigpicture/#beyondzero-grid

Haden, S. S. P., Oyler, J. D., & Humphreys, J. H. (2009). Historical, practical, and theoretical perspectives on green management: An exploratory analysis. *Management Decision, 47*(7), 1041–1055.

Hair, J. F., Sarstedt, M., Ringle, C. M., & Mena, J. A. (2012). An assessment of the use of partial least squares structural equation modeling in marketing research. *Journal of the Academy of Marketing Science, 40,* 414–433.

Hair, J. F., Hult, G. T. M., Ringle, C., & Sarstedt, M. (2014). *A primer on partial least squares structural equation modeling (PLS-SEM).* SAGE Publications. Incorporated.

Hair, J. F. Jr., Sarstedt, M., Matthews, L. M., & Ringle, C. M. (2016). Identifying and treating unobserved heterogeneity with FIMIX-PLS: Part I–method. *European Business Review, 28*(1), 63–76.

Halbesleben, J. R. B., Novicevic, M. M., Harvey, M. G., & Buckley, M. R. (2003). Awareness of temporal complexity in leadership of creativity and innovation: A competency-based model. *The Leadership Quarterly, 14*(4/5), 433–454.

Hart, S. L., & Dowell, G. (2011). Invited editorial: A natural-resource-based view of the firm: Fifteen years after. *Journal of Management, 37*(5), 1464–1479.

Hoffman, C. C. (2018). Civil service mandated cutoff scores: Challenges and practice recommendations. *Industrial and Organizational Psychology, 11*(1), 158.

Hoffman, B. J., & Dilchert, S. (2012). A review of citizenship and counterproductive behavior in organizational decision-making. In *The Oxford handbook of personnel selection and selection* (pp. 543–569).

Howell, J. M., & Avolio, B. J. (1993). Transformational leadership, transactional leadership, locus of control and support for innovation: Key predictors of consolidated-business-unit performance. *Journal of Applied Psychology, 78,* 891–902.

Huang, L., Guo, Z., Deng, B., & Wang, B. (2023). Unlocking the relationship between environmentally specific transformational leadership and employees' green behaviour: A cultural self-representation perspective. *Journal of Cleaner Production, 382,* 134857.

Huang, X. X., Hu, Z. P., Liu, C. S., Yu, D. J., & Yu, L. F. (2016). The relationships between regulatory and customer pressure, green organizational responses, and green innovation performance. *Journal of Cleaner Production, 112,* 3423–3433.

Hu, X., Li, R. Y. M., Kumari, K., Ben Belgacem, S., Fu, Q., Khan, M. A., & Alkhuraydili, A. A. (2023). Relationship between green leaders' emotional intelligence and employees' green behavior: A PLS-SEM approach. *Behavioral Sciences, 13*(1), 25.

Ibrahim, M., & Mahmood, R. (2022). Proactive environmental strategy and environmental performance of the manufacturing SMEs of Karachi city in Pakistan: Role of green mindfulness as a DCV. *Sustainability, 14*(19), 12431.

Iqbal, Q., Hassan, S. H., Akhtar, S., & Khan, S. (2018). Employee's green behavior for environmental sustainability: A case of banking sector in Pakistan. *World Journal of Science, Technology and Sustainable Development, 15*(2), 118–130.

Jain, S. K., & Kaur, G. (2004). Green marketing: An Indian perspective. *Decision, 31*(2), 168–209.

Janda, K. F. (1960). Towards the explication of the concept of leadership in terms of the concept of power. *Human Relations, 13,* 345–363.

Jia, J., Liu, H., Chin, T., & Hu, D. (2018). The Continuous mediating effects of GHRM on employees' green passion via transformational leadership and green creativity. *Sustainability, 10*(9), 3237.

Jung, D. I. (2001). Transformational and transactional leadership and their effects on creativity in groups. *Creativity Research Journal, 13,* 185–195.

Jung, D. I., Chow, C., & Wu, A. (2003). The role of transformational leadership in enhancing organizational innovation: Hypotheses and some preliminary findings. *The Leadership Quarterly, 14*(4–5), 525–544.

Kawai, N., Strange, R., & Zucchella, A. (2018). Stakeholder pressures, EMS implementation, and green innovation in MNC overseas subsidiaries. *International Business Review, 27*(5), 933–946.

KCCI_Members Directory. Members Directory of Karachi Chamber of Commerce & Industry. (2021). https://www.kcci.com.pk/members-directory/. Accessed on January 7, 2023.

Keller, R. T. (1992). Transformational leadership and the performance of research and development project groups. *Journal of Management, 18*(3), 489–501.

Keller, R. T. (2006). Transformational leadership initiating structure, and substitutes for leadership: A longitudinal study of research and development project team performance. *Journal of Applied Psychology, 91,* 202–210.

Kolk, A., Levy, D., & Pinkse, J. (2008). Corporate responses in an emerging climate regime: The institutionalization and commensuration of carbon disclosure. *European Accounting Review, 17*(4), 719–745.

Koo, H., & Park, C. (2018). Foundation of leadership in Asia: Leader characteristics and leadership styles review and research agenda. *Asia Pacific Journal of Management, 35*(3), 697–718.

Kura, K. M. (2016). Linking environmentally specific transformational leadership and environmental concern to green behaviour at work. *Global Business Review, 17*(3_suppl), 1S–14S.

Makower, J. (2009). *Strategies for the green economy: Opportunities and challenges in the new world of business.* McGraw-Hill.

Mandip, G. (2012). Green HRM: People management commitment to environmental sustainability. *Research Journal of Recent Sciences, ISSN, 2277,* 2502.

Marsh, S. J., & Stock, G. N. (2006). Creating dynamic capability: The role of intertemporal integration, knowledge retention, and interpretation. *Journal of Product Innovation Management, 23*(5), 422–436.

Mittal, S., & Dhar, R. L. (2016). Effect of green transformational leadership on green creativity: A study of tourist hotels. *Tourism Management, 57,* 118–127. https://doi.org/10.1016/j.tourman.2016.05.007

Mohsin, M., Kamran, H. W., Nawaz, M. A., Hussain, M. S., & Dahri, A. S. (2021). Assessing the impact of transition from nonrenewable to renewable energy consumption on economic growth-environmental nexus from developing Asian economies. *Journal of Environmental Management, 284,* 111999.

Mumford, M. D. (2000). Managing creative people: Strategy and tactics for innovation. *Human Resource Management Review, 10,* 313–351.

Mumford, M. D., & Gustafson, S. B. (1988). Creativity syndrome: Integration, application, and innovation. *Psychological Bulletin, 103,* 27–43.

Mumford, M. D., Scott, G. M., Gaddis, B., & Strange, J. M. (2002). Leading creative people: Orchestrating expertise and relationships. *The Leadership Quarterly, 13*(6), 705–750.

Murga-Menoyo, M. (2014). Learning for a sustainable economy: Teaching of green competencies in the university. *Sustainability, 6*(5), 2974–2992.

Nier, S. L. (2013). *LMX as "silver bullet" to all things now experienced in US civil service.* Survey of 13,000 US Government Employees.

Norton, T. A., Zacher, H., & Ashkanasy, N. M. (2014). Organizational sustainability policies and employee green behavior: The mediating role of work climate perceptions. *Journal of Environmental Psychology, 38,* 49–54.

Ones, D. S., & Dilchert, S. (2012). Environmental sustainability at work: A call to action. *Industrial and Organizational Psychology, 5*(4), 444–466.

Paillé, P., & Boiral, O. (2013). Pro-environmental behavior at work: Construct validity and determinants. *Journal of Environmental Psychology, 36*(4), 118–128.

Podsakoff, P. M., MacKenzie, S. B., Moorman, R. H., & Fetter, R. (1990). Transformational leader behaviors and their effects on followers' trust in leader, satisfaction, and organizational citizenship behaviours. *The Leadership Quarterly, 1*(2), 107–142.

Przychodzen, W., Przychodzen, J., & Lerner, D. A. (2016). Critical factors for transforming creativity into sustainability. *Journal of Cleaner Production, 135,* 1514–1523.

Pujari, D., Wright, G., & Peattie, K. (2003). Green and competitive: Influences on environmental new product development performance. *Journal of Business Research, 56*(8), 657–671.

Qasim, M., & Kotani, K. (2014). An empirical analysis of energy shortage in Pakistan. *Asia-Pacific Development Journal, 21*(1), 137–166.

Ramasamy, B., Au, A., & Yeung, M. (2010). Managing Chinese consumers' value profiles: A comparison between Shanghai and Hong Kong. *Cross Cultural Management: International Journal, 17*(3), 257–267.

Ramus, C. A., & Killmer, A. B. C. (2007). Corporate greening through prosocial extra-role behavior–A conceptual framework for employee motivation. *Business Strategy and the Environment, 16*(8), 554–570.

Rego, A., Sousa, F., Cunha, M. P. E., Correia, A., & Saur-Amaral, I. (2007). Leader self-reported emotional intelligence and perceived employee creativity: An exploratory study. *Creativity and Innovation Management, 16*, 250–264.

Report of the World Commission on Environment and Development (WCED): Our Common Future. http://www.un-documents.net/our-common-future.pdf. Accessed on May 17, 2018.

Robertson, J. L., & Barling, J. (2013). Greening organizations through leaders' influence on employees' pro-environmental behaviors. *Journal of Organizational Behavior, 34*, 176–194. https://doi.org/10.1002/job.1820

Roe, B., Teisl, M. F., Levy, A., & Russell, M. (2001). US consumers' willingness to pay for green electricity. *Energy Policy, 29*(11), 917–925.

Rosenbach, W. E. (2018). *Contemporary issues in leadership*. Routledge.

Rugman, A. M., & Verbeke, A. (1998). Corporate strategies and environmental regulations: An organizing framework. *Strategic Management Journal, 19*(4), 363–375.

Rupp, D. E., Ganapathi, J., Aguilera, R. V., & Williams, C. A. (2006). Employee reactions to corporate social responsibility: An organizational justice framework. *Journal of Organizational Behavior: The International Journal of Industrial, Occupational and Organizational Psychology and Behavior, 27*(4), 537–543.

Salem, M. A., Hasnan, N., & Osman, N. H. (2012). Environmental issues and corporate performance: A critical review. *Journal of Environment and Earth Science, 2*(10), 112–122.

Sarros, J. C., Cooper, B. K., & Santora, J. C. (2008). Building a climate for innovation through transformational leadership and organizational culture. *Journal of Leadership & Organizational Studies, 15*(2), 145–158.

Schein, E. H. (1992). *Organizational culture and leadership*. Jossey-Bass.

Schneider, B., Ehrhart, M. G., & Macey, W. H. (2013). Organizational climate and culture. *Annual Review of Psychology, 64*(1), 361–388.

Scott, S. G., & Bruce, R. A. (1994). Determinants of innovative behavior: A path model of individual innovation in the workplace. *Academy of Management Journal, 37*, 580 607.

Sekaran, U., & Bougie, R. (2016). *Research methods for business: A skill building approach*. John Wiley & Sons.

Shah, D. S., & Syed, A. (2018). *Framework for SME sector development in Pakistan*. Planning Commission of Pakistan.

Shah, S. H., Raja, I. A., Rizwan, M., Rashid, N., Mahmood, Q., Shah, F. A., & Pervez, A. (2018). Potential of microalgal biodiesel production and its sustainability perspectives in Pakistan. *Renewable and Sustainable Energy Reviews, 81*, 76–92.

Shamir, B., House, R. J., & Arthur, M. B. (1993). The motivational effects of charismatic leadership: A self-concept-based theory. *Organization Science, 4*, 577–594.

Sheu, J. B. (2014). Green supply chain collaboration for fashionable consumer electronics products under third-party power intervention—A resource dependence perspective. *Sustainability, 6*(5), 2832–2875.

Shin, S. J., & Zhou, J. (2003). Transformational leadership, conservation, and creativity: Evidence from Korea. *Academy of Management Journal, 46*, 703–714.

Shrivastava, P. (1994). Castrated environment: Greening organizational studies. *Organization Studies, 15*(5), 705–726.

Silva, A. (2016). What is leadership? *Journal of Business Studies Quarterly, 8*(1), 1–5.

Singapore Business Review. (2018, January 1). *Six in 10 Singaporeans want more eco-friendly firms.* https://sbr.com.sg/markets-investing/news/six-in-10-singaporeans-want-more-eco-friendly-firms

Snook, E. (2017). *Women, reading, and the cultural politics of early modern England.* Taylor & Francis.

Stolp, S., & Smith, S. C. (1995). *Transforming school culture: Stories, symbols, values and the leader's role.* ERIC Clearinghouse on Educational Management, 5207 University of Oregon, 1787 Agate Street. OR 97403-5207.

Tierney, P., Farmer, S. M., & Graen, G. B. (1999). An examination of leadership and employee creativity: The relevance of traits and relationships. *Personnel Psychology, 52*, 591–620.

UNEP World Conservation Monitoring Centre. (2010). *Are you a green leader. Business and biodiversity: Making the case for a lasting solution.*

USAID Report. (2022). *Pakistan – Floods fact sheet #3, fiscal year (FY) 2022.* https://reliefweb.int/report/pakistan/pakistan-floods-fact-sheet-3-fiscal-year-fy-2022. Accessed on January 14, 2023.

Voon, M. L., Lo, M. C., Ngui, K. S., & Ayob, N. B. (2011). The influence of leadership styles on employees' job satisfaction in public sector organizations in Malaysia. *International Journal of Business, Management, and Social Sciences, 2*(1), 24–32.

Waldman, D. A., & Bass, B. M. (1991). Transformational leadership at different phases of the innovation process. *Journal of High Technology Management, 2*(2), 169–180.

Wang, C. J. (2014). Do ethical and sustainable practices matter? Effects of corporate citizenship on business performance in the hospitality industry. *International Journal of Contemporary Hospitality Management, 26*(6), 930–947.

Weinberg, A. S. (1998). Distinguishing among green businesses: Growth, green, and anomie. *Society & Natural Resources, 11*(3), 241–250.

Wensen, K. V., Broer, W., Klein, J., & Knopf, J. (2011). *The state of play in sustainability reporting in the EU. Publication commissioned under the European Union's Programme for employment and social solidarity–Progress (2007–2013).* 2011."INFORMATIK 2015" was the 45th annual meeting of the Gesellschaft für Informatik and took place at the Brandenburgische Technische Universität Cottbus-Senftenberg in Cottbus. The guiding theme of the meeting was the interplay between interdisciplinary methods relating the fields of computer science. In Energy and Environment. This volume contains contributions from the workshop program, the student and doctoral symposium, and the tutorials.

Werff, E. V. D., Steg, L., & Keizer, K. (2014). I am what I am, by looking past the present. *Environment and Behavior*, 46626–46657. https://doi.org/10.1177/0013916512475209

World Bank Report. (2022, October 28). *Pakistan: Flood damages and economic losses over USD 30 billion and reconstruction needs over USD 16 billion – New Assessment.* https://www.worldbank.org/en/news/press-release/2022/10/28/pakistan-flood-damages-and-economic-losses-over-usd-30-billion-and-reconstruction-needs-over-usd-16-billion-new-assessme. Accessed on January 14, 2023.

Yang, M. G., Hong, P., & Modi, S. B. (2011). Impact of lean manufacturing and environmental management on business performance: An empirical study of manufacturing firms. *International Journal of Production Economics*, *129*(2), 251–261.

Yukl, G. (2001). *Leadership in organizations* (5th ed.). Prentice Hall.

Zhao, H., & Guo, S. (2014). Selecting green supplier of thermal power equipment by using a hybrid MCDM method for sustainability. *Sustainability*, *6*(1), 217–235.

Zhou, S., Zhang, D., Lyu, C., & Zhang, H. (2018). Does seeing "mind acts upon mind" affect green psychological climate and green product development performance? The role of matching between green transformational leadership and individual green values. *Sustainability*, *10*(9), 3206.

Chapter 14

Green Marketing Mix From the Perspective of Service Sector: Leveraging Marketing of Services With Green-SIVA Marketing Mix Elements

Muhammad Faisal Sultan, Muhammad Nawaz Tunio, Ghazala Shaukat and Muhammad Asim

Abstract

The shift in consumer focus towards green marketing mix elements is not a unique thing. Especially in recent times, most organizations are trying to implement green marketing strategies in order to influence customers as well as to reduce the negative impacts of environmental footprints. However, in recent times service marketing requires thorough implementation of a Green Marketing Mix as evidenced by Asian countries. However, research also claims that the use of a traditional green marketing mix is not a guarantee of success in the long run and therefore has been criticized by several researchers and scholars. Hence, there is a need to follow the Green-SIVA (Solution, Information, Access, and Value) concept in order to create a long-lasting impact on consumer buying and to discuss the application of tools in a more comprehensive manner. Although the linkage of Green-SIVA marketing might provide a new way to develop an effective marketing mix strategy for services. Hence, this chapter has been written purposely to discuss GMM elements with reference to the service industry of Pakistan and tries to develop an association with green-SIVA marketing practices in order to optimize service marketing practices.

Keywords: Green marketing mix; SIVA-green marketing mix; service marketing; green product; green purchase; Pakistan

Entrepreneurship and Green Finance Practices, 267–283
Published under exclusive licence by Emerald Publishing Limited
doi:10.1108/978-1-80455-678-820231014

1. Introduction

Green marketing is also known as sustainable marketing. In fact, the concept is the contemporary requirement of developing sides of the world. The concept came into the limelight due to the increase in consumer concerns towards the environment and hence preferred to use those products that do not cause a negative impact on the environment. The concept was initiated back in the 1970s due to a significant rise in environmental issues. Thus, by the start of the 1990s, most marketing philosophers started to criticize firms for their actions. Thus, the concept of Green Marketing was introduced through which people satisfy their needs and want by utilizing products that are environmentally safe. In short, we can easily state that Green Marketing includes all forms of transactions that provide value to the company and customers without creating harm to the environment. However, it is also fruitful to understand that Green Marketing is not indulged in Societal Marketing, as the concept is directed towards improvement in marketing processes physically with an inclination towards social responsibility (Abzari et al., 2013).

In recent times, there is a massive increase in the level of consumer environmental awareness throughout the world. There are several environmental problems like non-biodegradable solid waste, the harmful impact of pollutants, etc. Other than these there are some issues that need global concern e.g. global warming and pollution. Hence, marketers and consumers are getting seriously aware of the need for green products and services and hence consumers are inclined towards environmentally friendly products (Mahmoud, 2018). Therefore, each of the consumers has to make their decision to purchase on the grounds of ethics, benefits to the community, and conversion of resources and waste. These forms of consumers are known as 'Green Consumers'. The study further elaborated that Green Consumers as the ones who prefer environmentally friendly products in order to produce a positive impact on the environment. Hence, day after day there is an increase in consumer preference towards environmentally friendly organizations and therefore organizations are also trying to increase the green footprints of their business activities (Karunarathna et al., 2020).

These requirements might be induced through the addition of environmentally friendly features to the company's offerings (Karunarathna et al., 2020) regardless of the risk that the shift towards green might become costly in the short run. However, the masses are still in favour of the shift and believe that the shift will be fruitful and will depreciate its cost in the long run (Rahbar & Wahid, 2011). Hence, it is also better to use green marketing strategies that are purposefully executed to make customers aware of those products and services that are environmentally safe (Karunarathna et al., 2020). Studies, e.g. Mahmoud (2018), also indicated that a company's inclination towards environmentally safe products and services also reflected positively on consumer buying decisions. Similar studies have been indicated by several studies, e.g. Ansar (2013); Karunarathna et al. (2020), etc. Although there is a difference in opinion regarding the range of green marketing mix elements, studies like Viani Parlan et al. (2016) indicated that there are four major marketing mix elements that are applicable on traditional as well as green marketing. However, studies like Eneizan et al. (2016) postulated that the green marketing mix might also range up to seven and their implementation is also full of challenges.

On the other hand, one of the latest studies by Mehraj and Qureshi (2020) considered GMM as a multi-dimensional construct and provides illustration with reference to the industrial perspective. In fact, it has been emphasized that companies must incorporate the production of harmless, biodegradable goods and services by engaging in recyclable and eco-certified packaging, sustainable manufacturing, and use of energy efficiently.

2. Factors Lead to the Use of Green Marketing Mix Elements

Tiwari et al. (2011) postulated the following reasons for adopting the strategy of green marketing. However, there are some other reasons for adopting green marketing strategies like social responsibility, government and competitive pressure, etc., which are highlighted by Abzari et al. (2013); Alwis and Manel (2021), and Tiwari et al. (2011), etc.

2.1 Social Responsibility

In recent times firms are getting more aware of the fact that focussing merely on profitability is not a guarantee of success. Therefore, there is a need to understand that companies are also an active part of society and therefore societal objectives must also be incorporated into their culture (Tiwari et al., 2011). Similar research has been indicated by Alwis and Manel (2021) as the implementation of a green marketing mix has several other objectives other than the enhancement of marketing efforts. In fact, implementation will also result in influencing stakeholders towards green products and green business activities. However, it is totally dependent upon the firm's strategy to use their societal concern in their marketing strategies or not. Examples include Coca-Cola which is one of the well-known names that does not use its societal concerns for marketing purposes. Although, the efforts of the company towards the betterment of environmental foot-steps are not lacklustre as the company is actively involved in recycling and also focusses on the improvement of packaging styles to produce a positive impact on environmental footsteps (Tiwari et al., 2011).

2.2 Governmental Pressure

There is a significant rise in governmental pressure as governments are much inclined towards the protection of society and consumers (Tiwari et al., 2011). Therefore, we are observing an increase in modification of industrial norms to reduce the manufacturing of harmful products. Similarly, governments are providing support to consumers in the evaluation of environmental concerns related to production. Hence, hindering the production of harmful products for human health and environment (Tiwari et al., 2011).

2.3 Competitive Pressure

Competitive pressure also makes firms modify their detrimental environmental behaviour. Due to this Xerox started to use 100% recycled paper for photocopy. In fact, there are several examples when competitive pressure makes the entire industry modify their philosophy for conducting business operations and business practices (Tiwari et al., 2011).

2.4 Issues of Cost and Profit

Reduction of harmful waste might also be the reason for the decrease in cost. Similar research has been quoted by the study through the development of symbiotic relationships which makes one firm use the waste of the other. Moreover, to reduce waste, the firm might also revamp its production method which may not reduce waste but may aid production by using waste as the raw material of some other process (Tiwari et al., 2011).

2.5 Revolutionizing of Own Business Activities

One of the other reasons quoted by Alwis and Manel (2021) in revolutionizing the activities of one's own business is required due to the changing conditions of the modern world. Hence, use of Green Marketing Mix Elements might be fruitful for the adjustments that are the major characteristics of the modern world. The study also indicated that opting for GMM elements and Green Practices will optimize the firm.

2.6 Need of Developing Sides and Sustainability

The study also indicated that opting for Green Marketing Mix Strategies is one of the real challenges in developing sides of the world. Although the effective implementation of GMM is recommended to make developing sides of the world attain sustainability (Alwis & Manel, 2021).

3. Need of Research

Rahbar and Wahid (2011) pinpointed the fact there is a severe lack of research with reference to environmental or green marketing. Similar has also been indicated by Mahmoud (2018), however, each and every firm has to develop a unique blend of marketing mix elements as the weightage of every marketing mix might be different for different firms. However, an in-depth study on marketing mix may assist companies in influencing consumer buying behaviour in an effective way (Delafrooz et al., 2014).

In fact, one of the studies also indicated that companies are developing their own marketing mix strategies though the real challenge is to use the strategy of the marketing mix in a unique manner. Therefore, it is legitimate to believe each and every marketing mix element has its unique role and significance for the maintenance and enhancement of customer satisfaction which is also related to increasing customers' willingness for future activities and purchases (Chairunnisa et al., 2019). On the other hand, one of the latest studies by Mehraj and Qureshi (2020) indicated that traditional green marketing mix elements are criticized by several researchers and scholars. In fact, scholars emphasized the point that the use of traditional green marketing mix elements is not consistent with modern marketing trends and practices and neither has the ability to provide benefits in the long run. Moreover, the change of focus of marketing activities from a traditional to a Green Marketing Mix could not overcome the lack of studies that may provide viewpoints on marketing efforts and practices with reference to the industry. However, the use of the SIVA Marketing mix may provide more value to the customers (Hsu et al., 2021).

Hence, this chapter also reflected upon requirements to follow the SIVA Marketing mix and logic to transform SIVA Marketing mix elements into Green-SIVA Marketing mix by incorporating (Mehraj & Qureshi, 2020). Though the major focus of this chapter is on the use of Green-SIVA Marketing Mix with respect to service-oriented companies according to Alwis and Manel (2021), in recent service-oriented companies from Asian sides of the world are getting more involved in green marketing practices.

4. Purpose and Significance of the Study

The purpose of writing this chapter has two significant folds, as it is not only directed towards the importance of the green marketing mix in the service industry but also provides the way through which service marketing may become more optimized. In fact, this chapter will shed light on new aspects of Green Marketing i.e. Green-SIVA Marketing which is not only an emerging topic but also a unique blend of strategies that may be used for making a green marketing mix also related to other stakeholders like the environment, etc. The special concern towards the developing Asian market is also one of the plus points of the study that may substantiate the value of the study. Hence, the study is significant for researchers, scholars, and academicians that may not only use that teaching and class discussion but may also extend research work in this vein.

5. The Concept of Green Marketing Mix and the Way Forward

5.1 Green Marketing Mix

The wish to have a greener economy can only be fulfiled through introducing a range of new products and technologies that are produced and generated through the green concept. However, for effective and green production there is a need for high-level integration and communication, good information, precise attention to concepts of the environment, senior management support, and using a person-alized approach for measurement and benchmarking. Thus, there is a challenge for marketers to revamp marketing mix elements into green marketing mix elements (Abzari et al., 2013). On the other side, little emphasis on the subject from academics and researchers also resulted in hindrance in the application of the concept in a broad manner. However, the concept is also termed *environmental marketing* and *responsible marketing*, etc., which means all the parties must pay focus on environmental sustainability and well-being (Mahmoud, 2019). Hence, legitimate to indicate that there is an area for discussions associated with the points indicated by Mehraj and Qureshi (2020). Thus, it is legitimate to extend research work by complying with Mahmoud (2019), to generate a substantial amount of literature on the subject to increase knowledge and research work.

5.2 Green Marketing Mix in Service Industry

Green Marketing has a significant impact on customer satisfaction as well as on the intention to repurchase which is perceived as the most important tool in analyzing customer satisfaction. In fact, each component (element) of GMM is significant in producing a favourable impact on customer satisfaction as well as intention to repurchase (Chairunnisa et al., 2019).

However, there is a severe lack of green products and services in the market (Delafrooz et al., 2014). Although service-oriented companies must try to be more inclined towards the implementation of GMM due to the higher rate of efficiency as compared to product-oriented firms. The statement looks valid as service-oriented firms contribute more than 61% to the global economy (Alwis & Manel, 2021). Moreover, the service sector also has more impact on the GDP of most countries around the globe, and therefore legitimate to believe most of the countries all over the globe are insisting on their service sector (Alwis & Manel, 2021). Although the service sector includes a range of business activities and therefore there is also a probability that business activities of the sector may create a negative impact on the environment. Thus, the service sector must be inclined towards the adoption of GMM elements in order to reduce the negative consequences of their activities (Alwis & Manel, 2021).

5.3 Mini Case Study 01

5.3.1 Effective Designing of Marketing Mix for Services – a Way Forward to All the Leading Service Brands

Marketing Mix elements have a massive importance in terms of the service sector in order to portray the desired impact of intangible offerings in the minds of the customers. The case study approach of research has been incorporated in order to develop a thorough flow of information. Thus, a detailed interview of 40 minutes has been conducted with executive-level employees of DHL-Logistic services (Oflac et al., 2015). Transcription of interviews and analysis highlighted that all the marketing mix elements are significantly important for brand positioning as well as customer satisfaction. In fact, the framework developed by DHL-Logistic might be found significantly important for the other service providers and may assist them in developing better marketing strategies (Oflac et al., 2015).

5.4 Green Marketing Mix Elements

The use of GMM also creates positive impacts on the level of customer satisfaction. Therefore, the description of each Green Marketing Mix has been written through considering a bunch of studies including Abzari et al. (2013); Alwis and Manel (2021); Chairunnisa et al. (2019); Tiwari et al. (2011) and Elgarhy and Mohamed (2022), etc.

5.5 Green Product

An increase in environmental concern resulted in the revision of new products through changes in the packaging, designing, as well as ways of formulating the products. Products that are designed to address ecological purposes are associated with lesser consumption of energy, resources, and pollution and result in environmental safety and survival of scarce resources (Abzari et al., 2013). Green Product is a form of product that is environmentally safe and has lesser or no negative impacts on society (Chairunnisa et al., 2019). A similar has been highlighted by Chairunnisa et al. (2019), but the use of green labelling may require certification from the authorized system for the overall system of the company. In fact, eco-labels are one of the most common and effective tools used by international hotels in order to portray a positive impact on consumers (Chan, 2014).

This is actually proof of environmental concern by the hotel in order to make customers believe that they are purchasing green products. The impact can be further enlightened by taking accreditations from internationally recognized environmental management systems like ISO 14000 and Grade Global 21 (Chan, 2014). Hence, in comprehensive manner green products are described as those products that are environmentally friendly and non-toxic in nature examples may include products that are biodegradable, recyclable, re-useable or grown originally, etc. (Odho & Maqsood, 2021).

5.6 Group Characteristics of Green Products

Abzari et al. (2013) pointed out some characteristics of Green Products that are as follows:

a. First group of characteristics of the Green Product is associated with the societal and environmental impact of the product must be viewed after consumption and therefore it must be designed in view with green marketing.
b. Second group of characteristics of Green Products is associated with the manufacturing process of the product in order to associate characteristics of the total product in green marketing.

It has been also recommended that the 5Rs (Repair, Reconditioning, Reuse, Recycling, and Remanufacturing) should be associated with the manufacturing of products to produce a better impact on environmental sustainability.

5.7 Empirical Evidence From Pakistan

Green Products are an important tool for the enhancement of customer satisfaction (Cheema et al., 2015). Similar has been indicated in studies from Pakistan e.g. Cheema et al. (2015); Mahmoud (2018); Mahmoud et al. (2017), and Odho and Maqsood (2021), etc. In fact, one of the initial studies by Cheema et al. (2015) reflected the positive impact of green products on customer satisfaction with reference to food restaurants through regression analysis. On the other side Mahmoud (2019) and Odho and Maqsood (2021) use regression to understand the impact of green marketing mix elements on customers' purchase intention and found that green product is always an impactful element on customers' purchase intention. Although according to Odho and Maqsood (2021), green product influences customer purchase intention in the most significant manner.

5.8 Green Price

Green price is perceived as the top-ranked element of the green marketing mix (Abzari et al., 2013) and is the form of the price that is charged due to an increase in the cost of production through low consumption of energy. Most of the time the Green Price is higher than the other competing products due to the following environmentally safe procedures that are not followed by the others (Chairunnisa et al., 2019). This phenomenon has also been highlighted by Kotler et al. (2018) that some consumers are willing to spend more money to purchase environmentally safe products. However, Green Pricing is also the most challenging element of the green marketing mix as it may make producers motivated if consumers are willing to pay more charges for social and environmental causes (Abzari et al., 2013). In fact, one of the studies from Pakistan indicated that environmentally focussed-consumers also have some limitations and they may not be willing to pay more price for environmentally safe products (Hayat et al., 2019). Hence, Green Marketing must be reasonable and competitive in order to attract customers towards the product and also to obsolete the negativity about overcharged products (Abzari et al., 2013). It has been indicated by Chan (2014) that prices of green hotels were not significantly different from the others that are not following green marketing strategies. Although some of the customers may still be ready to pay higher prices for green hotels especially when the percentage of the amount charged has been associated with the conduction of green activities.

5.9 Empirical Evidence From Pakistan

Empirical evidence from Pakistan is limited in this regard although most of the studies conducted e.g. Cheema et al. (2015); Mahmoud (2018); Mahmoud et al. (2017), and Odho and Maqsood (2021), etc., all indicated positive impact of green price either on customer satisfaction to purchase or re-purchase. The initial study by Cheema et al. (2015) was on customer satisfaction while the remaining three were on customer's purchase intention. However, most of the studies are empirical and use regression analysis to indicate that the perceived impact of green pricing is always positive in Pakistan.

5.10 Green Place

Green Place is defined as the process of distribution and includes all the forms of warehousing and logistic activities along with the recipient of orders. Although the real sense of green place lies in stores that are used to market the company's offerings, so as to make consumers feel protective about the environment (Chairunnisa et al., 2019). The concept is also termed Green Distribution and has been divided into internal and external aspects. The internal aspect of distribution deals with the place of production that must have tranquility for managers as well as employees along with the concern towards environmental issues. On the other hand, the external aspect of distribution deals with the place of offering products that may cause minimal harm to the environment (Abzari et al., 2013). Moreover, one of the studies by Goyal and Pahwa (2018) indicated that green places are also based on the decrease of carbon steps by diminishing the carbon emission in the process of transportation. Hence, opening branches with respect to customer convenience as well as selecting of distribution strategy that causes minimal carbon emission are the major requirements of the green place mechanism (Osiako et al., 2022).

5.11 Empirical Evidence From Pakistan

Among empirical studies from Pakistan, most of the work indicated that green place is also positively related to customer satisfaction. Although one of the studies by Odho and Maqsood (2021) indicated a negative association between green places and customers' purchase intention. Although the study was based on the textile industry and uses the concept of green logistics to evaluate the impact of green places on customers' purchase intention. However, other studies like Cheema et al. (2015) and Mahmoud et al. (2017), both have indicated a positive impact of green places on customer satisfaction as well as on intention to purchase.

5.12 Green Promotions

There are several data that emphasize environmental discussions for promotional activities (Abzari et al., 2013). Green Promotions can be any form of communication activity including advertisements, personal selling, point-of-sale communications, and direct marketing, etc., with a concern for the environment (Chairunnisa et al., 2019). In fact, green promotions are used to provide real environmental information to all the prospects that have any association with the offerings of the firm (Abzari et al., 2013).

Moreover, green promotions are directed to address ethical and legal considerations. These include messages to minimize air pollution, relate product characteristics to the environmental status, and indicate authentic data about the product advantage e.g. describe all the technical terms and explain the environmental advantages of the firm's offerings (Abzari et al., 2013). One of the other studies by Delafrooz et al. (2014) indicated the major elements of green advertisements i.e. corporate concern towards the environment, change in corporate procedure to show corporate's dedication towards the environment, and environmental action or impact for which corporate must be appraised. Abzari et al. (2013) also provides a classification of green advertisements that are as follows:

a. Advertisements that are used to reflect the relationship between the firm's offerings and the environment.
b. Advertisements that publicize green lifestyles through the use of the company's offerings.

In the case of the service industry, similar sort of indications was made by Chan (2014) that hotels must make their communications and advertisements reliable by developing some association with environmental associations or groups. These sorts of activities may make consumers believe in the green promotions of the company and not associate firms offering and promotions with the greenwash.

5.13 Empirical Evidence From Pakistan

Studies from Pakistan are mostly in favour of green promotions e.g. Mahmoud (2018); Mahmoud et al. (2017), Odho and Maqsood (2021), etc. Although one of the initial studies by Cheema et al. (2015) indicated that there is no impact of green promotions on customer satisfaction. Other than that, studies conducted on the food and textile sectors in recent years do acknowledge the role of green promotions and indicated a positive relationship between green promotions and customers' purchase intention.

5.14 Process

Processes are used to develop and ensure the relationship of organizational processes with green productive issues (Al-Majali & Tarabieh, 2020). The process can also be defined as the flow of activities in association with the main business of the service-based firm (Elgarhy & Mohamed, 2022). Chan (2014) indicated that genuine green products and services tend to play a positive impact on consumer perception. Therefore, environmental policies must be developed in order to assure the formulation of green products and services. A study by Al-Majali and Tarabieh (2020) also indicated that service-based firms also tend to follow laws and regulations that are implemented by the law-making bodies and government in order to devise offerings as per the green standards.

5.15 People

People refer to the employment of a skilled workforce in green businesses (Al-Majali & Tarabieh, 2020).

Chan (2014) indicated that marketers must motivate front-line managers in the hotel industry to initiate two-way communication with their customers in order to boost customers' confidence through discussions and feedback. Two-way communication is not only fruitful in the optimization of customer satisfaction but also in making improvements in the green product strategies of the firm. Moreover, the study of Al-Majali and Tarabieh (2020) also indicated that green businesses also motivate their employees to behave in a way that is in line with social responsibility and green marketing practices. In fact, companies must endorse the green behaviour of employees through various initiatives like training, awareness programmes, and performance management programmes.

5.16 Physical Evidence

Environment-friendly characteristics of service-oriented firms are a real example of physical evidence. It may include the design of the building, offices, gardens, and equipment with lesser carbon emissions and no wasteful energy, etc. (Zahmatkesh Saredorahi et al., 2021). The study of Chan (2014) indicated the implication of physical evidence with reference to the service industry in 2012 Fairmont Banff Springs which was awarded top environmental hotel by Fairmont Hotels and Resorts is willing to implement organic policies in the purchase as well as in customer service. These policies are in line with green marketing mix elements as hotels want to integrate green marketing mix elements into overall operations rather than to use less water and electricity city. All of these measures are believed to be an important component of hotels' green operations and are supposed to lead towards an increase in competitive advantage through diminishing consumer scepticism. In fact, impacts can further be optimized through disposable-free and paperless services and also by purchasing local, organic, and sustainable products to ensure the green philosophy of the company (Chan, 2014).

The examples of physical evidence vary with respect to the industry; for hospital physical evidence may include entrance, lobby area, waiting area, sewerage, transportation, uninterrupted lighting facilities and awards and recognitions of medical practitioners, etc. However, for transportation series physical evidence may include travel experience, accommodation, transportation, luxury, etc. Although regardless of the variation in the use and example of physical evidence it will remain as the tool to influence customers effectively and to charge a premium price for your offerings (Elgarhy & Mohamed, 2022).

5.17 Perspective of Green Marketing Mix With Reference to Pakistan

In Pakistan there is a significant rise in consumer concerns about environmental stability and consumers, as well as the court of law, are discouraging those products that may cause environmental degradation. Evidence includes an increase in plantation drives, a ban on the use of polythene bags, and Supreme Court orders for the protection of the environment and methods to diminish environmental degradation. Still, mass industrialization is perceived as one of the major reasons for the increase in the level of pollution in several rural and urban areas of Pakistan (Hayat et al., 2019). In fact, three major cities of Pakistan are also on the list of the top 20 polluted cities of the world. Hence, Pakistan is trying to implement different methods to cope with rising issues and to reduce environmental degradation. On the other hand, we are still observing a constant rise in the level of pollution in rural and urban areas of the country (Hayat et al., 2019), although in contemporary times service sector emerged as the major sector for Pakistan's economy as it contributes more than 50% to the GDP of the country (Ahmed & Ahsan, 2011). Although inhabitants of Pakistan do not have proper knowledge about green marketing strategies and the government is also not taking the required measures for the implementation of green marketing strategies (Siddique et al., 2013). Although according to research work, green marketing strategies might have a better impact on a firm's marketing performance, especially from the perspective of SMEs operating in Pakistan (Ahmad et al., 2020). Regardless of these reflections very limited work has been done on the perspective of green marketing with reference to Pakistan. Especially with reference to green marketing strategies of services and therefore most of the empirical evidence is either from green marketing of products or from other countries. However, the need to understand the role of green marketing mix elements with respect to the service industry is legitimate especially with respect to Asia where more and more companies are getting involved in green marketing of services (Alwis & Manel, 2021).

6. Methodology and Design

The study is conducted to generate knowledge and understanding about the green marketing mix with respect to the service sector as well as to shed light upon the use of green-SIVA marketing. Thus, the philosophy associated with the study is epistemology (Saunders et al., 2007), as the study is there to increase knowledge regarding green marketing which is still an under-research topic (Sharma, 2021), especially with respect to emerging countries (Agustini et al., 2021). The methodological choice is a mono method (qualitative); the research strategy is archival in nature and the time horizon is cross-sectional (Saunders et al., 2015).

6.1 Mini Case Study 02

6.1.1 Developing Sides of the World and Role of Green Marketing Mix
Studies from Sudan reflected that University students were also found to be inclined towards the green marketing mix as the country is also suffering from mass industrialization, urbanization, land degradation, soil erosion, and depletion of natural resources. Hence, companies are required to develop eco-friendly products that may create a better impact on the environmental condition of

developing countries where environmental pollution is ranked among the top problems. The study also shows that consumers are in fact inclined towards green businesses and green products and will never hesitate in paying more prices for obtaining eco-friendly products (Mahmoud, 2018).

6.2 Mini Case Study 03

6.2.1 Green Marketing Campaigns and Need to Develop More Elements of Green Marketing Mix

A study from Bangladesh indicated that consumers are highly inclined towards the green marketing mix elements and ready to pay more price for obtaining green products. In fact, the study recommended the formulation of new green marketing mix elements to produce a better impact on consumers. On the other hand, studies indicated that the major influence has been created by green products and green promotions, and therefore it is also recommended that marketers must try to use green promotional campaigns more and more to influence the consumers more in a desired manner (Hossain & Khan, 2018).

6.3 SIVA Marketing Mix Elements

SIVA Marketing mix elements are actually used to satisfy customer desires and expectations more precisely. Therefore, the concept has the ability to uncover the real needs and desires of customers and hence can generate more sales and profitability. The statement is legitimate and authentic as SIVA marketing mix is based on the real needs and desires of customers and therefore has the ability to develop better and more effective corporate strategies (Hsu et al., 2021).

6.4 Green-SIVA Marketing Mix Elements

A study by Mehraj and Qureshi (2020) postulated that GMM are multi-dimensional in nature and SIVA elements are somehow consistent with the GMM. Therefore, recommended to revamp GMM as Green-SIVA Marketing Mix In fact, SIVA Marketing Mix elements are perceived to be a latest upgradation in the marketing concept.

6.5 Green Solution

Solution refers to the value that has been generated through the consumption of a company's offerings. In fact, customers themselves become active members of the value-creation process through the addition of their own understanding of the process of consumption (Mehraj & Qureshi, 2020). In fact, one of the latest studies by Hsu et al. (2021), that instead of intense focus on the products there is a need that companies must shift their focus towards solutions for customer needs. Although green Solutions are actually based upon customers' desires from the company, that company will fulfil their needs with consideration towards environmental concerns. The requirement might be fulfiled by reducing pollution, and wastage, conserving energy, and saving scarce resources. The green solution can be indulged in the production process through having eco-certifications, control procedures, life cycle analysis, and pollution prevention (Mehraj & Qureshi, 2020).

6.6 Green Information

The information represents the totality of knowledge that the customer has about the marketers, offerings of the firm and marketing firm. It may not only include traditional marketing messages but also their customer's own experience of interaction with the social networks either through using offline or online modes of communication. Moreover, information may also include information through third parties through product reviews, blogs, and other resources (Mehraj & Qureshi, 2020).

Therefore, it is legitimate to believe that instead of promotions companies must try to provide authentic information (Hsu et al., 2021). However, Green Information is the term that is actually used to inform stakeholders about the plans, procedures, and intentions of the company for environmental protection and related areas. The purpose of green information is to make consumers aware of the practices and work activities that companies are using to decrease negative impacts on the environment (Mehraj & Qureshi, 2020). Therefore, the process strategically includes activities that may reduce the negative impacts of the organizational promotional campaigns. Green information may result in eco-friendly investment, eco-friendly product modification, and noticeable environmental engagements (Mehraj & Qureshi, 2020).

6.7 Green Value Practices

Value is termed as the cost that customers will bear against the bundle of benefits that they have through consuming the company's offerings. Value can be effectively determined through the customer's readiness to bear time cost, energy cost, pride, reputation, etc. (Mehraj & Qureshi, 2020). Hsu et al. (2021) indicated that the SIVA marketing mix also has the ability to endorse better relationships with other chain members so as to provide more value to the customers. Although green value practices include all forms of environmental as well as economic costs that may satisfy customers' requirements and will also provide considerable business and return to the firm (Mehraj & Qureshi, 2020).

6.8 Green Access Practices

Access refers to the delivery of the desired solution within adequate and reasonable cost and time so that customers may fulfil their needs in a desired way. Change in access and preference change the preference of the distribution channel preferred by the company in order to provide solutions to customers at their preferred place or location (Mehraj & Qureshi, 2020). It has been indicated by Hsu et al. (2021) that companies must try to provide solutions to the customers with respect to their feasibility and comfort. However, to endorse green practices in the green access practice there is a need to supplement eco-friendly practices in the area of supply chain management. The inclusion of eco-friendly practices in the area of the supply chain may take many folds as initially, it may include working with channel partners in order to increase product reuse and disposable arrangement. Working with supply chain partners may also result in the development of mechanisms through which customers may be able to provide recyclable material back to the company. Secondly, the green access process company may enforce practices in order to force suppliers and distributors to follow better cost-effective methods so as to attain their goals of marketing (Mehraj & Qureshi, 2020). Organizations may also develop alliances with channel members to revamp logistic arrangements in order to diminish the negative environmental impact of joint activities. Last but not the least, green access companies may be able to implement green supply chain tactics to improve the overall worth and impact of the product (Mehraj & Qureshi, 2020).

7. Conclusion

The world and its preferences are changing and hence we are observing the transformation of product-based economies into service-based economies. In fact, the contribution of the service sector is massive to the economies, especially in developing sides of the world. Therefore, the sector must transform its marketing strategies to green marketing strategies and use green marketing mix elements.

Although if the marketing mix elements have the flavour of SIVA marketing along with the concern towards the environment, then the marketing mix strategies may not only be beneficial for the growth of sales and profit but will also provide better solutions to the customer and meanwhile will also not produce a harmful impact on the environment. Therefore, the transformation towards Green-SIVA Marketing must be incorporated in order to leverage the holistic view of marketing management philosophies.

7.1 Policy Implications

This chapter may be utilized to make policymakers understand the role of green marketing from service companies. Hence, with this understanding individuals and institutions may not only increase further research but the light may also make the government implement some SOPs and KPIs for efficient and effective marketing campaigns. Moreover, understanding may also make institutions develop guidelines that may also place lenses on ways to perform green marketing practices that may also be effective for society, company, as well as consumers (Green-SIVA). In light of these parameters, the draft is significantly important for individuals, institutions, researchers, academicians, as well as policymakers.

References

Abzari, M., Safari Shad, F., Abedi Sharbiyani, A. A., & Parvareshi Morad, A. (2013). Studying the effect of green marketing mix on market share increase. *European Online Journal of Natural and Social Sciences: Proceedings, 2*(3(s)), 641.

Agustini, M., Baloran, A., Bagano, A., Tan, A., Athanasius, S., & Retnawati, B. (2021). Green marketing practices and issues: A comparative study of selected firms in Indonesia and Philippines. *Journal of Asia-Pacific Business, 22*(3), 164–181.

Ahmad, R., Ahmad, M. J., Farhan, M., & Arshad, M. A. (2020). The relationship within green marketing strategies and market performance of Pakistan SME's. *Hamdard Islamicus, 43*(2), 204–216.

Ahmed, A., & Ahsan, H. (2011). *Contribution of services sector in the economy of Pakistan*. PIDE Working Papers.

Al-Majali, M., & Tarabieh, S. (2020). Effect of internal green marketing mix elements on customers' satisfaction in Jordan: Mu'tah University students. *Jordan Journal of Busienss Administration, 16*(2), 411–434.

Alwis, P. D. S. M., & Manel, D. P. K. (2021). Green marketing inclination: A study of green marketing mix strategies for the service sector in Sri Lanka. *Sri Lankan Journal of Business Economics, 10*(11), 1–18.

Ansar, N. (2013). Impact of green marketing on consumer purchase intention. *Mediterranean Journal of Social Sciences, 4*(11), 650–655.

Chairunnisa, S. S., Fahmi, I., & Jahroh, S. (2019). How important is green marketing mix for consumer? Lesson from the body shop. *Jurnal Manajemen, 23*(2), 321–337.

Chan, E. S. W. (2014). Green marketing: Hotel customers' perspective. *Journal of Travel & Tourism Marketing, 31*(8), 915936.

Cheema, S., Durrani, A. B., Khokhar, M. F., & Pasha, A. T. (2015). Influence of green marketing mix and customer fulfillment: An empirical study. *International Journal of Sciences: Basic and Applied Research, 24*(6), 168–177.

Delafrooz, N., Taleghani, M., & Nouri, B. (2014). Effect of green marketing on consumer purchase behavior. *QScience Connect, 1*, 5. https://www.qscience.com/content/journals/connect

Elgarhy, S. D., & Mohamed, L. M. (2022). The influences of services marketing mix (7ps) on loyalty, intentions, and profitability in the Egyptian travel agencies: The mediating role of customer satisfaction. *Journal of Quality Assurance in Hospitality & Tourism*, 1–24.

Eneizan, B. M., Wahab, K. A., Zainon, M. S., & Obaid, T. F. (2016). Prior research on green marketing and green marketing strategy: Critical analysis. *Singaporean Journal of Business, Economics and Management Studies, 51*(3965), 1–19.

Goyal, M., & Pahwa, M. S. (2018). Green marketing mix: A model towards sustainability. *International Journal of Computer Science & Technology, 6*(9), 23–27.

Hayat, K., Nadeem, A., & Jan, S. (2019). The impact of green marketing mix on green buying behavior: A case of Khyber Pakhtunkhwa evidence from the customers. *City University Research Journal, 9*(1), 27–40.

Hossain, A., & Khan, M. Y. (2018). Green marketing mix effect on consumers buying decisions in Bangladesh. *Marketing and Management of Innovations, 4*, 298–306.

Hsu, T. H., Her, S. T., Chang, Y. H., & Hou, J. J. (2021). The application of an innovative marketing strategy MADM model—SIVA-need: A case study of apple company. *International Journal of Electronic Commerce Studies, 13*(1), 33–68.

Karunarathna, A. K. P., Bandara, V. K., Silva, A. S. T., & De Mel, W. D. H. (2020). Impact of green marketing mix on customers' green purchasing intention with special reference to Sri Lankan supermarkets. *South Asian Journal of Marketing*, *1*(1), 127–153.

Kotler, P., Keller, K. L., Ang, S. H., Tan, C. T., & Leong, S. M. (2018). *Marketing management: An Asian perspective.* Pearson.

Mahmoud, T. O., Ibrahim, S. B., Ali, A. H., & Bleady, A. (2017). The influence of green marketing mix on purchase intention: The mediation role of environmental knowledge. *International Journal of Scientific & Engineering Research*, *8*(9), 1040–1048.

Mahmoud, T. O. (2018). Impact of green marketing mix on purchase intention. *International Journal of Advanced and applied sciences*, *5*(2), 127–135.

Mahmoud, T. O. (2019). Green marketing: A marketing mix concept. *International Journal of Electrical, Electronics and Computers*, *4*(1), 20–26.

Mehraj, D., & Qureshi, I. H. (2020). Determinants of green marketing mix in developing economies: Conceptualisation and scale validation approach. *Business Strategy & Development*, *3*(4), 522–530.

Odho, F. N., & Maqsood, A. (2021). Impact of green marketing mix on consumer purchase intention in textile industry of Pakistan. *Social and Management Sciences Research Journal*, *1*(2), 1–29.

Oflac, B. S., Dobrucalı, B., Yavas, T., & Escobar, M. G. (2015). Services marketing mix efforts of a global services brand: The case of DHL logistics. *Procedia Economics and Finance*, *23*, 1079–1083.

Osiako, P. O., Wikurendra, E. A., & Abdeljawad, N. S. (2022). Concept of green marketing in environment conservation: A literature review. *Environmental and Toxicology Management*, *2*(2), 8–13.

Rahbar, E., & Wahid, N. A. (2011). Investigation of green marketing tools' effect on consumers' purchase behavior. *Business Strategy Series*, *12*(2), 73–83.

Saunders, M., Lewis, P., & Thornhill, A. (2007). *Research methods. Business students* (4th ed.). Pearson Education Limited.

Saunders, M. N., Lewis, P., Thornhill, A., & Bristow, A. (2015). Understanding research philosophy and approaches to theory development. In M. N. K. Saunders, P. Lewis, & A. Thornhill (eds), *Research methods for business students* (pp. 122–161). Pearson Education.

Sharma, A. P. (2021). Consumers' purchase behaviour and green marketing: A synthesis, review and agenda. *International Journal of Consumer Studies*, *45*(6), 1217–1238.

Siddique, M., Hayat, K., Akbar, I., & Cheema, K. U. R. (2013). Impediments of green marketing in Pakistan. *International Journal of Management & Organizational Studies*, *1*(2), 22–27.

Tiwari, S., Tripathi, D. M., Srivastava, U., & Yadav, P. K. (2011). Green marketing-emerging dimensions. *Journal of Business Excellence*, *2*(1), 18.

Viani Parlan, A., Kusumawati, A., & Mawardi, M. K. (2016). The effect of green marketing mix on purchase decision and customer satisfaction. *Jurnal Administrasi Bisnis (JAB)*, *39*(1).

Zahmatkesh Saredorahi, M., Boroumandzad, Y., Gharibzadeh, J., Siadatan, M., & Ardian, A. (2021). Analyzing the marketing role in the hotel industry brand by combining fuzzy cognitive mapping and social network analysis. *Journal of Tourism and Development*, *10*(2), 55–66.

Chapter 15

Understanding Green Entrepreneurship: Concept Implications and Practices

Muhammad Faisal Sultan, Muhammad Furqan Saleem, Sadia Shaikh and Erum Shaikh

Abstract

The concept of green entrepreneurship is still in its infancy stage and therefore there is no proper way to define and relate this form of entrepreneurship with the business or society. Although green entrepreneurship is the need of recent times in order to protect the environment. Therefore, there is a need to focus more intensely on the concept. On the other side, the support of the government and the lack of financial stability of entrepreneurs from developing sides of the world is hindering the path of green entrepreneurs from developing sides of the world. Therefore, this chapter has been purposely written to highlight the green entrepreneurial process along with the motivational model for green entrepreneurs. Hence, this chapter might be perceived as the cornerstone in the development of the concept of green entrepreneurship from developing sides of the world.

Keywords: Green entrepreneurship; social entrepreneurship; green business model and green entrepreneurs; emerging markets; green opportunity; Pakistan

1. Introduction

Social entrepreneurship is a form of entrepreneurship in which all the activities are directed towards the enhancement of socially responsible behaviour, environmental sustainability, and sustainable development of business. Firms that incorporate these practices are social enterprises and their preferences are to achieve social objectives in comparison to the market objectives (Tien et al., 2020). Hence, social enterprises are perceived as change makers that exist to

Entrepreneurship and Green Finance Practices, 285–297

increase economic well-being, environmental security, social inclusion, and market integration. Therefore, social entrepreneurship is perceived as a tool to serve the unmet needs of low-income groups with special emphasis on developing sides of the world. In fact, social entrepreneurship is an engine for social development and a strategic driver facilitating the adjustment to occurring changes in the community. Hence, a substantial difference exists in nature, motivation, and purpose as well as in business philosophies opted by social and commercial entrepreneurs. However, regardless of these massive differences between social and commercial entrepreneurs, there is a probability of collaboration to bridge social capital leading to the emergence of entrepreneurial capital and the development of both profit and non-profit activities. Among various types of social entrepreneurship, one that has received the least attention is known as Green Entrepreneurship (Tien et al., 2020).

According to research, initial signs of green entrepreneurship emerged in the 1960s when the developed and western world uncovered the negative impacts of industrialization. In fact, this is one of the prime reasons behind the formulation of (EPA) the Environmental Protection Agency whose purpose is to trace major reasons for environmental degradation. Formulation of the agency also resulted in various occupational opportunities and also provided some alternative opportunities for businesses to get involved in eco-friendly products. Hence, it is appropriate to state that agencies actually trigger the new, innovative, and eco-friendly use of raw materials (Haldar, 2019).

However, the concept gained mass recognition and attention in the 1990s and the concept of Green Entrepreneurship gained popularity due to its prime focus on environmental sustainability (Mohsen, 2018). Especially there is a significantly lower focus on the motives and influences of Green Entrepreneurship (Tien et al., 2020). In fact, the term Green Entrepreneurship is not easy to explain as it is a hybrid of a series of philosophical and semantic arguments. The concept was first coined by Berle in 1991 and even after 31 years there is a need for clarity of concepts that constitutes Green Entrepreneurship and those that have created the distinction between green entrepreneurs and non-green entrepreneurs (Haldar, 2019). In fact, one of the latest studies, Rahmawati et al. (2021), defines Green Entrepreneurship as a form of business that has implications for the entire globe with high concern for environmental protection. Although the idea must also not reflect negatively upon the financial streams of the firm. Thus, Green Entrepreneurship is leveraging society with innovative ideas for the reduction of poverty, unemployment, and environmental harm. On the other side outbreak of COVID-19 also produced a considerable impact on the procedural requirements for green startups (Nguyen et al., 2022). On the other side consumers from Pakistan do not have a positive attitude towards the green purchase and therefore there is a need for concern about the issue. Hence, optimal to design effective awareness and marketing campaigns in order to shed light on individual, organizational, and societal contributions that must be initiated to protect the environment and society as a whole (Moon et al., 2021).

In recent times, considerable attention has been placed on the 'Green Business Model' due to the sustainability that these models might bring to society. The need for green entrepreneurship became more vibrant as business processes and activities became the major reason for the increase of pollution and environmental degradation. Legal actions and instruments are also failing in assisting society in curing these harmful activities and processes (Muo & Azeez, 2019).

Hence, there is a need to harness the concept of green entrepreneurship in such a way that it may be able to curtail the propensity of environmental incidents in our society (Muo & Azeez, 2019). In fact, the research of Mohsen (2018) reflected that it is imperative to conduct further research on the topic of Green Entrepreneurship as the form of entrepreneurship is advantageous for startups as well as existing firms. In fact, focussing on environmental sustainability will not only create a point of differentiation but will also induce profitability of the firm. The findings will be especially beneficial for Pakistan as the youth of Pakistan may be found more inclined towards owning green startups as the soil may encourage these forms of endeavours. In fact, the government must also provide a thorough push for green initiatives by focussing more on sustainability education and green education (Soomro, Ghumro, & Shah, 2020). Although it is quite certain that small- and medium-sized firms (SMEs) tend to face challenges and obstacles that often slowed down the implementation of environmentally sound practices, studies indicated around seven types of major obstacles that may confront SMEs in implanting environmentally friendly practices and among these obstacles one is technology as SMEs cannot afford to invest heavily in technology (Rajkamal et al., 2022).

1.1 Need of Research

Green Entrepreneurship is in its infancy stage and scholars and practitioners are still exploring the new elements of Green Entrepreneurship so as to have a thorough understanding of basic programmes, processes and principles, etc., involved in green entrepreneurship management (Muo & Azeez, 2019). In fact, the study of Mohsen (2018) reflected that most of the developing sides of the world perceive Green Entrepreneurship as a way to produce cheaper products to satisfy the lower-income side of society. On the other side, developing countries also try to develop environmentally safe products to strive towards the transformation of the economy. In short, it is legitimate to state that lack of knowledge about eco-friendly products and the segment that may invest in green entrepreneurial ventures are the legitimate challenge in the way of green business and green entrepreneurial ventures.

The study further indicated that the concept of Green Entrepreneurship is in its infancy stage, especially in developing sites of the world, and hence it is not implemented thoroughly in these sides of the world (Mohsen, 2018). Although in Pakistan there is a massive opportunity for green entrepreneurship (Soomro, Mirani, et al., 2020) hence there is a significant need that prevails to investigate the concept as well as its social and economic benefits for the country (Hussain et al., 2021). However, most of the studies are quantitative e.g. Hussain et al. (2021); Moon et al. (2021) and Soomro, Mirani, et al. (2020), and either on green entrepreneurial intentions or on factors that may flourish green entrepreneurial intention in youth.

Although there is a lot to understand more about green entrepreneurship e.g. the green entrepreneurship process (Navarathinam & Amutha, 2022), etc., in order to enhance the conduct of comprehensive research with respect to Pakistan as indicated by Hussain et al. (2021).

1.2 Characteristics of Green Entrepreneurship

Green Growth and its determinants are one of the prime areas of discussion for policymakers. Although, in order to attain Green Growth, we must also understand the fact that there is also a paradigm shift towards green production and green consumption which eventually gives birth to Green Entrepreneurship. That is actually the relationship between the environment, sustainability, and entrepreneurs. Although can also be referred to as ecopreneurship; eco-entrepreneurship or environmental entrepreneurship. Although there are some distinctions between Green Entrepreneurship and Sustainable Entrepreneurship, as Green Entrepreneurship is for the generation of ecological and economic benefits. However, sustainable entrepreneurship is based on a triple-bottom-line approach that is exerted to generate a balance between the planet, people, and profit. On the other side study also indicates three major characteristics of green entrepreneurship among these one is almost similar to the other counterparts (Haldar, 2019):

i. Identify market opportunities and gain access to the resources in order to yield profitability in the long run. This entails involvement in innovative ventures that are associated with higher levels of risk and uncertainty of returns.
ii. There should be a positive net effect of entrepreneurial ventures on the natural environment and progress towards sustainability. Although this point has some variations according to authors like Schaper (2002), Green Entrepreneurship is a hybrid of several entrepreneurial efforts and it is impossible to gauge its impact.
iii. Intentions and values of Green Entrepreneurs are also the major distinctions between the path and activities opted by Green Entrepreneurs and Traditional Entrepreneurs. The major difference is the preference for sustainable business strategies by Green Entrepreneurs that are implemented to protect the environment and to attain goals of sustainable development. Hence, the ventures are accelerated by ecological sustainability as well as means to attain economic gains.

2. Relating Ability, Motivation, and Opportunity Theory (Amo) With Green Entrepreneurship

The theory that is used to gauge the impact of Green Entrepreneurship on society is known as AMO theory. However, these forms of impact were rarely addressed and discussed with respect to developing countries like India, Pakistan, Bangladesh, etc. The theory proposed that three different elements related to work systems i.e. AMO affects the operative traits of the entrepreneur and resulted in the success of the firm. Actually, the AMO model resulted in the transformation of Skills, Incentives, and Entrepreneurial Education (SIE), and these three elements are discussed below (Mia et al., 2022).

Skills: New generation of Green Entrepreneurs are surely in need of a certain set of skills and therefore youth that is focussed on green and ethical entrepreneurial ventures need to polish the inventory of their skills set.

Moreover, there is also a need for a thorough mindset and therefore potential green entrepreneurs must try to revamp their knowledge by obsoleting the vague parts of the knowledge and must try to apply innovation and critical thinking in the process of decision making. Study also mentioned some of the skills that are required by Green Entrepreneurs like persuasiveness, bravery and learning abilities i.e. entrepreneurial thinking, innovation, team building, networking, etc.

Incentives: The incentives of Green Entrepreneurship are not only with respect to the financial or non-financial returns to the entrepreneur but the terminology is also associated with the incentives for the society. The concept holds the relationship as Green Entrepreneurship is for the betterment of society and sustainability and therefore businesses may become more socially oriented by excluding the hazardous effects of operations from society along with the extensive financial motivation for the attraction of young entrepreneurs.

Entrepreneurial Education: The strategy to combat present and future needs is to supplement youth with entrepreneurial education. The purpose of entrepreneurial education has two folds as it is directed towards the replacement of harmful behaviours with those which are in benefit of individuals and society. Moreover, entrepreneurial education also makes individuals supplemented with necessary skills like intelligence, knowledge, and ethical responsibility. Through this, we may be able to induce problems solving abilities in individuals and may foster their motivation to assist society and humanity in the desired and effective way. Hence, entrepreneurial education is the major contributor to the green business model that is a need of social scenarios to bring positive changes. Thus, entrepreneurial education is the real hope for humanity for attaining sustainable growth.

2.1 The Process of Green Entrepreneurship

According to Navarathinam and Amutha (2022), the process of green entrepreneurship is a unique blend that describes the way to deal with environmental challenges in order to fulfil social and economic requirements. Hence, use the reference of Sharma and Kushwaha (2015) to elaborate on the four components that are required for effective green entrepreneurship.

a. *Green Challenges*: Businesses in pursuit of glory need to encounter various challenges among these there are some that are related with environmental well-being and sustainability. For example, businesses have to counter problems related with natural resource depletion, global warming, energy consumption, climate change, waste management, etc.

b. *Social and Economic Goals*: Business exists in order to achieve economic and social goals for business activities as well as for stakeholders. Therefore, a concrete-level focus is required to attain the required social and economic goals along with the societal and environmental obligations.

c. *Green Business*: Through green business, we term an enterprise that actually works for the betterment of the environment. The purpose can be attained by reducing the negative impact of business on the environment or by developing ways or products that may produce a better impact on the environment. Making eco-friendly products is associated with the way by which companies may produce a better impact on the environment and therefore we must include green as well as green–green businesses in this category.

d. *Green Idea and Innovation*: The final component of the green entrepreneurship process is actually the one that provides a solution to the environmental problem by relating innovation with the processes, design, and business activities.

2.2 Intentions for Being a Green Entrepreneur

Entrepreneurial Attitudes are actually one's ability to become an entrepreneur. Elaborating on the statement, we may state that the positive or negative abilities of an individual to become an entrepreneur are reflected in the entrepreneurial attitude. Similarly, attitude towards green business is based upon likeness or dislikeness of the green business. In fact, a similar theory has been highlighted by the theory of reasoned actions that whenever people come in contact with any object, they will develop a specific mindset and on the basis of the particular mindset (i.e. judgement), people will accept or reject the product. Studies indicated that there are various reasons why people may prefer entrepreneurship over full-time or part-time employment. Similarly, there are definite reasons to prefer green entrepreneurship (Nguyen et al., 2022).

a. *Educational Support towards Green Entrepreneurship*:

It has been observed that problems pertaining to the support of startup businesses have a significant impact on the success of student businesses Hence, universities are recently found to encourage green businesses. Hence, green entrepreneurship must be included in educational support programmes administered by different universities. Universities that encourage green business may also be able to make students leveraged with business-related skills and knowledge that may cause empowerment of student ventures. In fact, the value of green businesses and the intention to be a green entrepreneur may be more enlightened through a proper understanding of the goals and objectives of green businesses.

Thus, it is legitimate to consider university-level education as one of the major ways that may transform green entrepreneurial intentions into the green.

b. *Subjective Norms*:

Subjective Norms are the perceived normative ideas from friends, family, and other social groups. The ideas also have the ability to influence entrepreneurial decisions as indicated by TRA theory that subjective norms are the perception of anyone who has any sort of belief related to the positive or negative act of the entrepreneur. Hence, subjective norms are perceived as potent predictors of entrepreneurial intention. However, starting a new business may have a stronger effect on an individual's thoughts about entrepreneurship and career.

c. *Self-Efficacy towards Green Entrepreneurial Intentions*:

The theory of planned behaviour indicated that an increase in business performance is directly associated with business intentions. Similarly, there is a significant relationship between university students' overall performance and their desire to start a business.

Individuals face several issues and hurdles in starting green entrepreneurial ventures compared to other forms of start-ups. Some of the major reasons for these forms of hurdles are the complexity and cost associated with obtaining green technologies along with the infancy stage of green businesses. Hence, study predicted that self-efficacy is one of the major predictors of green entrepreneurship.

Studies further indicate that self-efficacy is not only a motivational factor but through this one may also be able to control the social environment; therefore, self-efficacy is also reflected as one of the major indicators of green entrepreneurship.

d. *Risk Aversion*:

Risk Aversion is one of the major indicators of research related to investment making and in fact, the indicator has a significant impact on investment decisions across the globe. The reason for the extreme influence of risk aversion on investment decisions is elaborated as each and every investor has a different mindset as well as investment ability. Along with these elements risk tolerance is the other major indicator and therefore risk aversion acts as the major difference between the entrepreneurial mindset of entrepreneurs and non-entrepreneurs. Hence, people who are risk-averse are more inclined towards entrepreneurship.

e. *Need for Achievement*:

According to the theory of planned behaviour achievements are based upon behavioural attitudes, subjective standards, and perceived behavioural controls. Therefore, people with a high need for achievement are often willing to take risks, tackle hindrances, have confidence, thorough visions and leadership abilities, and these would contribute significantly to green entrepreneurship.

2.3 Mini Case Study 01

2.3.1 Mitti Coll Clay Creations

Mitti Cool Clay Creations deals in the manufacturing and sales of innovative clay products. The owner of the company is Mr Mansukhbhai Prajapati who was featured in the list of Forbes's top seven rural entrepreneurs for the year 2010. He was exposed to the manufacturing of clay products due to his family's occupation. Still, due to high entrepreneurial intent, he took a loan of 30,000 from a local money lender back in 1988 to set up an earthen plate manufacturing factory. He registered his firm as Mansukhbhai Raghavbahi Prajapati in 1990 where he experimented on clay to devise a mix that is more resilient and heat resistant. However, due to the earthquake in 2001, Manukhbhai Raghavbahi Prajapati suffered from severe loss as the stock got destroyed. Although, a massive loss could not break down the entrepreneurial intent of Manukhbhai who devised inspiration to develop a clay fridge from an article published in the daily Sandesh, a Gujrati Newspaper (Haldar, 2019).

For this purpose, Mansukhbhai obtained a loan from his friends and also mortgaged his father's house to obtain a three years loan from the bank. The design for the clay fridge was approved in 2005 and the innovation was designed with the consultation of Gujrat Grassroot Innovation. The fridge works on the principle of evaporation as the unit gets cool through the distillation of water to the lower chambers which eventually got evaporated to make the unit cool without any consumption of electricity. Mansukh Bhai made his firm registered in 2007 as Mitti Cool Clay Creations. Mansukh Bhai was also involved in the production of several other environmentally safe products like cookware with environmental concerns. After crossing the breakeven stage, Mitti Cool Clay Creations started to supply its products all over India in 2010.

Moreover, due to cheaper, innovative, and environmentally safe products, the company also received export orders from 41 countries across the globe. Recently the company is getting well established with a turnover of 45 lakhs and an employee base of around 40 employees (Haldar, 2019).

2.4 Association and Explanation

This case study has been associated with Berly (1991) that there are business opportunities that may not only induce one's earnings but may also produce a positive impact on the earth. Similarly, the case is also consistent with Farinelli et al. (2011) as business activities are produced due to hazardous impacts on the natural environment. In fact, activities are also causing negative impacts on wildlife, natural habitats, climate, and biodiversity. There is a need to move towards an environmentally sustainable development path through the imple- mentation of sustainable practices. A study by Farinelli et al. (2011) further indicated that for now, sustainability is the central part of the business plans by companies operating all over the globe, and green entrepreneurs are a major source behind sustainability. The statement is valid as green entrepreneurs are committed to fulfiling needs of the society through efficient utilization of resources that are in line with environmental as well as social concerns.

2.5 Mini Case Study 02

2.5.1 Green Oil Energy Sciences

Mr Anupam Jalote who served Airtel till 2008 as the chief process officer is the owner of Green Oil Energy Sciences (Pvt.) Ltd. It is an innovative firm sourced by the motive of green entrepreneurship to devise energy from waste. The motivation behind this cause is to reduce environmental degradation and to reduce the impact of long-lasting hazards. Hence, Mr Anupam Jalote actually works to leverage residents of rural areas to generate low-cost and renewable energy from their own resources. Initially, Mr Anupam Jalote also faced adverse conditions due to the delay in receiving payments, which was eventually received in 2012. After that, he started to develop organic manure on a small scale with the brand name 'Green Oil Karishma' and recently the company is able to develop over 1,000 tons of organic manure through the processing of farming and other forms of waste. Thus, able to generate revenue of 3–4 lakh/month with the intention to develop at least 10 power plants with a capacity of 1 MegaWatt/plant in the span of five years. Although for now 30% of the shares have been sold to Zurich-based companies in order to earn revenue for the purpose of research and development so as to foster environmental as well as socio-economic benefits for the residents and locality (Haldar, 2019).

2.6 Association and Explanation

This case study is also consistent with Farinelli et al. (2011), as providing low-cost manure to the inhabitants of rural areas is not only cost-effective but will also not produce negative impacts on the environment. Hence, the point is aligned with the major purpose of green entrepreneurs. Moreover, the intention to be a green entrepreneur has been based on self-efficacy, risk aversion, and the need for achievement as highlighted by Nguyen et al. (2022). Last but not the least the process that Mr Anupam Jalote has followed has been based upon the entrepreneurial process reflected by Navarathinam and Amutha (2022).

2.7 Mini Case Study 03

2.7.1 Green Entrepreneurship in Pakistan: Opportunities and Role of Government to Induce Green Businesses

Pakistan is one of the developing sides of the world where the temperature of rural areas of Sindh and other provinces fosters the need to use green products.

Especially by youth as the youth is the major influencer and decision makers for the utilization of resources. Youth contribution to the overall Pakistan population is more than 50%, in fact the contribution of youth in the population of Pakistan reaches its all-time highest level. Hence, there is a massive opportunity for young entrepreneurs in Pakistan to attract youth towards green products and increase business growth through the persuasion power of young customers. In fact, the government of Pakistan must take necessary steps to support SMEs that are involved in the green business as the consumption of green products. This can be done in multiple ways and funding and sponsoring green businesses is not the only way to support green entrepreneurship. In short, support might become conducive through supporting marketing and promotional activities of green businesses and also through implementing penalties on those businesses that are harmful to society (Soomro et al., 2020).

2.8 Association and Explanation

This case study is also consistent with Farinelli et al. (2011), but in a bit different way in comparison to case study number 01 and case study number 02. The difference is legitimate as this study has been associated with the preferred way of entrepreneurship for developing sides in comparison to the developed sides of the world. In fact, the study emphasized the point that developed and developing sides of the world have differences in focus towards Green Entrepreneurship. Developed sides of the world are mainly inclined towards Green Businesses, while the developing sides are majorly inclined towards low-cost entrepreneurship. The study also quoted the examples of Indian and Chinese entrepreneurs who are developing cheaper products that suit the needs of the poor. However, the study also emphasized that there is still a need for green inclination in order for the proper functioning of green entrepreneurship. On the other side, studies mentioned that developed sides have sufficient resources to develop new and innovative products but do not have entrepreneurs that may push prototypes towards commercially acceptable products.

2.9 Hurdles for Green Entrepreneurship and Green Businesses

Rajkamal et al. (2022) indicated that the implementation of green entrepreneurship is complex for SMEs as well as for large-sized firms. Hence, also identified a few of the major obstacles that may hinder the implementation of conventional business, which are as below:

a. *Management's commitment:* There is a severe lacking in a managerial commitment to implement green practices. The concern is lacking due to threats due to enlarged and unseen threats that may hinge due to over-innovation.
b. *Lack of governmental support:* Government usually does not offer any sort of relaxation like a reduction in tax rates or low-interest loans to green

businesses. Thus, it is also a significant barrier in the way of new or young entrepreneurs that have the potential to flourish in green business.

c. *Cost:* SMEs are mostly unknown of the incentives and schemes that may be given to businesses that may assist the environment and society. Therefore, they always try to increase their output through productivity and therefore face severe challenges associated with the cost of expensive raw materials.

d. *Lack of support from business partners:* In order to assure green output green business also needs support from other partners along the supply chain. However, due to the unavailability of green support, it is quite difficult to pursue green business.

e. *Technology:* SMEs mainly rely on ready-to-market technology and cannot support technological development through research and development processes. Hence, SMEs also face challenges due to technology as they cannot optimize it through time or input from stakeholders. On the other side, lack of knowledge, as well as the shortage of skills, also hamper the growth OF green startups.

f. *Unpredictability of payback period:* Prior studies also raised the concern about the issue that in green business there is a severe unpredictability of recovery. Therefore, it is a serious concern that is obstructing the way of green entrepreneurs.

g. *Customer knowledge:* Lack of customer knowledge about green products and their benefits is also impairing the conduction of green business.

2.10 Drawbacks of Green Entrepreneurship

In addition to obstacles, RajKamal et al. (2022) also indicated that green entrepreneurship is also associated with some major drawbacks that are as follows:

a. *Expenses:* The material that is required for initiating green business is significantly expensive as compared to the raw material required for conventional business.

b. *Time:* In green business, there is a need for intense planning in order to avoid any negative impact of the company's offering on the environment. Thus, it will also need a substantial amount of time for thorough analysis and forecasting and hence the time taken for decision-making is a bit lengthier than a conventional business.

c. *Meagre Savings:* One of the major issues that have been faced by green entrepreneurs is of saving due to the intensive need of financial needs of green businesses.

d. *Hesitation in Purchase from Buyer:* Due to the high cost of raw materials associated with green business the market price of offerings may also be higher than the competing products. Thus, buyers may feel reluctant in purchasing green products in comparison to the conventional products available in the market.

3. Research Methodology and Design

The study uses epistemology as the philosophy as the major purpose of the study is to increase knowledge regarding '*Green Entrepreneurship*', with special emphasis on green entrepreneurship from developing sides of the world.

Hence, in connection with Saunders et al. (2007), it is optimal to use epistemology as the philosophy of the study with methodological choice is mono-method (qualitative), research strategy is archival and time horizon is cross-sectional.

4. Conclusion

Green Entrepreneurship is the contemporary requirement of the world and therefore there is a need to support the process and entrepreneurs who are willing to serve society and humanity. Although developing sides of the world have perceived green entrepreneurship in the right way. Therefore, this chapter has been written to clarify the process as well as motivational factors for green entrepreneurship. Moreover, case studies from developing sides of the world are also indulged in this chapter to make it more relevant and authentic for readers. Thus, it is legitimate to consider this chapter as the pervasive work in the field of academia and research to make academicians, researchers, and policy makers inclined towards the topic.

5. Policy Implications

In addition to its theoretical and academic importance, the study is also important for policymaking as it may push policymakers to start initiatives and programmes that may make youth, academicism, and researchers aware of the incentives that green businesses may earn from governments and agencies in order enlarge efforts as a whole towards the betterment of society and community through green startups and businesses.

References

Berle, G. (1991). *Business opportunities that can save the earth and make you money.* Liberty Hall Press.

Farinelli, F., Bottini, M., Akkoyunlu, S., & Aerni, P. (2011). Green entrepreneurship: The missing link towards a greener economy. *Atdf Journal, 8*(3/4), 42–48.

Haldar, S. (2019). Green entrepreneurship in theory and practice: Insights from India. *International Journal of Green Economics, 13*(2), 99–119.

Hussain, I., Nazir, M., Hashmi, S. B., Di Vaio, A., Shaheen, I., Waseem, M. A., & Arshad, A. (2021). Green and sustainable entrepreneurial intentions: A mediation-moderation perspective. *Sustainability, 13*(15), 8627.

Mia, M. S., Rahman, S. M., Alom, S., Ahmed, F., & Longpichai, O. (2022). An insight on green banking practices in Bangladesh: A study on commercial banks. *International Journal of Education, Business and Economics Research, 2*(5), 23–33.

Mohsen, A. (2018). Green entrepreneurship in Afghanistan: Prospects and challenges. *The Asian Journal of Technology Management, 11*(1), 46–56.

Moon, M. A., Mohel, S. H., & Farooq, A. (2021). I green, you green, we all green: Testing the extended environmental theory of planned behavior among the university students of Pakistan. *The Social Science Journal, 58*(3), 316–332.

Muo, I., & Azeez, A. A. (2019). Green entrepreneurship: Literature review and agenda for future research. *International Journal of Entrepreneurial Knowledge, 7*(2), 17–29.

Navarathinam, K., & Amutha, V. (2022). Green entrepreneurship: A sustainable development initiative with special reference to selected districts. *Journal of Positive School Psychology, 6*(3), 7517–7526.

Nguyen, T. L., Pham, N. A. N., Nguyen, T. K. N., Nguyen, N. K. V., Ngo, H. T., & Pham, T. T. L. (2022). Factors affecting green entrepreneurship intentions during the COVID-19 pandemic: An empirical study in Vietnam. *The Journal of Asian Finance, Economics and Business, 9*(2), 383–393.

Rahmawati, R., Suprapti, A. R., Pinta, S. R. H., & Sudira, P. (2021). Green entrepreneurship: A study for developing eco-tourism in Indonesia. *The Journal of Asian Finance, Economics and Business, 8*(5), 143–150.

Rajkamal, S. V., Velmurugan, J. S., & Suryakumar, M. (2022). Green entrepreneurs challenges and innovation: The struggles they face. *International Journal of Professional Business Review, 7*(2), e0482–e0482.

Saunders, M., Lewis, P., & Thornhill, A. (2007). *Research methods. Business students* (4th ed.). Pearson Education Limited.

Schaper, M. (2002). The challenge of environmental responsibility and sustainable development: Implications for SME and entrepreneurship academics. In *Radical changes in the world: Will SMEs soar or crash* (pp. 541–553).

Sharma, N. K., & Kushwaha, G. (2015). Emerging green market as an opportunity for green entrepreneurs and sustainable development in India. *Journal of Entrepreneurship and Organization Management, 4*(2), 2–7.

Soomro, B. A., Ghumro, I. A., & Shah, N. (2020). Green entrepreneurship inclination among the younger generation: An avenue towards a green economy. *Sustainable Development, 28*(4), 585–659.

Soomro, R. B., Mirani, I. A., Ali, M. S., & Marvi, S. (2020). Exploring the green purchasing behavior of young generation in Pakistan: Opportunities for green entrepreneurship. *Asia Pacific Journal of Innovation and Entrepreneurship, 14*(3), 289–302.

Tien, N. H., Hiep, P. M., Dai, N. Q., Duc, N. M., & Hong, T. T. K. (2020). Green entrepreneurship understanding in Vietnam. *International Journal of Entrepreneurship, 24*(2), 1–14.

Chapter 16

Green Banking Practices: A Bibliometric Analysis and Systematic Literature Review

Ahsan Riaz, Nimra Riaz, Hamad Raza and Farhan Mirza

Abstract

Purpose: This chapter review studies on green banking practices and identifies information gaps to justify future research approaches.

Design methodology/approach: A systematic literature review has been conducted by analyzing 44 Scopus-indexed articles on adopting green banking practices through the PRISMA flowchart and analyzed through Vosviewer software.

Findings: The findings indicate that survey studies comprised 82% of the selected papers. The *Journal of Cleaner Production* was the most-cited publication, with 471 citations. France was most frequently involved in collaborative research, with connections to six other countries. Notably, two-thirds of the listed countries had collaborated internationally in publications, but with less than 10 countries involved, based on the 44 studies included in the analysis.

Originality: According to the authors' best knowledge, no systematic literature review on green banking practices from the Scopus database utilizing the PRISMA approach has been published in academic literature.

Research implication: The pitfalls observed in previous research, such as the paucity of an empirical and conceptual methodology and a systematic investigation of theory development, give numerous opportunities for future research. Following this, many new trends in green banking are outlined to assist researchers in identifying gaps in the literature and future study directions.

Practical Implication: The study aids researchers, professionals, and managers in understanding green banking adoption's significance. Banks can increase their economic scenarios by using this concept in new markets with

Entrepreneurship and Green Finance Practices, 299–317
Copyright © 2024 Ahsan Riaz, Nimra Riaz, Hamad Raza and Farhan Mirza
Published under exclusive licence by Emerald Publishing Limited
doi:10.1108/978-1-80455-678-820231016

excessive potential for employment and business avenues. In addition, the study highlights the value of sustainable practices, environmental concerns, and the importance of green banking.

Keywords: Systematic literature review; green banking; PRISMA; bibliometric analysis; Scopus database; sustainable practices

1. Introduction

The last three decades have seen a dramatic upsurge in focus on environmental protection and Sustainable Development Growth (SDG) in response to intensifying concerns about the effects of human activity on the planet's natural resources on present and future generations (Aruna Shantha, 2019; Tara et al., 2015). Environmentalism, or Green Politics, was thus named the 1990s' most crucial business challenge (Grove et al., 1996). To address environmental issues such as global warming, acid rain, air and water pollution, ozone layer depletion, and climate change, global leaders have collaborated on future responsibility paradigms for their development activities through voluntary codes of conduct such as the United Nations Environment Programme-Finance Initiative (UNEP-FI), the Equator Principles for Project Finance, and the UN Principles for Responsible Investment (UNPRI) (World Bank, 2017). Because of the growing threat of climate change and global warming, the finance industry intends to adopt 'Go Green' (Bouteraa et al., 2021; Samina & Hossain, 2019; Yin et al., 2019; Zhixia et al., 2018). Environmental sustainability and reduced carbon emissions are the goals of Green Banking.

The rapidly increasing and pervasive awareness of the dangers of pollution on the environment as a result of economic activities must have piqued stakeholders' interest in learning about the environmental and social costs of goods and services produced, as well as attempting to force enterprises to manage their business in a context of sustainable development. As a response, businesses are becoming more vocal about their efforts to promote sustainable development to gain stakeholder support and credibility. Businesses need to create innovative sustainable production techniques and approach to reduce the adverse effects of their operations on the environment if they want to contribute to sustainable development.

At this crucial juncture in the journey towards sustainable development, numerous stakeholders, like banks, have started acknowledging and working towards minimizing, reducing, and eliminating environmental waste. Green Banking (Käufer, 2011, p. 2016) is a corrective and control method implemented by the global banking sector in response to its accountability and responsibility for resource and environmental deterioration. Green banking is recognized worldwide as a pillar of the standard financial system and a separate banking institution, such as the Connecticut Green Bank and the New York Green Bank. However, Green Banking adoption in emerging and developing economies is distinct in terms of sustainable management activities.

A literature review was the foundation for any research and stimulated the researchers' interest. This chapter will review the research on adopting green banking practices with a systematic literature review and bibliometric analysis technique. The study's specific objectives are to:

- Compile a review of existing studies on the adoption of green banking practices.
- Organize the articles in a logical order to facilitate research.
- Sort research publications that adopt green banking practices into categories based on their methodology and approach.
- Examine existing challenges in adopting green banking practices literature and propose a study outline for future research.

In addition to the purposes listed above, the authors concentrated on the following research questions:

- How are articles on the adoption of green banking placed in time?
- What research has been done on the adoption of green banking practices?
- What kind of research methods were used?
- What are the most influencing articles on the subject?

The rest of the chapter is organized as follows. First, green banking practices are explained, and then the research design. Second, an article classification technique and a review of the selected publications are provided. Finally, the summary of significant findings evaluated implications, and proposed future study areas are explained.

1.1 Concept of Adoption of Green Banking Practices

Banks are one of the financing sources for organizations, particularly in developing and emerging markets. By supporting enterprises that actively pollute our planet, banks could aid the deterioration of the environment and threaten the population of humans. As per a study (Schücking et al., 2011), 93 banking institutions spent €232 billion on coal financing between 2005 and 2010. Green Banking adoption is helping to raise awareness of banks' role in environmental degradation, and steps are being taken to reduce banks' harmful environmental activities while enhancing significant contributions to an environmentally friendly society (Bukhari et al., 2020).

On the other hand, Green Banking is a broad term that banks use to refer to activities beyond profit-making, including improving people's lives. It achieves sustainable development by intertwining economic, environmental, and social considerations to achieve social equity while reducing ecological risks (Bouteraa et al., 2021). It enables banks to conduct environmentally friendly financial transactions by combining technological advancements with organizational changes. Green banks should constantly monitor transaction processing to meet all legal and environmental criteria, as any breach could lead to banks' adverse selection. Green banking is financial goods and services that considerably use information systems and paperless banking transactions. It offers e-banking, SMS banking services, phone banking, e-statements, electronic bank account registration, e-payment, e-investment, ATM use, e-Fund Transfer Network, as well as other mobile monetary benefits such as e-currency 24 hours a day, seven days a week (Aktar & Masukujjaman, 2014; Choudhury et al., 2013).

2. Methodology

A literature review aims to discover and evaluate the review of research to identify possible research areas and knowledge gaps. The systematic literature review outlines appropriate protocols, including relevant keywords, literature searches, and analysis. This study adopted a systematic literature review and bibliometric analysis technique on green banking practices, a modified review process for identifying issues and possible pathways (Bouteraa et al., 2021).

2.1 Systematic Review

An essential step in any systematic review is defining the research question that helps to achieve the desired goal. The first step involves deciding on the best search method, such as digital sources (libraries and indexing systems), and determining the search terms. Initially, EBSCO, Elsevier Science Direct, and Emerald explored article searching. Scopus was chosen as the digital source for the literature review, and the following keywords were used to find the titles and abstracts of the papers. The keywords are 'green banking adoption; green banking practices; sustainable practices; green banking AND sustainability'. Initially, a keyword search offered a large amount of information. The authors developed some delimiting boundaries for screening the literature because reviewing all the available literature was impossible. Table 16.1 shows the following criteria for accepting and rejecting the papers:

Table 16.1. Acceptance and Rejection Criteria for the Refinement of Literature.

Criteria for Acceptance	Criteria for Rejection
Papers published from the year 2007–2021 were included.	Non-English language article was excluded.
The paper's title related to adopting green banking practices was selected. Only papers from Scopus digital sources were included.	Book chapters, master/doctoral theses, conference papers, reviews, reports, Retracted, Editorial, Notes, Short surveys, and unpublished working articles were eliminated. Missing record papers were also excluded.

To avoid receiving many papers during the literature search, only those published between 2007 and 2021 were considered. The initial investigation attempted to identify 3,038 articles in the Scopus database. The results of the above keyword search were saved in the green banking practices folder with information related to all identified papers, including authors' names, article titles, journal names, volume, issue numbers, affiliation, keywords, abstract, and document type. A few papers overlapped due to the repeating of keywords. There were 2976 papers after removing duplicates and missing records such as authors' names and journals.

The second step involves screening the papers based on titles and abstracts after applying the inclusion and exclusion criteria listed in Table 16.1 and eliminating 129 studies that did not fit the study's goal. Studies focussing on the link between adopting green banking practices and sustainability are included. However, 738 articles were eliminated from a single database because they did not meet the study's requirements (Books, Notes, Conference papers, Editorial, notes, Reports, Retracted, Reviews, and Short surveys). The whole text of these articles was evaluated in the last step, and 44 papers were selected for analysis and classification, as shown in Fig. 16.1. As explained above, all of these steps for systematic review were completed in the PRISMA diagram, as suggested by Page et al. (2021).

2.2 Database (Publisher) Research Protocol

The authors choose different publishers for data collection of articles based on titles, keywords, and abstracts, such as Associate management consultant Pvt Ltd, Ciber Institute, Cogent OA, Elsevier, Emerald, IGI Global, Inderscience Publisher, John Wiley and Sons Ltd, MDPI, Politchnika Lubelska, Sage Publications Ltd, Springer Netherland, Taylor & Francis Ltd, Universiti Malaysia Terengganu, and Scopus. The initial time frame of the search was from 1985 to 2022, and the sample comprised articles (2007–2021) that met all of the delimiting criteria for further evaluation. A literature search was undertaken in a selected database using the terms 'adoption of green banking practices' searched in the title, keywords, or abstract. At first, the database search with defining restrictions retrieved 1754 articles. Additional processing steps were necessary to ensure the papers discovered were pertinent to green banking practices. It has been done by reading and analyzing the articles and thinking about how they relate to the challenges. After a thorough investigation, 44 articles directly related to adopting green banking practices (please see Table 16.2).

3. Results and Analysis

The analysis is based on 44 selected articles established on publication year, journal, country, nature of papers, and bibliometric analysis. This analysis will provide insight into the topic, highlight key trends, and identify future research gaps and opportunities. It is done to figure out what is happening in the literature regarding adopting green banking practices.

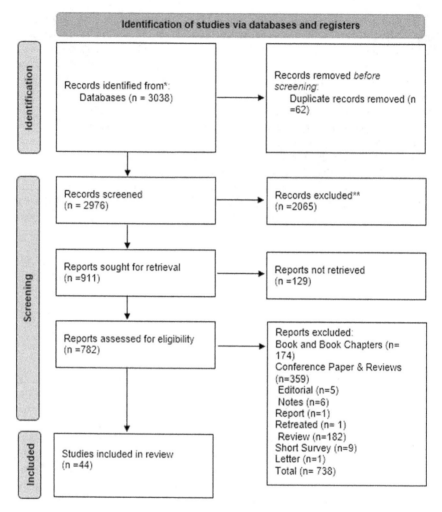

Fig. 16.1.   PRISMA Flowchart for the Papers Selection Process.

3.1 Distribution Based on Publication Year

The articles were published regularly from 2007 to 2021, according to the investigation of the papers by year of publication. As seen in the bar chart in the figure, only a few publications were released in 2007 and 2008. The graph also shows an upward trend in publications since 2007 that could be attributed to the recent economic slowdown, highlighting the importance of green banking adoption. Most research articles will be published between 2019 and 2021, as shown in Fig. 16.2. In 2021, 12 articles were published on the underlying topic that proves the emerging significance of this area among researchers.

Table 16.2. Research Protocol by Publisher.

Publisher	Scope	Time Horizon	Total Number of Articles	Number of Selected Articles
Associated Management Consultants Pvt. Ltd.	Title/ Abstract/ Keywords	1985–2022	2	1
CIBER Institute	Title/ Abstract/ Keywords	1985–2022	1	1
Cogent OA	Title/ Abstract/ Keywords	1985–2022	6	1
Elsevier	Title/ Abstract/ Keywords	1985–2022	655	16
Emerald	Title/ Abstract/ Keywords	1985–2022	121	8
IGI Global	Title/ Abstract/ Keywords	1985–2022	8	1
Inderscience Publishers	Title/ Abstract/ Keywords	1985–2022	48	1
John Wiley and Sons Ltd	Title/ Abstract/ Keywords	1985–2022	89	2
MDPI	Title/ Abstract/ Keywords	1985–2022	270	4
Politechnika Lubelska	Title/ Abstract/ Keywords	1985–2022	4	1
SAGE Publications Ltd	Title/ Abstract/ Keywords	1985–2022	29	1

Table 16.2. *(Continued)*

Publisher	Scope	Time Horizon	Total Number of Articles	Number of Selected Articles
Springer Netherlands	Title/ Abstract/ Keywords	1985–2022	12	1
Taylor and Francis Ltd	Title/ Abstract/ Keywords	1985–2022	83	1
Universiti Malaysia Terengganu	Title/ Abstract/ Keywords	1985–2022	1	1
Scopus (Journal Not Mentioned)	Title/ Abstract/ Keywords	1985–2022	425	4

3.2 Analysis by Research Method and Methodology

The table presents the numerous methods examined and employed in the litera-ture. Whether a paper is based on empirical analysis or primary research depends on the type of paper reviewed. There are three categories of papers that have been

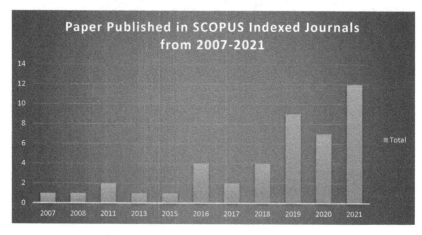

Fig. 16.2.   Distribution Based on Publication Year.

Table 16.3. Articles by Research Methods.

Research Methods	Number	Percentage (%)
Empirical	6	14
Conceptual	2	4
Survey	36	82
Total	44	100

published. The empirical survey and conceptual studies are part of green banking practices research. As per the analysis in Table 16.3, a questionnaire survey was the most prevalent primary methodology incorporated in the study, with 82%. On the other hand, only six empirical studies and two papers are from conceptual methods.

3.3 Distribution Based on the Journal

Table 16.4 shows the journal's frequency of articles publishes the maximum number of papers published on green banking adoption. Journal of cleaner production is the journal that addresses this issue more frequently. Nine papers have a 20.45% success rate, and Sustainability (Switzerland) has a 9% portion (4 articles). In three articles, business strategy and the environment contribute 7% of the subject matter. Innovative and Sustainable Built Environment and the International Journal of Production Economics have two articles, with 4.5%. The 24 remaining papers were distributed across 44 journals, with 54.55%.

Table 16.4. Frequency of Articles Published by Journals.

Frequency of Papers Published by Journals		
Journal Name	Number of Papers	Percentage (%)
Journal of Cleaner Production	9	20.45
Sustainability (Switzerland)	4	9
Business Strategy and the Environment	3	7
Smart and Sustainable Build Environment	2	4.5
International Journal of Production Economics	2	4.5
Others	24	54.55

3.4 Articles by Country Studied

The next part highlights the research on green banking practices based on country. The research articles for sample selection are primarily listed in Western countries, as per Fig. 16.3. Green banking adoption research appears to be very popular in the European and Australian continents, as many researchers are from Spain, Finland, the Netherlands, France, and Australia. It is observed from the review articles that researchers focussed their research on a single country. A few articles report cross-sectional studies that indicate a lack of systematic literature that allows researchers to compare findings across contexts and cultures. A list of nations with several journal articles published is shown in the graph. The selected published articles were dispersed, driven by economic development, empirical techniques, and a country-by-country classification. Based on their economic growth, countries are classed as developed or developing, and the number of articles published is depicted in the graph. The United States and Western European countries are formed, while Brazil, India, Malaysia, Iran, and Pakistan are emerging economies. It suggests that studies investigating green banking adoption have recently paid much attention to developing countries.

3.5 Adoption of Green Banking Classification

Fig. 16.4 represents the number of papers published by developed and developing countries. The graph shows that 14 countries are developing economies with 44% and 18 developed countries with 56% of the total population. Over the last few years, research investigating green banking practices has required to pay attention from developed countries.

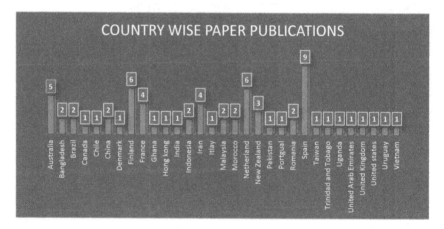

Fig. 16.3.   Country-Wise Paper Publication.

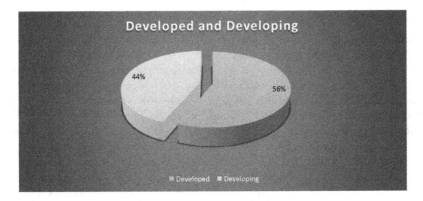

Fig. 16.4.   Classification by Type of Economy.

4. Citation Analysis

4.1 Author Citation Analysis

Citations are when someone refers to another author's work(s). Citation analysis examines many cited articles to determine the most significant works. This section examined the cited references for articles and identified the essential articles on green banking practices. The Scopus database is used for citation information for 44 articles under consideration for citation analysis, and most articles were published between 2007 and 2021. Table 16.5 displays the most-cited articles with at least 140 citations. The most-cited article is Chan et al., 2018; Darko et al., 2017; Deng & Ji, 2015; Niaki et al., 2019; Rantala et al., 2018 were also among the top five most-cited papers on green banking adoption.

Table 16.5. List of Citations Adoption of Green Banking.

Serial No.	Articles	Number of Citations
1.	Chan et al. (2018)	140
2.	Niaki et al. (2019)	82
3.	Darko et al. (2017)	79
4.	Deng and Ji (2015)	54
5.	Rantala et al. (2018)	50
6.	Millar and Russell (2011)	43
7.	Piyathanavong et al. (2019)	41
8.	Azeem et al. (2017)	32
9.	Liu et al. (2019)	24
10.	Shubham et al. (2018)	23

4.2 Journal Citation Analysis

However, because different papers have different effects, the number of papers published per journal is not a good benchmark for evaluating journals. As a result, when interpreting the above results, consider the impact of journal papers on the following studies. The authors rely on each journal's citations from the Scopus database to address this problem, as Scopus has the most reliable information for journal evaluation. The most common method for determining a publication's importance is conducting a journal citation analysis. The citation and citation rank of the journals of the 44 final papers selected are shown in Table 16.6. For example, it was discovered that the most cited journals related to adopting green banking practices were the Journal of Cleaner Production, which has 471 citations and the highest citation rank in the citation analysis. On the other hand, the top-cited journal's findings were remarkably consistent in the top half of the table with the top three, generating identical results in both analyses.

5. Bibliometric Analysis

A complete bibliometric analysis of the 44 selected articles based on two essential factors. The first is text mining to pinpoint the vital keywords (terms) studied together, which provides us with the concept of clustering the critical research areas in the field. A VOS-viewer (version 1.6.15) software was used for bibliometric analysis. 164 author keywords were documented, among which 164 were used only once, 26 keywords occurred twice, seven were used three times, and 6 were more than three times. After re-labelling synonymic single terms and congeneric phrases, 164 terms met the minimum threshold of 1 occurrence for the mapping in VOS-viewer. Fig. 16.5 reveals the outcomes of text incidence based on the co-occurrence of the correlated keywords. Each circle in the figure indicates a keyword in the dataset. The higher the number of author keywords that co-occurred (used), the closer they are placed on the map. The findings revealed nine significant clusters represented by circles in different colours that signify different keywords used in 44 included studies. The most prominent is a light green cluster, which shows that sustainability was frequently confronted with keywords with 24 occurrences and 48 links to other keywords. The second most reoccurring keyword was green banking adoption, which appears in an orange cluster with eight circumstances and 22 connections. The following other authors' keywords based on links and groups can be summarized as environmental sustainability (light blue labelled), green practices (yellow labelled), stakeholder theory (dark green labelled), barriers (Dark blue labelled), technology adoption (brown labelled), supply chain management (red labelled), and innovation adoption (purple labelled).

The second significant analysis examines the countries' collaborative attempts to find alternatives to the issues. Fig. 16.6 shows that France was the most associated country in collaborative research, which linked six countries. The list was followed by India, Australia, the United Kingdom, and China, with five links to other countries. Whereas the United States (4), Pakistan (4), Malaysia (2), and

Table 16.6. Analysis of a Journal Based on Citations.

Analysis of Journal by Citations

Journal Names	Number of Papers	Citation (Total Cited)	Citation Rank
Journal of Cleaner Production	9	471	1
Sustainability (Switzerland)	4	60	5
Business Strategy and the Environment	3	70	4
Smart and Sustainable Built Environment	2	36	8
International Journal of Production Economics	2	25	12
Building and Environment	1	0	24
Cogent Business and Management	1	4	18
Ecological Economics	1	23	14
Engineering, Construction, and Architectural Management	1	22	15
Environmental Innovation and Societal Transitions	1	33	11
European Journal of Innovation Management	1	1	23
Industrial Management and Data Systems	1	44	7
International Journal of Ethics and Systems	1	2	21
International Journal of Green Economics	1	0	25
International Journal of Production Research	1	66	6
International Journal of Technology and Human Interaction	1	0	26
Journal of Applied Business Research	1	12	17
Journal of Business Ethics	1	226	2
Journal of Sustainability Science and Management	1	0	27
Management of Environmental Quality: An International Journal	1	35	9
Plant Engineer (London)	1	0	28

Table 16.6. *(Continued)*

Analysis of Journal by Citations

Journal Names	Number of Papers	Citation (Total Cited)	Citation Rank
Prabandhan: Indian Journal of Management	1	3	19
Problemy Ekorozwoju	1	18	16
Quality and Quantity	1	35	10
Resources Policy	1	0	29
Resources, Conservation and Recycling	1	24	13
Social Responsibility Journal	1	2	12
South Asian Journal of Business and Management Cases	1	3	20
Technological Forecasting and Social Change	1	83	3

Ghana have (2) links. It was also revealed that 2/3 of the listed countries had an international collaboration in publications with less than 10 countries based on 44 included studies.

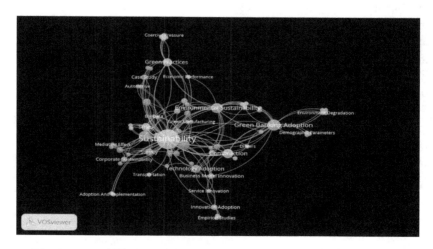

Fig. 16.5.   Bibliometric Map Created Based on Author Keywords Co-Occurrence Using Network Visualization of VOS-viewer. Minimum Occurrences of a Keyword are Set to Two.

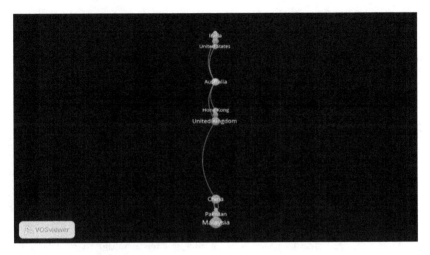

Fig. 16.6.   Bibliometric Map Created Based on Co-Authorships With Network Visualization Mode of VOS-viewer.

6. Findings From the Systematic Literature Review

6.1 The Dominance of Survey Research

Most research articles are on primary data and are based on a survey or questionnaire (Piyathanavong et al., 2019). Only a few researchers, such as Bukhari et al., 2020, used a conceptual approach to identify green banking adoption in various economic settings, whereas (Sharma et al., 2020) used empirical research to compare green banking adoption across India and assess the impact of environmental dimensions on it.

6.2 Lack of Inter-Country Research

All research publications were assessed using a sample of a single country for the analysis. Only a few studies (Ainin et al., 2016; Baig et al., 2020; Millar & Russell, 2011; Thomas et al., 2021) tried to compare the adoption of green banking across countries.

6.3 Emerging Topic

Green Finance is a significant and emerging issue in today's business settings. Banks can increase their economic prospects further by dipping into new markets with great potential for employment and business opportunities.

6.4 Adds Value

Businesses, Banks, and corporations can add value to their portfolio by enhancing and publicizing their engagement in green finance. Thus, they can give their business a green edge and attract more environmentally conscious investors and clients.

7. Conclusion

The primary purpose of this review was to conduct a systematic literature review with bibliometric analysis to identify and analyze the essential aspects of adopting Green Banking practices literature to contribute to a more thorough understanding of the research domain. We found and evaluated 44 research publications adopting Green Banking between 2007 and 2021. Although the quantity of research articles on Green Banking Adoption has increased, the articles' quality has been criticized due to repetitions of one or two original ideas and a low citation count. In order to adopt Green Banking, the banking business requires a thoughtful process (marked by or demonstrating considerable compassion) atmosphere. In this sense, an expanded environment involves the essential resources and aid in developing the competencies required for Green Banking adoption (Bukhari et al., 2020). Some key research opportunities and gaps have been identified for future attention based on the above findings and analysis, which include:

(1) As per findings, it is observed that most of the studies on green finance are from developed countries. The banks in developing countries (bank-dominated economies) have tremendous opportunities to increase the number of banks and shift the current system on green finance to claim the status of an environmentally friendly organization.

(2) In addition, future research could replicate this study with clients and owners to assess their perceptions of various dimensions and sources of green finance and sustainable practices and assess the significant challenges of green financing in different emerging economies.

(3) The researchers suggest that similar investigations be conducted in various literature parameters such as geographic contexts and databases.

(4) Finally, expanding the green finance 'Go Green' concept will mean comparative advantage and sustainability.

A few limitations in the current chapter need to be addressed. Firstly, the articles included in this review are restricted to the Scopus database and the time frame mentioned above. Further research could consist of scholarly articles from other sources, such as the (Web of Science) and a more extended period, resulting in more exciting research findings. Secondly, it is primarily associated with a failure to consider organizational or financial institution factors such as the size of the company or banking industry, the number of employees, the size and composition of the board of directors, a company's economic resources, financial performance, and sustainability performance. Future studies can incorporate these factors into their framework to verdict new evidence. They can also use quantitative research methods to examine the impact of these factors on the motivation for such disclosures. Third, although this article only used one software, VOS viewer, other bibliometric analysis tools, such as R programming (Biblioshiny), could be used in future studies.

8. Statements and Declarations

On behalf of all authors, the corresponding author states that:

- There is no conflict of interest.
- The authors declare that no funds, grants, or other support were received during the preparation of this manuscript.
- The authors have no relevant financial or non-financial interests to disclose.
- The authors have no competing interests to declare relevant to this article's content.
- All authors certify that they have no affiliations with or involvement in any organization or entity with any financial or non-financial interest in the subject matter or materials discussed in this manuscript.
- The data will be furnished upon request.
- The authors have no financial or proprietary interests in any material discussed in this article.
- The research has no involvement of Human Participants or Animals.
- The research has no requirement for informed consent from any party or agency.

References

Ainin, S., Naqshbandi, M., & Dezdar, S. (2016). Impact of adoption of green IT practices on organizational performance. *Quality and Quantity, 50*(5), 1929–1948.

Aktar, S., & Masukujjaman, M. (2014). Reasons to create intention of entrepreneurship among university students: A study on Bangladesh. *Journal of Entrepreneurship and Management, 3*(2), 15–25.

Aruna Shantha, A. (2019). Customer's intention to use green banking products: Evidence from Sri Lanka. *International Journal of Scientific and Research Publications (IJSRP), 9*(6), 9029.

Azeem, S., Naeem, M., Waheed, A., & Thaheem, M. (2017). Examining barriers and measures to promote the adoption of green building practices in Pakistan. *Smart and Sustainable Built Environment, 6*(3), 86–100.

Baig, A., Khaleeq, A., Ali, U., & Syeda, H. (2020). Evidence of the COVID-19 virus targeting the CNS: Tissue distribution, host–virus interaction, and proposed neurotropic mechanisms. *ACS Chemical Neuroscience, 11*(7), 995–998.

Bouteraa, M., Raja Hisham, R., & Zainol, Z. (2021). Exploring determinants of customers' intention to adopt green banking: Qualitative investigation. *Journal of Sustainability Science and Management, 16*(3), 187–203.

Bukhari, S., Hashim, F., & Amran, A. (2020). Green banking: A road map for adoption. *International Journal of Ethics and Systems, 36*(3), 371–385.

Chan, A., Darko, A., Olanipekun, A., & Ameyaw, E. (2018). Critical barriers to green building technologies adoption in developing countries: The case of Ghana. *Journal of Cleaner Production, 172,* 1067–1079.

Choudhury, T. T., Salim, M., Al Bashir, M., & Saha, P. (2013). Influence of stakeholders in developing green banking products in Bangladesh. *Research Journal of Finance and Accounting, 4*(7), 67–77.

Darko, A., Chan, A., Owusu-Manu, D., & Ameyaw, E. (2017). Drivers for implementing green building technologies: An international survey of experts. *Journal of Cleaner Production, 145,* 386–394.

Deng, Q., & Ji, S. (2015). Organizational green IT adoption: Concept and evidence. *Sustainability, 7*(12), 16737–16755.

Grove, S., Fisk, R., Pickett, G., & Kangun, N. (1996). Going green in the service sector. *European Journal of Marketing, 30*(5), 56–66.

Käufer, K. (2011). *Banking as if society mattered: The case of Triodos Bank* (p. 2016). Retrieved March 4.

Liu, Y., Zhang, Y., Batista, L., & Rong, K. (2019). Green operations: What's the role of supply chain flexibility? *International Journal of Production Economics, 214,* 30–43.

Millar, H., & Russell, S. (2011). The adoption of sustainable manufacturing practices in the Caribbean. *Business Strategy and the Environment, 20*(8), 512–526.

Niaki, M., Torabi, S., & Nonino, F. (2019). Why manufacturers adopt additive manufacturing technologies: The role of sustainability. *Journal of Cleaner Production, 222,* 381–392.

Page, M. J., Moher, D., Bossuyt, P. M., Boutron, I., Hoffmann, T. C., Mulrow, C. D., Shamseer, L., Tetzlaff, J. M., Akl, E. A., Brennan, S. E., & Chou, R. (2021). PRISMA 2020 explanation and elaboration: Updated guidance and exemplars for reporting systematic reviews. *BMJ, 372.*

Piyathanavong, V., Garza-Reyes, J., Kumar, V., Maldonado-Guzmán, G., & Mangla, S. (2019). The adoption of operational environmental sustainability approaches in the Thai manufacturing sector. *Journal of Cleaner Production, 220,* 507–528.

Rantala, T., Ukko, J., Saunila, M., & Havukainen, J. (2018). The effect of sustainability in the adoption of technological, service, and business model innovations. *Journal of Cleaner Production, 172,* 46–55.

Samina, Q., & Hossain, M. (2019). Current position of banks in the practice of green banking in Bangladesh: An analysis of private sector commercial banks in Bangladesh. *SSRN Electronic Journal,* 516–525.

Schücking, H., Kroll, L., Louvel, Y., & Richter, R. (2011). *Bankrolling climate change* (urgewald, groundWork, Earthlife Africa Johannesburg & BankTrack).

Sharma, R., Singh, G., & Sharma, S. (2020). Modeling Internet banking adoption in Fiji: A developing country perspective. *International Journal of Information Management, 53,* 102116.

Shubham, Charan, P., & Murty, L. (2018). Secondary stakeholder pressures and organizational adoption of sustainable operations practices: The mediating role of primary stakeholders. *Business Strategy and the Environment, 27*(7), 910–923.

Tara, K., Singh, S., & Kumar, R. (2015). Green banking for environmental management: A paradigm shift. *Current World Environment, 10*(3), 1029–1038.

Thomas, A., Scandurra, G., & Carfora, A. (2021). Adoption of green innovations by SMEs: An investigation about the influence of stakeholders. *European Journal of Innovation Management, 25*(6), 44–63.

World Bank. (2017). *World development report 2017: Governance and the Law.* The World Bank.

Yin, W., Kirkulak-Uludag, B., & Zhang, S. (2019). Is financial development in China green? Evidence from city-level data. *Journal of Cleaner Production, 211,* 247–256.

Zhixia, C., Hossen, M., Muzafary, S., & Begum, M. (2018). Green banking for environmental sustainability-present status and future agenda: Experience from Bangladesh. *Asian Economic and Financial Review, 8*(5), 571–585.

Index

Printed in the USA
CPSIA information can be obtained
at www.ICGtesting.com
JSHW011252180424
61427JS00004B/41